MYTHOLOGY AMONG THE HEBREWS

MYTHOLOGY AMONG THE HEBREWS

AND

ITS HISTORICAL DEVELOPMENT

BY

IGNAZ GOLDZIHER, PH.D.

MEMBER OF THE HUNGARIAN ACADEMY OF SCIENCES

TRANSLATED FROM THE GERMAN, WITH ADDITIONS BY THE AUTHOR

BY

RUSSELL MARTINEAU, M.A.

OF THE BRITISH MUSEUM

A MARANDELL BOOK

COOPER SQUARE PUBLISHERS, INC.
NEW YORK
1967

Published 1967 by Cooper Square Publishers, Inc.
59 Fourth Avenue, New York, N. Y. 10003
Library of Congress Catalog Card No. 66-23969

Printed in the United States of America

TO

PROFESSORS

H. L. FLEISCHER
FRIEDRICH MAX MÜLLER
H. VÁMBÉRY

THE PIONEERS OF SEMITIC, ARYAN, AND TURCO-TATARIC PHILOLOGY

This Work is Dedicated

BY THE AUTHOR AND THE TRANSLATOR

Errata.

P. 13 line 5 from below, *for* 'with all his advanced ideas' *read* 'notwithstanding the progress of modern ideas.'

P. 209, first line of note, after 'ball,' *insert* that descended from heaven.' Whether this feather-ball

TRANSLATOR'S PREFACE.

Conscious that Comparative Mythology is not very generally studied even in England, where some of the earliest and ablest expositions of its principles have appeared, I foresee that this work is likely to fall into the hands of many who have not the preliminary intellectual training necessary to an appreciation of its principles. If anyone takes up the book with an idea that it will settle anything in the history of the Jews, he will be disappointed. Its aim is not theological nor historical, but mythological; and Mythology precedes History and Theology, and has nothing to do with them, except as a factor that may to a certain extent determine their form. To understand this book fully, some previous knowledge of what has already been done on the field of Comparative Mythology is essential. This is easily obtained by reference to the various works of Prof. Max Müller and Rev. G. W. Cox, which are frequently quoted.[1] Such studies will enable the reader to see how far Dr. Goldziher is merely treading in the foot-

[1] Especially Max Müller's essay on *Comparative Mythology* (*Chips* etc., II. 1), and the ninth in the second series of his *Lectures on the Science of Language*; and Cox's introductions to his *Manual of Mythology*, *Tales of the Gods and Heroes*, and *Tales of Thebes and Argos*.

steps of others, and how far he has struck out a new track. Speaking generally, it may be said that he acknowledges the principles of the science as laid down by Kuhn and Max Müller, but that the application to the Semitic nations is his own. This application was, indeed, first attempted, fifteen years ago, by Professor H. Steinthal of Berlin with reference to one special mythological cycle, in Essays which, on p. xxix of his Introduction, Dr. Goldziher urgently recommends the reader to study as a suitable preparation for this book, since they 'showed for the first time and on a large scale how the matter of the Hebrew legends yields to mythological analysis,' and contain matter which is left out here precisely because it is to be had there. Through the obligingness of the publishers I am enabled to present the English reader with a translation of these Essays, whereby he is put in a position of no disadvantage as compared with the German. They will also serve the purpose of showing that the principles of Semitic Mythology were asserted in weighty words by a philosopher of high repute many years ago. But Dr. Goldziher has in the present work for the first time extended the application of the principles of Comparative Mythology to the entire domain of Hebrew Mythology, and laid down a broad foundation of theory, on which the elaboration of special points may be subsequently built up. Both these authors, it will be seen, regard a systematic working out of the results of Psychological science as the fundamental pillar of Mythological studies; and the reader will consequently find some psychological preparation not less necessary to the full understanding of the book than a knowledge of what has been written on Comparative Mythology.

The translation has received so many additions and corrections made expressly for it by the author, that it is far superior to the original German edition; moreover, it has been thoroughly revised by the author in proof.

I have added a few notes, where they seemed to be wanted; they are always distinguished (by 'Tr.') from the author's own. The Index is also compiled by me.

References to the Old Testament are made to the original Hebrew; in the few cases where the chapter or verse bears a different number in the English and other modern versions, the reference to the latter is added in brackets.

I have adopted a few peculiarities of orthography, which I ought to confess to, the more so as I hope others may be convinced of their reasonableness. *Nazirite*, *Hivvite*, are corrections of positive blunders in spelling of the English Bible. *Hivite* was probably written in obedience to an unwritten law of English spelling which forbids the doubling of *v*; whether there is now any sense in this precept (which must have originated when *vv* would be confounded with *w*) or not, at least it ought not to be extended to foreign names. The tendency of the age to dispense with the Latin diphthongs *æ*, *œ* (which were a few generations ago used in *æra*, *œconomy*, *Ægypt*, etc.), I have ventured to anticipate in similar words, such as *esthetic*, *Phenicia*, *Phenix*. The anomaly of the French spelling of the Greek word *programme*, alongside of *anagram*, *diagram*, *parallelogram*, seems to me sufficient condemnation of the form.

In the Hebrew and Arabic quotations the Latin alphabet has been used throughout. The transliteration of the following letters should be noted, as being the only ones about which there could be any doubt:—
א ا commencing a syllable in the middle of a word = ʼ. ע ع = ʻ. غ = ġ. ج = j. ح = ḥ. ח خ = ch. כ ك = k. ק ق = ḳ. ת ت ة = t. ט ط = ṭ. ظ = ẓ. ס שׂ س = s. שׁ ش = sh. ث = th. ذ = ḏ. צ ص = ṣ. ض = ḍ. ו as consonant generally = v, but و = w. י ى as consonant = y. The aspirated ב כ פ ת are written bh (to be pronounced v), kh, ph, th. In Hebrew ă ĕ ŏ denote either the ordinary short vowels or the châṭêph vowels; and ĕ also the vocal sheva. In Arabic texts the iʻrâb is omitted in prose, but preserved in verse on account of the metre. These principles of transliteration are the same which the author adopts in the German edition, with a few modifications which seemed desirable for English readers, especially the use of the letters j, th and y with their usual English force.

RUSSELL MARTINEAU.

LONDON: *January* 1877.

CONTENTS.

———◦◦◦———

CHAPTER I.

CHAPTER II.

CHAPTER III.

CHAPTER IV.

CHAPTER V.

CHAPTER VI.

CHAPTER VII.

CHAPTER VIII.

CHAPTER IX.

CHAPTER X.

APPENDIX.

Two Essays by H. Steinthal.

INTRODUCTION.

The following sheets make no claim to present a *system* of Hebrew Mythology. I have left out much that would necessarily be included in a system, and confined myself to a limited portion of what can be proved to be the matter of the Hebrew myths. Even within the actual domain of my labours, I was not anxious to subject the extant narratives in all their minutest features to mythological analysis. The application of the certain results of the science of Mythology in general to a domain hitherto almost ignored with reference to this subject, could only be accomplished by some self-limitation on the part of the author; and my immediate task was only to show that Semitism in general, and Hebrew in particular, could not be exceptions to the laws of mythological enquiry established on the basis of psychology and the science of language, and that it is possible from Semitism itself, on psychological and philological principles, to construct a scientific Semitic Mythology.

By blindly tracing out copious matters of detail, the investigator of myths is very easily and unconsciously seduced to the slippery ground of improbabilities; and therefore I preferred, in the first instance, to enlarge only on subjects on which I was confident of being able to present what was self-evident, and in these only, so to speak, to reveal the first cellular formations, from which later growths were produced, and to leave the analysis of the entire substance, and of the separate elements which complete the conception of the mythical figures, to a future time, when the science will have gained a firmer footing even on the Semitic domain, and will have less distrust and misunderstanding to contend against. I am myself responsible for this limitation of the subject, in the service of which, encouraged by kind friends, I resolved to publish the following pages. In mythological affairs I acknowledge myself a pupil of the school established on the Aryan domain by Ad. Kuhn and Max Müller. Only in certain points, which, however, occasionally touch upon first principles, I have been compelled to differ from the masters of Comparative Mythology. It may be boldly asserted that, especially through Max Müller's literary labours, Comparative Mythology and the Science of Religion have been added to those chapters of human knowledge with which certain borderlands of science cannot dispense, and which can claim to have become an essential portion of general culture.[1] This conviction must excuse frequent copiousness of exposition, which I have adopted knowingly and intentionally. I have had in my eye not only the small circle of professional mythologists on the Aryan and other domains, but also the larger circle

[1] Both in England and in France the attempt has been made with much taste to introduce the results of comparative mythology in the instruction of youth; in England by Rev. G. W. Cox in his *Tales of the Gods and Heroes*, *Tales of Thebes and Argos*, *Tales from Greek Mythology*, *Manual of Mythology in the form of question and answer*, 1867, and *Tales of Ancient Greece*, 1870, the last two of which have just been translated into Hungarian, and published by the Franklin Society; in France by Baudry and Delerot (Paris 1872). Still more recently the results of comparative mythology have also been summarised in two excellent books for children by Edward Clodd, *The Childhood of the World: a simple account of Man in Early Times*, 1873, and *The Childhood of Religion; embracing a simple account of the birth and growth of Myths and Legends*, 1875.

of educated readers who will be interested in learning how the results of Comparative Mythology shape themselves when applied to Semitic nations. But, on the other hand, I must crave the indulgence of the latter readers, if I have not always succeeded (especially in the fifth chapter) in making my meaning as intelligible as I could wish. For it is a fact that the Semitic still remains further removed from the mind of educated society than the Aryan, which, through the study of classical antiquity, has so ensnared us from our school-days with its irresistible charms, that it can never cease to determine the direction of our thought and action. Therefore I have had resort to foreign examples, sometimes non-Semitic instances from antiquity, sometimes instances from modern poets, for illustrations of particular assertions, which otherwise would appear improbable, but could thus be brought nearer to the understanding. From the figures used by poets the wealth and variety of the mythical apperception of the primeval man is truly elucidated. Here and there I have also permitted myself to make reference to Hungarian idioms, which was very natural, as I originally composed this book in my Hungarian mother-tongue for the purpose of University lectures, and then translated it myself into German. Some parts of these essays have been already published in Hungarian, in a different connexion and with special reference to linguistic results, in the first and second parts of Vol. XII. of the *Nyelvtudományi Közlemények* (Philological Essays), edited by Paul Hunfalvy for the Hungarian Academy of Sciences.

In adducing Aryan parallels, I am very far from thinking that where the Hebrew exhibits a striking similarity to something Aryan it has borrowed from the latter, or that, as a recent scholar tried to make out, the

Hebrews themselves were originally Aryans, who afterwards took a Semitic language and preserved their Aryan habits of thought. I start from the conviction that the Myth is something universal, that the faculty of forming it cannot *a priori* be denied to any race as such, and that the coincidence of mythical ideas and modes of expression is the result of the uniformity of the psychological process which is the foundation of the creation of myths in all races; and this very uniformity of mythical ideas may consequently serve to psychologists as an argument for the thesis of the psychological uniformity of all races.[1] 'Where no historical transference of myths can be proved,' says Bastian very justly,[2] 'the uniformity must be referred to the organic law of the growth of the mind, which will everywhere put forth similar products, corresponding and alike, but variously modified by surrounding influences.' The oldest history of paleography exhibits on the ideographic and figurative stage the most striking similarities in the modes of apperception belonging to nations of the most various races. Lenormant says: 'Nous pourrions faire voir, si nous voulions nous laisser aller à la tentation d'entreprendre un petit traité de l'écriture symbolique chez les différents peuples, comment certaines métaphores naturelles ont été conçues spontanément par plusieurs races diverses sans communication les unes avec les autres, et comment, par suite, le même symbole se retrouve avec

[1] This psychological uniformity of all races of men is independent of the question of the monogenetic or polygenetic origin of races. The psychological uniformity of different races is especially conspicuous when we observe and compare individuals of the separate races in infancy, when the distinctions produced by history, education, instruction, etc., are not yet present (see Frohschammer, *Das Christenthum und die moderne Naturwissenschaft,* Vienna 1868, p. 208. When we are considering the growth of mankind in general, the stage when myths are created corresponds to the infancy of the individual.

[2] *Das Beständige in den Menschenrassen und die Spielweise ihrer Veränderlichkeit,* Berlin 1868, p. 78.

le même sens dans plusieurs systèmes d'origine tout-à-fait indépendante. L'exemple le plus frappant peut-être de ce genre est celui du symbole de l'abeille, qui, ainsi que nous venons de le dire, signifie *Roi* dans les hiéroglyphes égyptiens, et se reconnaît encore clairement dans le type le plus ancien de l'idéogramme doué du même sens dans le cunéiforme anarien.'[1] The same lesson is taught by Prehistoric Archeology, the comparative study of which among the various races would present very instructive examples. In our museums we see identical implements used by men of the most various races at the same primitive stage of civilisation,[2] yet in this case the idea of one having borrowed from another enters no one's head. Why should we be surprised at meeting with the very same phenomenon in Comparative Mythology?

The uniformity of the Hebrew myths with those of nations belonging to other races only becomes an obvious fact when we apply the method of modern mythological enquiry to Semitic stories. But, even without the help of this method, the mere outside of the Hebrew stories attracted the attention of many enquirers. It occasionally gave rise to the absurdest aberrations, which even now shoot out into a fresh crop of mischief. One answer, of course, was always at hand—that Greek and Egyptian narratives and 'theogonies' were bad translations or 'diluted' versions of the Hebrew; or else, as it has often been attempted in recent times to prove, the Egyptian was the original, from which everything else had flowed. The eighteenth century was especially rich in literary productions of the first species, following the

[1] François Lenormant, *Essai sur la Propagation de l'Alphabet phénicien dans l'ancien monde,* Vol. I. (2nd ed., Paris 1875), p. 17.

[2] Tylor, *Primitive Culture,* I. 6.

lead of Gerhard Johann Voss, Huet,[1] Bochart, and others whose labours had prepared the way. G. Croesius published at Dort, in 1704, '"Ομηρος Ἑβραῖος, sive Historia Hebraeorum ab Homero Hebraicis nominibus ac sententiis conscripta in Odyssea et Iliade,' and V. G. Herklitz at Leipzig two years later, 1706, 'Quod Hercules idem sit ac Josua.' At Amsterdam a book was published in 1721 entitled 'Parallela τῆς χρονολογίας et Historiae Sacrae,' having the same object; and in 1730 a book in two volumes, of similar tendency, by Guillaume de Lavaur, an *avocat*, was published at Paris in French, and translated into German by Johann Daniel Heyden (Leipzig, 1745).[2] But it was reserved for the end of the century to produce the most curious specimen, in the work entitled 'Histoire véritable des Temps Fabuleux: ouvrage qui, en dévoilant le vrai que les histoires fabuleuses ont travesti et altéré, sert à éclaircir les antiquités des peuples et surtout à venger l'histoire sainte,' by the Abbé Guérin du Rocher. I have not seen the original edition of this work, but have consulted a later edition prepared by the Abbé Chapelle, an admirer of the author (Paris and Besançon, 1824), in five volumes, of which the first three contain the original work, and the fourth and fifth are taken up by the editor with a recapitulation of principles and a defence against the attacks of antagonists, who count among their number such men as Voltaire, De la Harpe, De Guignes, Du Voisin, Dinouart, and Anquetil du Perron. The author undertook to prove that the entire ancient history of the Egyptians and other nations is only a repetition of Biblical narratives: that thus what is related of Bothyris,

---

[1] On these two see Pfleiderer, *Die Religion, ihr Wesen und ihre Geschichte*, II. 8.

[2] The title is 'Conférence de la Fable avec l'Histoire sainte, où l'on voit que les grandes fables, le culte et les mystères du paganisme ne sont que des copies altérées des histoires, des usages et des traditions des Hébreux.'

Orpheus, Menes, Sesostris, and others, is identical with the Biblical history of Abraham, Jacob, Lot, Noah, and others; even the Egyptian Thebes is not a city, but Noah's ark. The influence which this sensational book exercised on the learning of the period is very characteristic of the times. Dr. Asselini, vicar of the diocese of Paris, who had to pass judgment on it for the censorship (1779), regards it as a vindication of the Bible. The Sorbonne appropriated Guérin's theorems, and made them the subject of theses for graduation. The King of Poland read the work through, and sent his compliments to the author. The French government accorded the Abbé an annual pension of 1,200 livres. One reviewer compares Guérin's discoveries to those of Columbus and Newton; and a poetical panegyrist sees in them a French counterpoise to the superiority in science then possessed by England in virtue of discoveries of the first rank in physical science. He says—

> Fière et docte Albion, qui dans un coin des mers
> Prétends aux premier rang de la littérature,
> Pour avoir à vos yeux dévoilé l'univers
> Et le vrai plan de la nature,
> De tes discours hautains rabaisse enfin le ton;
> La France, ta rivale, va égaler ta gloire.
> Ce que pour la physique a fait le grand Newton,
> Du Rocher l'a fait pour l'histoire.

But even on the very threshold of the second part of our century, in 1849, a systematic argument was conducted, to show that Livy had read the Bible, and based his description of T. Manlius Torquatus' battle with the Gauls on that of David and his battle with the Philistine giant; and twenty-two similarities between the respective stories had to do duty as demonstrations.[1] The unscientific

---

[1] Edward Wilton in the *Journal of Sacred Literature*, 1849, II. 374 *et seq.*

mode of regarding these subjects prevailing up to the most recent time has not yet ceased to generate absurdities.

We see old-fashioned absurdities still finding a way to the general reading public by means of encyclopedias, as in a 'Dictionary of the Mythology of all Nations,' of which a third edition was recently published.[1] This work in its new form comes before the public with a touching delivery against modern physical science by way of introduction. Here we read under *Abraham*, 'Some scholars are inclined to make this celebrated Patriarch of the Jewish nation either the god Brahma himself or a Brahman who was obliged to leave India in the contest between the worshippers of Siva and those of Brahma. *In truth, there is much that might lead to such a conjecture.* In Sanskrit the word 'earth' is often expressed by *Brahm* or *Abrahm.* Abraham's wife was named Sarah; Brahma's wife was Sara (Sarasvati)' etc. But sins of a different kind also are committed up to the present day. The Hebrews are said to have borrowed their myths from foreign parts. It is not only by Voltaire and men of his age and spirit that this assumption is made. It is expressed in a recent article by a learned German investigator intended for the widest circulation. Sepp writes, 'No nation has been so clever as the Hebrews in appropriating to themselves the property of others, both intellectual and material. What can we say to the fact that the sun's standing still at Joshua's bidding, with the purpose of enabling the Hebrews to complete the slaughter of the Amalekites, is *directly borrowed from Homer* (*Il.* ii. 412), where the poetical hyperbole 'Let not the sun go down, O Zeus,' etc., is put into the mouth of Agamemnon? . . . To be brief, the popular

---

[1] Dr. Vollmer's *Wörterbuch der Mythologie aller Völker*, newly revised by Dr. W. Binder, with an Introduction to Mythological Science by Dr. Johannes Minckwitz, 3rd ed., Stuttgart 1874.

hero Samson has had the Twelve Labours of the Lybian Herakles transferred to him, and bears the doors, as Sandon or Melkart the pillars of the world, on his shoulders.'[1] The reader will agree with me in regarding it as superfluous at the present day to attempt a serious refutation of the hypothesis of *borrowing*, which assails the originality of the most primitive mythological ideas known to the nation under review. But it is impossible to evade the obligation to find an explanation of the manifold coincidences exhibited in the independently produced myths of nations belonging to quite different races. Under the new method of mythological enquiry this obligation is doubly pressing; for the coincidences appear yet more surprising, and occupy a more extensive sphere when the myths are considered analytically by the light of the new method, and from a linguistic point of view. Only then does the identity become psychologically important. And then it can in my view be explained only by the rejection of the prejudice that there are unmythological races, or at least one race incapable of forming any myths—the Semitic. If the Myth is a form of life of the human mind psychologically necessary at a certain stage of growth, then the intellectual life of every individual, nation, and race must pass through it. 'The tendency of modern enquiry is more and more toward the conclusion that if law is anywhere, it is everywhere,' as Tylor maintains.[2] This means, applied to the present question, that if the formation of myths is a natural law of the ψυχή (mind) at a certain stage, it must necessarily occur everywhere where there is a beginning of intellectual life, unless we could speak of whole races or tribes as psychologically patho-

[1] See the Augsburg *Allgemeine Zeitung*, 1875, no. 169, p. 2657.
[2] *Primitive Culture*, I. 22.

logic,[1] and make the whole Semitic race thus pathologic on account of its alleged incapacity to form myths—which would, after all, be rather a curious proceeding. No doubt we often read in ethnological works of nations without a trace of Mythology. But we ought not to forget either that such informants understand by Mythology only complicated stories and fables, which in my view represent the more advanced stage of mythic development, or that they identify Mythology with heathen religious ideas, and confound absence of religion or atheism with want of myths. So, e.g., Sir John Lubbock says, quoting Sibree,[2] 'Even in Madagascar, according to a good authority, "there is nothing corresponding to a Mythology, *or any fables of gods or goddesses*, amongst the Malagasy;"' but this want of stories of gods and goddesses is very far from demonstrating the absence of myths of all and every sort.

It would be worth while in this connexion to pursue a thought raised by Schelling, with the aid of the present more advanced ideas on the psychology of nations. According to Schelling,[3] a nation becomes a nation through community of consciousness between the individuals; and this community has its foundation in a common view of the world, and this again in Mythology. Consequently in Schelling's system absence of Mythology can only occur in circles of men in which nationality is as yet unformed, and the necessary community undeveloped. But to Schelling 'it appears impossible, because inconceivable, that a *Nation*

---

[1] See Virchow in the *Monatsbericht der königl. preuss. Akademie der Wissenschaften*, January 1875, p. 11.

[2] *Origin of Civilisation*, 3rd ed., p. 330, quoting Sibree's *Madagascar and its People*, p. 396.

[3] *Einleitung in die Philosophie der Mythologie*, pp. 62, 63. This is the idea to which Max Müller refers in noticing the lectures of the philosopher of Berlin, in his *Introduction to the Science of Religion*, p. 145.

should be without Mythology.' However the question may stand with reference to savage tribes, modern science cannot possibly support the old thesis concerning the Semitic Hebrews of their incapacity for Mythology.

Guided by this conviction, I lay down at starting the necessity of subjecting the material of the Hebrew myths to the same psychological and linguistic analysis which has contributed so much light to the consideration of the beginnings of intellectual life in the Aryan race.

I do not conceal from myself that the acknowledgment of the legitimacy of this method for Semitic things may be exposed to many attacks. For even on Aryan ground the results which the school of Kuhn and Max Müller have brought to light do not enjoy that general acceptation which ought to reward such sound investigations—investigations, moreover, the basis of which is being constantly extended by later writers such as G. W. Cox and De Gubernatis. Both in Germany and in England this school has notable adversaries. I do not speak of Julius Braun, who, in his *Naturgeschichte der Sage* (Natural History of Legend), thought to undermine the solid substratum of Comparative Mythology by extending to the domain of mythology the consequences of his theory of the history of art and of Röthe's assumptions, and by fetching from Egypt the foundation-stone on which to construct a Science of Mythology—an attempt which turned out most unfortunate, especially in etymology. But some worthy partisans of the study of classical literature refuse to receive the results of the science of Comparative Mythology. One of these is K. Lehrs;[1] another is the latest German editor of Hesiod, who objects to the

---

[1] See his *Populäre Aufsätze aus dem Alterthum, vorzugsweise zur Ethik und Religion der Griechen*, second edition, Leipzig 1875, especially p. 272 *et seq.*

modern science of Mythology that it ignores historical and philological criticism and seizes upon every passage of an author that suits its theory, without regard to its value and genuineness.[1] Among the English scholars it is no less a writer than Fergusson who declares, 'So far as I am capable of understanding it, it appears to me that the ancient Solar Myth of Messrs. Max Müller and Cox is very like mere modern moonshine.'[2] And Mr. George Smith, the renowned pioneer of the ancient Assyrian literature, seems not to have much confidence in the latest method of mythological investigation; for he says in his latest book,[3] 'The early poems and stories of almost every nation are by some writers resolved into elaborate descriptions of natural phenomena; and in some cases, if that were true, the myth would have taken to create it a genius as great as that of the philosophers who explain it.' So that the so-called 'Solar theory' is far from being generally adopted even on the domain where it was first brought out and has been most firmly established. But the adherents of the school of Max Müller may take comfort from the consideration that the accusations made against them hit only those who have ridden the theory too hard, since, as Tylor says, no allegory, no nursery-rhyme, is safe from the speculations of some fanatical mythological theoriser. 'Much abused' is a correct epithet used of the Solar theory by a learned English Assyriologist, himself a friend of it.[4] If, then, on Aryan ground the legitimacy of the new method is not undisputed, how will it be on Semitic, and especially on Hebrew ground, which a prejudice prevalent far and wide has

---

[1] Flach, *Das System der Hesiod. Kosmogonie,* Leipzig 1874; see *Literar. Centralblatt*, 1875, no. 7.

[2] *Rude Stone Monuments in all Countries*, p. 32, note 2.

[3] *The Chaldean Account of Genesis*, p. 302.

[4] Sayce in the *Academy*, 1875, p. 586.

decided to be occupied by a race and a nation with no mythology at all? Nevertheless, I hope I have kept myself free from abuse and extravagance in these essays. I have endeavoured sedulously to avoid whatever, on the Aryan domain, aroused the distrust of the hesitating, by showing no anxiety to gain immediate command of the whole extent of the mythological field. The essential point at the commencement of these matters is not the elucidation of all the minute details, but rather the solution of the general questions that arise, and the accurate laying down of a sound method of investigation. What I have brought forward I wish to be regarded as a collection of examples of the application of the method.

The reader will observe that I have given to the conception of the myth a narrower scope than is usually done. I believe it necessary to separate it strictly from the conception of religion, and especially to exclude from the sphere of primitive mythology the questions of Cosmogony and Ethics (the origin of Evil). The latter point was of especial importance in reference to the Hebrew Myth, since, as I show in the last chapter, the solution of these questions by the Hebrews was produced in the later period of civilisation and from a foreign impulse. There is an immense difference between the ancient mythical view of the origin of nature and that later cosmogonic system. So long as mythical ideas are still living in the mind, though under an altered form, when the times are ripe for cosmogonic speculations, a cosmogony appears as a stage of development of the ancient myth. But when the myth has utterly vanished from consciousness, then the mind is ready to receive foreign cosmogonic ideas, which can be fitted into the frame of its religious thought and accommodated to its religious views. This was the case with the Hebrews; and hence it will be understood why I have not treated as Hebrew mythical matter the Cosmogony of Genesis, which, moreover, according to all appearance, is to be regarded rather as a mere literary creation than as a view of the origin of things emanating directly from the mind of the people.

It appeared desirable to give a few chapters to show what I imagined the course of development of the primitive myths to have been, before they attained the form in which they are presented to us in literature. The mythological question is indeed quite distinct from that concerning the history of literature, and there is only a distant connexion between the two. The purpose of the following pages is, strictly speaking, attained where that of the literary history of the Canon commences; and I would gladly have kept aloof from the literary question, which cannot yet be regarded as even nearly settled. But when I included in my task the description of the further course of development of the myth, it was obviously impossible to stand so entirely aloof. I have on many points deviated from the current views, without being able either to enter into so complete a justification of the deviation as is generally reasonably expected, and the importance and scope of the subject would demand, or to refer to all the suggestive and original works contributed, especially by Germany and Holland, to the elucidation of the problems in question. For this point, which is only accessory to the real subject of my work, would require to be treated in a separate monograph, which it was not my intention to give. On the other hand, it was impossible to leave these questions quite on one side. On the Pentateuch question I start from the principles of Graf, which at first were adopted solely by the learned Professor Kuenen of Leyden, but have recently found zealous promoters also in England[1] and Germany—in the latter country especially in the works of Kayser (Strasburg, 1874), and Duhm (Bonn, 1875).[2] Nevertheless, the section on Jahveism and Prophetism has turned out more lengthy than considerations of symmetry would sanction. I must confess that my personal sympathy with and affection for this portion of the history of religion places me too close to it to allow me, when once brought face to face with it, to impose on my pen a reserve which perhaps is desirable for the sake of equilibrium. All this obliges me to count on the kind indulgence of my readers for the second portion, which may be termed the historical.

It remains to say a few words about previous works of the same character. Some earlier writings there are on Hebrew Mythology. But it needs not to be specially insisted on that Nork's muddle-headed works, such as his 'Biblical Mythology of the Old and New Testament,' his 'Etymological-symbolical-mythological Cyclopedia for Biblical Students, Archeologists, and Artists,'[3] and other books of his, and similar attempts by others,[4] which have tended to discredit the school of Creuzer rather than to gain lasting adherents to it, do not deserve to be regarded as anything but passing aberrations. Braun's 'Natural History of Legend: Reference of all

---

[1] The *Academy*, 1875, no. 184, p. 496. The promoters of the *Theological Translation Fund*, by whom Kuenen's *Religion of Israel* was published, Dr. J. Muir of Edinburgh, who wrote some letters to the *Scotsman* on the Dutch Theology, and to a certain extent Bishop Colenso, besides many others who have not avowed their views so publicly, indicate the progress of opinion in England.—Tr.

[2] See *Literar. Centralblatt*, 1875, no. 49, p. 157.

[3] *Biblische Mythologie des Alten und Neuen Testaments*, 2 vols., Stuttgart 1842; *Etymologisch-symbolisch-mythologisches Realwörterbuch für Bibelforscher, Archäologen und bildende Künstler*, 4 vols., Stuttgart 1843–5.

[4] I have not succeeded in obtaining a sight of Schwenk's *Mythologie der Semiten*, published in 1849; but Bunsen's condemnation of it in *Egypt's Place in Universal History*, IV. p. 363, made me less anxious to get it.

Religious Ideas, Legends, and Systems to their Common Stock and Ultimate Root'[1] maintains a more serious and dignified tone, but is a kind of anachronism built on an antiquated theory, and not happier in its etymological identifications and derivations than Nork's writings. I think that no branch of the science of History and Civilisation can be advanced to satisfactory results when the following thesis is laid down as an axiom: 'It is a fundamental law of the nature of the human mind never to invent anything as long as it is possible to copy'—which is the starting-point of Braun's studies. It would be quite as difficult to rest satisfied at the present day with the method which Buttmann follows in treating of Hebrew Mythology.

There are many smaller excursus by Biblical expositors and historians, who set out from the standpoint of the earlier views on the relation of the Myth to the Legend, and more frequently from the exegetical point of view. Among these ought especially to be named Ewald's section on the subject in the first volume of his 'History of Israel,' Tuch's short treatise 'Legend and Myth' in the general introduction to his Commentary on Genesis, as well as several dissertations by the indefatigable Nöldeke in his '*Untersuchungen*' (Investigations) and elsewhere. It is obvious that these performances, though in every sense noteworthy and of permanent value, could not draw into their sphere of observation those preliminary questions which in the subsequent investigations of Kuhn and Max Müller removed to a greater distance the goal of mythological enquiry. Steinthal, who did so much for the psychological basis of the new tendency of mythological science, was the first to merit the praise of making Com-

[1] *Naturgeschichte der Sage. Rückführung aller religiösen Ideen, Sagen, Systeme auf ihren gemeinsamen Stammbaum und ihre letzte Wurzel*, 2 vols., Munich 1864–5.

parative Mythology fruitful on Hebrew ground. His dissertations on the Story of Prometheus and the Story of Samson[1] showed for the first time, and on a large scale, how the matter of the Hebrew legends yields to mythological analysis. I would on this occasion beg the reader to have the kindness to read these pioneer-articles of Steinthal's, to complete the matter left undiscussed in my work, as I considered it superfluous repetition to work up a second time what was sufficiently expounded there. Steinthal must consequently be regarded as the founder of mythological science on Hebrew ground. He has again recently given some suggestive hints on this subject in a short article, in which he again defends the capacity of the Semitic race to form myths.[2] It is only to be regretted that the commencement made by Steinthal in this science has not been followed up for more than fifteen years.[3] Steinthal's two dissertations gave me the first impulse to the composition of this work; and my purpose was confirmed by the words of the ingenious Italian Angelo de Gubernatis, who, in his 'Zoological Mythology' (which appeared at the very time when I was maturing my purpose of putting together into one work this series of essays originally written as lectures), eloquently designates the subject of my researches the next problem of Comparative Mythology.[4] The words in which he recommends the study of Hebrew Mythology in

---

[1] In Vol. II. of his *Zeitschrift für Völkerpsychologie und Sprachwissenschaft*, translated and appended to this volume.

[2] *Der Semitismus*, in *Zeitsch. für Völkerpsychologie etc.*, 1875, VIII. 339–340.

[3] It would be unfair not to mention the Dutch Professor Tiele as a worker on this field. In his *Vergelijkende Geschiedenis der oude godsdiensten*, Vol. I.: *De egyptische en mesopotamische godsdiensten* (Amsterdam 1872) he has occasionally inserted explanations of Hebrew myths, to which I have referred at the proper places.

[4] II. 421 *et seq.*; see his *Rivista Europea*, year VI. II. 587. Cf. his review of the German edition of this work in the *Bollettino italiano degli studj orientali*, 1876, I. 169–172.

the spirit of the new method seem to me very striking. It is my earnest conviction that not only the interests of learning, but also preeminently the religious life of the present age make it important to gain for this subject an acknowledged position in learned literature. For he who feels the true meaning of religion must welcome these studies as a step in advance towards the highest ideal of religion, towards Monotheism pure and unsullied by anything coarse or pagan, which is independent of legends and traditions of race, and has its centre, its exclusive element of life, and its impulse towards never-resting enquiry and self-perfection, in aspiration after the single living Source of all truth and morality. I am convinced that every step which we take towards a correct appreciation of the Mythical brings us nearer to that centre. The confusion of the Mythical with the Religious makes religious life centrifugal; it is the duty of the progressive tendency on this domain to confirm a centripetal tendency.[1] The recognition of this relation between pure Monotheism and the oldest historical portion of the Biblical literature does not date from yesterday or to-day; the most ideal representative of Hebrew Monotheism, in whom Jahveism as an harmonious conception of the universe attained its climax, the Prophet of the Captivity himself, described this relation in clear terms (Is. LXIII. 17; see *infra*, p. 229).

But while, on the one hand, the investigation of Hebrew myths gives a stimulus to religious thought to advance in the direction of a Monotheism purified from all dross; on the other, the employment of the method offered to the Hebrew stories by Comparative Mythology in its

---

[1] In reference to this I may refer to the eloquent expressions of Steinthal in his lecture *Mythos und Religion*, p. 28 (in Virchow and Holtzendorff's *Sammlung gemeinverständlicher Vorträge*, Bd. V. Heft 97).

latest stage, paves the way for a more serious treatment of the old Biblical stories. It cannot be denied that there is no little frivolity in the idea that those stories were invented at a certain time, no matter whether *bona* or *mala fide*, by persons guided by some interest, or affected by some leaning, of their own. It is no more satisfactory to be told that the stories were not *invented*, but *sprang up* naturally, and then to find that no answer is forthcoming to the question, *How* that could be? The modern science of Comparative Mythology has washed the teachers of the human race clean of the suspicion of mystification and deceptive principles. The origination of the stories is, at the outset, claimed for an antiquity higher than even the most orthodox apologists could ever exhibit. Now for the first time we can learn to appreciate them as spontaneous acts of the human mind; we perceive that they arose through the same psychological process which gave us language also; that, like language itself, they were the very oldest manifestation of activity of the mind, and burst forth from it φύσει, not θέσει, at the very threshold of its history; and subsequently transformed and developed themselves again quite spontaneously, on the attainment of a higher stage of civilisation, by processes of national psychology, and most certainly not by the cunning ingenuity and the worldly wisdom of certain leading classes.

Last year Dr. Martin Schultze announced a 'Mythology of the Hebrews in its connexion with those of the Indogermans and of the Egyptians'[1] as about to appear. The method followed by the author in a preliminary specimen[2] was not such as to induce me to delay the

[1] *Mythologie der Ebräer in ihrem Zusammenhange mit den Mythologien der Indogermanen und der Ægypter*. Nordhausen 1876.

[2] *Ausland*, 1874, p. 961 *et seq.*, 1001 *et seq.*

publication of my work and wait for his, even though he promised to give a complete system, which was not my intention.[1] My manuscript was already in the publishers' hands, when the papers announced the publication of a learned book by Dr. Grill, 'The Patriarchs of Mankind: a contribution towards the establishment of a Science of Hebrew Archeology;'[2] and more than ten sheets were printed before I could gather, from a review of it in the *Jenaer Literaturzeitung*, in how close a connexion it stood to the subject of my book; for from the title alone I was not likely to suspect anything on Mythology. I cannot pretend to explain in a few lines my opinion of so large a book as Dr. Grill's. But as he starts with the assumption of the impossibility of a Semitic Mythology, and endeavours to establish the view that the Hebrew Myth is that of an Indogermanic people, that the Hebrews were Indogermans, and that the Hebrew mythological proper names can find an etymology only in Sanskrit, I have great pleasure in referring him to p. 25 and to Chapter V. of my book, where he may convince himself that no very daring etymological leaps nor arbitrary assumptions of phonological laws of transformation are necessary to explain the Hebrew mythological figures and their appellations from the Semitic languages themselves. It must, no doubt, be admitted that in some cases—but the minority—the formation of the proper names used in Mythology is not quite in accordance with grammatical analogy. I account for this by the peculiar feature of the Semitic languages, that an appellative on becoming a proper name often takes a peculiar form, differing in some respect from that of the original appellative: 'al-'adl li-l-

---

[1] The above-named work was published immediately after the conclusion of this Introduction.

[2] *Die Erzväter der Menschheit: ein Beitrag zur Grundlegung einer hebräischen Alterthumswissenschaft.* Leipzig, Fues 1875.

'alamîyyâ,' as the Arabian grammarians say.[1] There will always be *cruces*. Is it possible to indicate a satisfactory etymon for every proper name of the Greek mythology? and if not, ought we on that account to explain the Greek out of Semitic, whenever a case occurs which tempts us to do so, as our learned ancestors did?[2] For transformation is always easy to find; since etymology is allowed to be a science in which the consonants go for but little, and the vowels have nothing at all to say for themselves! It certainly seems a pity to waste ingenuity in trying to banish out of the Semitic stock names which sound Semitic and can be recognised as such without the employment of any law of transformation at all, like Yiphtâch (Jephthah), Nôach (Noah), and Debhôrâ (Deborah), and in dissolving by Sanskrit solvents the Hebrew impress of a word like Yehôshûa' (Joshua), produced by Jahveism out of the original Hôshêa', and not even mythical at all, in order to make it into a 'Dog of Heaven,' instead of 'He has holpen' or 'enlarged [the people's possessions],' i.e. 'The Helper.'[3] Pinechas (Phinehas), no doubt, is a word that might drive the etymologist to despair. But there is far more intrinsic probability in Lauth's Egyptian interpretation[4] than in Grill's Sanskrit *tour de force*, especially considering that Egyptian proper names cannot be explained away out of the Old Testament, and have in history a positive reason

---

[1] Ibn Ya'îsh's Commentary on the Mufaṣṣal, p. 74 (of the edition now being published by Dr. Jahn of Berlin). See *Fables* de Loqman le Sage (éd. Dérenbourg), Introduction, p. 7.

[2] I may refer on this point to Von Gutschmid's excellent critique on Bunsen's attempt to explain Athene as Semitic, in the former's *Beiträge zur Geschichte des alten Orients*, Leipzig 1858, p. 46.

[3] Stade (*Morgenländische Forschungen*, p. 232) justly insists on the good Hebrew character of the names occurring in the Hebrew stories, even against the false supposition of the original Aramaic character of the Hebrew people.

[4] *Zeitsch. d. D. M. G.*, 1871, XXV. 139; see Lepsius, *Einleitung zur Chronologie der alten Ægypten*, I. 326.

for existence. Then why hover in the dream-land of a prehistoric connexion with the Aryans?

When the Arabian traditionary stories are once subjected to etymological treatment, it will appear how far Semitism is from utter deficiency of Mythology. In certain instances I have taken occasion to demonstrate this with reference to Arabian tradition in the course of this work (e.g. p. 182 *et seq.*, p. 334 *et seq.*). In other cases no reference to the etymological meaning of the proper names is required to recognise true Arabian myths. Instances are found especially in the stories about the constellations. Al-Meydânî informs us that 'the old Arabs say that the star al-Dabarân wooed the Pleiades, but the latter constellation would have nothing to do with the suitor, turned obstinately away from him, and said to the Moon, 'What must I do with that poor devil, who has no estate at all?' Then al-Dabarân gathered together his Ḳilâṣ (a constellation in the neighbourhood of al-Dabarân), and thus gained possession of an estate. And now he is constantly following after the Pleiades, driving the Ḳilâṣ before him as a wedding-present.'[1] 'The constellation Capricorn killed the Bear (na'sh), and therefore the daughters of the latter (binât na'sh) encircle him, seeking vengeance for their slain father.' 'Suheyl gave the female star al-Jauzâ a blow; the latter returned it and threw him down where he now lies; but he then took his sword and cut his adversary in pieces.' 'The southern Sirius (al-Shi'ra al-yamânîyyâ) was walking with her sister the northern Sirius (al-Shi'ra al-shâmîyyâ); the latter parted company and crossed

[1] See Ibn Ya'îsh's Commentary on the Mufaṣṣal of Zamachsharî, p. 47, in which the name of the constellation al-'Ayyûḳ (Auriga, 'The Hinderer') is imported into this story, as hindering al-Dabarân from coming up with his beloved.

the Milky Way, whence her name (al-Shi'ra al-'abûr). Her sister, seeing this, began to weep for the separation, and her eyes dropped tears; therefore she is called the Wet-eyed (al-ġumeyṣâ).'[1] The existence of similar Hebrew myths may be inferred from the names of constellations in the Book of Job (XXXVIII. 31, 32), especially from the Fool (kesîl, Orion) bound to heaven.[2] Are not these genuine Nomads' myths, produced through contemplation of the constellations and their relations to one another?

In conclusion, I must observe that in many passages, especially of the later chapters, a fuller citation of literary apparatus would have been desirable. The want of this is to be ascribed in part to the peculiar design of the book, and in part to the deficiency of aid from libraries for the exegetical department in my dwelling-place.

---

[1] al-Meydânî, Majma' al-amthâl (ed. of Bûlâḳ), II. 209.

[2] See Nöldeke in Schenkel's *Bibellexikon*, 2nd ed. IV. 370.

MYTHOLOGY AMONG THE HEBREWS.

CHAPTER I.

ON HEBREW MYTHOLOGY.

§ 1. At the very foundation of the investigations to which this book is devoted, we find ourselves in opposition to a wide-spread assumption: that in regard to Mythology nations may be divided into two classes, Mythological and Unmythological, or in other words, those which have had a natural gift for creating Myths, and those whose intellectual capacity never sufficed for this end. It is therefore desirable to lay down clearly our position in regard to this assumption, before we advance to the proper subject of our studies.

The Myth is the result of a purely psychological operation, and is, together with language, the oldest act of the human mind. This has been shown conclusively by the modern school of mythologists who are also psychologists. Assuming then, what can scarcely be called in question, that the same psychological laws rule the intellectual activity of mankind without distinction of race, we cannot *a priori* assume that the capacity for forming myths can be given or withheld according to ethnological categories. As there is only one physiology, and every race of mankind under the influence of certain conditions produces the same physiological functions in accordance with physiological laws, so it is also with the psychological functions, given the stimulus necessary to their production. And this stimulus acts upon mankind everywhere alike. For it is clearly proved that the Myth tells of the operations of nature, and is the mode of expressing the perception which man at the earliest stage of his intellectual life has of these operations and phenomena. These form the substance of the Myth. Consequently, wherever they act as attractions to the youthful human mind, the external conditions of the rise of Mythology are present. Not unjustly, therefore, it seems to me, has a recent psychologist spoken of the 'Universal Presence and the Uniformity' of myths.[1] Undoubtedly the direction of the myth will vary with the relation of natural phenomena to mankind; the myth will take one direction where man greets the sun as a friendly element, and another where the sun meets him as a hostile power; and in the rainless region the rain cannot act the same part in Mythology which it plays in the rainy parts of the earth. The manners and usages of men must also exercise a modifying influence on the subject and the direction of the Myth. As in the course of our further inquiries we shall recur to this point, I will here only refer to one example of the latter. It is well known that in the Aryan mythology, 'the milking of cows' is a frequently recurring expression for the shining of the sun, or as some say for the rain. In tribes which do not milk their cows, like some Negro peoples,[2] or the American natives, this mythical expression can of course not arise.

§ 2. There are two points of view, from which the Mythical faculty has been denied to certain sections of the human race—on the one side a *linguistic*, on the other an *ethnological*. As to the first, we must especially name Bleek, the distinguished investigator of the South African languages, who, in the introduction to his work

[1] *Zeitschrift für Völkerpsychologie und Sprachwissenschaft*, 1869, VI. 207.
[2] Theodor Waitz, *Anthropologie der Naturvölker*, II. 85.

on the Story of Reynard the Fox in South Africa, makes the remark that a mythological genius is peculiar to nations in whose languages a distinction of gender in nouns finds expression, whereas those whose languages possess no formal distinction of gender in nouns, have no proper mythology, but their religion stands on that original stage which is the starting-point of all human religion, namely that of the cultus of their ancestors.[1] It is obvious that this learned linguist's distinction involves a confusion of Myth and Religion, which we shall find in the course of our subsequent investigations to be untenable. At present we will disregard this point, and only refer to the mythologies of the Finnish-Ugrian nations—peoples whose languages do not indicate any distinction of gender in their nouns. Or can it be said that the substance of the epos of Kalevala is not proper mythology? To be sure, in nations whose mind never evolved the category of grammatical gender in their languages, the myth will take such a direction as will give to the sexual idea, so charming a feature in the Aryan mythology, much less prominence. For the mode of conception which is conveyed by the distinction of '*die* Sonne' and '*der* Mond,' or '*hic* sol' and '*haec* luna,' cannot arise where this distinction is not made. But the figures of a mythology not only vary as to sex and genealogy, but act also; they are busy, they fight and kill, and the story of these actions and fights is quite independent of the gender-idea in language. Stories of them, consequently, which we call Myths, may exist even where the genius of language has opposed the distinction of gender.

§ 3. The second point of view, from which some have denied to a section of the human race the faculty and tendency to form myths, is *ethnological*. Either the Semites in general or the Hebrews specially fell a sacrifice to this

---

[1] W. H. I. Bleek, *Reynard the Fox in South Africa*, 1864, pp. xx–xxvi. See Max Müller's *Introduction to the Science of Religion*, London 1873, p. 54.

view. The exclusion of the Semites from the domain of Mythology is announced most emphatically by the ingenious member of the French Academy, Ernest Renan, in the words, 'Les Sémites n'ont jamais eu de mythologie.'[1] This arbitrary assertion is deduced from a scheme of race-psychology invented by Renan himself, which at the first glance seems so natural and sounds so plausible when described with all the elegance of style of which he is master, that it has become an incontestable scientific dogma to a large proportion of the professional world—for even the territory of science is sometimes dominated by mere dogmas—and is treated by learned and cultivated people not specially engaged in this study as an actual axiom in the consideration of race-peculiarities.[2] The foundation of this scheme is the idea that in their views of the world, the Aryans start from multiplicity, the Semites from unity; and not only in their conception of the world, but also in politics and art. On intellectual ground, therefore, the former create mythology, polytheism, science, which is only possible through discursive observation of natural phenomena; the latter create monotheism, ('the desert is monotheistic,' says Renan), and have there-

---

[1] *Histoire générale et Système comparé des Langues sémitiques*, p. 7.

[2] Two instances will suffice to show how Renan's hypothesis became the common property of educated people. It is treated as fully made out, both by Roscher, the German political economist, and by Draper, the American naturalist and historian of civilisation. The former says: 'Life in the desert seems to be an especially favourable soil for Monotheism. It wants that luxuriant variety of the productive powers of nature by which Polytheism was encouraged in remarkably fruitful countries, such as India' (*System der Volkswirthschaft*, 7th ed., Stuttgart 1873, II. 38). The latter: 'Polytheistic ideas have always been held in repute by the southern European races; the Semitic have maintained the unity of God. Perhaps this is due to the fact, as a recent author has suggested, that a diversified landscape of mountains and valleys, islands, rivers, and gulfs, predisposes man to a belief in a multitude of divinities. A vast sandy desert, the illimitable ocean, impresses him with an idea of the oneness of God' (*History of Conflict between Religion and Science*, London 1875, p. 70). This view has also passed into Peschel's *Völkerkunde*, and Bluntschli also, in his lecture on the ancient oriental ideas of God and world in 1861, echoed Renan's hypothesis of 1855.

fore neither mythology nor science. 'If it is difficult,' justly observes Waitz, 'to estimate the capability of single individuals well known to us, it is a far more dubious task to gauge the intellectual gifts of whole nations and aces. It seems scarcely possible to find available stanards for the purpose, and consequently the judgment is almost always found to be very much founded on personal impressions. The various nations stand at various times on very different stages of development, and if only actual performances permit a safe induction as to the measure of existing capabilities, then this measure itself seems not to remain the same in the same nation through the course of time, but to vary within very wide limits, especially if we are to assume in all cases that a state of original savageness preceded civilisation.'[1] In fact, the words of this cautious psychologist apply admirably to Renan's scheme of race-psychology; for history is just what that scheme disregards. He does not observe that Polytheism and Monotheism are two stages of development in the history of religious thought, and that the latter does not spring up spontaneously,[2] without being preceded by the former stage, and that Polytheism itself is preceded by a preliminary stage, that of the mythological view of the world, which is in itself not yet a religion, but prepares the way for the rise of religion.

To form some idea of the arbitrariness of schemes founded upon some universal characteristics, we have only to glance over the literature which sprang up as soon as Renan's dictum was uttered, either to refute it, or to work his hypothesis still further—a regular host of dissertations fighting on this side or on that.[3] On reading these,

---

[1] *Anthropologie der Naturvölker*, I. 297.

[2] On the other side, Renan says (*Hist. gén.* 4th ed., p. 497) 'Cette grande conquête (the recognition of Monotheism) ne fut pas pour elle (i. e. for the Semitic race) l'effet du progrès; ce fut une de ces premières aperceptions.'

[3] Much of this literature has been unnoticed, as e.g. a late pamphlet by Léon Hugonnet: *La civilisation arabe, défense des peuples sémitiques en réponse à M. Renan*, Geneva 1873.

we see clearly how worthless such clever fancies are, that enable one to embrace with a stroke of the pen a domain which geographically fills more than half of the inhabited world, and chronologically stretches from the highest antiquity down to the most recent time. For even Renan's antagonists have fallen into his radical error: they have taken one-sided schemes and characteristics, only *different* ones from Renan's. How passive and elastic these schemes are, shall be shown by an example of some importance, which will convince us that the inferences drawn from ethnological characteristics are never anything higher than arbitrary sleight-of-hand, which any investigator can manipulate to his own purpose. To this end we will place side by side the inferences which Renan has tacked on to his hypothesis, and a talented German's conclusions, which also essentially take Renan's basis as the correct starting-point. We speak of Lange, who also starts from the principle that the Semites grasp natural phenomena in combination, the Aryans in multiplicity, and that therefore the former naturally incline towards Monotheism, and the latter towards Polytheism. But let us see to what windings and deductions this dogma leads on both sides. We hear Renan say: 'Or la conception de la multiplicité dans l'univers, c'est le polythéisme chez les peuples enfants; c'est la science chez les peuples arrivés à l'âge mûr.'[1] Quite the contrary is affirmed by the German historian of Materialism, who says: 'When the heathen sees gods everywhere, and has accustomed himself to regard every separate operation of nature as the domain of a special demonic action, he throws in the way of a materialistic explanation difficulties a thousandfold, like the offices in the Divine household . . . But Monotheism here stands in a very different relation to science.' 'If a uniform mode of work on a large scale is attributed to the one God, the mutual connexion of things in their origin and action becomes

[1] *Histoire générale*, p.

not only a possible, but even a necessary consequence of the assumption. For if I saw a thousand and again a thousand wheels in motion, and believed them to be all driven by one agent, then I should have to conclude that it was a piece of machinery, the minutest portion of which had its movement absolutely determined by the plan of the whole.' [1] 'The fact that Islâm is the religion in which that advancement of the study of nature, which we attribute to the monotheistic principle, shows itself most clearly, is connected with the peculiar talents of the Arabs . . . , but also undoubtedly with the circumstance that Mohammed's monotheism was the severest of all.' [2] Auguste Comte also draws the same inferences from the tendency of Monotheism to develop a scientific conception of the world, and makes Monotheism and Scientific treatment exert a reciprocal influence on each other.[3] To which of these opposite deductions from the same premisses shall we hold? 'Which is right?' every educated man will ask, and immediately infer the inadequacy of such general characterisations, and the wide room thereby opened to arbitrariness and error, in case it should be attempted to erect upon them a history of civilisation or an ethnology.

Now this foundation is exactly that on which Renan's assumption of the absence of mythology from the Semites rests—an assumption which can by no means be admitted, first, because it is unhistorical; and secondly, because it would necessarily follow from it that race-distinctions differentiate the psychological bases of intellectual activity. 'The Semites cannot form a myth,' is a proposition the possibility of which could be allowed only if such an assertion as 'This or that race has no digestive power, or no generative power,' could be treated otherwise than as an

---

[1] *Geschichte des Materialismus*, 1st ed., 1866, p. 77. See 2nd ed., 1873, I. 149.

[2] Ib. p. 83. See 2nd ed., p. 152.

[3] *Cours de Philosophie Positive*, éd. Littré, Paris 1869, V. 90, 197, 324.

a priori absurdity. But it is even more remarkable that Renan, notwithstanding his conviction of the 'uniform psychological constitution of the human race,' in which he finds the justification of a common story of the Deluge springing up everywhere without borrowing,[1] and although he finds the gaps in the chronology of the antediluvian period of the Biblical history filled up, 'par des noms d'anciens héros, et peut-être de divinités qu'on retrouve chez les autres peuples sémitiques,'[2] still speaks of the possibility, indeed of the necessity, that the Semitic race should be destitute of myths.

Renan's hypothesis had to encounter many a hard battle soon after its publication. The theologians were highly pleased at what was said about the monotheistic tendency of Semitism, but thought it blasphemy for Renan to find in Monotheism *le minimum de religion* and in Polytheism a higher and more civilised stage of religion. And philologists, historians and philosophers assailed the foundations of Renan's pile. Steinthal subjects the notion introduced by Renan, of a monotheistic *instinct*, to acute psychological criticism. Max Müller does the same, and points to the history of the Hebrews and the other Semites, to resolve the dreams of Semitic Monotheism into their nullity. Abraham Geiger and Salomon Munk (Renan's successor in the chair of the *Collége de France*) wish to limit to the Hebrew nation the assertion of Semitic Monotheism. Yet what is said about Mythology is not much objected to by any of these critics (with the exception of Steinthal). Indeed, one of the pioneers of modern Comparative Mythology, while combating the monotheistic instinct, takes up a position on the mythological question

[1] *Histoire générale*, p. 486: 'L'unité de constitution psychologique de l'espèce humaine, au moins des grandes races civilisées, en vertu de laquelle les mêmes mythes ont dû apparaître parallèlement sur plusieurs points à la fois, suffirait, d'ailleurs, pour expliquer les analogies qui reposent sur quelque trait général de la condition de l'humanité, ou sur quelques-uns de ses instincts les plus profonds.'

[2] Ib. p. 27.

not very far from Renan's own: 'What is peculiar to the Aryan race is their mythological phraseology, superadded to their polytheism; what is peculiar to the Semitic race is their belief in a national god—in a god chosen by his people, as his people had been chosen by him.'[1]

Mythological science has at the present day ceased to hold fast to the divisions of race in relation to the formation of myths. At least it has acted so in relation to that class of nations which, though not exhibiting a single race or several closely connected races, has (*faute de mieux*) been termed the *Turanian*—a purely negative designation, which only asserts its members to be neither Semites nor Aryans. Max Müller himself wishes to see the Turanian mythology investigated by the same method which is employed in the Aryan; and he is not shaken by the result, which exhibits a striking identity between Aryan and Turanian myths. He is not shaken even by consideration of the psychological force, which must be taken into account in the first instance in the criticism and valuation of myths. 'If people cannot bring themselves to believe in solar and celestial myths among the Hindûs and Greeks,' says this leading investigator, 'let them study the folk-lore of the *Semitic* and Turanian races. I know there is, on the part of some of our most distinguished scholars, the same objection against comparing Aryan to non-Aryan myths, as there is against any attempt to explain the features of Sanskrit or Greek by a reference to Finnish or Bask. In one sense that objection is well founded, for nothing would create greater confusion than to ignore the genealogical principle as the only safe one in a scientific classification of languages, of myths, and even of customs. We must first classify our myths and legends, as we classify our languages and dialects . . . But there is in a comparative study of languages and myths not only a philological, but also a philosophical

[1] Max Müller, *Chips from a German Workshop*, I. 370.

and more particularly a psychological interest, and though even in this more general study of mankind the frontiers of language and race ought never to disappear, yet they can no longer be allowed to narrow or intercept our view.'[1] Thus Müller also lays especial stress upon the psychological point of view, and, whatever he concedes to race-distinctions, still takes for granted the universality of the formation of myths as a psychological postulate. He exhibits, however, the application of his principle to the Turanian only in concrete examples. The Semitic, which, as we saw above, cannot be excluded in reference to the universality of the formation of myths, is left out altogether. Yet Müller appears in respect of the Semitic to have passed beyond the position on which he stood in 1860, when writing his essay 'Semitic Monotheism.'[2] Advancing in the footsteps of the master, a recent American mythologist, John Fiske, has drawn the Turanian into the domain of comparative mythology, and worked out a portion of the American stories collected by Brinton,[3] according to the laws of the new method,[4] while the German Schirren, and also Gerland less completely, had already subjected the Polynesian myths to a similar treatment.[5]

This circumstance, that the stories of the so-called Turanian humanity lend themselves to the comparative method of investigation quite as easily as the legendary treasure of the Aryan nations, is a proof how common to all mankind is the mythological capacity, how false it is to follow ethnological categories and assign it to one race and deny it to another; and on the other hand, how the

---

[1] *Introduction to the Science of Religion*, p. 390 *et seq.*

[2] In *Chips*, &c., I. p. 341.

[3] In *The Myths of the New World*, New York 1868. See Steinthal's criticism of this collection in the *Zeitschrift für Völkerpsychologie und Sprachwissenschaft*, 1871, Bd. VII.

[4] *Myths and Myth-Makers*, Boston 1873, p. 151 *et seq.*

[5] In the sixth vol. of Waitz's *Anthropologie der Naturvölker*, where I obtained information about Schirren's works.

subject-matter, the perception of which forms the groundwork of the oldest mythology, is everywhere the same—the phenomena of nature and the contests of alternating elements. For very many and various races, incapable as yet of linguistic classification, endowed with the most diverse physical constitutions, inhabiting the most differing climates from the highest northern to the furthest southern latitudes, and speaking languages the most incongruous, have taken refuge in the vast unlimited house of Turanism, until legitimate parents are found for them. Turanism is therefore the best test of the controverted universality of mythological capacity. There is then no tenable reason why, for the sake of fair-sounding but meaningless distinctions, we should introduce the Semites into history with the loss of a nose, as it were, and interpret the history of the intellectual development of that race by a principle which essentially proclaims that the Semites were not born into life as infants, and never saw the sunlight till they were men, or even old men.

§ 4. Such reflections may have determined the French Assyriologist François Lenormant quite recently, to claim mythology for the Semitic race also; although in so doing he does not mention the Hebrews at all.[1] For, notwithstanding the alluring mythological subject-matter deposited in the literature of its traditions, the Hebrew nation has always been a stepchild of mythological inquiry, and still awaits an investigator to do full justice to it. It is easy to be understood that a mistaken religious interest, which identified itself with the Biblical literature and warned off mythological inquiry with an energetic *Noli me tangere*, sharpened, it may be, with a dose of canonical or uncanonical excommunication, blockaded the passage of investigation on this path. I call it a *mistaken* interest, because the true interests of religion are advanced, not imperilled, by the results of science. Disregarding men

[1] *Les premières civilisations,* Paris 1874, II. 113 *et seq.*

of the calibre of Nork and a few other inferior disciples of the school of Creuzer, we can affirm that, with the exception of a few essays, even the freest and most earnest interpreters of the Bible have examined, and do still examine, the Biblical books only as products of literature, bringing to light valuable results as to the times and tendencies of the original composition and subsequent editing of the several parts of the Canon. But on the origin and significance of the persons themselves who figure in the Biblical stories, even the freest interpreters are silent, as if the Hebrews were a people quite apart, and not to be measured by the measure of History and Psychology.

Even those who are willing to know something of Semitic myths in general resist the assumption of Hebrew myths. No one has defined his position on this point so unambiguously as Baron Bunsen, who has thought so much and so profoundly on religious matters. It is really extraordinary that this immortal man, who exerted so stimulating an influence on the studies of his young friend Max Müller, and who welcomed the latter's pioneer-essay 'Comparative Mythology' with 'especial pleasure' at the 'pure popular poetry of the feeling for nature,' exhibited so little comprehension of the aims of the new direction given to mythological studies by Müller. His view of the connexion of the Aryan mass of mythology is consequently very confused. This is especially to be regretted, because the displacement of the true point of view in mythical speculation, and the continual concessions to Creuzer and Schelling, hindered him from making permanently useful the philosophical labour expended on the understanding of the Egyptian theology. Bunsen did not separate Religion from Myths, and consequently he sees what he calls Consciousness of a God in a genealogised and systematised Mythology. It is therefore not surprising that he advanced no further than his predecessors in relation to the Hebrew myths. He speaks of the 'spirit of the Jewish people, historically penetrated through and through with aversion to mythology,'[1] and concentrates his thoughts on this theme in the sixth, seventh, and eighth of the theses in which he exhibits the relation of the Egyptian mythology to the Asiatic. According to these, 'the Bible has no Mythology; it is the grand, momentous, and fortunate self-denial of Judaism to possess none.' As if a myth—which Bunsen himself had called '*pure* popular poetry of the feeling for nature' —were an abomination, a defilement of the human mind, a sinful act voluntarily performed, which the Elect can *deny themselves!* On the other hand, 'the national sentiment mirrored in Abraham, Moses, and the primeval history generally from the Creation to the Deluge, and the expression of it, are rooted in the mythological life of the East in the earliest times,' and 'in the long period from Joseph to Moses, there have been interwoven with the life and actions of this greatest and most influential of all the men of the first age [Abraham] and the history of his son and grandson, many ancient traditions from the mythology of those tribes from whose savage natural life the Hebrews were extracted, to their own good and that of mankind and for higher ends.'[2] According to this there are Myths belonging to the Hebrews, but not Hebrew Myths —only borrowed ones, obtained from 'Primeval Asia.'

I have exhibited Bunsen's position at some length, because, with all his advanced ideas on the essence and significance of Mythology, he still to this day dominates the minds of those who, while admitting the possibility of Semitic Mythology, are up in arms against the existence of Hebrew myths.

§ 5. Nevertheless, I hope it is clear from the above that Hebrew mythology is *a priori* possible. The following

---

[1] *Gott in der Geschichte*, I. 353; a passage which, with a large part of the volume, is omitted in the greatly abridged English translation.

[2] *Aegyptens Stelle in der Weltgeschichte*, V. ii. 18–19 (English tr. IV. 28–29).

chapters will give occasion to prove in what this existence consists. It will then appear that the Hebrew myths, necessarily owing their existence to the same psychological operation as the Aryan or the so-called Turanian, must consequently have the same original signification as these. Hence the figures of Hebrew mythology denote the very natural phenomena whose appellations lie before us in those figures' names. These names, however, are *not symbolic*,[1] but are antiquated appellatives of the natural phenomena denoted by them, just as the words, *Sun*, *Moon*, *Rain*, &c. This must be distinctly proclaimed, as some who misunderstand the modern method of Mythology pervert it in a false and antiquated way by the introduction of symbolism.

We must also beware of confounding the original Myth with Religion or, still worse, with the Consciousness of God. This confusion is the source of most of the erroneous estimates and notions of Mythology, which even the latest methods of investigating myths has not entirely removed. The very earliest activity of the human intellect can only work upon what falls immediately under the cognisance of the senses, and upon what through its frequency and the regularity of its return prompts men most readily to speech. Such things are the daily natural phenomena, the change of light and darkness, of rain and sunshine, and all that accompanies these changes. What primitive man spoke on these things, is the Myth. It is psychologically impossible that the earliest activity of the human mind should have been anything else but this. We cannot speak of a consciousness of God, a *sensus numinis*, as existing in the earliest Mythological period. Not till later, when some process in the history of language

---

[1] Even old Plutarch observed in reference to the then favourite explanation of the myths *ex ratione physica*: Δεῖ δὲ μὴ νομίζειν ἁπλῶς εἰκόνας ἐκείνων (i.e. of the sun and moon) τούτους (Zeus and Hera), ἀλλ' αὐτὸν ἐν ὕλῃ Δία τὸν ἥλιον καὶ αὐτὴν τὴν Ἥραν ἐν ὕλῃ τὴν σελήνην (*Quaestiones Romanae*, 77). See Cicero, *De Nat. Deorum*, III. 24: Longe aliter rem se habere, atque hominum opinio sit: eos enim, qui dii appellantur, *rerum naturas* esse, non *figuras deorum*.

gives the ancient myths a new direction, do they turn into either History or Religion. The latter always arises out of the materials of Mythology, and then finds its historical task to be to work itself upwards into independence. Then, while the mythology out of which it sprang is growing less and less intelligible, and therefore also less and less expressive, Religion must in the progress of its development sever its connexion with Mythology, and unite itself with the scientific consciousness, which now occupies the place of the mythological.

How Mythology becomes Religion is shown most clearly by *Dualism.* Nothing can be less correct than the belief that the dualistic system of religion had from its very origin an ethical meaning. This, as well as the limitation of Dualism to Irân and Babylon,[1] is refuted by the frequent occurrence of the dualistic conception of the world among the most various savage peoples.[2] The ethical significance of Dualism is decidedly secondary; it is the form of development of the main theme of all mythology, the relation of light to darkness, proper to a higher stage of culture. Many mythological fancies, and especially the Sun's voyage by ship in the nether world, became religious eschatological ideas when the mythical meaning itself was lost from the mind, and gave rise to new ideas of life in the nether world, resurrection, ascent to heaven, &c.; this was first established in reference to the old Egyptian mythology.[3] So also Dualism as it appears in Irân is a myth that has taken an ethical sense. This is best seen in the facts that the northern Algonquins, with whom Dualism is almost as fixed a principle as in Irân, call the good and evil principles respectively Sun and Moon,

---

[1] Spiegel still does this up to a recent date in his *Eranische Alterthumskunde*, II. 19.

[2] See Tylor, *Primitive Culture*, II. 287 *et seq.*

[3] The story of Osiris and Typhon *e.g.* originally personified the vegetative life of nature and the struggles incident to it, but was afterwards transferred to the destinies of the human soul. See Ebers, *Durch Gosen zum Sinai*, Leipzig 1872, p. 477.

and that among the Hurons the Evil principle is the grandmother of the Good:[1] the Night is the mother or grandmother, or, in general, the ancestress of the Day. Here religious dualism has not quite put off the character of its origin in Mythology. On the other hand, the Iranic system at a very early age (that of the Avesta) elevated Dualism into the region of pure morals, and yet at a later (the epic period) formed out of the original myth the localised story of the war of Zohak against Ferîdûn.[2]

That Dualism as a religious conception is a further development of the myth, and not first excited by the moral problem of the strife of the good against the evil, becomes evident also from the consideration of a peculiar form of dualistic religion which we find in many Semitic nations. We here frequently find a deity regarded as male, who has a corresponding female to represent, as it were, the reverse side of the same natural force, and then the two forces unite to produce a natural phenomenon. So, for instance, Sun and Earth, Baal and Mylitta, the factors of procreation. This likewise is a dualistic tendency, in which however the two deities are not represented as mutually hostile. We are justified in placing this phenomenon in the chapter on Dualism, because two such deities in the course of history are often joined together into one.[3] Now this side of dualistic religion can be traced back only to Mythology as its source and point of departure. The Hebrew myth of Judah and Tamar, which we shall consider further on (Chap. V., § 14), exhibits a mythical prototype of such dualistic views of religion.

---

[1] Waitz, *Anthropologie der Naturvölker*, III. 183.

[2] See Roth in the *Zeitschrift der deutschen morgenländischen Gesellschaft*, 1848, II. 217; Albrecht Weber, *Akademische Vorlesungen über indische Literaturgeschichte*, Berlin 1852, p. 35.

[3] See Kuenen, *The Religion of Israel*, London 1874, I. 226.

CHAPTER II.

SOURCES OF HEBREW MYTHOLOGY.

§ 1. If it is now established that we are justified in speaking of a Hebrew Mythology, in the same sense as of the mythologies of Indians, Hellenes, Germans, &c., then the question naturally arises, Can we come upon the track of those forms of expression and those figures which generally make up the elements of the Hebrew Myth; and Are these elements when found recognisable as elements of myths, i.e. Are they expressions and stories in which the ancient Hebrew, standing on the myth-creating stage of his intellectual development, spoke of the operations and changes of Nature? That in the abstract he was as capable as the Aryan on the same stage of development of speaking myths, we have admitted in assuming the *universality* of the formation of myths; and of what those expressions exactly consist, and what are the mythical figures which he formed, it will the business of a subsequent chapter to exhibit.

In this chapter our task will be limited to the discovery of the sources which we have to estimate by the method of Comparative Mythology, in order to discern the various expressions and figures of the Hebrew myth. Now both the incitement to the formation of myths and the course of development through which they pass before they are noted down in a literary age and then stiffen and undergo no further change, are based on psychological operations, the laws of which are not governed by categories of race and ethnology. It is therefore obvious, that for the understanding of the Hebrew myths we must betake ourselves to the very same class of sources which the mythologist finds fruitful on Aryan territory. Fortunately such sources are open to us on Hebrew ground also. They have, indeed, a less copious stream than those of Aryan mythology, but yet suffice to give us a picture of what the ancient Hebrew on the mythic stage thought and felt, and how he found expression in language for these thoughts and feelings. It is true, this investigation cannot be separated from another closely connected with it—what method we must employ to arrive at the germ of the myth hidden in these sources. But for the present we must still put off this second question, and content ourselves with the search for the sources of mythical matter. It will, however, not be always possible to avoid an indication of the method; and this is the case now with the first of the sources which we have to bring forward.

§ 2. *a.*) We shall have to speak again further on of the question, What factors in the minds of the Hebrew people produced the conception of those *Patriarchs*, whose destinies form the most illustrious portion of their national historic writing? It will then become clear that this Patriarchal character represents only a later historical stratum of mythical development, produced by those very factors. Originally the names of the Patriarchs and the actions which are told of them signified nothing historical, but only something on the domain of Nature. The names are appellations of physical phenomena, and the actions are actions of Nature. For surely we must at the outset come to a clear understanding on the question, What is the origin of persons like Abram, Sarah, Jacob and the rest, who fill the Hebrew Patriarchal history? whence, how, and by what psychological law did they enter into the mind of the primitive Hebrews? The facile assumption that these persons and the actions with which they are concerned are mere *Fiction* with no external foundation, is so cheap and meaningless a way of getting over the difficulties which their existence in poetry presents to the investigator, that it as impossible to adopt it as to admit the opposite equally arbitrary opinion, which makes them historical in the same sense as Goethe or Frederick the Great. Certainly they are fictions, if by that we mean that no historical persons correspond to them as human individuals; but by no means in the sense that their origin, or rather the conception of them, has no other foundation but the fancy of the poet or writer. In this sense they have actual realities corresponding to them—the events and operations of Nature, which are the main-springs of mythical language. And it is not conceivable that the oldest utterances of the human mind should have begun from anything else but from the sensations which the operations of Nature aroused in their breasts. As soon as they perceived these, occasion for myths was present; and the myths show how they became fully conscious of the operations of Nature.

The Patriarchal stories are therefore an important source for the knowledge of myths. If we loosen stratum after stratum which has been formed through the agency of psychological and historical factors over the primitive form of the myth, and have at length penetrated back to the stage at which many of the mythical appellations, through the disuse of multifarious synonymous terms, were individualised and personified, then it is easy to pick the primitive germ, the original mythic elements, out of the shell in which they had been encased. Hence it appears that the most fruitful field for mythological investigation on Hebrew territory is the Book of GENESIS, the greater part of which brings together the stories which the Hebrew people connected with the names of the Patriarchs.

§ 3. *b.*) The Patriarchal legends, in such fulness and artistic finish as the remains of old Hebrew literature have preserved for us, are a distinguishing characteristic of this literature. Other nations have failed to transform their myths into such a wealth of reports about their first progenitors. What meagre accounts the Hellenes give of their national ancestors, in comparison with this rich and varied Patriarchal history! A special peculiarity of the historical development of the Hebrew people was active here, bringing the *national* idea into the foreground, and exerting its influence in this direction on the transformation of the primitive mythological materials.[1] But instead of this, other nations, among whom our above-named example, the richly endowed Hellenes, are to be reckoned, have chosen rather to transform the figures of their myths into Gods and godborn Heroes.

The figures of Gods, which were developed out of Hebrew myths, very early retired into the background. It was partly the Canaanite influence to which the Hebrew people very early succumbed, and partly the progressing monotheistic tendency, that allowed no theology consistently developed out of mythology to maintain itself for any length of time. Of Heroes, however, there is no want in the memory of the Hebrews. In that region as well as elsewhere, the Heroes had originally borne a different meaning and belonged to mythology; and their heroic character is, on the Hebrew as well as on the Aryan domain, secondary, produced by the psychological and linguistic process which caused the natural meaning of mythological figures to vanish from the mind.

Now although these Heroes are originally gigantic persons bound to no definite place or time, yet they are gradually condensed into individuals and regarded as more and more concrete and definite. What is told of them puts off its generality and indefiniteness. They are conceived as belonging to certain places where their heroic deeds were performed—in other words, the legends of Heroes are localised. Their activity is assigned to a definite time, they are inserted in a chronological frame,

[1] We shall treat of this in the Third Section of Chapter VIII.

in which they take up a definite position as to time. What more natural localisation of the activity of the Heroes could there be than to imagine them living in the same geographical districts as those who tell of them? The localisation of heroic legends is always enlisted in the service of patriotic feeling. Herakles and Theseus are *Greek* patriots, heroic benefactors of the Grecian people. The determination of the time when they lived was influenced mainly by the endeavour, natural to every civilised nation, to gain a clear, comprehensive, and continuous picture of its own history. But truly historical memory does not generally go far enough back to explain with proper fulness the entire past doings of a nation. The historical beginnings of a people are lost in the mist of indefiniteness and uncertainty. What is easier than to fill up this obscure period of history by telling of the doings of the Heroes? Why, the human temper in its pessimistic mood is always inclined to fancy the very oldest age peopled with men of gigantic proportions of both body and mind, in comparison with whom the enervate present generation is a mere shadow. So we find the stories of Heroes always at the head of the national history. The history of the Greek people begins with their heroic age; and the obscure period of Hebrew history between the first entrance into Canaan and the creation of the Monarchy, the so-called time of the Judges, is likewise the frame which must hold the Hebrew heroic legends. The stories of the Hebrew Heroes group themselves round the history of this period. The second important source of knowledge of the materials of the Hebrew mythology is accordingly the cycle of stories to be found in the canonical Book of Judges. This is the mine of mythology, whose treasures Professor Steinthal has brought to light with such critical acuteness in his dissertation on the story of Samson,[1] which breaks up entirely new ground. Here for the first

---

[1] Translated and given as an Appendix to this volume.—Tr.

time the method and results of the modern science of mythology were independently applied to the domain of Hebrew antiquity. It must be called a happy accident that the mythical character of the Hebrew heroes could be proved by so convincing an example as Shimshôn (Samson); for even the wildest scepticism cannot doubt that this name is equivalent to shemesh, 'sun,' and that this fact gives us an undeniable right to maintain the *solar* significance of the hero, and to see in his battles the contest of the Sun against darkness and storms.

§ 4. *c.*) But the Old Testament stories do not cease to be a source for mythological investigation exactly where the traditions of Genesis and the Book of Judges are succeeded by really historical accounts. For it is an admitted fact that, as soon as ever the myths have lost their original meaning by the personification of their figures, mythical characteristics are not limited to their proper domain, but often actually attach themselves to historical persons and historical actions. Alexander the Great, for example, is a phenomenon whose historical character could not be shaken by the very boldest criticism. Yet the story even of Alexander's acts and fortunes has been forced to bear some characteristics of the Solar myth, traits which were originally peculiar to the Sun-hero, as especially the journey into the realm of darkness.[1] Accordingly, not every phenomenon in the traditional characteristics of which we discover solar features is mythical, even though, strictly speaking, it can scarcely be classed with history (as e.g. William Tell). It is highly erroneous to speak, as is often done, of myth and history as two opposites which exclude any third possibility.

However, there are two points to which we ought to attend when considering the attachment of mythic ele-

[1] How readily Alexander's history was combined with the Solar myth is best proved by the fact that Arabian tradition gives Alexander a Sun-name, the variously interpreted Ḏû-l-karnein = the Horned, i.e. the Beaming.

ments to historical phenomena. First, it is usual, as we have just mentioned, to find one or another mythical characteristic attached to historical phenomena, as we may observe (to keep on specifically Hebrew ground) in the portraiture of the character of David or of Elijah (see Chap. VI. § 8). The residence of the Hebrews in Egypt, and their exodus thence under the guidance and training of an enthusiast for the freedom of his tribe, form a series of strictly historical facts, which find confirmation even in the documents of ancient Egypt. But the traditional narrative of these events, elaborated by the Hebrew people. was involuntarily associated with characteristics of that Solar myth which forms the oldest mental activity of mankind in general. Thus, for example, the passage through the sea by night is to be compared with the myth of the setting sun, which travels all night through the sea, and rises again in the morning on the opposite side. Similarly, we find attached to the picture of the life of Moses, which the Biblical narrative presents with a theocratic colouring, solar characteristics, indeed more specifically features of the myth of Prometheus. These have been clearly exhibited by Steinthal in his fine Treatise on the Prometheus-story, to which I will here only refer without reproducing its contents.[1] Secondly, we must consider the converse relation—that historical facts, the names of the agents of which have not been preserved in the popular mind, may be attached to mythical names. We can go back to the time of the Judges for an example of this. It is evidently real history that we read of the embittered contests waged by the Hebrews in that age against the Philistines and other tribes of Canaan. Remembrance of these contests, in the absence of historical names, helped itself out by the mythical appellations which, after the individualising of mythical figures, had obtained significance as personal names. In the first case the bearers of the names are historical per-

[1] Translated and given as an Appendix to this volume.—Tr.

sons, and the features of the story belong to mythology; in the second, history is wedded to mythical names. In both directions, accordingly, the Hebrew history treated critically is a source for mythological investigation.

§ 5. *d.*) One of the most reliable, but at the same time most hazardous, sources of Hebrew, as of Aryan, mythological investigation is the *language* itself, and above all, the appellations to which the myth is attached. These appellations, which in the process of transformation of the original meaning of the myth became personal names, are in their proper original sense appellatives; and we have to find the appellative signification in order to establish the mythological character. In this investigation it is best to follow the method, the use of which in Aryan mythology has brought such brilliant results to light. In many appellations the appellative sense can be found without much difficulty, being explicable from the language itself, in our case from the known treasures of the Hebrew tongue. In others the known material of the Hebrew language refuses its aid, and we must then take refuge in a cautious employment of the group of allied languages, i.e. the Semitic stock. In this connexion we must never leave out of sight the fact that the treasury of Hebrew words which is contained in the books of the Old Testament does not even approximately embrace the wealth of the ancient Hebrew vocabulary which we are enabled to infer from this fraction. In the proper names much ancient linguistic property is preserved which occurs nowhere else. The discovery of the appellative signification of mythological proper names consequently does an important service to mythological investigation, by finding a tangible starting-point for the determination of the mythical sense of the root-word in question. But it does more: it also fills up gaps in the Hebrew lexicon, and rescues many an old component part of that important language, which otherwise would remain utterly unknown.

An example will make this clear, and show that linguistic investigation and mythology have an equal share in the instruction to be derived from such inquiries.

We often meet in Hebrew with the verb hishkîm, denoting 'to perform some occupation early in the morning' (the occupation itself being determined by a dependent verb), ὀρθρεύειν. It represents the so-called *Hiph'îl*-stem, which has regularly the sense of a factitive, but is not unfrequently used to express the entrance into a certain time or place, the doing of an act in certain conditions of time or place. In this case the Hiph'îl verb is always derived from the noun which describes this place or time. Here the conditions of time concern us most. We say, for instance, he'erîbh with the sense 'to enter on the evening,' 'to do something in the evening;' e.g. 'the Philistine came near *morning and evening*,' hashkêm we-ha'arêbh (1 Sam. XVII. 16). The last word is derived from the noun 'erebh, 'evening.' From the word shachar, which denotes 'the dawn,' is formed at a late stage of the language hishchîr, 'to do something at that time;' and this Hiph'îl form of shachar can then appear beside that from 'erebh exactly like hishkîm in an earlier age.[1] Now of course this verb hishkîm must have a noun for its basis, which would denote 'morning.' But no such is found in the known Hebrew thesaurus, for the nominal form belonging to this root, shekhem, means 'neck,' and etymologists have given themselves much useless labour in trying to find any tolerable connexion between the meaning of this noun and hishkîm. The most bearable which they could give is that one who rises early to go after his business loads his neck with labour.[2] But any one may reply, Does one who does his work after dinner or in the evening load his neck with no labour? Considering the relation in which these Hiph'îl-forms stand to the nouns from which they are derived, we might almost *apriori* assert that in the ancient language

[1] *Wayyiḳrâ rabbâ*, sect. XIX.: hishchîr we-he'erîbh.

[2] See Gesenius, *Thesaurus*, p. 1406. *b*.

shekhem must have denoted 'morning' also. And in this instance mythological inquiry offers us the safest clue. The name *Shekhem* [Shechem] figures in the Hebrew myth as the ravisher of Dinah, Jacob's daughter. Without anticipating the analysis of this myth, which fits into the context of one of the next chapters, we immediately recognise in the mythic name *Shekhem* the noun from which the verb hishkîm is derived. Thus the mythical appellation refers to the early morning, the red glow, as the ravisher of the sun; and the same amorous connexion is expressed in various ways in the Aryan mythology also.

No one can deny that the consideration of the myth has here enriched the knowledge of the old Hebrew vocabulary; and thus, even on Hebrew ground, mythology and linguistic studies go hand in hand. This makes the investigation of language one of the richest sources for the discovery of the mythical ideas of early humanity.

§ 6. *e.*) While the circle of thoughts which guide the prose style moves on the level of the general principles current at the time of the writer, poetical language and style, on the other hand, have a tendency to adopt modes of expression produced in a long past age in accordance with the ideas then prevalent. These modes of expression, when they arose, corresponded accurately with the general ideas of the time, and had the signification which the *literal sense* yields; they were used whenever occasion offered for their employment, and everyone understood what was meant by them, for the thought would in that age never be expressed otherwise. The poetical language of a later time preserves such modes of expression even when their significance in the general conception of things is lost, and the occurrences thereby indicated are imagined in a different way altogether; the language then becomes *figurative*, as it is called.[1] Thus the language of the

[1] See Hermann Cohen's dissertation, *Die dichterische Phantasie und der Mechanismus des Bewusstseins*, in the *Zeitschrift für Völkerpsychologie*, &c. 1869, VI. 239 *et seq.*

Hebrew poetry and of those writers who speak in a lofty style bordering on that of poetry, and are called Prophets, preserves many of the modes of expression derived from the ancient mythological ideas of the world. Mythical material may consequently be found now and then here also.

When e.g. Isaiah says (XIV. 28), 'I will sweep it with the besom of destruction,' this is what we call a poetic figure—destruction being pictured as a broom that sweeps away from the surface of the earth those who are to be destroyed. But from another side it is seen to be something more and different from a mere poetical figure, since its origin is due, not to an artistic idea of the speaker, but to an old-world mythical conception here employed figuratively, a conception which occurs in many cycles of mythology. For instance, the Maidens of the Plague are represented with brooms in their hands, with which they sweep before house-doors and bring death into the village.[1] But Isaiah says again (XXVII. 1) that 'Jahveh with his sore and great and strong sword shall punish Leviathan the piercing serpent, even Leviathan that crooked serpent, and he shall slay the dragon (tannîn) that is in the sea;' and Job (XXVI. 13), in his grand picture of the contest which Jahveh wages against the tempest, and the defeat of the latter by the omnipotence of Jahveh, says 'By his breath the heavens are brightened; his hand has pierced the flying serpent (nâchâsh bârîach)'; and the prophet living in the Babylonian captivity addresses Jahveh in the following words (Is. LI. 9): 'Awake, awake, put on strength, O arm of Jahveh! awake, as in the ancient days, in the generations of old! Art thou not it that didst kill the monster (rababh), and wound the dragon (tannîn?)' &c.[2] In these expressions we observe that

[1] On the German legends in which this idea occurs see Henne-Am-Rhyn, *Die deutsche Volkssage*, Leipzig 1874, p. 268 *et seq.*

[2] See Ps. LXXIV. 13–14; LXXXIV. 11. There is nothing to justify those interpreters who, caring nothing for the remains of ancient myths, always wish to understand by *Rahabh* and *Tannîn* the kingdom of Egypt.

prophets and poets employ the long outgrown and obsolete notions of the myth of the battle of the Sun against the flying serpent (Lightning) and against the recumbent or curved serpent (Rain)—the monsters which want to devour the Sun, but which the Sun shoots down with his arrows (Rays) or wounds with a volley of stones; or else of the myth of the battle of the Sun already set against the monster that lies in wait at the bottom of the sea to devour him (a myth which is also preserved in the story of Jonah), only that the monotheistic mind substituted Jahveh for the Sun. Many prophets frequently speak in a perfectly general way, without reference to a definite historical event, of a passage through the sea. This is by no means a reminiscence of the Passage of the Red Sea, as an event in the primeval history of the Hebrew people, unless a pointed reference is made to that; it is another application of an old mythical notion of the course taken by the Sun-hero after sunset through the sea, so as to shine again on the following morning on the opposite shore. Indeed, that Hebrew story of the Exodus itself, as we have indicated, is only a myth transformed into history by a process which we can follow, step by step, in the history of the evolution of Mythology. This becomes very clear when we examine the sequel of the above-quoted words of the anonymous Prophet of the Captivity (Is. LI. 10): 'Art not thou it whichd ryeth the sea, the waters of the great deep; that maketh the depths of the sea a way for the ransomed to pass over?' What is pictured in this verse is in the mind of the speaker an event of the same character as that referred to in the preceding verse—the killing of the Rahabh and the wounding of the Tannîn. The description of Canaan, too, as a land 'flowing with milk and honey,' points back to the myth of a sun-land; for the myths call the rays of the sun and moon 'milk and honey,' regarding the moon as a bee[1]

[1] Angelo de Gubernatis, *Zoological Mythology*, II. 217. On the meaning of

and the sun as a cow. In Excursus E we shall speak of the mythological conception of rays of light as fluids. Palestine, which the writer wished to pourtray as possessed of every blessing, thus receives attributes which the myth gave to a place above the earth, whence the blessings of light streamed down to it. It is noteworthy that in the Çatapatha Brâhmana the same mythic conception which is employed poetically in Hebrew meets us tinged already with an eschatological colour. This work (XI. 5. 6. 4) makes *milk and honey* flow in the abodes of the Blest.[1] We also see from this that the notion of a 'poetical figure' requires frequent limitation. Many apparently poetical figures have their origin in an ancient mythical conception. Not everything that has the look of a poetical or rhetorical figure is one. Who would doubt, for instance, on a superficial glance, that such a phrase as nâr al-ḥarb, 'the fire of war,' was a figure of poetry or rhetoric? Yet it is not; it is not derived from what only exists in the fancy of the speaker, but from something which has a concrete, objective existence. We learn this from the Arabic commentary on the proverb Nâr al-ḥarb as'aru, 'the fire of war is burning.' The scholiast[2] says 'When the ancient Arabs began a war, they used to light a fire, to serve as a beacon for those eager for the fight.' It is also said (of the Jews): 'As often as they light a fire for war, Allâh extinguishes it.'[3] Thus the fire of war of which the ancient Arabs spoke was only a material or natural one.

§ 7. *f.*) The Hebrew mythic tradition is not contained exclusively in the Old Testament. This canon, indeed, was very far from receiving all the remains of the old myths that were current among the people in an historical transformation. Much of it is contained in the tradition

---

milk and honey in the Hebrew myth, Steinthal has written exhaustively in his Treatise on the Story of Samson, given in the Appendix.

[1] See Weber in the *Zeitschrift der D. M. G.*, 1855, IX. 238.

[2] Al-Meydânî, *Majma' al-amthâl*, II. 203.

[3] *Korân*, Sûr. V. v. 69.

which was not incorporated with the canon, especially in the so-called Rabbinical *Agâdâ*, which contains many a treasure of as high an antiquity as the mythological sources which we have named within the canon. In the discovery of such elements in the Agâdâ circumspection and cautious criticism are necessary, because the valuable portion is only an excessively small fraction of the whole, and has to be picked out of a preponderating mass of very different character. Still we must acknowledge the Agâdâ as a source for the discovery of the old Hebrew myths. It has indeed already been employed for this purpose, though not always wisely. The learned Professor F. L. W. Schwartz has referred to this source,[1] and Julius Braun goes even too far in his mythological estimate of the Agâdâ, when he says without limitation,[2] 'The Rabbinical stories are anything but arbitrary inventions; they are echoes of primeval memories only refused entrance into the Bible by the compilers of the canon. If Rabbinical erudition sometimes makes unfortunate attempts to confirm extrabiblical tradition by a Biblical quotation, and to prove its existence in Biblical times by imagined allusions, this is no proof that the whole tradition is only a speculation derived from misunderstood Bible-words.' But Braun makes a very bad use of the Rabbinical tradition, and vies with the foolish writer Nork in taking from right and left without selection or judgment whatever he can find, not caring whether it is Veda or Bible, Homer or the Fathers, cuneiform inscriptions or some obscure allegorical writer.

The Agâdâ in many places gives names to persons who are mentioned in the Bible without name; and these names have frequently so antique a stamp, that we cannot suppose them to be due to the capricious invention of the Agadists.[3] I believe that when these names appear justi-

---

[1] *Sonne, Mond und Sterne* [i.e. Bd. I. of *Die poetischen Naturanschauungen, &c.*], p. 4.

[2] *Die Naturgeschichte der Sage*, I. 127.

[3] See Excursus A.

fied by internal evidence (i.e. when they show themselves quite fitting to the nature of the myth), they may be ancient and important for mythological inquiry. Of course we must not be ruled by excessive optimism, nor ever forget the freedom with which the Agadic fancy rules in its own sphere.[1] The same may be said also of the identifications, of which the Agadists are very fond, and of the genealogical statements, which, though deserving little attention from the historical point of view, may have their origin in an old myth. So e.g. the Targûm on 1 Sam. XVII. 4 calls Samson the father of Goliath.[2] Now Goliath is the giant whom 'the reddish hero with fine face' overcomes by throwing stones; in other words, the Sun-hero throws stones at the monster of the storm. Thus the myth may very well say that the Sun (Samson) is the father of this hostile giant of the night, just as the Sun in various forms frequently appears in the character of father or mother of the Night.

It is easily intelligible how difficult it must be to determine the mythological value of every such statement; and we have consequently made very scanty use of this source. It might be relatively safer to use them when they speak not merely of names and genealogies, but of actual stories. The Abram-story especially has preserved in its Agadic form much matter from ancient myths, the valuation of which by B. Beer, in a lucid compilation on this very portion of the Agâdâ,[3] is easily accessible. So e.g. the battle of Abram against Nimrod, which the myth-investigator must take as the contest between the Nightly heaven and the Sun, is known only

[1] Such names have often planted themselves firmly in popular tradition, and are accordingly mentioned in various quarters with perfect uniformity. So e.g. Ιαννῆς and Ιαμβρῆς, who appear both in Rabbinical writings and in 2 Tim. III. 8 (see Jablonski, *Opuscula*, ed. Te Water, II. 23).

[2] See Wilhelm Bacher's treatise, *Kritische Untersuchungen zum Prophetentargûm* (*Zeitschrift der D. M. G.* 1874, XXVIII. 7).

[3] *Leben Abraham's nach Auffassung der jüdischen Sage*, Leipzig 1859. Another good compilation is that of Hamburger, *Geist der Hagada*, Leipzig 1857, I. 39-50.

from the Agâdâ; the Scripture says not a word of it. For the solar character of Nimrod, which is however independently clear from the Biblical statements, the Agâdâ has again preserved a valuable datum, viz. that 365 kings (equal to the days of the solar year) appear ministering to him.[1] This is the same conception of the myth as that Enoch, of whom again the solar event of the Ascension is preserved only in tradition, lived 365 years; or that Helios had herds of 350 cattle (7 herds of 50 each); and that in the Veda the Sun-god is blessed with 720 twin children, i.e. 360 days and nights,[2] and that his chariot is drawn by seven horses, i.e. the seven days of the week.[3]

The Agâdâ, again, has preserved the following mythical expression, which Professor Schwartz interprets in this sense:[4] 'Abraham was in possession of a precious stone which he wore round his neck all his life; when he died, God took the stone and hung it on the Sun.'[5] As has been fully proved with regard to Aryan mythology, especially by Schwartz and Kuhn, the myth calls the sunshine and other luminous bodies stones in general, or more specifically precious stones.[6] By night, as long as Abraham (the nightly heaven) lives, he bears the precious stone himself; when the night dies, God takes this stone (the moonlight) and hangs it on the sun.

How cautiously we must proceed in the mythological application of the Agâdâ, is obvious to all who know the nature and origin of the Agâdâ and the Agadic collections. I will adduce one other example to show how easily one might be led astray by yielding too trustingly and unconditionally to the temptation to employ this source in the interpretation of myths.

---

[1] *Bêth ham-midrâsh : Sammlung kleiner Midrashim und vermischter Abhandlungen aus der jüdischen Literatur*, ed. Ad. Jellinek, Vienna 1873, V. 40.

[2] Max Müller, *Essays* [German translation of *Chips*], II. 147; not in the English.

[3] Rigveda, L. 8; CCCXCIX. 9.

[4] *Sonne, Mond und Sterne*, p. 4.

[5] Bab. Bâbhâ bathrâ, fol. 16. *b*.

[6] See Kuhn, *Ueber Entwickelungsstufen der Mythenbildung* (*Abhandl. der kön. Akad. d. W.* 1873, Berlin 1874), p. 144.

In the course of our investigations, it will become certain that Jacob belongs to the series of mythical figures which are connected with the nightly heaven. How easily would this conception be disturbed, if we were to accord to all the Agâdâ an absolute voice among the sources of Hebrew mythical investigation! For there it is said in reference to Gen. XXVIII. 11: 'He (Jacob) reached that place and passed the night there, for *the sun was come* (kî bhâ hash-shemesh), i.e. had set.' On this the Agadist Chaggî of Sephoris remarks, 'This sentence indicates that Jacob, when he was in Bethel, heard the welcoming voices of the angels: "The Sun is come, the Sun is come," i.e. Jacob himself. Many years later, when Jacob's son Joseph told his father the dream in which an allusion is made to Jacob as if he were the Sun (XXXVII. 9, 10), Jacob thought to himself, 'Who has informed my son that my name is Sun?'[1]

I must point out one other peculiarity in this part of the subject. Sometimes the Agadists utilise mythological elements, by supplementing the old mythic tradition with something added by themselves, *based on some one of their hermeneutic principles*, but which could not possibly be also a portion of the old myth. An example will elucidate this. We will not lay down dogmatically, nor on the other hand dispute the possibility, that the name Bile'âm *Balaam* is mythical. It signifies 'the Devourer,' and has consequently been identified for centuries with the Arabic Loḳmân, which has the same meaning.[2] Accordingly Balaam would originally have been a name of the monster which devours the sun. It is not uncommon in mythology to find wisdom, cunning and prudence attributed to the powers hostile to the sun. Hence the serpent appears in the myth endowed with wisdom. This justifies Balaam's character as sage and prophet; the serpent delivers oracles, or is *οἰωνός*.[3] Balaam is son of

[1] Berêshîth rabbâ, sect. 68.

[2] See on the other side Ewald, *History of Israel* (2nd or 3rd ed.), II. 214.

[3] Welcker, *Griechische Götterlehre*, Gottingen 1857, I. 66.

Be'ôr, or 'the Shining'—a mythical expression which often occurs when the darkness is described as springing from the daylight; and the Agâdâ may be using mythic elements in identifying this Be'ôr with Lâbhân 'the White.'[1] So this myth, like many others, would then have been *nationalised* by the influence of factors, which will be fully described in the Seventh Chapter. The Devourer of the Sun became a Devourer of the Hebrew people, just as the Sun-hero became the Hebrew national hero. Personations of the storms are often exhibited in mythology as lame and limping.[2] This feature, which is not ascribed to Balaam in the Bible, is found in the Agâdâ, which says, Bile'âm chiggêr beraglô achath hâyâ, 'Balaam was lame of one foot.' So far all is regular. But then follows, Shimshôn chiggêr bishtê raglâw hâyâ, 'Samson was lame of both feet'[3]—a feature which does not suit the Sun-hero. We must consider that this latter is an inference drawn by the Agâdâ in virtue of one of its hermeneutic principles, thus: Balaam's lameness is attached to the word shephî, 'hill, high place,' Num. XXIII. 3; the word shephîphôn, 'serpent,' Gen. XLIX. 17 (in the declaration concerning Dan, which the Agadists take as referring to Samson the Danite), must according to the Agadists' hermeneutics express by its form a doubling of the notion conveyed by shephî.[4]

Thus only what is said about Balaam could possibly belong to the old myth; what is said about Samson is late Agadic induction, which has no importance whatever for mythology.

---

[1] I find this identification, it is true, only in later books, Tânâ de-bhê Elîyâ, c. 27; Sêder 'ôlâm, c. 21; see Halâkhôth gedôlôth (hilkhôth haspêd). In the Sêder had-dôrôth, under the year 2189, Beor is called son of Laban. On Laban see Chap. V. § 11. Besides the name Loḳmân, which in signification corresponds with Bile'âm (Balaam), we find in the Preislamite genealogy of the Arabs, which in my opinion is largely mixed up with mythical names, the chief Bal'â'u, who is said to have been a leper (Ibn Dureyd, *Kitâb al-ishtiḳâḳ*, p. 106. 8). It should be observed that this is a man's name with the grammatical form of a feminine adjective.

[2] See Chap V. § 10 end. [3] Sôṭâ, fol. 10, *a*. [4] See Excursus B.

CHAPTER III.

THE METHOD OF INVESTIGATING HEBREW MYTHS.

§ 1. The method of investigation is intended to discover —how the original myth is to be reached through the sources described in the preceding chapter, how the primitive germ of the myth is to be freed from the husk which in the course of its growth has been formed around it, and further how the progress and lapse of this growth itself are to be recognised. Then we shall be enabled to determine how stratum upon stratum has fastened itself round the original myth until it reached that configuration which is the concrete material of our investigation. The development of the myth in any nation is mainly determined by two factors, which give to this development the direction actually taken. One group of these factors is *psychological*, the other belongs to the *history of civilisation*.[1] The psychological factors in the development of all myths are the same, not changing with the special character of the people whose myths form the subject of our consideration. For the same general laws everywhere determine the life of the soul; no difference in them is introduced by the ethnological life and the peculiarity of race of the people in question. There is a psychology of mankind, or as it was called when Lazarus introduced the science, a Psychology of Nations (*Völkerpsychologie*).

[1] 'Die andere *culturhistorisch.*' I am obliged to render this convenient adjective by a circumlocution, as 'civilisation-historical would be too cumbrous and hardly intelligible.—Tr.

This is not a contemplation of the modes in which the intellectual life of various nations exhibits itself as acting in opposite directions, but of the modes in which the same laws find their expression and validity in the intellectual life of the most various nations. But there is no special psychology of races. On the other hand, the factors belonging to the *history of civilisation* are not everywhere alike, but are as various as the historical fates of the nations among themselves are various. We shall subsequently come back to the subject to show more fully that myths share in the historical vicissitudes of their nation, that they are always transformed in accordance with the stages of civilisation which the nation itself passes through in its historical development, and that accordingly the configuration of the myth is a faithful mirror of the stage of civilisation at which it has taken this particular configuration. Obviously therefore, we can duly estimate the myth through all its stages of development only in connexion with a comprehensive view over the historical development of the civilisation of the nation itself. And to gain this view we must especially attend to those phenomena which might produce an altered direction of the mind, and thus impress a new form on the myth also. But as in the methodical observation of the intellectual development of a nation in the course of its history psychological points of view must again occupy the foreground, we may assert that psychological observation must take up a prominent position in the method of mythological investigation; for the question will always be, What transformation does this or that historical vicissitude produce in that which makes up the sum of the human mind? The answer will however evidently turn out different according to the nature of these historical vicissitudes. But there is one special step of transformation which stands earlier than and in no connexion with the separate history of the nation, and is produced by a purely psychological operation. This transformation is therefore common to all myths—so much so that most inquirers, and especially Max Müller, make the life of the myth to begin only at this stage.

It is the stage of mental development which is signalised by a remarkable fact in the history of language: viz., that an endless multitude of names, bestowed upon the phenomena and processes of nature, in virtue of various features of which there is a preponderating consciousness at the moment of perception, gradually lose their meaning; while some few features of the total phenomenon are retained, to represent all those particular factors and supply comprehensive general terms for their sum total. For example, the Sun has at first a countless number of designations. It is not merely that, in its various aspects, the Sun is treated as the subject of detached observation unrelated in thought to that of other aspects of the same Sun; but the very same aspect, on repeated notice, is regarded as something different every time, and is accordingly denoted by other names. In other words, borrowed from the terminology of modern psychology, no *fusion* (*Verflechtung*) has yet been effected. Long-continued observation of the same aspects gives consciousness of their identity under repetition, and makes possible the fusion of their ideas. Next, by a further advance in development, the psychological change emerges, through which the various features of the same phenomenon cease to be essential difference-marks in the idea, and, dropping into the background, give place to a general conception gained by their fusion, an aggregate of fusion (*Verflechtungsmasse*), the product of often-repeated fusion.[1] The effect on language of this psychological change is that, through its gradual operation, the meaning is lost from the great majority of those expressions which arose merely because the particular observations of the same aspect of a phe-

[1] I must refer those readers who are not sufficiently familiar with the terminology to Steinthal's *Abriss der Sprachwissenschaft*, Berlin 1871, vol. I., where all this is fully discussed in the section *Elementare psychische Processe.*

nomenon, or the various features of the same phenomenal aggregate had not yet been brought into unity by the process of fusion or blending.

By the abandonment of the difference-marks, the sum total of all the aspects, now regarded as forming one unity, is given over to one single word, and a vast number of old designations, which stood in connexion with one particular aspect or one particular condition of observation, lose in the mind of the speaker all connexion with the physical phenomenon in question. The multiplicity of names becomes objectless, loses all psychological basis, and vanishes.[1] What vanishes, however, is only the consciousness of the connexion of the multifarious names with the physical phenomenon; in other words, the names cease in great part to be designations of the phenomena, yet remain in existence. But they have a very different value to the mind from their original one. They become *Proper Names*; and what the sentences in which these names figured as subjects and objects originally predicated of physical phenomena, they now say of persons and individuals. The transition is facilitated by the fact that the physical phenomena themselves, whose names they were in an earlier stage of intelligence, are conceived under the figure of human actions, as loving, fighting, persecuting, &c. We must here observe emphatically that from this process in the history of language the Semitic area was not excluded. In the course of the following expositions we shall have occasion to convince ourselves that mythological appellatives forfeited their appellative character just like those of the Aryan myths. The Hebrew said 'he laughs,' 'he hides,' 'he trips up,' he increases,' &c. in a strictly mythical sense; in later times the meaning of these assertions was forgotten, and a proper name took the place of each.

[1] But it is to be observed that some of the expressions produced by Polyonymy [multitude of names] survive the process of fusion and remain with the original signification; thus e.g. several names for Moon in Hebrew. On such names Synonymy, a secondary function of conscious speech, then performs its work.

What Max Müller says of Semitic speech, that 'those who used the word were unable to forget its predicative meaning, and retained in most cases a distinct consciousness of its appellative power,'[1] is not true, at least of this portion of Semitism.

Now this is the very earliest step in the transformation of the myth. As we have seen, this transformation is conditioned only by a psychological operation, and is therefore common to every mythology. Some scholars are inclined to draw nothing that precedes this transformation into the domain of myths at all, and to say that these begin only when, as Max Müller says, *the language* (i.e. the living consciousness of the original signification of the multifarious names) *dies*. But we hold that there is every reason to regard the stage at which those expressions lived in the human mind with their original appellative sense, as one of the proper mythic stages. That event which Max Müller treats as the commencement of the development of the myth, indicates the first link in the long chain of transformations which make up the history of the myth. It is not a characteristic of the myth, that the speaker is no longer conscious of speaking of physical phenomena. As soon as ever he perceives physical phenomena as events in human life, he has at once made a myth; and every name by which he designates a physical phenomenon forms a myth. For if unintelligibility or obsoleteness of language were a condition of a myth's existence, then there could be no myth when the Greek calls Hêlios the brother of Selênê, since both these names have been retained in their original sense, and the Greek knew that the former name meant Sun and the latter Moon, though of Hêraklês and Helenê he had no similar consciousness left. Similarly, it could not be a myth when the Roman said that Aurora opens the gates of the Sun and strews roses on his way, since every Roman knew that the name Aurora denoted the Dawn.

---

[1] *Chips*, First Series, pp. 356, 361.

§ 2. It is easy to see that the first step in the formation of myths could not be a short and quickly passing stage. If it were so, the appellations of physical phenomena could not have become so firmly established as to prolong their existence even after a great majority of them had become linguistically meaningless, and to become objects of mythical transformation. The psychological process which brought about the identification of an object with itself must therefore have taken place late in the development of the human mind. Men had already expressed most various notions of the phenomena of nature and observed them in many phases, long before they attained to the power of identifying one such repeatedly occurring phenomenon with itself, notwithstanding the regularity of its appearance.

One other psychological consideration, however, demands our attention here—one among many; for a systematic presentation of all the psychological forces with which we have to reckon in investigating myths and the history of their growth belongs to a Philosophy of Mythology, which it is not our intention to give here.

Among the various categories, that of Space is the earliest to become an object of consciousness to the human soul, both in the genetic development of the individual mind and in that of the human race. The attachment of a notion to space is the earliest developed; indeed the notion of a thing without the notion of space is impossible. Even beasts distinguish things by their space. Hence L. Geiger correctly said that Language, the origin of which also marks the first phase of the power of thought, 'springs from' the organ of the discrimination of space, 'the Eye and Light.' With the category of Time it is otherwise. The discrimination of things in time is unfolded relatively later; it postulates a more delicate degree of observation. The notion of Space emanates from that sense, the use of which man acquires the earliest and the most easily of all except that of touch—the sense of Sight; the excitement of which also gives the first impulse to the formation of language. But the notion of Time demands more than a mere sensuous perception. We need not therefore be surprised if the notion of Space, both in the individual and in history, is older than that of Time, nor that, as language teaches, all the finer distinctions of opposite terms emanate from the notion of Space,[1] and the very distinctions of Time itself were originally conceived from the point of view of Space. To verify this, we only need to observe the expressions still in daily use, which can be applied to time, such as, *before, after, thereafter, space of time, short* or *long* time. The Semitic is very instructive on this point. The Hebrew shâm, originally used of place (*there*) is found applied to time (*then*); in Arabic these two significations are divided between thumma 'then' and thamma 'there.' Hebrew words, such as liphenê 'before' and acharê 'after,' ḳedem, ḳadmôn, 'old, olden time,' bring before our eyes a very clear view of the transition from local to temporal distinctions, when we take into consideration their original significations. The Arabic beyna yedeyy, or beyna eydî, is also especially instructive. This phrase signifies 'between the hands,' and is used very commonly for 'before,' of space. But even in early classical texts (e.g. in the Ḳorân) it passes over into the 'before' of time. 'Between the hands of the Prophet,' thus means either *standing before him* as to place, or *preceding him* in time. Now that which we meet thus at every step in the Semitic and Aryan, is found also in the third great stock of languages. The time-particles of the Anaric languages often go back to relations of space; and what the German *Zeitraum* 'space of time,' and the Arabic *muddá* (properly 'extension,' but generally in the sense of a 'period of time') exemplify to us, we see also e.g. in the Finnish *kausi*,

[1] On the Pronoun Wilhelm von Humboldt's essay, *Ueber die Verwandtschaft der Ortsadverbien mit dem Pronomen*, Berlin 1830, still deserves study. See also what is said below (Chap. V. § 6) on Âshêr.

which is used to express a *piece of time.* It properly signifies a *direction* or *way*, in a local sense; and the related Esthonian word *kaude* is still used exclusively to denote local relations.[1]

In myths also we find the conception of Space and of motion in space predominant. A large group of names of the Dawn in the Aryan mythology is formed by composition of adjectives with εὐρυ and its etymological relatives, and yields variations on the notion 'shining afar,'[2] always bearing witness to local extension and motion. And in the Hebrew myths a number of solar names designate the solar figures, as *going*, *moving*, &c.[3] Even in cases where *rapid* motion is spoken of, a great result of such motion is not treated as attained in a *short time*; but described rather by the *space* that has been passed through.

On the other hand, when we consider the notion of Time, and the question how far it is acknowledged in myths, we observe that at the earliest mythical stage the distinction of Time is only very feebly presented. We must demonstrate this at this place while treating of the method of mythology. The myth makes a distinction between the bright radiant sunny heaven and the dark heaven. Now as to this darkness, it is indifferent whether it is the darkness of night or that of the overclouded heaven by day. The myth notices only the phenomenon of the dark sky, darkness as a physical fact or state, considers only *What* is there? but does not distinguish the *When*?—the time in which this darkness occurs. Hence in the myth the nightly heaven and the stormy or cloudy heaven are synonymous, since it does not distinguish day and night as alternate periods of time, but only brightness and darkness as phenomena. Hence it comes that even in later poetry and language the notions of *Rain* and *Night* are so closely connected, that rain is more naturally

[1] Budenz, in the Hungarian review *Magyar Nyelvőr* ('Guardian of the Hungarian Language'), 1875, IV. 57.

[2] Max Müller, *Chips*, II. pp. 93–106.

[3] See Chap. V. § 5, 6.

thought of in union with night than with day; therefore it is said in Arabic, 'more liberal than the rainy night' (anda min al-leylâ al-mâṭirâ).[1] Not only the rain, but the *Wind* also, in contrast to the merry laughing sunshine, is conceived as closely connected with the night.[2] In the Mohammedan cosmogonic legend it is said that the rough Wind lives on the curtain of the Darkness.[3] Hence also we see that the myth does not distinguish between the *Morning Glow* and the *Evening Glow*, but denotes the phenomenon by itself, without caring whether it precedes or follows the night. In connexion with this stands the fact that, as Steinthal has recently briefly noted,[4] mythic thought did not attain to the category of Causality; for this category presupposes a clear consciousness of succession, or of one event following another in time. Only thus can we explain myths which speak of the Dawn now as the daughter, now as the mother of the Day. On the domain of language some phenomena in the semasiology of Arabic words can be explained from this fact of the development of conceptions, as e.g. when the lexicographers translate the verb safar II. IV. to 'pasture *early* or *late*': IV. V. 'to come at the *morning* or *evening* glow'.[5] Except by the operation of the above-named psychological fact, the express combination of these two definitions of time in one word would seem to be impossible.

But the very fact just mentioned, that it is characteristic of mythical ideas to put one phenomenon into a family relation towards another, and to speak of mother, brother, son, daughter, &c., furnishes the first elements of and impulses towards the discrimination of *Succession in*

---

[1] *Kitâb al-aġânî*, I. 133. 19. Compare *al-Meydânî*, ed. Bûlâḳ, II. 262. 4.

[2] Both wind and rain are placed in connexion with the night in the *Dîvân of the Hudailites*, ed. Kosegarten, p. 125, v. 5: ta'tâduhu rîḥu-sh-shimâli biḳurrihâ * fî kulli leylatin dâjinin wa-hutûni, 'the Northwind blows over it with his coldness every cloudy rainy night.'

[3] Yâḳût's *Geogr. Dictionary*, I. 24. 2.

[4] *Zeitschrift für Völkerpsychologie*, &c. 1874, VIII. 179.

[5] See Böttcher's article on this group of roots in Höfer's *Zeitschrift für die Wissenschaft der Sprache* (Greifswald 1851), III. 16.

time, though the discrimination itself may at the mythic stage not yet break forth into life. Phenomena occurring one after another or simultaneously are conceived in the light of the most primitive relations of the family; and when the myth-forming man speaks of father and child, the very use of these terms rouses and encourages in his mind a new category, that of *Succession in time*, or more definitely *Causality*.

Another point follows naturally from this, enabling us to fix the chronological position occupied by certain myths in relation to others. If in a myth we find the fact of the temporal succession of a phenomenon treated as important, or see that a following event is in its very name described as such in relation to what preceded it, then we can justly draw the conclusion that a myth of this form belongs to an advanced stage of development, and that in determining the time of its origin we must choose a later period than we should for myths in which no conscious notion of time is visible. We shall have occasion to insist on this inference when we come into the presence of such mythic expressions as Yiphtâch *Jephthah*, i.e. the 'Opener,' and Ya'aḳobh *Jacob*, i.e. the 'Follower.'

§ 3. What has to be said on the *historical* aspect of the method of mythical investigation follows from the mode in which the myth grows under the influence of historical factors. If, after the first transformation of the myth occasioned by a purely psychological process, there are factors which immediately cause its further development, it is of course the business of mythic investigation to find out those transformative forces which have fastened themselves on a previous stage of development. Beginning therefore from the latest aspect of the myth, we have to follow it further and further up, to arrive by help of the thread of historical research at a knowledge of the process of historical development which operated on the myth and caused the transformation. Thus we ascend step by step to the point at which the above-described psychological process caused the individualising of the mythic figures. From this point it is only a step to the original formation of the myth, at which the appellations proper to the mythic figures are not proper names but appellative nouns. It is easy to see that, while investigation takes a retrograde course, beginning with the latest form of the myth and going back to arrive at its original form, exposition will take the contrary direction and pourtray its historical transformation in the natural order of growth, beginning with the primitive form discovered by analysis, and demonstrating successive transformations by the aid of history.

It is advisable, before we proceed to the materials of Hebrew mythic investigation, to elucidate the course of this historical method by a well-known example.

Let us take the story which is presented in Genesis, chap. XXII. Abraham, the forefather of the Hebrew people, at the behest of Elôhîm, is about to offer his only son Isaac as a sacrifice, but is prevented by an angel of Jahveh, who shows him a ram entangled in the thicket, which he may offer as a sacrifice to Jahveh instead of his son. The various religious tendencies connected with the two Divine names, Elôhîm and Jahveh are scarcely so prominent in any part of the Pentateuch as in the small passage under consideration. We see here the divergence of the religious ideas on both sides in reference to the value of *human sacrifice.* Not yet fully released from the Canaanitish system, the early Elohistic religious tendency as yet regards it as an unobjectionable performance. Jahveism abominates it, and is satisfied with the *temper* which is ready to sacrifice—the *intentio*; though this may very well be brought to express itself in the substituted sacrifice of a beast or something else. Hence our story makes Elôhîm demand the human offering, and Jahveh recommend the substitution.[1] The present form of the legend

[1] See especially the lucid exposition of Dr. Abr. Geiger, in his *Das Judenthum und seine Geschichte* (2nd edit.), I. 51.

is accordingly the product of the religious polemic waged by the Prophets against the popular view of religion which still clung to the Canaanitish system; and the apologists of the Jahveistic idea intend to show by it the advance which their own religious views had taken beyond those of earlier times.[1] The divergent ideas held by these two Hebrew religious parties on human sacrifice are also to be seen in the legislative portions of the Bible. In these we can distinguish passages in which the sacrifice of the first-born of beasts is not clearly discriminated from the sanctification of the first-born child, from others in which the latter has already gained a merely theocratic meaning and is put in connexion with the deliverance of the people out of Egypt. Therefore, what is deeply impressed on these passages of legislation, viz. the battle between the Canaanitish religious tendency and the national Hebrew idea of Jahveh according to the Prophets, finds a memento in the conformation of the existing very late myth of the sacrifice of Isaac. It has the same purpose as the passage of Deuteronomy (XII. 31), in which the polemic against human sacrifice as a religious institution of the Canaanites comes most prominently forward: 'Thou shalt not do so unto Jahveh thy God; for every abomination to Jahveh which he hateth have they done unto their Elôhîm; for even their sons and their daughters they have burned in the fire to their Elôhîm.' This polemic tendency in the service of the Jahveh-idea, and the religious views attached to it, gave the myth in question the form in which it is known to us. But that cannot be the original form. Stripped of its Jahveistic coating, the myth remains in the following form: 'Elôhîm demanded from Abraham the sacrifice of his only son, and Abraham was willing to sacrifice Isaac for Elôhîm.' But again, the

---

[1] In other countries also human sacrifices have been abolished by a reform of religion, and sacrifices limited to beasts and vegetables; e.g. in Mexico, where the reform is attributed to Quetzalcoatl. See Waitz, *Anthropologie der Naturvölker*, IV. 141.

myth could take this form only in a time when the religious idea of Elôhîm had already gained such full life in the Hebrew people as to impel them to sacrifice what was dearest to them. When the myth had this form, accordingly, there was in Canaan already a monotheistic religion, the centre of which was Elôhîm the object of adoration, while the ancestors of the Hebrew people were his pious servants and favourites. This coating also must be stripped off, if we wish to trace the myth analytically to its primitive form. When we have stripped off the religious coating, we have still not yet penetrated to the central germ; for, independently of any religious tendency, Abraham remains as Patriarch, as a national figure; and this brings us into the historical epoch when the Hebrew people, attaining to a consciousness of national peculiarity and opposition to the surrounding Canaanitish peoples, constructed their own early history. Accordingly, the national coating has now to be thrown off; and then Abraham meets us as a (so to say) cosmopolitan figure—not yet transformed into the likeness of one nation, but still as a person, an individual. This stage of mythic development brings us to the psychological process which caused the mythological *persons* to come forth at the beginning; and behind this stage we find the original form of the myth: 'Abram kills his son Isaac.' At that primitive stage these expressions naturally signified no more than the words imply. 'אַבְרָם Abh Râm, the *Lofty Father*, kills his son יִצְחָק Yiṣchâḳ, the *Laugher*.' The Nightly Heaven and the Sun, or the Sunset, child of the Night,[1] fell into a strife in the evening, the result of which is that the Lofty Father kills his child; the day must give way to night.

In the above example we have endeavoured to give a short sketch, less of the progress of development of the Hebrew myth, than of the method by which, observing

[1] The Sunset is child of Night only if we keep before our eyes the mythical identity of the Morning and Evening Glow, according to § 2 of this chapter.

the most prominent forces in the historical development of the intellectual life of the Hebrews, we can rise by analysis from the latest form of the myths to the original. Having reached this, we must confide ourselves to the guidance of the Science of Language; for that particular source for mythic inquiry which was treated in § 5 of the preceding chapter has chiefly to do with the primitive form of the myth. The myth is accompanied through all its stages of development by the same constant terms of language: these are, accordingly, the oldest matter for investigation on the mythological field.

Thus, taking it all together, the Method of mythic investigation turns on three hinges: 1. Psychology, 2. History, 3. Science of Language.

CHAPTER IV.

NOMADISM AND AGRICULTURE.

The basis of all modern Comparative Mythology, and the principle from which we start on the present studies, is that the Myth is only the expression in language of the impression made on the men of ancient time by the physical events and changes under the immediate influence of which they lived. If this is true, it cannot be questioned that the tendency and quality of the Myth must change, independently of the matter and contents which remain the same, in obedience to the advancing civilisation of men. For all progress in civilisation is marked, speaking generally, by continual development of the relation in which man stands to external nature. When a nation emerges from the stage of Nomadism and advances to an agricultural life, its relation to external nature is changed. The same thing happens when a people that lived exclusively by the chase and fishing advances to Nomadism. Since a new epoch in the development of human civilisation has commenced in our own times through the progress made in physical science, our relation to nature has again entered on a new phase. The spirit of modern civilisation has been characterised by the common-place, that reason has subdued nature.

The Myth accompanied mankind from the first germ to the highest stage of mental culture, always adapting itself to man's intellectual field of view and changing with the measure of this field of view. It is therefore a faithful mirror of the ideas of the world held by the men of each age; and these ideas are nowhere so clearly reflected as in myths. The configuration and tendency of the myths is always dependent on the ideas of men at that particular stage of civilisation which gave the myth its form and guided it to its special tendency. The traces of these historical transformations of the myths are scarcely distinguishable for small chronological divisions; but when the larger epochs of civilisation are under consideration, they cannot fail to be noted by the explorer's eye. And the discovery and demonstration of these transformations of the tendency of the myths in their relation to the great epochs of civilisation is one of the special problems of Comparative Mythology.

The solution of this problem has an intimate connexion with the answer to the question, 'When does the life of the Myth begin, and when does it end? what is its *terminus a quo*, and what its *terminus ad quem*?' This question is obviously closely bound up with the results of the psychological inquiry into the essence and conditions of production of the myth. The myth lives from the moment that man begins to interpret physical phenomena through processes brought before his eyes by his own every-day life and action; and as soon as the human mind uses in the interpretation of the phenomena of nature utterly different means from those prevalent in all myths, i.e. as soon as the phenomena of nature are not interpreted from human conditions, the myth has ended its life, and yields up its elements for other combinations. It is self-evident that the commencing point of the creation of myths cannot be later than the first beginnings of language; for Myth and Language are two modes of utterance of the same intellectual activity, and the oldest declarations of the human mind. Even in the Miocene age we find man —the so-called fossil man—in possession of fire: so that even then the conditions were already present for the first growth of the elements of a Prometheus-myth. In the Postpliocene age we find him already endowed with the first breath of religious feeling, if, as is generally done, we can allow the careful graveyards found at Aurillac, Cro-Magnon and Menton, to pass as historical data.[1] The end of the life of the myth coincides with the moment at which is formed out of the elements of the myth a *religious* conception of the world peopled with gods. The living and conscious existence of the myth is finished when the mythical figures become gods. Theology hurls the myth from its throne. But this is the end only of the living existence of the primitive myth; the myth transfigured and newly interpreted in a religious sense lives on, and only now begins to pass through a rich and various series of stages of development, each marked by a corresponding stage of the religion and civilisation of the men who possess it. There then spring from mythic elements, sagas, fables, tales, legends. And as religion in its primal origin appears in history not in opposition to myths, but as a higher development of them, the life of religion does not absolutely exclude that of myths. There remain, beside the myth which has been transformed into religion, other portions of the mythic matter which religion has not yet touched, and these live on as myths, so long as the process of religious transformation has not drawn them into its domain. Pure and free Monotheism in its highest development is the first force that comes forward as a denial of the mythic elements in religion. The religious history of the Hebrews reached this stage when Jahveism was fully developed.

We will for the present not trouble ourselves with these scions of the transformed myth. We will first study it only at the early stages when it still lives an unclouded, young, fresh life, untroubled by misunderstanding—the life that precedes the origin of religion from mythic elements. There are two successive stages in the historical development of mankind, which have to be con-

[1] See Sir Ch. Lyell, *The Geological Evidence of the Antiquity of Man* (4th ed. 1873), pp. 122 *et seq.* and 228. See also F. Lenormant's essay, 'L'Homme Fossile,' in his *Les premières Civilisations*, I. 42.

sidered in the course of the expositions to which this chapter is devoted, the *Nomadic* and the *Agricultural.* In the former commences the chain of development, which is closed by the formation of perfect, true Society. First are formed communities which, though still standing only on the base of the Family, yet represent a broadening of this base insofar as the notion of the family is first enlarged into the institution of a Tribe, and then this institution cannot always refuse to take in foreign elements (prisoners of war, or clients claiming protection). The nomadic stage is in its element in constant wandering from pasture to pasture, in unceasing change of residence; and is accordingly completed, whether with regard to its intrinsic character or to the experience of history, by passing over to the stage of the stationary agriculturist. The gathering of wild fruits, by which huntsmen and primitive nomads find some vegetable nourishment, forms the first impulse to pass over to an agricultural life, as Waitz observes.[1] It must be noticed that a pastoral life is frequently combined with tillage. The Nomad's relation to nature is a very different one from the Agriculturist's. But the consciousness of union among men—of their belonging to one another—was first excited at the nomadic stage; and it is therefore not surprising if a large proportion of the names of nations point back to that age.

A nation calls itself by a common name when the consciousness of the union of its members first arises. Names in which the nation confesses itself to be a wandering, restless society, point back to the nomadic stage of civilisation. That the contemplation of their own wandering mode of life, is with the nomadic peoples one motive for the national appellation, is shown in many instances which Bergmann has correctly explained in this sense.[2] The Kurdic nomadic tribes still call themselves

[1] *Anthropologie der Naturvölker*, I. 407. Compare Hehn, *Culturpflanzen und Hausthiere*, 2nd edit., p. 103.

[2] Bergmann, *Les peuples primitifs de la race de Jafète*, Colmar 1853,

Kötsher, i.e. 'wandering,' and despise and persecute their settled brethren.[1] The national appellation of the Zulus denotes the 'homeless,' 'roaming.'[2] According to the etymological explanation given by an old Hebraist, Clericus, the name of one of the peoples which are mentioned as aborigines of Canaan, the Zûzîm, is to be referred to this notion; it is so if we can cite for its explanation the late Hebrew *zûz*, 'to move from place to place.'[3] Another Canaanite national name, Perizzî, also according to many expositors points to nomadic life.[4] The name Pûṭ, by which the Egyptians called many nomadic tribes that came into their country, and which is also given in the list of nations in Gen. X. as the name of a son of Ham, likewise belongs to the same class. From their wandering life they were called by the Egyptians the 'Runners,' and the graphical power of the name is shown in the hieroglyphs by the picture of the quickfooted hare.[5] The name of the Hebrews also, 'Ibhrîm, belongs to the same series; it denotes 'those who wander here and there,' the Nomads. For the word 'âbhar, from which the national name 'Ibhrîm or Hebrews is derived, denotes not merely *transire*, 'to pass through a land, or to cross a river,' but rather 'to wander about' in general; for which sense many Hebrew texts might be quoted. The Assyrian is instructive on the point; there the phonetically corresponding verb is used of the sun, which *i-bar-ru-u kib-ra-a-ti* 'marches, wanders through the lands.'[6] A similar wandering through various lands is the foundation of the appella-

pp. 42, 45, 52, 53 apud Renan, *Hist. gén. d. langues sém.*, p. 39. It is interesting that the ancients explained the hard-bested name of the Pelasgians from this point of view, making Πελασγοί equivalent to πελαργοί = storks (Strabo, V. 313; Falconer, ed. Kramer, V. 2, § 4). Compare Pott, *Etymologische For schungen*, 1836, II. 527.

[1] Blau in the *Zeitschrift d. D. M. G.*, 1858, II. 589.

[2] Waitz, *ibid.* II. 349.

[3] Gesenius, *Thesaurus*, p. 410. *a.*

[4] Munk, *Palästina*, Germ. transl. by Levy, Leipzig 1871, p. 190.

[5] Ebers, *Aegypten und die Bücher Moses*, I. 70.

[6] See the passage in Schrader, *Keilinschriften und das A. T.*, p. 64. 20.

tion 'Ibhrîm 'Hebrews,' so that it denotes 'the Wanderers here and there,' the Nomad-people.[1] In opposition to these national names others are formed, which speak of the sedentary mode of life; a name of this kind is that of the South Arabian people Joḳṭân, which, as Freytag conjectured,[2] comes from ḳaṭana 'to take up a fixed abode.'[3]

We must not overlook the fact that such national names as these, derived from and referring to a certain stage of life and civilisation, are preserved by the same nation, even when that stage has been long passed. We see this most clearly in the case of the Philistines, who lived chiefly in towns, and preserved not even a tradition to remind them of a former nomadic life. Yet their name Pelishtîm is itself a reminiscence of this kind. Whether the name is to be combined with the Semitic (Ethiopic) palasha 'to wander,' as most of the Semitic philologists say,[4] or is to be explained from the Aryan, as others say; in either case it is a living witness and reminiscence of the nomadic stage of the Philistine people, at which they gave themselves this name. Similarly the Accadians still called themselves by that name, which means 'Highlanders,' long after they had chosen a new habitation in the plains.[5]

The herdsman finds his happiness in the well-being of his herds; his wealth depends on the quality of the pasture which he can get for them; to seek this is the constant object of his endless wanderings. Good, fresh, sound pasture is the sum of his modest wishes: 'green pastures beside still waters,' as a Hebrew Psalmist (Ps. XXIII. 2) expresses it. The cloudy heaven, which sends rain to his fields, is in his eyes a most friendly element, to which he gladly gives the victory over the scorching glow of the

---

[1] See Böttcher, *Ausführl. Lehrb. d. hebräischen Sprache*, edited by Mühlau, p. 7, *note*.

[2] *Einleitung in das Studium der arab. Sprache*, p. 19.

[3] Compare the Hottentot national name *Saan*, from *sâ* 'to rest,' i.e. 'the Settlers' (F. Müller, *Allgemeine Ethnographie*, p. 75).

[4] J. S. Müller, *Semiten, Chamiten und Japhetiten*, &c., p. 257.

[5] Lenormant, *Études Accadiennes*, pt. 3, I. 72.

sun, which dries up his pastures. The nomad calls himself 'Son of the water of heaven,' i.e. the rain. 'By banû mâ al-samâ (Sons of Rain),' says an Arabic commentator on Muslim's collection of traditions, 'the Arabs are to be understood . . . For as the greater part of them are owners of herds, they supported themselves mainly by the goodness of the pastures.'[1] Thus this appellation 'Sons of the water of heaven' could then come to have the general meaning 'rich people,' as e.g. in a sensible verse of 'Anbar b. Samâk:[2]

falâ tathiḳan min-an-nauka bishay'in
walau kânû banî mâ'i-s-samâ'i :

'Confide thou not in anything in fools,
E'en were they *sons of water of the heaven,*'

i.e. however rich they might be. The Bedawî of Somali, Isa, call their Ogas, i.e. chief, by the name *Roblai,* which, according to Burton, denotes Prince of the Rain.[3]

The nomad must be constantly wandering and seeking good pasture, if he is to gain a comfortable position. The glowing heat of the sun is in this respect his terrible enemy and continual adversary.

The starry heaven by night and the moon he recognises as his friends and protectors; and he gladly welcomes the moment when these guardians overcome the enemy, and drive off the beaming sun, when noon is followed by afternoon, and the evening comes on with its cool breeze, on the track of the departed solar heat. Then he is delivered from the tiresome ḳail, 'midday sleep,' which the noon-day heat had brought on. He therefore likes best to begin his journey in the afternoon, and continues it till night or during the night.[4] 'In their journeys and

[1] *Al-Nawawî* (the Cairo edition of Muslim's collection, with Commentary), V. 169.

[2] *Kitâb al-aġânî,* XVI. 82 *penult.*

[3] Burton's *First Footsteps in East Africa,* London 1856, p. 174.

[4] See *al-Nâbiġâ,* XXXI. v. 4 (Derenbourg).

expeditions with caravans or for plunder,' says Sprenger of the Arabs, 'they generally travel during the night. When one rides on a camel at a slow pace through the monotonous desert, the nights seem very long. But the heart is filled with quiet delight by the stillness of the night and the enjoyment of the fresh air, and the eye involuntarily looks upwards. Hence we find even in the Ḳorân and in the poetry of the Bedawî frequent allusion to the starry heaven and its motion.'[1] The caravan-songs (ḥidâh) accordingly refer mainly to night-travelling, as e.g. one quoted by Wetzstein:

O how journey we, while dew is scattered out
And desert-dust bedecks the lips of sumpter beasts.
O how journey we, while townsmen sleep
With limbs involved in coverlets;[2]

and when he travels by day he follows the course of the clouds, seeking coolness and shade. The Arabic poet Abû-l-'Alâ al-Ma'arrî, who, like all the later writers of ḳasîdâs,[3] makes the horizon of Beduin life the background of his poetry, says somewhere of his beloved,

As though the cloud were her lover, she always turns her saddle
To the quarter where the cloud is moving;

and the scholiast observes on the passage, 'that is, she is a Beduin, and the Bedawî always follow the rain and the places where raindrops fall from heaven.'[4] The old Arabian poet wishes for rain also on the grave of his friend; he cannot bear to see it scorched by the sun's heat. 'Drench, O clouds, the earth of that grave!' is a frequently recurring formula in the old Arabic poetry; and the later poetry, with its imitation of old forms, has

---

[1] On the Calendar of the Arabs before Moḥammed (in *Zeitschrift der D. M. G.*, 1859, XIII. 161).

[2] *Sprachliches aus den Zeltlagern der syrischen Wüste*, p. 32, *note* 21 (a reprint from *Zeitschrift der D. M. G.*, 1868, XXII.).

[3] A species of lyric poem or elegy.—Tr.

[4] *Saḳt al-zand* (Bûlâḳ edition of 1286), II. 34. Yet *Aġânî*, I. 147. 20, in a poem of Nuṣeyb: wa lam ara matbû'an aḍarra min-al-maṭari.

received this phrase into its inventory.[1] It is connected with this preference of the nomads for the heavens by night, that Hind, daughter of 'Otbâ, says on the day of the battle of Oḥod to the Koreyshites, the opponents of Islâm: 'We are the daughters of the Star,' (naḥnu binât Ṭâriḳ),[2] thereby claiming descent for herself also from the nightly heaven. We put this exclamation of the brave Arab woman in the same category with the above-mentioned reference of the origin of the Arabs to the Rain, and consider ourselves justified in rejecting the explanation given by al-Jauharî, who finds in it a simile, with the sense, 'Our father excels others in nobility of birth, as that brilliant star excels the other stars.'[3] It is then quite indifferent which star Ṭâriḳ is, whether the morning star, according to most lexicographers, or Zoḥal, (Saturn, or another of the five Chunnas-stars),[4] as al-Baiḍâwî explains it.[5] The point lies only in the fact that the Arab woman calls herself 'Star's daughter;' and this designation falls into the same category with Banû Badr 'Sons of the Full Moon,' Banû Hilâl 'Sons of the New Moon,' adopted by some Arabian tribes, and compared even by Bochart[6] with the name of the people Jerah.[7] Thus also several clans of Arabian tribes, especially the Banû Temîm, Banû Ḍabbâ, and Banû Azd called themselves 'Sons of Night,' (Banû Ṣarîm).[8] On the other hand, the townsman of Mecca called himself 'Child of the Sun,'—a name which has survived to the present time, as is to be seen from an interesting communication of Kremer.[9]

---

1 See an example in *Zeitschrift der D. M. G.*, 1857, V. p. 100, l. 14.

2 *Kitâb al-aġânî*, XI. 126.

3 Ṣaḥâḥ, s.r. *ṭrḳ*.

4 Chunnas, 'planet,' i.e. Saturn, Jupiter, Mars, Venus, or Mercury.—Tr.

5 *Commentary on the Ḳorân* (Fleischer's edition), II. 397. 6.

6 *Phaleg* (ed. Frankfort), II. 124.

7 Yerach (pausal yârach), Gen. X. 26, 1 Chr. I. 20; elsewhere yerach denotes 'month' and yârêach 'moon.'—Tr.

8 Ibn Dureyd, *Kitâb al-ishtiḳâḳ*, p. 99. 9.

9 *Culturgeschichtliche Streifzüge auf dem Gebiete des Islams*, Leipzig 1873, p. viii.

The relation of the Agriculturist to the two warring elements of the sky is very different. Storm, wind, and excessive rain are the declared enemies of his life, whereas the warm sun's rays, which heat and bring to perfection the fruits of the field, are gladly welcomed by him, and their victory over the dark gloomy sky gives him joy. An old Hellenic name of the sun is *Zeus Talaios*, or *Tallaios*, or simply *Talos*, which denotes 'encouraging growth,' as has been proved long ago.[1] It is Zeus who watches the cornfields and sends bountiful harvests;[2] and even clouds and rain are connected with him, insofar as their powers are beneficial to the agriculturist. For this reason Zeus himself becomes the *νεφεληγερέτα*, the Thunderer and Rain-giver.[3] This variety of relation to nature will be found reflected in the myths formed at these two stages respectively. The altered relation to external nature works a change even in the old and already fully formed myths, and lays down for them a new tendency in accordance with the altered conception of nature. Thus the myth which was already formed at an earlier stage of civilisation frequently still possesses enough power of resistance to preserve, in spite of adaptation to new views, much of the character formerly impressed on it by a past stage of civilisation. But the new myth must bear only the impress of the new stage at which its existence begins. For as the capacity for creating language does not exhaust all its force at once, but still continues to form new modes of speech whenever an alteration of circumstances demands them, so it is with myths. As the agriculturist

---

[1] See Creuzer, *Symbolik und Mythologie der alten Völker*, 3rd ed., I. 38.

[2] Welcker, *Griechische Götterlehre*, I. 169.

[3] As the myth grows more and more into a religion, and the conception of a mighty god who excels all others becomes fixed, the production of thunder and rain, &c., is gradually transferred to this originally solar god (see also Max Müller, *Chips*, &c., I. 357 *et seq.*). The sharp division made above is therefore absolutely true only of the purely mythological stage. Conversely Indra and Varuṇa, originally figures belonging to the gloomy cloudy and rainy sky, which take the highest places in the Indian religion, are in the Vedic Hymns endowed with solar traits.

creates new words for his new circumstances and ideas, so also he creates new myths.

§ 2. What therefore especially distinguishes the Nomad's myth from the Agriculturist's is mainly referable to the different position occupied at these two stages by the dark night-sky on the one hand and the brilliant, warm, sunny sky on the other. The myth is not a merely *objective*[1] expression for the phenomena of nature. For what is ordinarily and in common life called purely objective description, is almost an impossibility, seeing that no one with all possible exertion, restraint and self-abnegation can put off all his individuality; and this is true, in a much higher degree, of the myth. It is incorrect to speak of objective reporters or historians. For how would it be possible for me, giving a report on an event, whether as eye-witness or as critical sifter of the statements of others, to speak of it without being *myself the Speaker*? And the single fact that *I* am the speaker, impresses on my report a different stamp from that which the report of another would have borne. Compare so-called objective historical narratives from different decads—not to speak of hundreds or thousands of years. How much more must the subjectivity of the myth-creators be impressed on the myths of different periods of civilisation! Now it is undoubtedy true that the special, sharply characteristic intellectual individuality of persons is only developed in direct proportion with the advance of the culture of the mind. The more education a man has, the more can he give expression to his inner self and make its influence felt; and with the advance of education, the just claims of Individuality will also receive more and more attention, both in society and in law.

[1] Those to whom the philosophical terms *objective* and *subjective* are not familiar must understand them respectively as *impersonal* or *impartial*, and *personal* or *partial*; the former being that which is outside the thinker's personality, the latter that which is within him, and therefore often the reflected image of external things on his own mind.—Tr.

This process can be traced upwards from animals of low organisation to man, and within the human race can be confirmed through its various stages of development, geographical and historical. At the myth-creating stage, intellectual uniformity prevails almost universally, in all individuals. Consequently here only the sum total of the men who are creating language and myth has any power; the individual could not effect anything of his own, different from the work of others. There is no such thing as either language or myth of a single individual;[1] and what Steinthal says in reference to national songs, is equally true of both of them, that the mind which produces them, 'is the mind of a multitude of persons without individuality, held together by physical and mental relationship; and whatever is mentally produced by this multitude is a creation of the common mind, i.e. of the nation.'[2] And just for this reason the common mind in each of the various epochs of civilisation has its own characteristic impress, a tendency and fundamental conception, which distinguish it from those of the preceding epoch.

Among the Nomads, then, the dark, cloudy heaven of night is the sympathetic mythical figure; they imagine it conquering, or if it is overcome, give to its fall a tragic character, so that it falls lamented and worthy rather of victory than of ruin; and the Nomad's grief for the defeated power is propagated from age to age far beyond the mythical period. The sacrifice of Jephthah's daughter is still lamented from time to time by the daughters of Israel. It is just the reverse with the myth of the Agriculturist. He makes the brilliant heaven of day-time conquer, and the gloomy cloudy heaven or the dark night

[1] On the disappearance of individuality in direct proportion to antiquity, see Wilhelm von Humboldt, *Ueber die Verschiedenheit des menschlichen Sprachbaues*, Berlin 1836, p. 4. Lazarus appears to concede to the individual too much influence on the origin of speech; see *Leben der Seele*, II. 115.

[2] See the article 'Das Epos' in *Zeitschrift für Völkerpsychologie*, &c. 1868, V. 8, 10.

fall; he accompanies the victory of the warm heaven of the day with cries of triumph and applause, and his hymns immortalise what he felt and thought on this victory. Here it is the defeat of the sunny heaven that attunes him to lamentation. The fallen Samson is a tragical figure. Every reader will be able himself to supply the application of these general propositions to the myth of the Hebrews, if he pays attention to the chapter in which the chief figures of the Hebrew mythology were brought forward, with the chief traits by which they are accompanied in Mythology. I should deem it superfluous to prosecute this application further, as it is to be found in every case in the nature of the myth itself.

But it is not only from a feeling of sympathy towards the heaven of night and clouds that the Nomad puts it in the foreground. This aspect of heaven is to him also the *datum*, the *prius*, the *natural*, which the heaven of day afterwards opposes as foe and persecutor. With the nature of Nomadism, and especially of the night-wanderings, is also connected the Reckoning of time by *Nights*. This has been best preserved by the Arabs, who count by nights, instead of days, as we do. It is especially marked in the determination of the distance between two places and of the length of a journey: e.g. 'His face perspires with desire for the payment held back for *long nights* (i.e. for a long time);'[1] 'Between Damascus and the place where Walîd b. Yazîd lived in the desert are *four nights*;'[2] 'I will give him five hundred dînârs and a camel, on which he can travel for *twelve nights*;'[3] in a poem of Abû Zeyd al-'Abshamî, 'When the tribe travels for *sixteen nights*' (iḏa-l-ḳaumu sârat sittat 'ashrata leylatan).[4] This Arabic idiom is so firmly established that in the opposite case, when a period is for once to be expressed in days, the equivalent expressed in nights is added as a more

[1] Nöldeke, *Beiträge zur Kenntniss der Poesie der alten Araber*, p. 185. 12.

[2] *Kitâb al-aġânî*, VI. 137. 17.

[3] *Durrat al-ġauwâs* (ed. Thorbecke), p. 178. 4.

[4] Yâḳût, I. 934. 2.

exact definition; e.g. 'So that there lay between them and their home a distance of *two days or three nights*.'[1] With the reckoning of time by nights two other practices are connected. *First*, the Night has priority before the Day; therefore among the Arabs and the Hebrews (as also among the later Jews), the two peoples which, as we shall see, preserved the feeling of nomadism longer than the Aryans, the day begins with the evening. 'There was evening, there was morning—one day.' A residuum of the old nomadic conception is found in the Egyptian myth that Thum, the form of the sun's nocturnal existence, was born before Ra, the sun's form by day. *Secondly*, chronology is thereby connected chiefly with the nocturnal heaven and the moon. It is to be observed on this subject that in nations which begin to count the day from the evening, the moon is the central figure and the starting point in the chronology of greater periods.[2] Seyffarth, in an essay entitled, 'Did the Hebrews before the Destruction of Jerusalem reckon by lunar months?' (published in 1848 in the *Zeitschrift der D.M.G.*, II. 347 sqq.), endeavoured to defend the thesis that the Hebrew chronology was originally founded on solar months, which were not supplanted by lunar months till between the second and fourth century after Christ; but he supports this theory by arguments which cannot stand against profounder criticism. It must rather be assumed that the original lunar year at the beginning of agricultural life was united with the observation of the solar periods (see Knobel, *Commentary on Exodus*, p. 95), so as to produce very early compensation of the difference between them; but that in the various attempts at compensation, which

---

[1] *Romance of 'Antar*, IV. 97. 2.

[2] This connexion is found among the Polynesians: 'The time-reckoning in all Polynesia conformed to the moon. They reckoned by nights,' &c., Gerland, *Anthropologie der Naturvölker*, VI. 71. Only the nights had names, the days had none, *ibid.*, pp. 72. Both the chronology according to moons and the counting of days by nights are linguistically demonstrated of the Melanesian group. See the comparison in Gerland, *ibid.*, pp. 616–619.

ended with the fixing of the calendar and the arrangement of the intercalary month, the reckoning by moons remained in the foreground, as is evident in the mode of compensation. In reference to the Arabs also, Sprenger has fully proved in the essay to which we have already referred in this chapter, that the solar element of chronology was subordinate, and that in the old times before Moḥammed the lunar reckoning was in force.

As on another occasion we shall recur to the fact that among the Aryans the Indians retained a certain degree of nomadic sentiment more distinctly than any other Aryans, and that this is impressed on their literature and on many of their institutions, so here we may observe the same in reference to their chronology. In the Vedas, the oldest literature of the Sanskrit people, we find the lunar year of twelve months, with the occasional addition of a thirteenth or intercalary month.[1] It is remarkable that on this subject we find still more reminiscences of the nomadic life among the Persians. In the whole book of Avesta, in passages where the shining heavenly bodies are enumerated, they appear in this invariable order: Stars, Moon, and Sun, the sun always occupying the last place. And we even find also the reckoning of time by nights exactly as it is among the Arabs; which enables Spiegel to draw the just inference that the ancient Persians reckoned by lunar years.[2] According to Bunsen[3] the Delphic myth of the purification of Apollo likewise points to the conclusion that the Hellenes in later times substituted the solar for the old lunar chronology.

The Solar chronology belongs to the Agriculturist, in opposition to the Nomad. As the night and the nocturnal sky forms the foreground to the nomad, so the agricultural stage of civilisation leads the sun to victory, and the sun

---

[1] Laz. Geiger, *Ursprung und Entwicklung der menschlichen Sprache und Vernunft*, II. 270.

[2] *Die heiligen Schriften der Parsen*, in German, II. xcviii. and III. xx.

[3] *God in History*, II. 433-5.

becomes the measure and the starting point of its chronology. With the advance to agriculture the lunar year is superseded by the *Magnus Annus*, or ἡλιακόν, which was also called ὁ θεοῦ ἐνιαυτός. Yet very curiously, as the remains of nomadism in general may be long visible and be unconsciously perpetuated in the ideas of the agriculturist, it is the mode of calculating time that echoes the nomadic ideas the longest, and even survives in ages of more advanced culture. Of the Gauls, e.g., Julius Caesar reports that they counted by nights, not by days.[1] Tacitus says the same of the ancient Germans.[2] In one case, namely in the English word 'fortnight,'[3] which is a speaking proof that the ancestors of those who now use the word reckoned time by nights, one of the most advanced nations of the present time has not yet left off counting by nights. Other languages also, spoken by nations which have long accepted the solar reckoning, preserve memorials of the old nomadic lunar reckoning. In Hungarian and other languages of the Ugric stock the expression 'hopping year' (szökő év) for leap-year,[4] in connexion with other similar phenomena, points to a chronology of lunar years, as the Hungarian Academician Paul Hunfalvy has very fully demonstrated, with important documents.[5] The residuum of the lunar chronology which has stood the longest, and which, despite the generally preponderating solar character of our reckoning of time, and despite the love of a decimal system inherent in the

---

[1] *De Bello Gallico*, VI. 18: 'Spatia omnis temporis non numero dierum, sed noctium finiunt; dies natales et mensium et annorum initia sic observant, ut *noctem dies subsequatur*.'

[2] *Germania*, XI: 'Nec dierum numerum, ut nos, sed noctium computant. Sic constituunt, sic condicunt: *nox ducere diem videtur*,' in connexion with the public assemblies at the changes of the moon. The fact must not be overlooked that, according to Caesar, *ibid.* 22, the Germans 'agriculturae non student, majorque pars victus eorum in lacte, caseo, carne consistit.' See also, on this subject, Pictet, *Les origines Indo-Européennes et les Aryas primitifs*, II. 588.

[3] And in 'Se'nnight.'—Tr.

[4] The identical English term 'Leap year' is another apposite example. —Tr.

[5] See the Hungarian review, *Magyar Nyelvőr*, I. 26–28.

first French Revolution, is now fixed firmly for a long future period, is the *Week*—a notion specifically connected with the Moon. Yet it has long been made evident that even this division of the month into four weeks was in antiquity sometimes exchanged for a solar division into three decads. This was due to the influence of the agricultural stage of civilisation giving prominence to the Sun. We know this, e.g., of the Egyptians, and it was therefore long doubted whether they knew the division into weeks at all. But Sir Gardner Wilkinson collected a series of proofs that among the Egyptians the later system of decads was historically preceded by the division of the months into four weeks of seven days each.[1] It is also tolerably certain of the Mexicans, that of their two methods of reckoning time, which in later times were in force side by side, the *Tonulpohualli* or 'solar reckoning' and the *Metzlapohualli* or 'lunar reckoning,' the latter was historically the earlier, but was retained in the time of the solar chronology, as is so frequently the case in computations of time.[2] We ought, moreover, also to consider the computation of longer periods of time by *Masika*, i.e. rainy seasons, which prevails among the Unyamwesi in Africa.[3] How powerful is the posthumous influence even on later times of the nomadic lunar division into weeks,—an influence which again and again obtained validity, even after it had been once supplanted by the solar reckoning by decads, we see best among the Romans. They had originally a consistent lunar computation; even their year consisted of ten months, the sun's cycle of twelve months being ignored; and they divided the month into four weeks.[4] Later, this fourfold division gave way to a threefold division into three decads, *nonae, kalendae, idus*; but yet

---

[1] In Rawlinson's *History of Herodotus*, App. to Book II. chap. VII. § 16–20 (ed. of 1862, vol. II. p. 282 *et seq.*).

[2] Waitz, *l. c.* IV. 174.

[3] See Karl Andree, *Forschungsreisen*, &c., II. 205.

[4] Mommsen, *History of Rome*, I. 217 (ed. 1862), 230 (ed. 1868).

they returned at last to the week again, and called its seven days by the names of the sun, the moon and the five planets. However, the division of the month into three decads is not always connected with solar chronology; it is also found in combination with lunar reckoning, when three phases of the moon are acknowledged (as in the three-headed forms of the moon in the Greek mythology).[1]

A *five-days'* period has been proved to exist in many nations as the equivalent of our week (among the Chinese, Mongol tribes, Azteks, and Mexicans.)[2] But this division into pentads must be connected with an original quinary system of numeration, to the linguistic importance of which Pott has devoted a special treatise.[3] In Old Calabar on the west coast of Africa a week of *eight days* occurs; most curiously, as the people cannot count beyond five.[4] *A priori* this would seem impossible; but it is vouched for by an observer so accurate as Bastian.

§ 3. As the Nomadic stage of civilisation of necessity historically precedes the Agricultural, so also that stage of the myths at which the nocturnal, dark or cloudy heaven has precedence of the bright heaven of day comes before the stage at which the latter occupies the foreground and plays the part of a beloved figure or favourite. Moreover, it cannot be assumed that this second stage of the formation of myths has grown up without being preceded by the first stage; for it is simply impossible that any portion of mankind should have lived through the stage of Nomadism, which perhaps lasted for thousands of years, without having thrown its conceptions of the world into mythic forms. Everyone knows, and no one now doubts, that the most prominent figure in the mythology of

[1] Welcker, *Griechische Götterlehre*, I. 555.

[2] Sir Gardner Wilkinson, in Rawlinson's *Herodotus*, ed. 1862, vol. II. p. 283, § 17.

[3] *Die quinäre und vigesimale Zählmethode*, Halle 1867.

[4] Waitz, *l. c.* II. p. 224, compared with Bastian, *Geographische und ethnologische Bilder*, Jena 1874, pp. 144, 155.

the Aryans, which later at the theological stage took the rank of a supreme god, was the brilliant sunny heaven, Dyu (Dyaus, *nom.*), Θεός, Zeus, on whom the powerful sympathy of the Aryan was concentrated, and to whom he turned with admiring devotion as soon as he began to pray and compose hymns. On the other hand, it could not escape the notice of the inquirer on the domain of Aryan mythology and history of religion, that the very oldest and most genuine representative of the Aryan mind seems itself to form a sort of exception to this universal idea. The Indians, namely, among whom Dyu certainly was elevated to theological importance,[1] do not make him their supreme god, but Indra, who, as his very name shows, (indu=' a drop ') is identical with the rainy sky (Jupiter pluvius),[2] and Varuṇa, who, in contrast to the shining Mitra, was the gloomy night-sky (from var=' to cover ').[3] Max Müller, whose merit it mainly is to have raised the Aryan Dyu to the high throne which he now occupies in the history of Aryan religion, explains this strange fact by supposing that Indra drove Dyu, the oldest of the gods, from the place which he had formerly held even among the Indians. 'If in India,' he thinks 'Dyu did not grow to the same proportions as Zeus in Greece, the reason is simply that *dyu* retained throughout too much of its appellative power,[4] and that Indra, the new name and the new god, absorbed all the channels that could have supported the life of Dyu,' [5] so that he died away.

From what has been explained above, it is evident that the subject might present itself in a different light. It is well known that the people of India represents, both

---

1 See on this J. Muir, *Contributions to a Knowledge of the Vedic Theogon and Mythology* (*Journal of Royal Asiatic Society*, N.S., 1864, I. pp. 54-58).

2 Max Müller, *Lectures on the Science of Language*, Second Series, p. 430.

3 Max Müller, *Chips*, &c., II. p. 65. Muir, *l. c.* p. 77 *et seq.*

4 This is connected with Müller's view that 'language must die before it can enter into a new stage of mythological life' (*Lectures on the Science of Language*, Second Series, p. 426).

5 *Lectures*, &c., Second Series, p. 432.

in its language and in its mythology, the oldest stage of the Aryan mind attainable by us, and after it follows the people of Iran. The ancient literature of these two nations, but that of the Indians more than that of the Persians, stands much nearer in its ideas to the nomadic life than any other documents of the Aryan mind which have been preserved to us. It is then no wonder if (it being a rule in all physical as well as intellectual development, that at a later stage of progress residua of a previous one remain behind unnoticed) these nations, which at the time of their oldest known intellectual productions were not far removed from nomadism, exhibit more traces of nomadism than others, even if they be found to have then fully passed out of the nomadic stage. We have already referred to this in treating of the nomadic elements in chronology, and now return again to the same point. In some things the Iranians preserved the traditions of nomadism more firmly and persistently than the Indians, who generally stood nearer to the original forms. This is to be explained from the fact that in Persia nomadism itself lived longer as an actual stage of civilisation, and was more fostered, than in India; for indeed it even now maintains its position there. For just as in the time of Herodotus (I. 125) the Persians were partly migratory nomads (*νομάδες*), partly settled agriculturists (*ἀροτῆρες*), so now a proportion, varying from a quarter to a half, of the population of modern Persia still leads a nomadic life.[1] One characteristic of the nomadic period is a social and political division into tribes, which in many civilised nations is retained into the time of fixed dwellings as a residuum of nomadism. Without pausing over the Thracians, who according to the account of Herodotus,[2] found it impossible to throw off all reference to tribe-differences and bring their power to bear through national

[1] Rawlinson, *History of Herodotus*, I. 211.

[2] V. 3: ἀλλὰ γὰρ τοῦτο ἄπορόν σφι καὶ ἀμήχανον μή κοτε ἐγγένηται· εἰσὶ δὴ κατὰ τοῦτο ἀσθενέες.

unity, we will refer to the Ionians as an example, whose divisions into φρατρίαι, γέιη, and γεννῆται, have been accurately traced.[1] Now among the Indians we find no trace of tribal divisions worth mentioning, but very soon come across the Caste—an hereditary division according to modes of occupation, which cannot be formed at any earlier stage than that of fixed dwellings, since this gave the first impulse to the practice of arts and trades, which is not conceivable at the nomadic stage. Among the Iranians, on the other hand, the tribal division maintained itself for a long time parallel with that according to occupation, which was better suited to the time of transition to a fixed life.[2] Even on the Caste system of the Parsees the tribal division still exerts a definite influence. The sacerdotal caste is a distinct tribe, a family, just like the Levites among the Hebrews;[3] and in ancient times many sacerdotal functions, 'the smaller and less important religious duties, were assigned to the heads of the various subdivisions of the tribe.' The name of the priests, môbed (which Spiegel explains as umâna-païti='chief head of the tribe or family,' perhaps equivalent to the Hebrew rôsh bêth âbh), in itself indicates the original universality of the bestowal of the sacerdotal functions on the head of the tribe.[4]

---

[1] The literature is clearly and concisely enumerated in G. Rawlinson's essay *On the Early History of the Athenians*, § 8-11 (*Hist. of Herod.*, Bk. II. Essay II.). But it must be added that the idea of the learned author—'The Attic castes, if they existed, belong to the very infancy of the nation, and had certainly passed into tribes long before the reign of Codrus'—does not agree with the historical sequence demanded by the connexion of the tribes with nomadic life and that of the caste with fixed tenure. In the very nature of the case the division into tribes is proper to nomadism, which knows of no systematic occupation with arts and trades, whereas the division into castes presupposes such an occupation with trades and arts as only a sedentary life renders possible. Therefore, between tribes and castes the priority will always have to be assigned to the former.

[2] Spiegel, *Ueber die eranische Stammesverfassung* (*Abhandlungen der kön. bair. Akad. d. W.*, 1855, Bd. VII.); *Kasten und Stände in der arischen Vorzeit* (*Ausland*, 1874, No. 36).

[3] *Die heiligen Schriften der Parsen*, in German, III. vi.

[4] *Ibid.* II. xiv.-xv.

As in Iran a fundamental social institution, so among the Sanskrit people a prominent mythological fact is the notable residuum of nomadism: viz. the fact that by them the first seat and highest rank among the figures of the myth and subsequently among the gods is assigned not to Dyu, but to Varuṇa and Indra. It is not to the field-guarding, harvest-sending, shining sunny heaven, but to Varuṇa the coverer and Indra the rain-sender, that the nomad directs his admiration and sympathy, his veneration and devotion. This relation towards Indra was preserved by the Indian from the nomadic period—from a time before that remarkable people had chosen a permanent abode on the banks of the Ganges and Indus. With this agrees very well the idea which Roth worked out in an essay on 'the highest gods of the Aryan peoples,' that Varuṇa is as old as the Aryan period, and is the common property of all members of the race; even the conception of Indra being later than that of Varuṇa, and specially Indian.[1] But it is not only among the Indians that we find this memory of nomadic life impressed on the mythology; its traces may be found also in the Hellenic mythology, not however as a positive, actual existence, as in India, but still as an historical reminiscence. According to Hesiod's *Theogony*, the dominion of Zeus was preceded by that of Uranus; i.e. before the Hellenic people, choosing a settled agricultural life, brought Zeus, the bright sunny heaven, into the foreground, the centre of their world was Uranus (Varuṇa), the gloomy overclouded sky. There is scarcely any serious reason for regarding, as Bunsen [2] and some writers on the history of religion do, the kingdom of Zeus alone as an original intellectual product of the Hellenic people, and putting aside Uranus as merely a result of Theogonic speculation, or for even seeing in Uranus a figure borrowed from a Semitic source. The succession—Uranus, Zeus—rather

---

[1] *Zeitschrift d. D. M. G.* 1852, VI. 67 *et seq.*

[2] *God in History*, II. 8.

corresponds perfectly with the successive stages of civilisation, nomadism and agriculture, and all that Hesiod did was to clothe an historical, natural and true tradition of the Hellenic people in the form of a theogonic story. With this, other points of the Theogony seem to be clearly and unmistakably connected, namely those in which we perceive the idea of the priority of the Night. Among the powers preceding the rule of Zeus in Hesiod's *Theogony*, *Chaos* is named—a word signifying according to its original sense 'darkness'—and *Tartarus*. We well know the theological meaning of the latter word—the subterranean place to which the souls of the dead go; but there is no doubt that it originally denoted 'a gloomy pit, never lighted by the sun,' or 'darkness' in general. Therefore Tartarus figures in Mythology as father of Typhon and Echidna, and therefore Nyx is his daughter. Then it agrees well with nomadic ideas that Tartarus is called 'father of waters and springs,' and that he bears the epithet 'the first born' (πρωτόγονος). On Hebrew ground also we meet a similar transition. In Job XXXVI. 20, the word laylâ 'night' is used quite in the sense of 'nether world;' which is true also of ṣalmâweth, denoting 'darkness' in general, and used only secondarily with special reference to Orcus.

§ 4. We have above just touched the confines of religious history, though it was strictly speaking, only a border territory of Mythology, which ought not to be confounded with religious history. But we must here allow ourselves an excursion into the neighbouring territory. For it ought not to pass unnoticed that, as the myth which has the night-sky in its foreground always precedes that which has the bright sky of day in its centre, the former corresponding to the nomadic, the latter to the settled agricultural life, the same sequence can also be observed in the history of religion. There are nations, which, when already standing at the nomadic stage, work out for themselves a theistic religion. As theistic religion always grows up out of the elements of myths, the religion of Nomadism must be essentially a worship of the night-heaven. Then, when the progress to the agricultural stage works the revolution in man's ideas of the world, and in the relation of his mind to external nature, of which I spoke above, when he cleaves more to the Sun and pays his reverence to him, then the worship of the nocturnal starry or overclouded rainy heaven is naturally supplanted by one of the diurnal heaven and the sun, and only residua of the ancient ideas and the ancient objects of worship are propagated into the new epoch, sometimes continuing and remaining in force unmodified, and sometimes interpreted anew in the sense of the new system. The religion and the worship of the nomad stand to those of the agriculturist in the same relation of historical succession as the two similar stages of mythology to each other. At the later stage, the elements of solar religion can undoubtedly stand peacefully side by side with the residua of the earlier stage of religion. Similarly, when nomads have relations with townsmen who have a solar religion already powerfully developed, many elements of the solar worship may find their way into the nomadic religion; of which the well-known accounts of the religion of some Arabic Beduin tribes furnish plenty of examples. To this an outside observer may probably reduce the report brought by William Gifford Palgrave, the daring explorer of Central Arabia, of the adoration of the Sun among the Bedawî.[1] But in the order of genesis the worship of the night-sky, inclusive of that of the moon, precedes that of the day-sky and the sun. It was observed long ago that wherever sun-worship exists, moon-worship also is always to be found, being a residuum of the earlier stage of religion; but not in the reverse order.[2] We shall have to revert in a subsequent chapter to this fact, in speaking of the

[1] *Narrative of a Year's Journey through Central and Eastern Arabia*, I. 8.
[2] See Welcker, *Griechische Götterlehre*, I. 551.

religion of the nomadic Hebrews, and will therefore only refer to a few points in the ancient Arabic religion. If Blau is right in interpreting the old Arabic proper name 'Abd Duhmân as 'Servant of the Darkness of Night,'[1] the theological importance of the night-sky to the ancient Arabs in general is proved; for it is well known that in Arabic proper names compounded with 'Abd 'servant' the second member of the compound is a god's name, or at least a name of theological meaning.[2] To the same class belongs the Moon-worship of the ancient Arabs, which is sufficiently attested.[3] The clearest evidence of a worship of the rainy sky and the storm among the Arabs is furnished by the name Ḳuzaḥ, to which storms and rainbows were attributed (see the following chapter § 12). Arabian etymologists, among whom may be mentioned the author of the Ḳâmûs and the author of the Supercommentary on that dictionary, publishing at Bûlâḳ, have tried many combinations in order to find a suitable explanation of this Ḳuzaḥ, with especial reference to the meaning 'rainbow;' all the derivative significations of the root ḳzḥ, *embellishment, variety of colour, lifting oneself*, are brought forward to yield a sufficient ground for the appellation. This proves how little the Mohammedan now knows of his heathen antiquity; the use of the name Ḳuzaḥ must have been interdicted. Al-Damîrî, in his work Almasâ 'il al-manthûrâ, finds a deep-seated error in the word itself, instead of which he wishes to read kaza'

---

[1] *Zur hauranischen Alterthumskunde* (*Zeitschrift der D. M. G.*, 1861, XV. 444).

[2] It should be noted that from Ibn Dureyd, *Kitâb al-ishtiḳâḳ*, p. 96. 11, it is evidently possible that in such compounds the word 'abd itself may belong to the idol; he writes wa-'abdu shams[in] za'amû ṣanam[un] wa-ḳâla ḳaum[un] bal 'aynu mâ'[in] ma'rufat[un] wa-hua ism[un] ḳadîm[un]: ''Abd Shams is in the opinion of some an idol, others say it is the name of a well-known spring of water: it is an old name.'

[3] Tuch, *Sinaitische Inschriften* (*Zeitschr. der D. M. G.*, 1849, III. 202).—Osiander, *Vorislam. Religion der Araber* (*Zeitschr. der D. M. G.*, 1853, VII. 483).

with *'ayn*, with the meaning 'cloud.' [1] But it is probable that this name Ḳuzaḥ is derived from the signification 'mingere,' which belongs to the corresponding verb (used specially of beasts), and that it is due to a mythological conception of the Rain. This circumstance tempts us to connect the Hebrew word bûl 'rain, rainy month' with the Arabic bâla, yabûlu 'mingere.' If so, the combination of this word with the name of the God Ba'al, which certainly does occur in Himyaric in the form Bûl, must have been made later, from a misunderstanding of the mythological relations.[2] The theological power of Ḳuzaḥ among the ancient Arabs is evident as well from its being explained by Moslem interpreters as the name of a devil or angel, as also from the fact that geographical appellations which are in force in the ritual of the old religion are connected with it.[3] These elements of the worship of the night and the cloudy and stormy sky must have priority before those of the solar worship which are found subsisting beside them. F. Spiegel states this succession to be a law in the history of religion. 'It is not the sun,' he says, [4] 'that first attracted the attention of the savage by its light . . . On the other hand, the night-sky, whose lights form a contrast to the darkness of the earth, is much more calculated to attract the gaze of the savage to itself. And among the heavenly lights it is the moon that first absorbs the sight, as well from its size as from its readily discernible changes; and after it a group of particularly brilliant stars. . . We find moon-worship among almost utterly savage tribes in Africa and America; and it is noteworthy that there the moon is always treated as a man, the sun as a woman; not till

---

[1] *Tâj-al-'arûs*, II. 209.

[2] Schlottmann, *Die Inschrift Eshmunazar's*, Halle 1868, p. 84.

[3] Yâḳût, IV. 85. See al-Jawâlîḳî's *Livre des locutions vicieuses* (ed. Derenbourg in *Morgenländ. Forschungen*), p. 153.

[4] *Zur vergleichenden Religionsgeschichte*, 1 Art. (*Ausland* 1872), p. 4. See also 1871, p. 1159.

later are these relations inverted. From this we may infer that *the lunar worship is older than the solar.*' We cannot, however, agree with Spiegel when he gives as the reason why darkness attracted the special attention of man, that the sun was to him a matter of course. We see the same story of the lunar religion repeat itself again in the history of the Babylonian-Assyrian religion. Hur-ki (Assyrian Sin) is historically the older and earliest prominent object of worship of the ancient Accadian kingdom; and the further we advance towards the beginnings of the history, the more does the worship of the moon preponderate. The monarchs of the first dynasties regard her as their protector, and the name of the moon often enters into composition to form their proper names.[1] In the later empire, that of Assyria, this prevailing pre-eminence of the moon gradually ceases. She is supplanted by the sun, under whom she descends to be a deity of the second rank, the 'Lord of the thirty days of the month,' and 'Illuminator of the earth.'[2] That Samas, the sun, is called in the Assyrian epic of Istar *the son of Sin*, the moon-god (IV. 2), 'points,' as the learned German interpreter of the cuneiform inscriptions observes, 'to a veneration of the moon-god in Babylonia earlier than that of the sun-god,'[3] or else to the conception of the night preceding the day. Among the Egyptians, too, it is a later period at which the dominion of the sun is recognised. The older historical epoch—whether permeated, as Bunsen expresses it somewhat obscurely,[4] by a '*cosmogonic-astral*' idea, or, as Lenormant describes it in a few bold strokes,[5] possessing very little positive religion at all—knows as yet nothing of solar worship. The solar worship of the Egyptians is undoubtedly the product of a later development of high culture.

[1] Compare also the Himyaric proper name Ben Sîn (Halévy, *Études sabéennes* [*Journal Asiat.* 1874, II. 543]).

[2] Lenormant, *Les premières civilisations*, II. 158.

[3] Schrader, *Die Höllenfahrt der Istar*, p. 45.

[4] *Egypt's Place in Universal History*, IV. 342.

[5] In his essay on the Egyptian antiquities at the Great Exhibition of 1867 at Paris.

This phenomenon, the priority of the lunar to the solar worship, is asserted also by the adherents of a theory of the history of civilisation usually called the *Gynaecocratic*, which was founded and worked out by the Swiss savant Bachofen in a large book entitled 'The Gynaecocracy of Antiquity.' To the adherents of this theory, who suppose the lordship of man to have been preceded by a long period in which the female sex bore rule, the lunar worship is closely allied to the importance of woman, while the solar worship is connected with the rule of man. I do not, of course, deem it a part of my present task to criticise the Gynaecocratic theory, which has certainly had but small success in the learned world, or to take up a position either for or against it. Yet it is satisfactory that the phenomenon in the history of religion which we have brought into prominence may find confirmation in another quarter, where the premisses are utterly different.

§ 5. The first founder of Comparative Mythology, Professor A. Kuhn, starting from the truth 'that every stage of social and political growth has a more or less peculiar mythological character of its own, and that the fact of these, so to speak, mythological strata lying side by side or crossing one another often renders the solution of mythological enigmas more difficult,' insisted, primarily with reference to Aryan mythology, that the mythological products of each of the great epochs of civilisation ought to be sifted with reference to the cycles of myths peculiar to each epoch.[1] He himself ventured on the first beginnings or elements of such a sifting in a very interesting and instructive academical treatise 'On stages of development in the formation of Myths.'[2] Kuhn finds the criterion of a myth's belonging to one or another period

---

[1] I must explain that the preceding four sections were already written down, before I could get a sight of Kuhn's essay, which appeared later.

[2] *Ueber Entwickelungsstufen der Mythenbildung*, Berlin 1874; from the *Abhandlungen der königl. Akademie d. Wiss. zu Berlin* (*phil.-hist. Klasse*), 1873, pp. 123–137.

of civilisation mainly in the notions and objects with which the myth has to do. Sun's hunts were spoken of in the hunting period, the sun's cattle in the nomadic, &c.; and the formation of myths which employed these notions commenced 'as soon as the following period had lost the understanding of the language of the preceding' (p. 137).

I do not think that a definition of the periods of myth-formation which starts with the Material of the myth can always afford a strictly reliable rule for judging a mythic stratum and assigning it to this or that period of civilisation. For it must not be left unnoticed that, when once the notion of hunting or of herds has come into existence, it does not vanish from the mental inventory of man as soon as ever the stage of civilisation is passed on which that portion of mankind occupies itself with hunting or keeping herds. On the other hand, the entrance of a more advanced stage of civilisation does not imply the utter banishment out of human society of everything connected with the preceding, though, speaking generally, this was now passed and gone. Otherwise, how could we at the present day, when the hunting age is left so many thousand years behind us, still have our hunting adventures and enjoy all the pleasures belonging to the sportsman's life? And must there not be shepherds even in agricultural countries, although the agriculturist has long passed the stage of nomadism? Consequently, from the phraseological material employed in the myth it is only possible to infer the *terminus a quo* referring to its origin, but not the *terminus ad quem.* Else we should be entangled in the same mistakes into which the earlier Danish antiquaries fell, when from the occurrence of stone, bronze, or iron instruments in a tumulus or avenue, they inferred that the tumulus or avenue was so and so old; not considering that the material of a completed period is propagated into the next epoch, as is shown in all those prehistorical finds in which instruments of all possible materials appear promiscuously, as James Fergusson has convincingly proved.[1] We are in the same case with the phraseology of the Myth. On the ascent out of each of the great periods, the ideas connected with it, which began with the entrance into it, cannot disappear. The idea, having once been grasped by man, remains always present to him, and can be conveniently used to give names to natural phenomena connected with the same circle of ideas; and he does not cease to take notice of natural phenomena while forming myths. Thus even the agriculturist may have spoken of the Sun's hunts; and even at the agricultural stage myths may still have arisen which spoke of the Sun as a sportsman armed with arrows with which he slays the dragon. It is accordingly not the mythic material that is of the highest moment in sketching the chief stages of development in the formation of myths, but rather the *Tendency* of the myth—the position occupied by man in relation to external nature, so far as appears from the myths in question. How, according to this scale of development, the stages of the myth among the Aryans are reflected in their mythology, I do not presume to judge, being on Aryan ground only a *dilettante*. I will, however, quote some examples from the special ground of these studies, to illustrate what has been expounded. Looking at the myth of Jacob, observing the centre of the cycle, whose name—as is demonstrated at the proper place—is an appellation of the starry heaven, how he strives against the *Red*, 'Edôm,' and the *White*, 'Lâbhân,' and seeing that the myth-maker's sympathy always inclines to Jacob, that his over-reaching of his enemies always appears in a light favourable to him, and that his defeats always wear a tragic colour, I can conclude that this cycle of myths belongs to Nomadism. The same inference must be drawn from an examination of the myth of Joseph. But if I look at the hymn to Judah, or consider the myth of Samson and what the Hebrew told of

[1] *Rude Stone Monuments in all Countries, their Ages and Uses,* London 1872, pp. 9 *et seq.* and 28.

the Sun-giant with his long locks, of his being blinded, and of his fall, then I know that I have to do with myths of agricultural people. With regard to the antipathy felt towards the scorching sun, I will finally call attention to the ideas held by the tribe of Atarantes in Herod. IV. 184, where it is said: *οὗτοι τῷ ἡλίῳ ὑπερβάλλοντι καταρέονται, καὶ πρὸς τούτοισι πάντα τὰ αἰσχρὰ λοιδορέονται, ὅτι σφέας καίων ἐπιτρίβει, αὐτούς τε τοὺς ἀνθρώπους καὶ τὴν χώρην αὐτῶν.*[1]

§ 6. It is a remarkable fact in the history of the human mind that many nations which made the advance from the nomadic to the agricultural life under the condition that either Nomadism still continues to vegetate in the nation as an isolated residuum of the previous stage, or that the advance affects only a part, though an influential one, of the nation, whilst another equally considerable portion remains at the old stage of civilisation, not only have no consciousness that the transition is an advance, but even hold to a conviction that they have taken a step towards what is worse, and have sunk lower by exchanging pasture for crops. The nomad cherishes the proud feeling of high nobility and looks haughtily down on the agriculturist bound to the clod. Even the half-savage Dinka in Central Africa, who leads a nomadic life, calls the agriculturist Dyoor 'a man of the woods,' or 'wild man,' and considers himself more privileged and nobler.[2] Everyone who knows anything of the nature and history of Arabic civilisation knows the pride of the Bedawî and the ironical contempt with which they look down upon the Ḥaḍarî. For the Semites are especially characterised by this tendency.[3] The Hellenic mind is totally

[1] The same is stated of some American tribes by Sir J. Lubbock, *The Origin of Civilisation*, ed. 3, 1875, pp. 273, 306, *et seq.*

[2] Georg Schweinfurth, *The Heart of Africa*, I. p. 200.

[3] But we cannot on this account characterise the Semites generally by the assertions, 'The Semites are in general a pastoral people,' 'the Semites live in tents,' as Friedrich von Hellwald does in his *Culturgeschichte in ihrer natür-*

different. To the Hellene the agricultural life only is a morally perfect condition; his poet has given expression to this feeling in the beautiful words :—

> Τῆς πᾶσιν ἀνθρώποισιν εἰρήνης φίλης
> πιστὴ τροφὸς ταμία συνεργὸς ἐπίτροπος
> θυγατὴρ ἀδελφὴ πάντα ταῦτ' ἐχρῆτό μοι
> σοι δ' ὄνομα δὴ τί ἐστιν; ὅτι γεωργία. .[1]

And to the Roman poet of a period troubled by wars peaceful agriculture is not only the most ideal condition of human life, but also the happy state of innocence of primeval mankind :—

> Ut *prisca gens mortalium*
> Paterna rura bobus exercet suis,

says Horace in his celebrated epode 'Beatus ille'; and of any more ancient period he had never heard.[2] George Rawlinson very oddly says, 'It was a fashion among the Greeks to praise the simplicity and honesty of the nomade races, who were less civilised than themselves ;[3] for the passages of literature quoted by him in confirmation of this assertion lay no stress on the *nomadic* element. But

---

lichen Entwickelung, p. 134. A glance at the sedentary Phenicians and the settled Semites of Mesopotamia shows at once the important exceptions. It must also not be overlooked that agriculture was in practice to no small extent among the Phenicians; even the Romans call a kind of threshing machine, the 'Punic:' Varro, *De re rustica*, I. 52; cf. Lowth, *De sacra poesi Hebraeorum*, Oxford 1821, Prael. VII. p. 62. The commerce with Egypt, which von Hellwald brings into prominence, is no sufficient reason why the favourite characterisation of the Semites does not apply to these nations. The Hebrews continued their nomadic life for a long time after they had made intimate acquaintance with Egypt; and the nomadic Arabs were not materially influenced by communication with sedentary nations.

[1] Given by Josephus Langius, *Florilegii magni seu Polyantheae . . . libri XXIII.*, Lugduni 1681, I. 120, as by Aristophanes; but the author and the translator have searched the works and fragments of Aristophanes in vain.

[2] Ovid also begins with the life of the fields; his golden age is distinguished from the others only in this, that:

> Ipsa quoque immunis, rastroque intacta, nec ullis
> Saucia vomeribus, per se dabat omnia tellus;

and

> Mox etiam fruges tellus inarata ferebat:
> Nec renovatus ager gravidis canebat aristis.
> (*Metamorph.* I. 101–2, 109-10.)

[3] *History of Herodotus*, tr. G. Rawlinson, IV. c. 46, note 5.

the case is very different among the Semites. Let us first consider from this point of view the territory, richest among all those of the Semites, which yields the most copious evidence of the thoughts and feelings of its inhabitants—the Arabic. 'The Divine Glory' (al-sakînat = shekhînâ) it is said, in a speech of Moḥammed's, 'is among the shepherds; vanity and impudence among the agriculturists' (al-faddâdûn).[1] Another traditional sentence, which the propagators of Moḥammed's sayings – certainly not Bedâwî themselves—put in the mouth of the Prophet, is that every prophet must have been a shepherd for a long time.[2] How greatly Moḥammed approved the proud self-consciousness of the nomad, as opposed to the agricultural character, is evident from the following narrative belonging to the Islamite Tradition. 'The Prophet once told this story to one of his companions in the presence of an Arab of the desert. An inhabitant of Paradise asked Allâh for permission to sow, and Allâh replied, "You have already all that you can want." "Yes," answered the other, "but yet I should like also to scatter some seed." So (when Allâh had given him permission), he scattered seeds; and in the very moment that he was looking at them, he saw them grow up, stand high and become ripe for harvest; and they were like regular hills. Then Allâh said to him "Away from here, son of men; you are an insatiable creature!" When the Prophet had finished this story, the Arab of the desert said, "By Allâh! this man can only have been a Kureyshite or an Anṣârî, for they employ themselves with sowing seed, but we Desert-Arabs are not engaged in sowing." Then the Prophet smiled'—with manifest approbation.[3] The accredited collections of traditions tell also the following of Abû Umâmâ al-Bâhilî: 'Once on seeing a ploughshare and another agricultural implement,

[1] Muslim's *Collection of Traditions* (ed. of Cairo with commentary), I. 138; al-Jauharî, s.r. *fdd.* Cf. Dozy, *Geschichte der Mauren in Spanien*, Leipzig 1874, I. 17.

[2] Al-Buchârî, *Recueil des Traditions Musulmans* (ed. Krehl), II. 385 (LX. No. 29).

[3] Al-Buchârî, *Recueil* &c., II. 74 (XL I. No. 20).

he said: I heard the Prophet say, "These implements do not enter into the house of a nation, unless that Allâh causes low-mindedness to enter in there at the same time."'[1] So also, in his political testament the Chalîf 'Omar when dying recommended the Bedâwî to his successor, '*for they are the root of the Arabs and the germ of Islâm;*'[2] and how little this Arabian politician could appreciate the importance of agriculture is evident from the edict in which he most strictly forbade the Arabs to acquire landed possessions and practise agriculture in the conquered districts. The only mode of life equally privileged with the roving nomad life was held to be the equally roving military profession, or life of nomads without herds and with arms. Even in Egypt, a specially agricultural country, this principle was acknowledged and strictly carried out.[3] He was likewise hostile to permanent buildings and houses such as are erected in towns. Once, passing by the brick house of one of his governors, he obliged him to refund the money that had enabled him to enjoy such luxury; and when Sa'd b. Abî Waḳḳâṣ asked his permission to build a house, the Chalîf thought it was enough to possess a place that gave protection from the sun's heat and the rain.[4] And this same Chalîf, who may pass for a still better type of the true Semite than

[1] Al-Buchârî, *Recueil* &c. p. 67, No. 2. It is true these expressions might be balanced by a few somewhat opposite in character, such as that which declares that in the judgment of the Prophet the best business is Trade; according to other reporters Manufacture; according to others (whose version is regarded as the correct one) Agriculture (see al-Nawawî on Muslim's *Collection of Traditions*, IV. 32). Still such sentences, even when confirmed by others, cannot weaken the force of those cited in the text. I must also mention in conclusion that al Sha'rânî in his *Book of the Balance* (Kitâb al-mîzân, Cairo [Castelli], 1279, II. 68) mentions this question as a point of difference among the canonical authorities of Islamic theology: the school of al-Shâfe'î regards trade as the noblest occupation, whilst the three other Imâms (Abû Ḥanîfâ, Mâlik b. Anas, and Aḥmed b. Ḥanbal) declare for field-labour and manufactures.

[2] See Alfred von Kremer, *Culturgeschichte des Orients unter den Khalifen*, I. 16.

[3] Von Kremer, *ibid.* pp. 71, 77; *Culturgeschichtliche Streifzüge*, p. xi.

[4] Ibn 'Abdi Rabbihi, *Kitâb al-'iḳd al-ferîd*, ed. Bûlâḳ 1293 A. H., vol. III. p. 347.

Moḥammed himself, extends his preference for nomadism even to the mode of giving names. The nomad calls himself by the name of the tribe to which he belongs; the townsman, in whom all memory of tribal life is already extinct, receives a name from his birth-place, or that of his ancestors, or from his occupation. 'Learn your genealogies,' said 'Omar, 'and be not as the Nabateans of al-Sawâd; if you ask one of them where he comes from, he says he is from this or that town.' This trait of glorification of the old-fashioned Beduin-life, to the disparagement of the free urbanity of the townsmen, runs through a considerable section of Arabic literature, which gladly encircled the rough manners of the sons of the desert with a romantic nimbus of transfiguration. In this connexion a passage in a work falsely ascribed to Wâḳidî [1] should be noticed, which describes the Bedâwî Rifâ'a b. Zuheir at the court of Byzantium, and after putting a satire against nomadism in the mouth of the emperor, gives a brilliant victory over this attack to the 'mouse-eating' [2] Bedâwî. This preference for nomadism, and the view that, although, having fewer wants, it be a simpler and more uniform stage of human development than city-life, it nevertheless surpasses the latter in nobility and purity, still live on in the system of the talented Arabian historian Ibn Chaldûn. He devotes several sections of his historical 'Introduction' to the glorification of the Bedâwî against the townsmen.' [3] What was thus established theoretically is presented in

---

1 *Futuh as-Shâm,* being an account of the Moslem conquests in Syria, ed. Nassau Lees, Calcutta 1854, I. 9 *et seq.*

2 This satirical reproach of the Bedâwî often occurs, e.g. sometimes in the Romance of *'Antar* in passages which are not accessible to me at the present moment. We meet with it also in the Persian king Yezdegird's satire on the Arabs (*Chroniques de Tabari,* transl. by Zotenberg, III. 387). Later also, in Ibn Baṭûṭâ, *Voyages,* III. 282, where the Indian Prince describes his Beduin brother-in-law Seif al-Dîn Ġada, who had at first charmed him, but afterwards been disgraced for his want of manners, by the epithet *mûsh châr,* i.e. 'field-rat-eater;' 'for,' adds the traveller, 'the Arabs of the Desert eat field-rats.' See also *Aġânî,* III. 33, l. 4 from below, where Bashshâr b. Burd accuses a Bedâwî of hunting mice (ṣeydu fa'rin).

3 *Prolégomènes, trad. par de Slane,* pp. 255–273.

real life down to the present day. Still, as twelve centuries ago, the Bedâwî alone are quite strictly entitled to the name al-'Arab or al-'Orbân (Arabs), and the Arabic poetry of the townsmen is found to have its locality still in the desert. The old Arabic poet in forming his poetical figures always likes best to carry the camel in his thoughts. With the camel the great majority of his best similes are connected. In one verse the poet compares himself to a strong sumpter camel; and in the very same line he, the camel, milks the breast of Death, which again is regarded as a camel. Time is a camel sinking to earth, which crushes with its thick hide him on whom it falls; a thirsty camel, which in its eagerness for water (here *men*) swallows everything.[1] War and calamity also are camels. The poet Ḳabîḏa b. Jâbir cries to his adversaries in praise of the valour of his own tribe: 'We are not *sons of young camels with breasts cut off*, but we are sons of fierce battle,' where, according to the interpretation of the native commentator, the 'young camels with breasts cut off' are meant to denote '*weak kings*, who provoke the ardour of battle in a very slight degree.'[2] How frequently, too, has the comparison of men with camels both in a good and in a bad sense been employed! Even in the nomenclature of places and wells in the Arabian peninsula the camel often comes in, probably often as the result of comparisons of which the details have not been preserved.[3] The host of stars is to the nomad a flock, which feeds by night on the heavenly pastures, and in the morning is led back to the fold by the shepherd. A poet describing the length of a night, exclaims: 'A night when the stars move slowly onwards, and which extends to such a length that I say to myself "It has no end, and *the shepherd of the stars* will not come back to-day."'[4] Hartwig Derenbourg finds the same view expressed also in Ps. CXLVII. 4,

[1] A collection of similar poetical passages is to be found in Freytag's *Commentary on the Ḥamâsâ*, pp. 601 and 606. [2] *Ḥamâsâ*, Text, p. 340, 3 *infr*
[3] E.g. Yâḳût, *Geograph. Dict.*, II. 118. s.v. *gamal*. [4] *al-Nâbiġâ*, III. 2.

'Counting to the stars a number, calling them all [by] names;'[1] it is, however, doubtful whether this poetical passage is based on the conception of the starry heaven as a flock.[2] But also poems of non-nomadic poets have been written from a Beduin point of view. The Ḳasîdâs of the Andalusian Arabic poets are written as from the camel's back, and move in the scenery of the desert; and when a modern Arab writes a Ḳasîdâ for an English lady, as has been done, the circle in which he moves is the circle of Imrulḳais and 'Antarâ.[3] This is not the effect of the traditional canon of the Ḳasîdâ only, but of the Arab's belief that true nobility is only to be found in the desert. Therefore his national enthusiasm transports him into the desert, for only there is life noble and free, the life of towns being a degradation. 'Even the town-life of the Arabs,' says the celebrated African traveller George Schweinfurth,[4] 'is essentially half a camp life. As a collateral illustration of this, I may remark that to this day Malta, where an Arab colony has reached as high a degree of civilisation as ever yet it has attained, the small towns, which are inhabited by this active little community, are called by the very same designations as elsewhere belong to the nomad encampments in the desert.' We must add, that

---

[1] *Journal Asiatique*, 1868, II. 378.

[2] Just as can be said of another passage closely connected with the above, Is. XL. 26. On the contrary, especially in the latter passage, the host of stars is compared to a war-host, ṣâbhâ; and the idea that each star is a valiant warrior is also not strange to Arabic poetry (e.g. *Ḥamâsâ*, p. 36, l. 5, comp. Num. XXIV. 17); for the conception of ṣebâ hash-shamayîm 'host or army of heaven,' has taken as firm root among the Arabs as among the Hebrews. 'For thou art the Sun,' says al-Nâbiġâ (VIII. 10) to king No'mân, 'and the other kings are stars; when the former rises, not a single star of these latter are any longer visible.' With this is connected the expression juyûsh al-ẓalâm 'the armies of darkness' (*Romance of 'Antar*, XVIII. 8. 6, XXV. 60. 69). In the last passage, indeed, it stands in parallelism with 'asâkir al-ḍi'â w-al-ibtisâm 'armies of light and smiling,' just as with the synonymous juyûsh al-ġeyhab (*'Antar*, XV. 58. 11).

[3] On this peculiarity of the poets of the towns an opinion of 'Ajjâj very much to the point occurs in the *Kitâb al-aġânî*, II. 18.

[4] *The Heart of Africa*, I. 28.

even the so-called Moorish architecture is said by many art critics to point to nomadic life, and the onion-shaped domes, the thin columns, the horse shoe-arches and the double pointed arches to be transferred from the construction of the tent to stone. The wandering habits of the Arabs are also preserved to the present day. 'Even now,' says Gerhard Rohlfs,[1] this volatile people is engaged in constant wandering; the slightest reason is sufficient to make them pack up their little tents and seek another abode.' Yet this experienced traveller appears somewhat to overdo it when he adds: 'Their pleasure in roving has its root in the essence of the Mohammedan religion; wherever the Arab can carry his Islâm, he finds a home &c.' But Islâm has, on the contrary, rather contributed to give the Arab a stable, political, state-building character. Certainly it has rather hindered than promoted the development of the feeling of nationality—it has this in common with every religion of catholic nature; but it has not had the influence ascribed to it by Rohlfs for the maintenance of the nomadic tendency. Why, it is the Bedâwî himself who is the worst Mohammedan! With this tendency of the Arabian mind, finally, is connected the fact that the Central Arabian sect of the Wahhabites, the very branch of the Mohammedans which stands nearest to the old Patriarchal ways in faith and ideas of the world, and protests energetically against all novelties introduced by foreign civilisation and historical advancement, has a particular dislike to agriculture.[2]

The Hebrew conception of the world, like the Arabic, inclines to a glorification of the Nomadic life. In the last stage of their national development the Hebrews refer the origin of agriculture to a curse imposed by God on fallen humanity. What a charm tent-life had for them, is proved by the fact that the fair shepherdess of the Song of Songs (I. 5) compares her beauty with oholê Ḳêdâr, 'the tents of the Arabs.' Even the Hellenised Jew Philo, quite in

[1] *Quer durch Afrika*, I. 121. [2] Palgrave, *Central and Eastern Arabia*, I. 463.

opposition to Greek ideas, glorifies the shepherds as ideals of morality in contrast to the agriculturists.[1] Such a view could not but exert an influence on the figures of the myth. The persons of the myth who have our sympathy are generally presented as shepherds: Abel, Jacob, Moses, and David, are shepherds; whereas Cain is an agriculturist.

Moreover, the idea that the fall of the human race is connected with agriculture is found, besides the analogous cases commonly adduced by commentators, to be also often represented in the legends of the East African negroes, especially in the Calabar legend of the Creation communicated by Bastian,[2] which presents many interesting points of comparison with the Biblical story of the Fall. The first human pair is called by a bell at meal-times to Abasi (the Calabar God) in heaven; and in place of the forbidden tree of Genesis are put agriculture and propagation, which Abasi strictly denies to the first pair. The fall is denoted by the transgression of both these commands, especially through the use of implements of tillage, to which the woman is tempted by a female friend who is given to her. From that moment man fell and became mortal, so that, as the Bible story has it, he can 'eat bread only in the sweat of his face.' There agriculture is a curse, a fall from a more perfect stage to a lower and imperfect one. This view of the agricultural life is, however, not the conception of nomads only; it is proper also to nations which have not even reached the stage of nomadism, but stand a step lower—the hunters. To them their own condition appears the happiest, and that of the agri-

[1] *De Sacrificio Kajin*, p. 169, ed. Mangey, Oxford 1742. In another treatise Philo distinguishes two kinds of shepherds and two kinds of agriculturists, of which one kind is blameworthy, and the other praiseworthy. There is a distinction between *ποιμήν* and *κηνοτροφός*, and on the other hand between *γῆς ἐργάτης* (probably answering to the Hebrew 'ôbêd adâmâ), and *γεωργός* (probably intended to represent the Hebrew îsh adâmâ). See *De Agricultura*, p. 303 *et seq.*

[2] *Geographische und ethnologische Bilder*, pp. 191–97.

culturist condemned by a curse. 'The countries inhabited by savages,' as Montesquieu makes his Persian Usbek write,[1] 'are generally sparsely peopled, through the distaste which almost all of them have for labour and the tillage of the soil. This unfortunate aversion is so strong that when they make an imprecation against one of their enemies, they wish him nothing worse than that he may be reduced to field-labour,[2] deeming no exercise noble and worthy of them except hunting and fishing.' This contempt of a sedentary life and its usage is by the Bedâwî directed also especially against the practice of arts and manufactures. Hence it comes that such peoples as the Arabs, which even in a sedentary condition regard nomadic life as a nobler stage of manners than the agricultural life to which they have *fallen*, neglect manufactures and seldom attain to any perfection in them. This is especially true of the inhabitants of the holy cities of the Arabian peninsula, who give a practical proof of their preference for Beduinism by the fact that the Sherîf-families let their sons pass their childhood in the tents of the desert for the sake of a nobler education. 'I am inclined to think,' says the credible traveller Burckhardt in his description of the inhabitants of Medina,[3] 'that the want of artisans here is to be attributed to the very low estimation in which they are held by the Arabians, whose pride often proves stronger than their cupidity, and prevents a father from educating his sons in any craft. This aversion they probably inherit from the ancient inhabitants, the Bedouins, who, as I have remarked, exclude to this day all handicraftsmen from their tribes, and consider those who settle in their encampment as of an inferior cast, with whom they neither associate nor intermarry.'[4]

---

[1] *Lettres persanes*, Lettre CXXI.

[2] See Herberstein, *Rerum Moscoviticarum Commentarii*, Vienna 1549, p. 61, where a Tatar formula of execration is said to be 'ut eodem in loco perpetuo tamquam Christianus haereas.'

[3] *Travels in Arabia*, ed. Ouseley, 1829, p. 381.

[4] A notable illustration of this relation is presented by the Arabic proverb,

Burton compares the Arabs of the desert in this respect with the North American Indians of a former generation: 'Both recognising no other occupation but war and the chase, despise artificers and the effeminate people of cities, as the game-cock spurns the vulgar roosters of the poultry-yard.'[1] The same is true of the relation of the Bedâwî towards the townsmen in the Somali country.[2] Kant, who casually notices this remarkable trait of human ideas in a small tract, refers the peculiarity to the fact that not only the natural laziness, but also the vanity (a misunderstood freedom) of man cause those who have merely to live—whether profusely or parsimoniously—to consider themselves Magnates in comparison with those who have to labour in order to live.[3]

Thus is explained the conception which forms the basis of the Story of the Fall, and at the same time everything else in the older strata of Hebrew mythology in which the sympathy of the myth-forming people is given to the shepherds, to the prejudice of personages introduced as agriculturists. And now we will consider the most prominent of the figures forming the elements of the ancient Hebrew mythology.

'If you hear that the smith (of the caravan) is packing up in the evening, be sure that he will not go till the following morning' (*al-Meydânî*, Bûlâḳ edition, I. 34). Notice the occasion of the origin of this proverb, in the commentary on the passage.

[1] *Personal Narrative of Pilgrimage to Mecca and Medina*, 2nd ed. 1857, I. 117.

[2] Burton's *First Footsteps in Eastern Africa*, p. 240.

[3] Kant's *Kleinere Schriften zur Logik und Metaphysik, herausgegeben von Kirchmann*, II. 4 (*Philosoph. Bibliothek*, Hermann, Bd. XXXIII.).

CHAPTER V.

THE MOST PROMINENT FIGURES IN HEBREW MYTHOLOGY.

BATTLE and bloodshed, pursuit and suppression on the one side, love and union, glowing desire and coy evasion on the other, are the points of view from which the Myth regards the relations of day and night, of the grey morning and the sunrise, of the red sunset and the darkness of night, and their recurring changes. And this point of view is made yet more definite by the mythical idea that when forces are either engaged in mutual conflict, or seeking and pursuing one another in mutual love, as one follows the other, so one must have sprung from the other, as the child from the father or the mother; or else, being conceived as existing side by side in the moment of battle or of heavenly love, must be brothers or sisters, children of the same father or of the same mother, i.e. of the phenomenon that precedes both of them alike—as the bright day precedes the twilight and the night—or must be the parents of the child that follows them.

Therefore, still more definitely, murders of parents or children or brothers, battles between brothers, sexual love and union between children and parents, between brother and sister, form the chief plots of all myths, and by their manifold shades have produced that variety in our race's earliest observations of nature, which we encounter in the thousand colours of the Myth.

The talented founders of Aryan Comparative Mythology, especially Max Müller in the first rank, have set these themes of the myth on so firm and unquestioned a foundation both in relation to psychology and to philology, and have so completely introduced them to the mind of the educated class, that I may safely omit a new exposition of this axiom of all Mythology. I content myself with pointing once more to what was shown in the preceding chapters, that these fundamental mythical themes are not something specially Aryan, but lie at the bottom of the Myth of all mankind without distinction of race, and consequently must form a starting-point when we are about to investigate Semitic or Hebrew myths.

The task of the following chapter will therefore be to find a place in the category of what is *common* to the *whole* of human kind for the myth of the Hebrews; in other words, to prove the existence of the myth-plots on Hebrew ground. As it is not my object to exhaust all the materials, to present a system already perfectly worked out on every side, or to erect a building with all its rooms and stories stuffed full, I shall confine myself to that which, after competent and sober philological criticism, can be acknowledged as certain and indubitable. I hope that other investigators, who will gain from the method pursued here a rich treasury of material, will then follow up these safe results by gleanings of their own.

§ 1. In the designation of the Heaven the Semite starts from the sensuous impression of *height*, and therefore forms the names denoting it from the roots *samâ* (shama) and *râm*, both of which express the idea of 'being high.' To the latter group belongs e.g. the Ethiopic rayam,[1] which denotes *heaven*. Both roots are combined in the Phenician Shâmîn-rûm. One of the most prominent figures of Hebrew mythology belongs to this category: Abh-râm the *High Father*, with his innumerable host of descendants.[2] We have seen above that in

---

[1] Osiander (*Zeitschrift der D. M. G.*, 1853, VII. 437) is inclined to combine with this the old Arabic *Rayâm* or *Riyâm*.

[2] The added Abh in Abhrâm, compared with the other expressions in which

his view of nature the nomad begins with the sky at night. The sky by itself is the dark, nightly, or clouded heaven; the sunshine on the sky is an accessory. Hence it comes that in Arabic the word Sky (samâ) is very often used even for 'Rain;' and the notions of *rain* and *sky* are so closely interwoven that even the traces of rain on the earth are called sky.[1] In the language of the Bongo people there is only one word for sky and rain, hetōrro.[2] On Semitic ground the Assyrian divine name Rammanu or Raman must be mentioned here. If this name has any etymological connexion with the root *râm* 'to be high,' as Hesychius and some modern scholars say, though others derive it from *ra'am* 'thunder,' Ra'amân 'the Thunderer,'[3] then we find here again the primitive mythological idea that the intrinsically High is the dark stormy sky, or, personified, the God of Storms. So also in the old Hebrew myth the 'High' is the nightly or rainy sky. The best known myth that the Hebrews told of their Abh-râm is the story of the intended sacrifice of his only son Yiṣchâḳ, commonly called Isaac. But what is Yiṣchâḳ? Literally translated, the word denotes 'he laughs,' or 'the Laughing.' In the Semitic languages, especially in proper names and epithets, the use of the aorist[4] (even in the second person, e.g. in the Arabic name Tazîd) is very frequent where we should employ a participle.[5] So here. Now who is the 'He laughs,' the 'Smiling one'? No other but 'He who sits in heaven

the quality of *father* is not emphasized, finds an exact parallel in Δη(=Γη)-μητήρ and Γαῖα.

[1] *Opuscula Arabica* (ed. W. Wright, Leyden 1859), p. 30. 2; 34. 5. This usage is made possible by the signification *Cloud*, which is peculiar to the word samâ in Arabic (Sprenger, *Das Leben und die Lehre des Mohammed*, I. 544).

[2] Schweinfurth, *The Heart of Africa*, I. 311.

[3] See the Count von Baudissin, *Studien zur semitischen Religionsgeschichte*, Leipzig 1876, I. p. 306 *et seqq.*

[4] Or Future, or Imperfect, as it is more generally termed.—Tr.

[5] It is worthy of note that in Arabic *pluralia fracta* can be formed from this class of proper names. An interesting example of this is Tan'um[u] b. Ḳami'ata, the name of the ancestor of the tribe Tanâ'um. See Ibn Dureyd, *Kitâb al-ishtiḳâḳ*, p. 85 and gloss *h*.

and laughs' (Ps. II. 4), whom the mythology of almost all nations and their later poetry too likes to call the Laughing or Smiling one. When, as Plutarch tells in his Life of Lycurgus, that legislator consecrated a statue to Laughter (γέλως) and Laughter enjoyed divine honours at Sparta, we are certainly not to understand it of the laughter that plays round the lips of mortals, but of the celestial smile with which Mythology endows the Sun, as when the Indian singer calls Ushas (the Sun [1]) the *Smiling* (Rigveda, VI. 64. 10). With regard to the Sun's laughing in the Aryan mythology, we can refer to the learned work of Angelo de Gubernatis, 'Zoological Mythology' (vol. I. i. 1).

But there is a primitive connexion between the ideas 'to laugh' and 'to shine,' which is not, as might be thought, brought about *figuratively* by a mere poetical view, but rather, at least on the Semitic field, established at the very beginning of the formation of speech. An extraordinary number of the verbs which describe a loud expression of joyousness (to shout, bellow, laugh &c.), originally denoted to shine, dazzle, be visible, and the like; affording another confirmation of Geiger's thesis, that language owes its origin more to optic than to acoustic impressions (see *supra* p. 40) I give a series of linguistic facts as examples to prove this assertion. The Hebrew ṣâhal signifies both 'to shine bright' and 'to cry aloud,' and its phonetic connexion with ṣâhar, zâhar &c., proves the priority of the optical meaning. Similarly hillêl, which means 'to cry out, to triumph,' was originally 'to be brilliant,' as is proved by the derivative nouns hilâl (Ar.) 'new moon' and hêlêl (Heb.) 'morning star,' and the employment of the verb itself in Hebrew. Ṣârach, serach, ṣaraḥa, denotes 'to cry' in the chief representatives of Semitism; but the Arabic has also preserved the original sense 'clarus, manifestus fuit,' which appears in the Hebrew noun ṣerîach 'a conspicuous eminence,' or 'a high tower.' [2] The roots yâphaʿ (in Hiphʿîl)

[1] Strictly the Dawn.—Tr.

[2] This theory explains the connexion of ṣârach with zârach 'to be bright.'

'to be bright' and pâ'â 'to cry,' are through their etymological connexion brought into this group. The root of the Hebrew hêdâd 'cry of joy' is the same from which Hadad, the name of the Syrian god of the shining sun, can be etymologically derived. This root undoubtedly represents a reduplicated form of the radical of the solar name Yehûdâ 'Judah' (see § 14 of this chapter). The verbal root from which nahâr (Ar.) nehârâ (Heb.) 'daylight,' is derived has in one Arabic derivative form the meaning 'to cry.' So also ṣâchaḳ 'to laugh aloud' (compare ṣâ'aḳ 'to cry') must have originally expressed the idea of 'being bright, clear,' which is proper to the primitive Semitic root ṣaḥ, ṣach. If this be admitted, it follows that the name Yiṣchaḳ as a solar epithet was not formed by mere figurative or poetical metaphor, but is based on the original signification of the group of roots to which it belongs. Poetical phraseology then brought into general use what was based on etymology.

There is nothing more universal and more generally pervading all nature-poetry than the idea 'Like one *laughing gaily* the world shone,' as the Tatar poet says of the sunrise;[1] and in Arabic poetry, which has to be especially considered on these subjects, it is met with at every step. In the charming Romance of 'Antar, the cessation of night and the break of day is dozens of times expressed by the words 'until the black night went off and the *laughing morning* (al-ṣabâḥ al-ḍaḥik) arose;' or 'the morning arose and smiled (ibtasama) out of dazzling teeth.'[2] The old poet al-A'sha says of a blooming meadow that it rivals the sun in laughter (yuḍâḥik al-shams);[3]

Accordingly, I should like to place the Hebrew ṣâra'ath *lepra* in this same etymological group, as the relationship between ע and ח does not require demonstration; the signification would then be that of 'whiteness' (see Lev. XIII. 3, 4).

[1] Hermann Vámbéry, *Uigurische Sprachmonumente und das Kudatku Bilik*, Innsbruck 1870, p. 238 *a*.

[2] E.g. vol. IV. 26 ult.; XVIII. 3, 11. 19, 93. 11; XXV. 5. 12, 6. 6 &c. I always quote the octavo edition of the *Romance of 'Antar*, printed by Sheikh Shâhîn in thirty-two small vols., Cairo 1286.

[3] In De Sacy, *Chrestomathie Arabe*, II. 151. 13.

and in the last maḳâmâ of Ḥarîrî (de Sacy, 2nd ed. p. 673. 2,) it is even said that 'the tooth of the daybreak laughs' (ibtasama thaġr al-fajr), i.e. becomes visible, as the teeth of a person laughing become visible. This mythic view has become so incorporated in the Arabic language that the word *bazaġa*, denoting that the teeth are prominent, is also used of the rising of the sun. In a small Arabic tract[1] by the Sheikh 'Ulwân b. 'Aṭiyyâ of Ḥamâ, which brings forward the contest between Day and Night, a subject not infrequent[2] in Oriental literature, in which the two champions engage in a battle of respective excellence in prose and poetry, there also occurs a passage suitable for quotation here. The Night says in the course of her dispute: 'To the string of these thy blameworthy qualities this must yet be added—that thou art changeable and many-coloured in thy various conditions, and not stedfast; thy beginning contradicts thy end, and thy interior is different from thy exterior. O what an utterly culpable quality is this, which scratches out the face of every merit! *Thou laughest at thy rising*, when thou rememberest weeping and mourning; and at thy extinction thou clothest thyself in thy most gorgeous of raiments, instead of putting on mourning garments.' And the Day replies, in his own defence to his black antagonist: 'What rank takest thou in comparison with me? What is thy gloominess and thy sombre seriousness in comparison with my *gay smiles* (ḍaḥikî wabtisâmî)?'[3]

It is not only the clear shining sunny sky that is called by the Arab poet 'the Smiling;' this attribute is applied also to other luminous things, e.g. to the glittering *Stars*

---

[1] It is entitled *Nuzhat al-asrâr fî muḥâwarat al-leyl w-al-nahâr*, and is in MS. in the University Library at Leipzig: cod. Ref. no. 357, fol. 11–18.

[2] Of this literature I will now draw attention only to a Ḳasîdâ of the old Persian poet Asadî, which is now made accessible in the edition of Rückert's *Grammatik, Poetik und Rhetorik der Perser*, published by the care of W. Pertsch, Gotha 1874, pp. 59–63. But it contains little that harmonises with the argumentation of the above-employed Arabic tract.

[3] *Nuzhat al-asrâr* &c., fol. 14 *verso*, 17 *verso*.

(not to the night-sky itself),[1] and to the Lightning, which is even called al-ḍâḥik, 'the Laughing.' In the Romance of 'Antar there frequently occurs the expression 'the Lightning laughed '(al-barḳ yaḍḥak, e.g. XXIV. 65. 6).[2] Abû-l-'Alâ al-Ma'arrî, an excellent Arabic poet, says in an elegy on the death of his father:

> I disapprove of merriment even in the *laughing* (*i.e.* lightning) cloud,
> And let no cloud bring me rain, except a gloomy, dark one.[3]

We have in passing treated the words 'He who sits in heaven laughs' in the second Psalm as a mythical reminiscence, which originally referred to the Sun, but then, like similar instances which we shall see, was employed by the poet in another sense. But there is nothing to exclude the possibility that the Laughter of him who sits in heaven may refer in this passage not to the sweet smile of the bright sunny sky, but to the wild raging of the Thunderer, pictured in the myths as scornful laughter, as F. L. W. Schwartz[4] shows by many examples from classical antiquity. This conception would also be more suitable to the context of the passage in question in the second Psalm, where mention is made of derisive laughter. However this be, the 'Smiling one' whom the 'High Father' intends to slay, is the smiling day, or more closely defined the smiling sunset, which gets the worst of the contest with the night-sky and disappears.

§ 2. The same myth is also given as follows: '*Jephthah sacrifices or kills his daughter.*' In its later ethical or religious transformation given in Judges XI. 29–40, it is known to everyone. This story is especially worthy of consideration in connexion with the science of Mythology,

---

[1] E.g. Abû-l-'Alâ's Poems in the edition with commentary, Bûlâḳ 1286, II. 107, line 1: wa-tabtasimu-l-ashrâṭu fajran.

[2] See Abû-l-'Alâ, *ibid.*, p. 211, line 5: fî maḍḥaki-l-barḳi.

[3] Vol. I. 193. Compare a beautiful passage in a poem of Ibn Muṭeyr, given by Nöldeke, *Beiträge zur Poesie der alten Araber*, p. 34, to which we shall recur farther on.

[4] *Ursprung der Mythologie*, p. 109 *et seq*

because a Hebrew custom similar to the mourning for Osiris or Adonis and Tammûz was fastened on to it, as appears in v. 40; and it is well known that these latter rites stand in a very close connexion with physical phenomena, and with the myth which speaks of these phenomena.

What means Jephthah (Yiphtâch)? We have again an aorist form[1] exactly similar to Yiṣchâḳ; it denotes literally 'he opens, he begins,' thence 'the opener or beginner.' For the understanding of this mythical person we must note by anticipation that this Opener has a correlative in the After-follower Jacob (Ya'aḳôbh), 'he follows his heels.'[2] Both these expressions belong to one group of mythic conceptions; and it is remarkable that in these designations we find mythology already advanced to the stage which we characterised in the previous chapter as belonging to the ideas of the Agriculturist. For these two names and the cycle of myths coupled with them presuppose the view that in the order of time the Day is the earlier and is followed by the Night; and the very circumstance that the idea of time is impressed on these myths with something of precision (see above, p. 44), also indicates a relatively late formation of these designations and of the views that led to them. The Opener is the Sun, which first opens the womb (see Gen. XXX. 22; Ex. XIII. 2, 12), while the Night is called the After-follower; just as in the Rigveda (II. 38. 6) the Night follows on the heel of Sâvitri. To establish more certainly the meaning of the name Ya'aḳôbh it may also be mentioned that in Arabic the participial form of the same verb, ''Âḳib,' is exceedingly frequent in the same signification. According to Mohammedan tradition one of the many names of the Arabian Prophet is Al-'âḳib, with the sense that Moḥammed, the last of the prophets, followed after and concluded their

---

[1] Most persons know this tense as Future, or as Imperfect.—Tr.

[2] Similar correlative names in Hellenic mythology are Pro-metheus and Epi-metheus.

line.[1] We will now first return to Jephthah, the *Opening Sun*. This conception of the Sun as Opener receives a remarkable illustration in a passage of the Persian national epic by Firdûsî, in which occurs an expressive echo of this mythical view. The sun is there actually a *golden key*, which is lost during the night.[2] As the lighting up of the sun is conceived as an *unlocking*, so the darkness is a *locking up*. 'Who commandeth the sun and it riseth not, and who locketh up the stars,' is said in Job IX. 7, of the God who brings on darkness. The solar character of Jephthah receives confirmation from another side, but likewise on Semitic ground. In the version of the Phenician Cosmogony furnished by Damascius [3] it is related, on the authority of Mochus, that the spiritual God Ulômos begot Chrysoros τὸν ἀνοιγέα, 'the Opener.' The Sanchuniathon of Philo Herennius identifies this Opener with Hephaestus, who was the first inventor of iron implements (Tûbhal-Ḳayin of the Hebrews). Now, although in its latest development this cosmogony does not pretend to mean anything else than the opening of the Egg of the world,[4] there can be no doubt that this version belongs to a very late, perhaps the last phase of development of the myth which lies hidden in the background—a stage at which all that makes the myth a myth is quite washed out and changed by the prevalence of theological ideas into an artfully systematised cosmogony. But originally nothing else can have been understood by the Opener than the firstborn brother of the pair, Sun and Night. Another mythic trait which we know of this Opener testifies to his solar significa-

[1] Muslim's *Collection of Traditions*, edition with Commentary, Cairo 1284, V. 118. The commentator, Al-Nawawî, puts the name al-'Âḳib in combination with another name of the Prophet of identical meaning, viz. al-Muḳfî. The name al-'Âḳib occurs elsewhere also as a proper name, e.g. as the name of a friend of the poet al-A'sha (*Kitâb al-aġânî*, VI. 73).

[2] *Shâhnâmeh*, ed. Mohl, VII. v. 633, according to Rückert's ingenious interpretation in the *Zeitschrift der D. M. G.*, 1856, X. 145.

[3] *De Principiis*, ed. Kopp, p. 385.

[4] The sun itself is called a golden egg (Ad. Kuhn, *Zeitschr. für vergl. Sprachforschung*, I. 456).

tion in the myths on which the Phenician cosmogony was based. Philo Herennius' authority, who calls the opener *Chrysôr*, says of him: 'He was the first man who fared in ships.' This trait, which is far from fitting into the frame of the portrait of Hephaestus presents a very attractive and simple conception held by the men of the myth-forming age. We generally find in myths of the rising and setting of the sun, that the view which lives longest and conforms most naturally to the nature of the phenomenon is that the rising sun ascends out of the river or the sea, and that the setting sun sinks into the water.

> The gaudy, blabbing, and remorseful day
> *Is crept into the bosom of the sea,*

as Shakespeare says,[1] or as a German poet, feeling an echo of the meaning of the old myth, speaks still more expressively:

> '—that the sun was only
> A lovely woman, who the old sea-god
> Out of convenience married;
> All the day long she joyously wander'd
> In the high heavens, deck'd out with purple
> And glitt'ring diamonds,
> And all-beloved and all-admired
> By every mortal creature,
> And every mortal creature rejoicing
> With her sweet glance's light and warmth;
> But in the evening, impell'd, all-disconsolate,
> Once more returneth she home
> To the moist house and desert arms
> Of her grey-headed spouse.[2]

In a Swedish popular song, a King of England has two daughters, the elder *black as night* (Night itself); the other, younger, *beautiful and brilliant like the day* (Day itself). The latter goes forward followed by the other, who comes and throws her into the sea.[3] In this popular story, also,

[1] *King Henry VI.*, Part II. Act IV. beginning.

[2] Heinrich Heine, *The Baltic* [*sic*! i.e. 'die Nordsee' = the German Ocean], Part 2, No. 4 in E. A. Bowring's translation.

[3] In Henne-am-Rhyn, *Die deutsche Volkssage*, Leipzig 1874. p. 292, No. 544.

the sunset is viewed as a fall into the sea; but one new feature is here added, viz., that the two sisters fight, and the black one, the dark Night, throws the brilliant Sun into the sea. In the morning the Sun that had fallen into the sea rises up again out of her night's quarters. The Roman poet expresses the idea 'Never did a fairer lady see *the sun arise*,' by the words:

Ne qua femina pulchrior
Clarum *ab Oceano diem*
Viderit *venientem*; [1]

and because the sun rises out of the water, a Persian poet[2] calls water in general 'the Source of Light (tsheshmei nûr).' Connected with these ideas is that of the so-called *Pools of the Sun*,[3] which are assigned to the rising and setting sun alike.[4] But the morning sun is also made to come forth out of *mud* and *morass* (as in Homer from the λίμνη), as is described amongst others in the Arabic tradition.[5] It is obvious that this conception must have first arisen in countries whose horizon was not bounded by the sea. The same assumption must be made with regard to another conception also, found in the African nation of the Yorubas. These regard the town Ife as a sort of abode of gods, *where the Sun and Moon always issue forth again from the earth in which they were buried.*[6] No doubt this notion was formed among the portion of the nation that lived at a distance from the sea. A considerable part of the elements of the animal-worship which refers to water animals may be traced back to mythological conceptions which we have exhibited above.[7]

---

[1] Catullus, LIX. [LXI.] vv. 84–86.

[2] Emîr Chosrev of Delhi, in Rückert, *Grammatik, Rhetorik und Poetik der Perser*, p. 69. 6.

[3] See Excursus C.

[4] Pauly, *Realencyklopädie*, VII. 1277; Wilhelm Bacher, Niẓâmî's *Leben und Werke*, Leipzig 1871, p. 97, note 13.

[5] Al-Beiḍâwî, *Commentarius in Coranum*, ed. Fleischer, I. 572. 17. Bacher, *l. c.*

[6] Waitz, *Anthropologie der Naturvölker*, II. 170.

[7] See Excursus D.

When in ancient times men dwelling by the sea-shore saw the heavenly fire-ball in the evening dip into the sea, and the next morning issue shining at the opposite point of the sea-line, what other idea could he conceive of this but that down in the sea the sun was swallowed by a monster which spat out its prey again on the shore (see p. 28)?—or else that the sun undertook a voyage, starting over night?—or, as is so beautifully expressed in the Hellenic myth, that he took a bath, so as to shine on the sea-shore in the morning with new brightness and purified from all dinginess?

Navigation is the explanation of this daily phenomenon which prevails in the myth. It became so general that later among the Egyptians it was divested of its original associations and brought into connexion with the sun of day. In the Egyptian view the Sun's bark sails over the ocean of heaven:[1] *Ἥλιον δὲ καὶ σελήνην οὐχ ἅρμασιν ἀλλὰ πλοίοις ὀχήμασι χρωμένους περιπλεῖν ἀεί,* says Plutarch of the Egyptian view,[2] and adduces Homeric parallels.[3] The Jewish Midrâsh compares the course of the sun to that of a ship—and curiously enough to a ship coming from Britain,[4] which has 365 ropes (the number of the days of the solar year), and to a ship coming from Alexandria, which has 354 ropes (the number of the days of the lunar year).[5] The solar figures, then, are everywhere brought into connexion with the invention and employment of navigation. The sinking Apollo is with the Greeks the founder of navigation. Herakles receives from Helios the present of a golden bowl, which he used to employ as a bark when he sailed across the Okeanos. The voyage of the shining (*φαί-νω*) Phaeacians and Argonauts originally

---

[1] See e.g. Brugsch, *Histoire d'Égypte*, 1st ed., I. 37.

[2] *De Osir. et Isid.*, c. XXXIV.

[3] *De Pythiae oraculis*, c. XII., and compare the pseudo-Plutarch, *De vita et poësi Homeri*, c. CIV.

[4] So says Yalḳûṭ. Shôchêr Ṭôbh has the reading Akramânia, which is difficult of identification (Germania?).

[5] Yalḳûṭ and Shôchêr Ṭôbh on Ps. XIX. 7.

signified only the same sea-passage, which the sun makes every evening. Of Charon himself, the subterranean ferryman (whose name, Schwartz thinks, indicates his solar significance, χαροπός) it has also been proved that his subterranean navigation is only an eschatological development of the solar myth.[1] Indeed, eschatology and conceptions of the things after death and resurrection have their essential origin in the Sun's voyage under the sea and reappearance on the other side.[2] The Roman Sun-god Janus is also brought into connexion with navigation; this idea is unmistakably expressed on coins which bear the image of the two-headed god,[3] and is especially important here because Janus himself, as the etymology of his name declares, likewise belongs to the series of 'Openers.' 'This name was given him,' says Hartung, 'because the door represents in space exactly what formed the basis of his essence with regard to the relations of time and force. For every beginning resembles an entrance.'[4] The most prominent figure of the lately discovered Babylonian epos, Izdubar, and Ûr-Bêl (the Light of Bêl, *i.e.* the Sun), both of them purely solar figures, are provided with ships.[5] We cannot justly doubt, it is true, the historical character of the Biblical prophet Jonah. But, from what was discussed in the Second Chapter, this does not exclude the possibility that various mythical features may have been fastened on this undoubtedly historical personage, as is the case with many other persons of Hebrew history, for example, most strikingly with David. The most prominent mythical characteristic of the story of Jonah is his celebrated abode in the sea in the belly of the whale. This trait is eminently solar and belongs to the group on which we are now engaged. As on occasion of the storm the storm-dragon or the storm-serpent swallows the sun, so

1 *Ursprung der Mythologie*, p. 273.
2 See p. 15.
3 Compare Eckhel, *Doctrina Nummorum veterum*, V. 15.
4 *Die Religion der Römer*, Erlangen 1836, II. 218. Compare Mommsen, *History of Rome* (translation), I. 185, ed. of 1868.
5 Fr. Lenormant, *Les premières civilisations*, Paris 1874, II. 29-31.

when he sets he is swallowed by a mighty fish, waiting for him at the bottom of the sea. Then when he appears again on the horizon, he is *spit out on the shore* by the sea-monster.[1]

Accordingly, when Chrysôr is said to have been the *first navigator*, this must have the same meaning that it has when applied to Apollo, viz. that the Sun, sinking and going down into the ocean, is taking a journey by sea; or when applied to the Tyrian Herakles, the builder of the city (building of cities we shall see to be a specially solar characteristic), called the *inventor of navigation*;[2] or when used of Prometheus, recounting before the descendants of Okeanos his benefits conferred on mankind, and saying:—

> *βραχεῖ δὲ μύθῳ πάντα συλλήβδην μάθε,*
> *πᾶσαι τέχναι βροτοῖσιν ἐκ Προμηθέως.*
>
> Learn, in a word, the sense of all I mean:
> Prometheus gave all arts to mortal men;—

without forgetting to allude to the ships:—

> *θαλασσόπλαγκτα δ' οὔτις ἄλλος ἀντ' ἐμοῦ*
> *λινόπτερ' εὗρε ναυτίλων ὀχήματα.*
>
> The seaman's chariot roaming o'er the sea
> With flaxen wings none other found—'twas I.[3]

Now if this trait raises the solar character of Chrysôr to a certainty, then it cannot be doubted that his epithet the 'Opener,' which is identical with the Hebrew name

---

[1] It is well known that the story of Jonah was long ago connected with the myth of Herakles and Hesione, or that of Perseus and Andromeda (Bleek, *Einleitung ins A. T.*, Berlin 1870, p. 577). Tylor, *Primitive Culture*, I. 306, should also be consulted. What Emil Burnouf says in his *La Science des Religions*, Paris 1872, p. 263, is quite untenable; he finds in the myth 'un image de la naissance du feu divin et de la vie dont il est le principe.'

[2] Nonnus, *Dionysiaca*, XL. 443; Movers, *Religion der Phönizier*, p. 394.

[3] Aesch., *Prom.*, vv. 505, 467, Dind. I must also refer to Tangaloa, the chief figure in the Polynesian mythology, who is described as the first navigator. This characteristic, and the fact that Tangaloa is regarded as the originator of every handicraft (see the chapter on the Myth of Civilisation), with other features on which Schirren lays stress in determining his nature, seem to claim for him a solar character. Gerland (*Anthropologie der Naturvölker*, VI. 242) disputes this interpretation.

Yiphtâch (Jephthah) is an appellation of the Sun—the First-born. The Sun sacrifices his own daughter. In the evening the sunset sky is born from the lap of the sun, and in the morning, when in place of the red sunrise (which the myth does not distinguish from the red sunset) the hot midday sun comes forth, Jephthah has killed his own daughter, and she is gone.

Thus we see in the myths of Abram and of Jephthah the two sides of the same idea, each having its peculiar form and frame: the former tells of the victory of the Night, the dark sky of night over the Sun, the latter of that of the Dawn over the shades of Night. In Hebrew mythology the name Enoch (Chanôkh) belongs to this series. It was very happily explained by Ewald[1] as denoting the Beginner, *inceptor*, and is therefore a strict synonym of Jephthah.

We meet with one other 'Opener' on Semitic ground, the Libyan and especially Cyrenaic god of agriculture, whose name is preserved in the Grecized form Aptûchos ('Απτοῦχος). Blau[2] has already connected the name with the verb pâthach 'to open,' as opener of the ground by the plough. We must here refer in anticipation to the following chapter, which will elucidate the connexion in which the ancient religions put the rise of agriculture with the personages of mythology; and such a personage this Libyan 'Opener' undoubtedly is. Anyhow, we must hold fast to the identity of Aptûchos ('Απτοῦχος) and Jephthah.

§ 3. The myth of the death of Isaac, and that of his later life, which of course presupposes that he continued to live, are not contradictory to the mythical mind. At a more advanced stage of intellectual life, which had lost all share in and understanding of the nature-myth, and the mythical figures became *epic persons*, this con-

---

[1] *Jahrbücher für die bibl. Wissenschaft*, X. 21; *History of Israel*, I. 265 *et seq.*

[2] In his essay *Phönikische Analekten*, in the *Zeitschr. der D. M. G.*, 1865, XIX. 536.

tradition necessitated an arrangement or harmonising process; and in this lies the reason for the origin of the turn which occurred in the historical form of the legend of Isaac, substituting for the accomplished homicide an *intended* homicide; which latter, when religious feeling began to rule over the still existing mythic materials, became later simply an act of pious willingness to perform a sacrifice. Such contradictions do not present themselves distinctly to the mind of men at the stage of the actual formation of myths. The slain Isaac appears again on the arena a few hours after he was killed; he shews himself afresh. Some fifteen years ago when a Christian mission penetrated to the Central-African tribe of the Liryas, a great crowd collected round a priest, who began to expound to them the main principles of his religion. 'But when he came to the attributes of God, they absolutely refused to allow that he is very good. On the contrary, they said, he is very angry, and even bad, for he sends death; he is the cause of dying, and sends the sun, which always burns up our crops. *Scarcely is one sun dead in the west in the evening, than there grows up out of the earth in the east next morning another which is no better.*'[1] In this story we see the beginning of the transition from the formation of myths to religious reflexion: the sun that appears in the morning in the east is a different one from that which fell dead to the earth in the evening in the west. Yet, though substantially it is a different one and not identical with that of the previous day, it is still perfectly like it, and qualitatively not distinct from it. At the mythical stage, when it was still productive, Isaac reappearing is the same as Isaac already killed. He appears again several times; he marries Ribhḳâ (Rebekah); and again we meet him old and blind 'with weakened eyes,' sending his son Ya'aḳôbh (Jacob) into a foreign land, to return only after the death of the

---

[1] Sepp, *Jerusalem und das Heilige Land,* Schaffhausen 1863, II. 687.

old blind 'Smiling' one, with a large family, and prepared to take up again his old quarrel with his hairy brother Esau, the hunter. The living myth does not treat these events as following one after the other. To work up together the various members of the group of myths which assemble round a common centre or a common name, is not the business of the myth proper. The *epic* impulse first begins to act in this direction, and gives the first incitement to the harmonising of myths.

We will linger a few minutes longer with Isaac.

He loves and marries Rebekah, or as she is called in the Hebrew text, Ribhḳâ. The Dutch historian of religions C. P. Tiele sees in this name an appellation of the fruitful, rich *earth*,[1] a view which is partially supported by the etymology of the word. 'The laughing sky of day or the Sun-god (surely originally only the Sun?) is united in marriage with the fatness and fruitfulness of the earth.' This conception of the myth, notwithstanding its etymological correctness, has little to recommend it to my feeling, but I cannot propose any better in its stead. I only add, that if Tiele's conception is correct, we shall certainly understand better the feature of the myth which makes 'the Laughing one' (Isaac) of his two sons prefer Esau (who will be proved to be a solar character), while the mother's love attached itself more to Jacob. Esau is a mythical figure homogeneous with Isaac; but the fruitful earth is more closely connected with the dark rainy sky, as a kindred and homogeneous phenomenon.

Another notable point in the myth of Isaac is blindness. 'And when Isaac was old, his eyes became too dim to see' (Gen. XXVII. 1). It is an idea peculiarly mythical (which found an echo in poetry), to regard the Sun as an Eye, which looks down with its sharp sight upon the earth. In the Egyptian monuments and in the Book of the Dead the Sun is often represented as an eye, provided

[1] *Vergelijkende geschiedenis van de egyptische en mesopotamische Godsdiensten*, Amsterdam 1872, p. 434.

with wings and feet. To the same conception are also due the so-called mystic eye which is often met with on Etruscan vessels of clay, and the part played by the eye in the representation of Osiris.[1] The sun is called in the Malacassa language *masovanru*, and in Dayak *matasu*, both of which expressions denote *oculus diei.*[2] In the Polynesian mythology the sun is the left eye of Tangaloa, the highest god of heaven, hence the Eye of Heaven.[3] The sun accordingly possesses also the attributes of the eye. Thus in the Hebrew poetry we meet with the *Eyelashes*[4] (i.e. rays) of the Dawn, ʻaph-ʻappê shachar (Job III. 9, XLI. 10), as in the Greek with *ἁμέρας βλέφαρον* (Soph. *Ant.* 104),[5] and in the Arabic with ḥawâjib al-shams. This notion has so completely become an idiom of the Arabic language, where the mythical force of the 'sun's eyelashes' has retired into the background, that we even find the singular: 'the sun's eyelash is risen,' (ṭalaʻa ḥâjib al-shams) or 'set' (ġâba ḥâjib al-shams).[6]

Among more recent poets Shakespeare is most familiar with the expression *eye, eye of heaven*, as descriptive of the sun:

> Though thy speech doth fail,
> One eye thou hast to look to heaven for grace;
> The sun *with one eye* vieweth all the world.
> *King Henry VI.* Pt. I. I. 4.

---

[1] Julius Braun, *Naturgeschichte der Sage*, I. 41. See Tylor, *Primitive Culture*, I. 316.

[2] E. Jacques, *Vocabulaire Arabe-malacassa*, in *Journ. Asiat.*, 1833, XI. 129, 130.

[3] Gerland, *Anthropologie der Naturvölker*, VI. 242.

[4] 'Wimpern der Morgenröthe,' and so Ewald translates aphʻappayim in Job, i.e. eyelashes, *eyelids* being 'Augenlieder.' Yet Gesenius understands the word as *palpebrae*, i.e. eyelids (though both this word and *cilium* are occasionally used indiscriminately in either sense). Βλέφαρον is only 'eyelid;' the Arabic ḥawâjib is only 'eyelash.'—Tr.

[5] Gesenius, *Thesaurus*, p. 1003. *a*; compare Orph. VIII. I. 13. In the *Thesmophoriazusae* v. 17, Aristophanes makes Euripides call the eye 'the imitation of the disc of the sun;' compare *Acharn.* v. 1184: ὦ κλεινὸν ὄμμα, 'O glorious eye!' as an address to the Sun.

[6] Al Buchârî, IX. 30, 35.

Or with taper light
To seek the beauteous *eye of heaven* to garnish.
King John, IV. 2.

All places that the *eye of heaven* visits
Are to a wise man ports and happy havens.
King Richard II. I. 3.

When the *searching eye of heaven* is hid
Behind the globe and lights the lower world,
Then thieves and robbers range abroad unseen.
King Richard II. III. 2.

Hence also the Dawn is spoken of as *looking about*:-

Who is this that looketh forth as the morning?
Song of Songs, VI. 10.

At the theological stage the mythical view was subjected to several alterations. The holy book of the Parsees [1] calls the sun the *Eye of Ahuramazda.* Many regard the name ʿAnamelekh, who from 2 Kings XVII. 3 was a deity of the inhabitants of Sepharvaim (the Babylonian Sipar of the cuneiform Inscriptions), expressly designated in the national documents a solar town,[2] as contracted for ʿÊn ham-melekh, i.e. *Eye of the Sun-god Melekh,* and so probably the sun itself.[3] Even in the speech of a late Hebrew prophet (Zech. IV. 10) we find the same view, somewhat modified: '*These seven are the eyes of Jahveh,* that run over the whole earth.' Here Jahveh's eyes are undoubtedly to be referred to the sun, and the number seven allows us to think of the seven days of the week.[4] Similarly, it is said in the Atharvaveda IV. 16. 4 of the messengers of Varuṇa; 'descending from heaven they traverse the whole world, and *inspect the whole earth with a thousand eyes.*' [5] To the same tendency we must attribute

---

[1] *Yaçna,* I. 35, III. 49.

[2] Eberh. Schrader, *Die Keilinschriften und das Alte Testament,* p. 165.

[3] Haneberg, *Religiöse Alterthümer der Bibel,* Münich 1869, p. 49; Movers, *Die Phönizier,* I. 411, where other combinations are given.

[4] The seven days of the week are imagined to have a connexion with the sun. According to Diodorus, I. 272, the inhabitants of Rhodes at the time of Cadmus worshipped the Sun-god, who had begotten seven sons on that island.

[5] Muir, *Sanskrit Texts,* V. 64.

names of places such as *'Ên Shemesh*, 'Sun's Eye,' (e.g. Josh. XV. 7), and the Egyptian Heliopolis, Arabic 'ayn shams;[1] which suggests the obvious conjecture that the Hebrew 'Ir ha-cheres 'city of the sun' was originally and more correctly 'Ên ha-cheres. The emendation affects only the final consonant ר.

The Indian singer (Rigveda I. 164. 14), says that the sun has a sharp sight, and the same idea is preserved in a relic of Hebrew mythology, which has attached itself to an historical person. Of King David, an historical hero, it is written among other features borrowed from the myth of the Solar hero (to which also must belong the idea that he takes the life of his *giant* adversary by *hurling stones*), that 'he was ruddy, with beautiful eyes, and a good sight, admônî 'im yephê 'ênayim we-ṭôbh rô'î' (1 Sam. XVI. 12). The red colour itself which is praised, since the narrator evidently wishes to characterise David's handsomeness, shows us that these traits cannot have been invented directly for the hero of this story; for it can scarcely be proved that the Hebrews in ancient times considered reddishness an element of beauty. But the red colour is admirably fitted to figures of the solar myth, as we shall have further occasion to observe in the course of this chapter. With this are connected the beautiful eyes and the good sight, which are certainly taken from the mythical description of the blazing midday sun. They are the relics of a mythic cycle only preserved in fragments, and have been tacked on to the portraiture of an historical hero, who had, like the Solar hero, to fight with a hostile giant. When the sun appeared at noon with a red glow at its highest point in the heaven, the men of old said 'The Red one is looking down on the earth with his perfect eyes and sharp sight.' And he viewed the diminution of the solar rays and heat as a weakening of his sight, which ended at sunset with total blindness. Samson (Shimshôn),

[1] Yâkût, *Geogr. Wörterb.*, III. 762.

[2] See Excursus E.

the hero whose solar character Steinthal has raised above all doubt, ends his heroic career by being made blind. In the Greek mythology the significance of one-eyed and blinded persons is exhibited with equal clearness.[1] This mythical idea is very clearly reflected in language. In Arabic, for example, iṭlachamma or iṭrachamma signifies both *oculos hebetiores habuit* and *obscura fuit* [nox]. The verb aġdana, from which aġdan is derived, which is used of suffering from certain eye-diseases, expresses the idea of darkness, and the word inchasafa unites the two meanings *to be eclipsed* (of the moon) and *to lose one's sight.* Hence the expression, al-leyl a'war, 'the night is one-eyed.'[2] It becomes clear from all this what is the meaning of the mythical words, 'And when Isaac was old, his eyes became too dim to see.' It may also be mentioned here that Shakespeare calls night the *eyeless* :—

Thou and eyeless night
Have done me shame. *King John* V. 6.

§ 4. The battle of the Day with the Night is still more frequently represented as a *quarrel between brothers.* At the very threshold of the earliest Biblical history we meet a brothers' quarrel of this kind, the source of which is the nature-myth, spread out among all nations of the world without exception. It is not difficult to prove that Cain (Ḳayin) is a solar figure, and that Abel (Hebhel) is connected with the sky dark with night or clouds. Here, as everywhere, investigation must of course be guided by the nature of the personages in question, by the matter of the story, and by the appellative signification of the names. Cain is an agriculturist, Abel a shepherd. We have demonstrated in the preceding chapter that agriculture always has a solar character, whereas the shepherd's life is connected with the phenomena of the cloudy or nightly sky, Shepherds in mythology are figures belonging to the dark

[1] Hartung, *Religion und Mythologie der Griechen*, Leipzig 1865, II. 87-94.
[2] *al-Meydânî Majma' al-amthâl*, II. 111. 21.

or overclouded sky; whereas huntsmen and agriculturists are solar heroes. The heaven at night is a great tent or a group of tents, with a great piece of pasture close by, where the herds (the clouds) are driven to feed. In German, to be sure, the expression *Himmelszelt* (heaven's tent) is also used of the heaven by day, but this is a generalisation of the original limitation to the nocturnal and cloudy sky. This limitation is still acknowledged in the Hungarian language, where *sátoros éj* is said, 'the tented (provided with many tents) night;' e.g. by Vörösmarty at the commencement of the second canto of his national epic 'Zalán Futása' (the Flight of Zalán). And in Arabic, 'Night spread out its tent, and there arose thick darkness,' is quite a familiar expression.[1]

The shepherd Abel (Hebhel) is accordingly a figure of the dark sky. This is proved also by the signification of the name. For it denotes neither *childlessness*, as some try to explain it by the help of Arabic, and on the supposition that the first parents anticipated their son's future fate on giving his name, nor simply *son*, being explained from the Assyrian. The Hebrew language itself is adequate to establish the proper signification. The word denotes in Hebrew a 'breath of wind;'[2] and the wind stands in connexion with the dark sky. Another modification of the same appellation is known to Hebrew mythology. As in other classes of language *h* and *y* may interchange dialectically, so here beside Hebhel (Abel) we have Yâbhâl (Jabal). This latter appellation is etymologically either identical with the former, or if not, at least its mythological identity

---

[1] Wa-kân auwal mâ asbal al-leyl riwâḳah wa-ḳad iswadd al-ẓalâm biaġsâḳah, *Romance of 'Antar*, V. 170. 17. Accordingly, insadal is said of night as well as of a tent, e.g. *'Antar*, VI. 60. 14, 95. 5.

[2] I wish to mention here a suggestion received in a letter from Prof. de Goeje of Leyden, to take the name Hebhel in the appellative sense 'herdsman,' and compare it with the Arabic abil, the initial breathing being aspirated. The Hebrew âbhêl, 'pasture,' would then belong to the same group. But see also on the latter word an ingenious conjecture of Derenbourg in the *Journal Asiatique*, 1867, vol. I. p. 93.

can scarcely be questioned. Yâbhâl (from whence comes mabbûl, 'body of water,' hence of the Deluge) signifies Rain (like Indra). Rain and Wind are both attributes of the dark sky and the night-sky. In Arabic the verb gasaḳa denotes both the darkness of the sky, and the rain, and (what exactly suits the mythical circle of ideas) the flowing of milk from the udder. The rain is to the men of the myth-creating age a milking of the cloud-cows, which the shepherd leads out to pasture by night on the heavenly meadows. The verb aġḍana, of which Freytag, following al-Jauharî, gives only the meaning *perpetuo pluit coelum*, is known to the classical lexicographer of Arabic synonyms also in the sense *it is dark night*. Similarly, aġḍafa denotes both *obscura, atra fuit nox* and *ad pluviam effundendam paratum et dispositum fuit coelum*. In poetry also rain is often attached to night: an old poet quoted by Ibn al-Sîkkît says,[1] 'A dark night, during which a drenching rain pours down upon the streets.'[2]

The identity of Abel and Jabal appears conspicuously in another circumstance. Abel is introduced as a Herdsman. In the system of the harmonising genealogy of Genesis, in which Jabal appears some generations later, he is described as the '*Father of those that dwell in tents and with cattle*' (Gen. IV. 2, 20). Both features or rather this identical feature told of both these Patriarchs, have a foundation and are equally true. But in the method of the critical school of Biblical exegesis these two accounts involve a contradiction which it is attempted to solve, either by the usual supposition of different narrators, or by minutely pressing the literal meaning of words and setting up delicate distinctions. The acute Knobel, for instance, pretends to know that 'Even Abel had kept cattle, but only small cattle, and these only in his own district; Jabal invented the moving about with cattle from one

---

[1] Wa-leylatun ṭachyâ'u yarma'illu * fîhâ 'ala-l-shârî nadan muchḍallu, *MS. of Univ. Leyden, Cod. Warner*, No. 597, p. 345.

[2] See above, pp. 42, 43.

district to another.[1] It concerns us not to know how far Jabal extended the area of his pasture, and within what narrow limits Abel confined his: our assumption of the mythological identity of the two designations solves the inconsistency without any resort to minute distinctions.

Equally clear is also the Solar character of the name Cain (Ḳayin). This word, which, with other synonymous names of trades, occurs several times on the so-called Nabatean Sinaitic inscriptions,[2] signifies *Smith*,[3] maker of agricultural implements, and has preserved this meaning in the Arabic ḳayn[4] and the Aramaic ḳinâyâ, whilst in the later Hebrew it was lost altogether, being probably suppressed through the Biblical attempt to derive the proper name Cain etymologically from ḳânâ 'to gain.' In Hebrew therefore it appears only as the name of the first fratricide and of his duplicate Tubal-cain (Tûbhal-ḳayin), the brother of Jabal, who is called the founder of the smith's trade (Gen. IV. 22), and stands to Cain in very much the same relation as Jabal does to Abel.

Cain is accordingly the same mythological figure as Hephaestus and Vulcan with the Greeks and Romans. But there are some other points which determine his Solar character. First, there is the characteristic that after the murder of his brother he built the first city, and called it Enoch (Chanôkh, Gen. IV. 17). We have seen above, and I shall show still more clearly in the treatment of the Myth of Civilisation, that in the myths of all peoples the Solar heroes are regarded as the founders of city-life, and that a fratricide often precedes the building of the city. The agricultural stage, which is connected with the Solar worship, overcomes the stage of nomadic life, which holds to the dark sky of night or clouds; and, after conquering the herdsmen, the surviving agriculturists build the first

---

[1] *Die Genesis,* Leipzig 1860, p. 64.

[2] Levy, in the *Zeitschr. der D. M. G.*, 1860, XIV. 404.

[3] Compare Gelpke's article *Neutestamentliche Studien,* in the *Theo. Studien u. Kritiken,* 1849, pp. 639 *et seq.*

[4] See Excursus F.

city. It will not surprise us if the solution of the question raised by F. Lenormant, 'pour en suivre toutes les formes depuis Cain bâtissant le première ville Hanoch après avoir assassiné Abel, jusqu'à Romulus fondant Rome dans le sang de son frère Remus,'[1] proves the consistency and universality of the ideas of mankind at the mythic stage in reference to this point. Whether the connexion of the zodiacal figure of the Twins with this feature of the myth is so close as this acute French scholar imagines, is an independent question. The account of Cain as the first builder of a city is accordingly a testimony to his Solar character. But far more important testimony is afforded by the characteristic feature in the story of Cain, that after the commission of the crime that fratricide, laden with the curse of Jahveh, has to be 'a fugitive and a vagabond in the earth' (Gen. IV. 11). We will pause a little at this mythic feature, and passing beyond Cain, consider it in connexion with a larger group of myths which exhibit the same.[2]

§ 5. The word which preeminently denotes the Sun in the Semitic languages, and which, when the abundant synonyms produced by mythology to designate the Sun had vanished, drove all other names of the Sun into the background, viz. the Hebrew shemesh and the corresponding words in the cognate languages, has been proved to descend from the etymological basis of the idea of rapid motion, or busy running about. This original sense gives the point of connexion with the Aramaic terms shammêsh 'to serve' and shûmshemânâ 'an ant.'[3] The same function which language exhibits in the most prominent name of the Sun is also repeatedly shown in mythology.

[1] *Premières Civilisations,* II. 81.

[2] We do not wish to overlook the fact that the word Ḳayn in Himyaritic is a name of dignity, like Prince, Ruler, Lord, and may therefore, if this signification is adopted, be a synonym for Ba'al. See Prætorius in the *Zeitschr. der D. M. G.*, 1872, XXVI. 432.

[3] See Fleischer's *Nachträgliches* to Levy's *Chald. Wörterb. über d. Targ.*, II. 577. *b.*

The myth views the Sun from the point of view of his rapid course, hastening and continuous motion, or steady march forwards.

> Like a bridegroom coming out of the bridal chamber,
> Who exults like a hero to *run a course*. Ps. XIX. 6 [5].

Hence fiery, rapid horses are attributed to the Sun both in the classical mythology and in Indian and Persian,[1] and no less so in the Hebrew. The latter may be inferred from the fact that in the Hebrew worship in Canaan there were horses dedicated to the Sun. King Josiah, the zealot for Jahveh, was the first to abolish this worship (2 Kings XXIII. 11). And Heinrich Heine gives the jesting couplet:—

> Phoebus lashed his steeds of fire
> In the Sun's own cab with ire.[2]

To the same mythical conception must be referred the *Wings* assigned to the Sun or the Dawn, which are mentioned very frequently in the classical mythology.[3] Just as the Egyptians and the Assyrians[4] in their monuments express this aspect of the sun by the picture of a

---

[1] *Yaçna,* I. 35, XVII. 22; *Khordavesta,* III. 49, VII. 4; Spiegel, *Die heiligen Schriften der Parsen,* III. 27: 'The beautiful Dawn we praise; the brilliant, endowed with brilliant horses, who remembers men, remembers heroes, and is provided with splendour, with dwellings. The morning Dawn we praise; the cheering, endowed with fast horses.' *Vendidad,* XXI. 20: 'Rise up, O splendid Sun! with thy fast horses, and shine on the creatures. In the Sun's Yast (it is the sixth), in almost every verse from the invocation to the end of the prayer, this epithet is applied to the Sun; and in the tenth Yast chariots and flaming horses are assigned to Mithra (see the references in Spiegel, *l. c.* III. xxv.).

[2] A rough imitation of:

> Phöbus in der Sonnendroschke
> Peitschte seine Flammenrosse.
> *Atta Troll,* XXII. 1.

[3] Schwartz, *Sonne, Mond und Sterne,* pp. 106–109.

[4] According to Rawlinson this conception came from the Assyrians to the Persians. But the learned explorer of Assyrian antiquity seems to ignore the solar significance of the winged disc when he says: 'The conjecture is probable that . . . the wings signify Omnipresence and the circle Eternity' (*History of Herodotus,* note to I. c. 135, I. 215 of the edition of 1862).

winged solar disc, so the Hebrews, although they did not give expression to their ideas in monuments and imitations which might have been preserved to the present time, have in the extant fragments of their poetical literature left behind them confirmation of the fact that they conceived of the Sun and the Dawn in the same way. As they called the wind 'winged,' so that the monotheistic singer imagines Jahveh as 'flying on the wings of the wind' (Ps. XVIII. 11 [10]), so he binds wings also to the rapidly increasing light of the Dawn:—

> If I take the wings of the Dawn,
> And go down at the uttermost parts of the sea.[1]
>
> Ps. CXXXIX. 9.

Jahveh 'makes the Dawn *flying*' (literally *for flight*), as the prophet Amos (IV. 13) says. The prophet speaks in this verse of the regular phenomena of nature, not of exceptional physical changes, which would allow us to take 'êphâ as *obscuration*, as in Job X. 22; it is therefore best to keep to the sense of *flying*. Joel (II. 2) says, 'As the Dawn, spreading out her wings over the mountains.'[2] Accordingly the Dawn or the Sun is a bird, and the Persian expression murġ-i-saḥar 'Bird of the Dawn' becomes intelligible. When the sun sets, the runner has stumbled and fallen to the ground; or the bird gliding through the air has lost its power of flight and fallen into the sea. Hence comes the use of 'to fall' of the setting sun: *cadit sol*, and in Homer:[3]—

> Ἐν δ' ἔπεσ' Ὠκεανῷ λαμπρὸν φάος Ἠελίοιο,
> ἕλκον νύκτα μέλαιναν ἐπὶ ζείδωρον ἄρουραν.

And in Arabic they say of the setting of the sun, wajabat

---

[1] Hebrew scholars will observe that I here abandon the usual interpretation, and understand eshkenâ in the second member of the setting of the sun. In this way the first member speaks of the rising, the second of the setting of the sun (= bâ hash-shemesh), which dips into the water at the further edge (horizon) of the sea (acharîth yâm).

[2] See Excursus G.

[3] *Iliad*, VIII. 485. See Plutarch, *De vita et poes. Hom.*, c. CIII.

al-shams, or habaṭat al-shams,[1] verbs which are synonymous with waḳa'a, 'to fall.' We then understand (passing again to Hebrew) Isaiah's exclamation (XIV. 12), 'How art thou *fallen* from heaven, *Light-bringer, son of the Dawn!*'

As the rising Dawn is said to spread out her wings, so the setting evening sun *drops* her[2] pinions, bends her wings downwards. This expression, a relic of the mythic view, is retained in the Arabic language. The Arab says of the setting sun, janaḥat; but although this verb according to the lexicons denotes *inclinavit* in general, yet there can be no doubt that this *inclinatio* was originally something special, namely the bending of the wings, from whose name janâḥ, indeed, the above denominative verb is formed. Ḥassân b. Thâbit,[3] a poet contemporary with Moḥammed, says, 'The sun of the day bent herself (i.e. bent her wings) that she might set' (wa-ḳad janaḥat shams-al-nahâri litaġribâ). But when wings are attributed to the Night, the basis of the conception is quite different from that which gives wings to the Sun or the Dawn. In this case the thought is of covering and hiding.[4] In this sense are to be understood such phrases as kâna-l-leyl nâshiran ajniḥat al-ẓalâm, 'Night unfolded the wings of darkness,' or kâna-l-leyl ḳad asbala 'ala-l-châfiḳeyni ajniḥat al-ẓalâm, 'Night had thrown down over the ends of the earth the wings of darkness.'[5] The frequent expression fî junḥ or jinḥ al-leyl certainly belongs to this

---

[1] E.g. al-Suyûṭî in the *Ḥusn al-muḥâḍarâ*, &c.: 'fa idâ achadat fî-l-hubût' (ap. Weyer's *Diss. de loco Ibn Khacanis de Ibn Zeidun*, p. 87, n. 82).

[2] The Sun is in all the Semitic as well as in many Aryan languages grammatically feminine, and the myths frequently assign to the Sun a female form. It is therefore necessary sometimes to use the feminine pronoun.—Tr.

[3] In Ahlwardt, *Chalaf al-aḥmar*, p. 49. 1. See *Vita Timuri*, II. 48: 'ḳad janaḥat al-shams lil-ġurûb.'

[4] Compare Ps. XVII. 8, LXI. 5 [4]; and accordingly in tastîrêm besêther pânekhâ, Ps. XXXI. 21 [20], 'thou hidest them in the hiding-place of thy *face*,' we must emend pânekhâ 'face,' into kenâphekhâ 'wings.'

[5] *Romance of 'Antar*, V. 136 ult., 236 penult. In the Babylonian epos of *Istar's Descent to Hell*, v. 10 (Lenormant, *Premières Civilisations*, II. 85), Night is compared to a bird

category. Lexicographers who translate the word junḥ *pars noctis*, even on the authority of native lexicons, e.g. al-Jauharî, who explains it as ṭâ'ifâ minhu 'a portion of it,'[1] are mistaken. It must rather signify 'under the wings of Night,' which is also supported by the fact that, besides junḥ al-leyl, fî junḥ al-ẓalâm is also found,[2] where *wings* only can be understood.[3]

From all this it is easy to perceive that the solar figures of the myth are brought into connexion with the idea of swiftness, flight, and constant marching forwards; for rapid motion is one of the chief attributes of the Sun which naturally present themselves to the eye and the mind. From this mythical view of the rapid running of the Sun may also be explained a feature in the German mythology which Holtzmann[4] leaves unexplained. 'The *Osterhase* [Easter-hare],' he says, 'is inexplicable to me; probably the hare is the animal of Ostara [the goddess]; on the picture of Abnoba a hare is present.' If Ostara, as Holtzmann proves, is the sun or the sunrise, then the hare is easily explained as indicating the quick-footed sun. The connexion of ideas required to bring the hare into connexion with this view is one that needs no proof. In the hieroglyphs also, when there is free choice among

---

[1] This interpretation, here erroneously employed, is occasioned by the fact that in the Semitic languages the notion of 'part' is conveyed by words which properly denote 'side:' the two sides of a thing are two parts of it. Thus, even in literary Arabic the word ṭaraf, and in vulgar Arabic the word jânib (which is etymologically connected with the Hebrew kânâph 'wing') are used quite in the sense of ba'ḍ 'a part.' An interesting modern example of this lies before me in the Arabic text of the terms of the latest 5,000,000*l.* loan by the Egyptian Minister of Finance, in which the third article says: 'The shares fall under the ordinary laws regulating buying and selling and bequest—sawâ'an kâna fî jânib minhu au fîhi bil-kâmil—equally whether it concerns a portion of them or the whole' (*al-Jawâ'ib*, a weekly paper, XIV. No. 695, p. 2, c. 2, of the year 1291).

[2] E.g. *Romance of 'Antar*, V. 80 ult., 168 v. 6: Saarḥalu 'ankum lâ urîdu sawâ'akum * wa'aḳṣidukum fî junḥi kulli ẓalâmin 'I go away from you, I want not the like of you; but I shall seek you under the wings of all darkness.'

[3] *al-Aġânî*, II. 12. 3, is also noticeable: 'ḳamrun tawassaṭu junḥa leylin mubridi.'

[4] *Deutsche Mythologie*, p. 141.

various phonetic signs (e.g. with the vowel *u*), the figure of the hare is generally chosen when the word expresses a rapid motion.[1] So the Red Indians, in calling their Kadmus a great white hare, may have been influenced (independently of the false popular etymology of the word *michabo*[2]) by the conception of the Sun as a swift-footed hare.[3]

Abraham and his wife Sarah (the princess or queen of heaven—the Moon as we shall see) expel Hagar (Gen. XVI 6). The Moon is jealous of Hagar. What does Hagar signify in this Hebrew myth? The cognate Arabic language offers the most satisfactory basis of interpretation of this name. Hajara, the root of the name Hâgâr, denotes 'to fly,' and yields the word hijrâ, 'flight,' especially known from the flight of Moḥammed from Mecca to Medina. The mythic designation Hâgâr is consequently only one of the names of the Sun in a feminine form. The battle of the two figures of the night-sky against Hagar is again that inexhaustible theme of all mythology, the battle of Day with Night. With respect to this particular name the Arabic language gives us still further light. While ġaṭasha denotes both 'to be dark' and 'to move slowly,' the hot noonday sun is described by the Arabs by the participle of the verb from which we have explained the name Hagar, *al-hâjirâ* or *al-hijîrâ* 'the flying one.' That this is not mere chance, but is connected with the mythical order of ideas from which we deduced the designation Hâgâr for the Sun, is further confirmed by the word barâḥi or birâḥ, also denoting 'flight' (from the Hebrew and Arabic root *brḥ* 'to flee'), and yet belonging to the nomenclature of the Sun.

The case is the same with the 'fugitive and vagabond' life of Cain; after the conquest of Abel the Sun wanders from place to place, and leads a life of unrest and motion

---

1 Ebers, *Aegypten und die Bücher Mosis*, p. 70.

2 Fiske, *Myths and Myth-Makers*, pp. 71, 154.

3 The sun is called *celer deus* by Ovid, *Fasti*, I. 386; and Herodotus, I. 215, says: τῶν θεῶν ὁ τάχιστος. See Hehn, *Culturpflanzen*, etc., p. 38.

till night comes. A reminiscence of the solar significance of Cain is even found in the Agâdâ, which makes the sign granted for the safety of Cain to consist in the brightening of the sun; or, according to another interpretation, in a horn, which grew up on him from the moment of the promise.[1] It is well known that the sun's rays were mythologically called *horns*,—a meaning which the language preserved.

§ 6. With this group of Solar figures of the Hebrew mythology which are exhibited as *wandering* or *rapidly marching forward*,[2] I also class some others whose names alone lead us to recognise this mythological character. First and foremost we must consider a word which has been retained in the language beyond the mythical stage: the Hebrew shachar, Arabic saḥar, 'morning, dawn.' This word is doubtless connected with the verb sâchar, which denotes constant moving, wandering.[3] The Arabic sâḥir 'magician' is the same word as the Hebrew sôchêr 'merchant,' both signifying originally those who are always travelling about from place to place. The Hebrew verb shachêr 'to seek' relates originally to the *movement* of one who has lost something and goes about looking for it. Although in the course of this chapter I shall devote a special connected disquisition to Jacob's sons, yet I must here pick out a few beforehand to incorporate them in the class of solar figures whose characteristic feature is that here discussed. To this class belongs e.g. Âshêr, the name of a son of Jacob by his concubine Zilpah. The name cannot be explained (according to Gen. XXX. 13) as the 'Happy,' or 'Bringer of Happiness,' since this signification

---

[1] *Berêshîth rabbâ*, sect. 22.

[2] Even Philo lays the chief momentum of the story of Hagar on her flight: μέμνηται γὰρ (sc. ὁ ἱερὸς λόγος) πολλαχοῦ τῶν ἀποδιδρασκόντων, καθάπερ καὶ νῦν φάσκων ἐπὶ τῆς Ἄγαρ ὅτι κακωθεῖσα ἀπέδρα ἀπὸ προσώπου τῆς κυρίας (*De profugis*, p. 546, ed. Mangey).

[3] I leave it for the present undecided whether the name Terach, given to Abraham's father, belongs to this class. Ewald (*History of Israel*, I. 274) puts it in connexion with ârach 'to wander,' though in an ethnological sense.

of the root ('to be happy') is only secondary to the fundamental meaning—applied, not original. Language does not form originally expressions for ethical notions of this kind, any more than the notion itself rises without contact with something sensual, which may subsequently be transferred to the ethical. The Arabic words for similar ideas spring up in a similar way, e.g. muṣliḥ 'successful' denotes properly 'one who *penetrates* through something,' &c. The root of Âshêr, in Hebrew âshar, in Arabic athara (whence athar 'a trace'), originally denoted *to march, go forwards* (Prov. IX. 6); intensively ashshêr, *to make* some one *go forward, to lead*, and as a noun, ashûr 'way, path.' From the same root comes also the relative pronoun asher, which originally signified *place*, (compare the Aramaic athar 'place'); but we know that expressions which serve as exponents of the category of *relation*, both in time and space, generally start from the conception of space, as is clearly seen in the Hebrew shâm, indicating originally the idea of place, 'there' but also transferred to the expression of the idea of time, 'then.'[1] We see the same quite as clearly in the employment of the Aramaic athar in the combination bâthar (from ba-athar) to denote *after, afterwards*, properly *on the spot*.[2]

To this fundamental meaning of the root âshar 'to march, go forward' is added the secondary application 'to be happy,' properly 'to advance prosperously.' But the old mythical designation Âshêr is connected with the original sense: since at the time when this mythical word was first spoken the verb had not yet obtained its secondary sense, nor could yet obtain it, as ethical ideas were

---

[1] See above, p. 41.

[2] The first to discover this origin of the relative asher was the Hungarian Csepregi, pupil of the great Schultens, *Dissert.*, Lugd., p. 171 (quoted by Gesenius, *Thesaurus*, p. 165): he did not, however, follow out the idea very clearly. Compare also Stade's view, essentially the same, in the *Morgenländische Forschungen*, Leipzig 1875, p. 188; I could not get a sight of this till after the above was ready for the press. On the other side Schrader, *Jen. Literaturzeit.*, 1875, p. 299.

still non-existent. Accordingly Âshêr signifies 'he who marches on,' and is simply a solar name. Thus the ancient Hebrew called the Sun, when he noticed the continual change of his place on the horizon, and observed his constant movement. 'Through Asher,' it is said, in a fragmentary hymn on Asher in Gen. XLIX. 20, 'his bread is fat; he gives dainties for a king;' for the sun is to the agriculturist the beneficent element that hastens the ripening of his crops.

This simple and, I hope, obvious explanation throws light on another expression in Hebrew mythology, which stands in the closest connexion with Asher. I mean the feminine form derived from the masculine sun, the appellation Ashêrâ, on which Biblical interpreters and antiquaries have had so much to say. Ashêrâ, as the feminine form of Âshêr, denotes what the Hebrews regarded as the marriage-consort of the Sun. We know this of the Moon, as I hope to show more fully in speaking of Sarah. Ashêrâ is, therefore, an old Hebrew name of the Moon. In those passages of the Old Testament which speak of the idolatry of the Hebrews in Canaan, Asherah is named with Baal (the Sun-god): 'The vessels that were made for Baal and for Asherah and for all the host of heaven' (as though for Sun, Moon, and Stars), 2 Kings XXIII. 4; 'And the children of Israel did that which was evil in the sight of Jahveh, and forgat Jahveh their God, and served Baal and Asherah,' Judges III. 7. They probably served Asherah too at the altar of Baal (see Judges VI. 25); but this is quite in the spirit of the Canaanitish and Mesopotamian religious practice. One mode of doing homage to the supreme God was to offer sacrifices and build temples to his subordinate deity, just as any honour conferred on the Satraps conduced to the greater excellence of the 'King of kings.' This view is very general on the votive tables with cuneiform inscriptions; so e.g. in an inscription in the Temple of Mugheir: '*In honore* SIN *domini deorum coeli et terrae, regis deorum . . . templum* Iz *deae magnae condidi et feci.'*

Asherah is accordingly the *Wandering one*, and the moon is here made feminine. A masculine word for the Moon, which, being common to all the Semitic dialects (unlike the later, lebhânâ), must be one of the oldest Semitic names for *moon*, viz. yârêach, expresses the same idea; for it is derived from the noun ôrach, 'a path, way,' and stands for ôrêach with the initial hardened[1] (like yâchîd 'only,' with initial y, yet echâd 'one;' and yâshâr 'straight,' connected with the root under discussion, âshar 'to go forwards'). In Job XXXI. 26, the epithet hôlêkh, 'marching,' is applied to the moon. Therefore the two plural forms ashêrîm and ashêrôth are not identical (the former denoting *objects of worship*, and the latter as 'femininum vilitatis' declaring them to be in the opinion of the writer *objects of abomination*); [2] but the masculine form is derived from the singular Âshêr, and the feminine from the singular Ashêrâ.

§ 7. To the same series belong also the names Dân and Dînâ, which latter is only a feminine to the first, and occurs again as a proper name in Arabic.[3] It would be erroneous to regard the verb dîn 'to judge' as the etymon: for this would give no solution of the question concerning the nature and signification of the designations under review. Then, as the Hebrew language itself offers no satisfactory *points d'appui*, we are fully entitled to look for information to the cognate idioms. I believe that the fundamental idea contained in the group of consonants

---

[1] In Assyrian the Moon is called arḫu, with a mere hamzâ (Schrader, *Assyr.-babyl. Keilinschr.*, p. 282). In Arabic the reverse has happened; from warch (yârêach) has been formed the verb arracha 'to fix the time (by the lunar calendar), to date,' the *w* (Heb. *y*) being weakened into hamzâ (aleph). Whether the Coptic Ioh and Arabic yûḥ are connected with yârêach (the abrasion of *r* is not uncommon), is another question.

[2] So Böttcher, *Ausführl. Lehrbuch der hebr. Sprache*, I. 516–17.

[3] The poet Dîk al-Jinn had a mistress named Dînâ (Ibn Challikân, ed. Wüstenfeld, IV. 96. 7). See also Abû 'Uyeynâ al-Muhallabî (*Agânî*, III. 128. 2, 6).

Dn is extant in the Assyrian, where it expresses the idea of *going*;[1] whence the Arabic dâna 'to approach,' the secondary dana, and the adjective dunya, which denotes the near and visible world, in opposition to al-âchirâ, the life beyond.[2] Consequently, Dân and Dînâ must denote 'he or she who marches on, or comes nearer,' or 'goes' in general, synonymous with Âshêr, i.e. the Sun. In Arabic also al-jâriyâ 'who goes' is one of the many names of the Sun which are enumerated by Ibn al-Sikkît in his Synonymical Dictionary of the Arabic Language.[3] Whilst of Dan no actual myth has reached us, and etymology alone gives us any help in discovering his mythical character, of Dinah on the other hand the chief source of our knowledge of Hebrew antiquity has preserved a more material statement, telling of the love of Shechem for Dinah and their ultimate union, and of the immediately following murder of Shechem by Jacob's sons. These are the features which come under our view when we draw out the mythical kernel from the mass of epical description surrounding it (Gen. XXXIV). From the arguments of the Second Chapter the connexion of the noun shekhem with the verb hishkîm may surely be treated as removed beyond all doubt, as well as the fact that this word is a designation of the Morning-dawn. I will add at this place, to complete what was discussed at p. 26, that the Hebrew word shekhem seems to be etymologically connected with the Arabic thakam, which signifies 'way.' Like most Hebrew words denoting a *way*, this word shekhem must stand in connexion with the verbal idea of 'marching forwards'— either by the verb being a *denominative* (like the German *bewegen* from *Weg*), or inversely by the noun being a *deverbal*. The changes of consonants which we find here are in accordance with the law of the Semitic languages, namely:

---

[1] Edwin Norris, *Assyrian Dictionary*, I. 248.

[2] We find also al-'ulya opposed to al-dunya in Ibn Châkân ḳalâ'id al-'iḳyân, ed. Bûlâḳ 1284, p. 60 ult.: 'wa-dâmat laka-d-dunya * wa-dâmat laka-l-'ulya.'

[3] Cod. Leyden, Warner's Fund, No. 597, p. 325.

	Arabic ث th	Hebrew שׁ sh	Aramaic ת t,th
	ثلاثة thalâthâ	שְׁלֹשָׁה shelôshâ	תְּלָתָא telâthâ
	ثور thaur	שׁוֹר shôr	תּוֹרָא tôrâ
Therefore also:			
	ثكم thakam =	שְׁכֶם shekhem	—

The longing love of the Dawn for the Sun and her union with him—the same theme which Max Müller in his essay on 'Comparative Mythology' has so ingeniously traced in Indian and Hellenic myths—was told also by the Hebrews; only that the Hebrew inverted the relation. When the Dawn vanished and the Sun began to shine bright in the sky, the Hebrew said of the union between the Dawn and the Sun that the Dawn snatched up the Sun to himself and was united with her. Not long afterwards followed the vengeance taken by the sons of Jacob (the night-sky), who, enraged at the abduction of their sister, murder the ravisher and deliver her. This is only the disappearance of the Sun, while the evening glow comes forward, again independent, to inaugurate the dominion of the Night.[1] The myth makes no distinction between the morning and the evening glow, but treats them as identical phenomena. Therefore Shekhem is made a son of the Ass (Chamôr); and there is no doubt that chamôr (ass) has here the mythic significance which accompanies that animal whenever it appears in the Aryan mythology.[2]

Zilpah also, the mother of Asher, is to be classed in the same group. Any one who has cast even a superficial glance on the real meaning of the myths of the Aryan nations, as now discovered and recognised, must have noticed the peculiarity that the mythical relation of child

---

[1] It also deserves consideration whether Dînâ as the feminine of Dân denotes the Moon: compare Lâbhân, Lebhânâ; Âshêr, Ashêrâ. In that case the above myth would speak of the abduction of the Moon by the Morning-dawn, i.e. the disappearance of the moon at sunrise. It would then be the same myth as the Hellenic one of the abduction of Helenê (Selênê) by Paris.

[2] Angelo de Gubernatis, *ibid.* p. 278 *et seq.*

to parent does not always indicate a succession of what should precede and what follow, but that the child is not unfrequently only a repetition of the father or the mother, and is therefore to be considered identical with them.[1] The present is a case of this kind. Âshêr is only a repetition of his mother. The designation Zilpâ, the explanation of which has been sought in vain in Hebrew—for the meaning 'a drop' can hardly be maintained—finds a smooth and ready interpretation in Arabic, where zalafa, as well as *zlp, zlb* in Assyrian,[2] denotes 'to march on.' So that Zilpâ also is 'she that marches forward.' Another 'marcher forward' is preserved by Arabian tradition, viz. Zalîchâ. She is unmistakably a solar figure, and her name (*zlch* has the same signification 'to march forward') is perhaps even formally connected[3] with that of Zilpâ, with whom she is identical. The battle of the Sunshine with the Rainy Sky is the amorous contest of the beautiful Zalîchâ (or, as the name is commonly but erroneously pronounced, Zuleychâ) with Yôsêph 'the Multiplier.' Now, having been led into the above digressions by the explanation of Cain's flight, we return to Cain again.

§ 8. We have just alluded to the fact that in the Hebrew mythology the figures presented as children are frequently only *repetitions* of one of their parents.[4] This observation is found to be confirmed in the case of the posterity which the Biblical genealogy in Gen. IV. derives

---

[1] See *Zeitschr. d. D. M. G.*, 1855, IX. 758.

[2] Edwin Norris, *Assyrian Dictionary*, I. 347. The signification 'having locks' might also be mentioned as a possibility for zalîchâ. In that case we should have to notice the Syrian zelîchê of the Peshiṭṭô in *Song of Songs*, I. 11, where the parallelism to gedûlê demands something like 'locks of hair;' and this meaning agrees with that of zelach in Syriac: *fudit*.

[3] It is well-known that the gutturals ح ḥ and خ ch often change into ف f. The Arabic ḳadaḥ 'cup' becomes in Turkish ḳadef; the name Yehûd is pronounced in jest *Jufut*. Compare the Arabic naḳacha with naḳafa, and the Mehri ehû, denoting 'mouth,' with Arabic fû, Hebrew peh, etc.

[4] See *Zeitschr. d. D. M. G.*, 1855, IX. 758.

from Cain. Some of the descendants of Cain are quite as much solar figures as their ancestor himself; and in an age which had advanced beyond the stage of the formation of myths, and even beyond the after-sentiment of mythology, this identity occasioned the idea that these figures must stand in a genealogical connexion with the ancestor. The same psychological process which in the employment of language produces a specialisation or limitation in the sense of words originally synonymous, is at work here also, forming from the numerous synonyms of mythology genealogies, in which identical designations, after their substratum has been personified, become his sons, grandsons, and great-grandsons. Thus among Cain's descendants none but solar figures are to be found. In the demonstration of this fact, I limit myself to those names which can be interpreted without at all forcing their meaning. The very first, Enoch (Chanôkh), the son of Cain, from whom he names the first city he built, is of pure solar significance. We have above already, with Ewald, put his name in the class in which the Sun is presented as the 'Opener.' The solar character of Enoch admits of no doubt. He is brought into connexion with the building of towns—a solar feature. He lives exactly three hundred and sixty-five years, the number of days of the solar year; which cannot be accidental.[1] And even then he did not die, but 'Enoch *walked* with Elôhîm, and was no more [to be seen], for Elôhîm *took him away.*' In the old times when the figure of Enoch was imagined, this was doubtless called Enoch's Ascension to heaven, as in the late traditional legend. Ascensions to heaven are generally acknowledged to be solar features. Herakles among the Greeks, Romulus the city-founder among the Latins, and several heroes of American mythology,[2] agree in this. The same feature also often attaches itself even to historical persons—e.g. to the legend of the Prophet

---

[1] See Pfleiderer, *Religion und ihre Geschichte,* II. 271.

[2] Brinton, *Myths of the New World,* pp. 159 *et seq.*

Elijah, the 'hairy man' who ascends to heaven on 'a chariot of fire and horses of fire,' [1] indeed this as well as other mythical features has been better preserved in the case of this favourite hero of Israelitish prophecy than in that of the former purely mythical personage.

Wachsmuth [2] expressed a conjecture that the old Greek god Helios, who drives round the vault of heaven on a fiery chariot, has a share in the phenomenon, so frequent in modern Greece, that the prophet Ilias (Elias or Elijah) is especially venerated on mountain-tops. The temples and altars of Helios in ancient times were similarly situated on high hills; and the casual similarity of sound between Ilios and Ilias, together with the identity of the myths concerning each, in this case caused the old heathen worship to be preserved and transferred to the name of the Biblical prophet. But this certainly cannot have taken place, as Otto Keller lately flippantly declared in a lecture on the 'Discovery of Troy by Henry Schliemann,' 'from a sort of childish attention to the wants of great Prophet, inasmuch as the people wished to make the fiery journey as easy as possible for him, and therefore made him mount the chariot at the nearest point to heaven.[3]

Enoch (Chanôkh) is introduced in another version of the genealogy (Gen. V. 18), as son not of Cain but of Jered, who is separated by five generations from Seth, Adam's third son. But this genealogy has but little importance for mythological investigation; indeed its two chief original creations (Seth and Enos), do not belong to mythology at all. The feeling of a later time rebelled against deriving all mânkind from the hated fratricide who bore the curse of God, and thus gave rise to the two interpolated patriarchs and the Seth-genealogy, which runs parallel with that of Cain: moreover, in proof of the

---

[1] 2 Kings, I. 8, II. 11. Compare the fiery, flame-red chariot of Ushas (*Rigveda*, VI. 64. 7).

[2] *Das alte Griechenland im neuen*, p. 23.

[3] Supplement to the Augsburg *Allgem. Zeitung*, 1874, No. 344. p. 5377.

honourable origin of mankind, the son of Seth was made the author of the worship of Jahveh, which is said to have begun in his time. The Seth-genealogy, which answered better to the feeling and the ethical need of mankind, then utterly expelled the Cain-genealogy. The author of the Book of Chronicles, who knows only Adam, Seth, Enos, &c. as first-fathers, seems either not to have known or intentionally to have ignored the other genealogy, and keeps strictly to that in Gen. V. It is remarkable that even in the Seth-genealogy among the ancestors of Enoch a Cainan (קֵינָן Ḳênân) is named—a word which will be recognised by everyone who knows the laws of the Semitic formation of words as a so-called nunnated form of the word קַיִן Ḳayin, so that the two are really perfectly identical.[1]

Let us continue the consideration of Cain's descendants. One prominent figure is Lemech.[2] An obscure song, which he declaims before his two wives, has given the interpreters much trouble with regard both to its language and to its subject; and legend has made free with this song, as it has with anything problematical. For us here this only is important, that the song contains a self-accusation on the part of Lemech before his wives, of having killed his own child. As Jephthah killed his daughter, so the myth spoke of Lemech as a similar solar hero who killed his child. The Sun today kills her child, the Night, whom she bore yesterday evening. Among the children of Lemech we actually find Jabal (Yâbhâl), of whom we have already spoken at length as denoting the Rainy Sky. No doubt the ancient myth spoke of Jabal as the son who was murdered by his solar father Lemech. Accordingly, the genealogy does not continue the line of Jabal. Next to him his brother Jubal (Yûbhâl), inventor

---

[1] Compare Renan, *Hist. génér. des Langues sémitiques*, p. 28.

[2] Called in the English Bible Lamech, which is derived from the pausal form Lâmĕkh through the LXX. Λάμεχ, as is the case with many names, e.g. Abel, Japheth, Jared, though not all; cf. on the other side Jether, Zerah, Peleg. The ordinary form, such as Lĕmĕch, ought to be preferred.—Tr.

of musical instruments, the Hebrew Apollo, is mentioned. It is to solar gods such as Apollo, and heroes, that the invention of music, a product of the settled mode of civilised life, was everywhere attributed. But his name seems to have been chosen only on account of its assonance to Jabal (a favourite practice with the Semites), and not to belong to the ancient myth, but to owe its origin to the later legend of civilisation.

That the brothers Tubal-cain and Jabal are only a repetition of Cain and Abel I think I have already made evident. It must here be added that the mother of Tubal-cain, the solar man, is named Zillah (Ṣillâ), 'she who *covers, overshadows*'—the Night, mother of the Sun or of the Day. The Seth-genealogy concludes with one who is called son of Lemech—Noah (Nôach), the founder of improved agriculture, who 'gave men rest from their work and the toil of their hands proceeding from the earth which Jahveh cursed' (V. 29). What else can this mean, but that Noah invented agricultural implements? The Seth-genealogy accordingly disputes the invention of these by Cain or Tubal-cain, and gives to the etymology of the name Nôach, which really does denote 'rest,' an application which makes it as impossible for it to belong to the ancient myth as for the names Shêth and Enôsh. Noah is a regular hero of the legend of civilisation; and the larger part of what the myth tells of him is a product of the victory of Solarism, i.e. of agricultural life. He is the first vine-grower, and a new ancestor of the human race, since all mankind is derived from his three sons. The regular operation of the laws of nature (Gen. VIII. 22), and social order and legality, are also brought into connexion with him. The protection and forbearance, secured to the beasts by the Nomad, ceases; the Agriculturist subdues the beasts. But, on the other hand, with him begins the protection and security of human life (Gen. IX. 2–5). Yet side by side with this legend of civilisation we have in connexion with Noah a true *old* solar myth, which well deserves attention.

After the introduction of vine-cultivation Noah once makes overfree use of his discovery and gets drunk; and in that condition 'uncovers himself'—takes off his clothes (Gen. IX. 21). Only this last feature has any mythological interest; for the previous one, which was attached to this germ, belongs to another and later stage of formation of legends, since nothing could be told of intoxication till the free use of wine was known and practised. The word Nôach denotes 'him who *rests*.' While the Sun of Day is called 'he who *goes, runs, wanders*,' the Evening Sun, preparing to set, is 'he who *rests*.' 'Noah uncovers himself:' after setting, the Sun is shrouded in a covering which darkens his light, but in the morning he throws off the clothes and becomes visible, spreading light and brightness abroad. In a hymn to Ushas, the Dawn, the ancient Indian poet says that she 'uncovers her bosom' (Rigveda, VI. 64. 2, 10). If the intoxication is also to be accounted for, then this prominent circumstance must describe the reeling motion with which the Sun, exhausted by his long course, staggers towards his repose. The Agadic tradition has preserved another element of the Noah-myth. The wicked black son Ham (Châm), emasculates his father (Sanhedrîn, 70 a). The emasculation of the Sun, when the Sun is male, is an expression of Aryan mythology denoting the weakening of his rays before and at sunset.[1] The black son, the Night, overcomes and emasculates his father, takes all power from his rays and drives him to ruin.

§ 9. Thus we find Cain's posterity to be repetitions of their ancestor, mere solar figures of the old myth, brought by an unmythological age into a genealogical connexion with the wandering and fratricidal solar hero. It is the genealogy of the solar figures to which the data of the legend of civilisation are attached; for the agriculturist always puts civilisation into conjunction with

[1] Schwartz, *Ursprung der Mythologie*, pp 138-150.

the sun.[1] But besides this solar pedigree, we possess also a nomadic one, starting from the myth of the dark Night-sky—the genealogy of Abram (Gen. XI. 10 sq.), which begins with his ancestor Shem. But the name Shêm has the same signification as Abhrâm itself, according to the lexicon. As Abhrâm is the '*High* Father,' so also the name Shêm denotes the 'High;' and from this name the Semitic appellation of heaven, Hebrew shâmayim, Arabic samâ, is derived. Like Abram, Abel, Jabal, Jacob, Lot &c., Shem too possesses tents. 'Elôhîm opens out (room) for Jepheth;[2] he (Jepheth) dwells in the tents of Shem' (Gen. XI. 27), is said in the extant fragment of an ancient hymn. Jepheth (Yepheth) signifies the 'Beautiful, Brilliant,' if it is connected with yâpheh; or 'who spreads himself out,' if the root pâthâh is its origin; or 'who opens,' if with Gesenius and some later writers we lay stress on the connexion of the sounds of pâthâh with pâthach; but in any case it is a solar name. As the sun of the daytime is observed wandering from place to place, it is not an unnatural idea that the sun takes up his abode in the *tents* of high heaven. 'For the sun he made a tent in them (the heavens).'[3]

It cannot be denied that in Abraham's genealogy, as given in the Book of Genesis, there occur some ethnographical appellations which have no mythological meaning (e.g. Arpachshad). Still, the majority of names are of a mythical character. Unfortunately, they must remain mere names to us, as no material myth connected with these names is extant. Although they seem to invite etymological attempts, as e.g. the names Shelach and 'Êbher, yet I shall resist the temptation, as it is not my business here to indulge in vague speculations. But I may be allowed to remark that there is one sentence in this

---

[1] See the whole of Chapter VI. [2] See note 2, p. 129.

[3] Ps. XIX. 5 [4]. We have already remarked (p. 111) that the tents which originally belonged to the sky at night are frequently transferred to the sky of daytime; see also Is. XL. 22. And Noah uncovers himself, bethôkh oholô 'in the middle of his tent' (Gen. IX. 21).

genealogy which reflects the nomad's life again. 'Peleg begat Re'û:' that is, taking these words, as they were originally understood, appellatively and translating them literally, 'The stream produces the pasture-land;' the nomad owes his meadow-land to the stream that meanders through the pasture and keeps the grass fresh and green. So instead of 'to lead the cattle to pasture,' he says also, 'to lead them to the waters of rest.' The psalmist of Ps. XVIII. 1, 2, says 'Jahveh is my shepherd, I want nothing. He makes me lie down in green pastures, he leads me to waters of rest.'

§ 10. We will now continue our contemplation of the contests which the myth tells of the sky at night, in which we have already seen the dark sky either conquering or conquered by his brilliant father or brother. One of the most conspicuous names of the dark sky of night or clouds in the Hebrew mythology, and containing a rich fund of mythical matter, is Jacob. Etymologically we have already done justice to him. Now let us see what the myth has to say of him. He endures hard struggles. His father, 'the *laughing* sunny sky,' loves him not. The hatred of his brother Esau drives him from house and home; and at the place where he takes refuge, he has to struggle against 'the white one' (Lâbhân), who, if not his brother, is at least his near relative, and in the original form of the myth was perhaps presented as his brother (see Gen. XXIX. 15). We must examine more closely the mythical character of these two hostile brothers of Jacob. To make short work of it—both Esau and Laban are solar figures. What we learn of them in the epic treatment of the old myth found in the Old Testament, presents a multitude of solar characteristics. We especially note this in Esau, whose *heel Jacob grasps at their birth* (Gen. XXV. 26). This mythical expression is in itself clear enough: 'Night comes into the world with Day's heel in his hand,' or, as we should say, Night follows close upon Day, driving him from his place. Nevertheless, we can further confirm this signification of the mythical expression for the benefit of hesitating doubters by showing that the same conception is found even in the later Arabic poetry, where it is doubtless a residuum of an old mythical idea. For Tha'labâ b. Ṣu'eyr al-Mâzinî [1] says of the breaking of the dawn: 'The shining one stretches his right hand towards him who covers up;' the Sun puts out his hand towards the Night, grasps him, and pulls him forward, whilst he himself retires; here therefore it is the same relation, only inverted. Similarly, the poet al-'Ajjâj says: 'till I see the shoulder of the brilliant dawn, when he springs upon the back of the black night.' [2] This is spoken in quite a mythical tone, and expresses the same idea as the Hebrew when he said 'Jacob holds the heel of his red brother in his hand,' only that the Arabic words quoted speak of day following after night.

'Esau is a hunter, Jacob a herdsman, dwelling in tents.' *The Sun is a hunter*: he discharges his arrows, i.e. his rays, and does battle with them against darkness, wind and clouds. Why should I adduce examples from Aryan mythology, where this view occurs in manifold variations and is one of the commonest? [3] The Sun's arrows are golden, wherefore Apollo is called χρυσότοξος Πύθιος (Pindar, *Ol.* XIV. 15). This mythical idea is frequently reflected in the composition of language. In Egyptian, the combination *st* denotes 'flame, ray, and arrow,' all at once; and the Slavonic strêla, with which the German *Strahl* 'ray' is connected, means 'arrow.' [4]

---

[1] In al-Jauharî, s.r. *kfr*.

[2] In Ibn al-Sikkît, p. 193; ḥatta ara a'nâḳa ṣubḥin ablajâ * tasûru fî a'jâzi leylin ad'ajâ. The expression a'jâz al-leyl also occurs in a verse of Farazdaḳ, *Kitâb al-Aġânî*, XIV. 173. 19, and of Ashga', *ibid.* XVII. 35. 13.

[3] See also *Shâhnâmêh*, VII. 395, with Rückert's conjecture suggested in *Zeitsch. der D. M. G.* 1856, X. 136.

[4] Lazarus Geiger, *Ursprung und Entwickelung der menschl. Sprache und Vernunft*, I. 447.

'The Sun can no longer bend his bow' = he has lost his power, is therefore an expression for the setting of the sun. When Herakles finds himself too weak to bend his bow and shoot his arrows, he feels that his end is approaching. When the Sun regains his powers at the outburst of spring, after a long winter in which his arrows had been at rest, Odysseus (Ulysses), a solar wanderer like Cain, seizes his bow to shoot off his shafts again.[1] We see the same in the myths of the Semites. An epithet of the Sun-god Bêl is Nipru, which, according to Sir Henry Rawlinson, signifies 'hunter;'[2] and the city Resen, the building of which is attributed in the Bible to Nimrod, is called in the historical cuneiform inscriptions the 'City of the Hunter.'[3] This Nimrod himself, against whom Abraham the Nomad contends in the same sense in which Jacob the Nomad against Esau the Hunter, is a hunter (Gen. X. 9). The etymological explanation of the name Nimrôd cannot be established until the really primary signification of the root mârad has been satisfactorily traced; for it may be considered certain, that at the myth-creating stage mankind had no sense of the idea of 'insurrection,' which could only be formed after some advance in social life, and could not therefore endow a word with that special meaning. This signification can consequently only be secondary and metaphorical.[4] As to the grammatical form of the name Nimrôd, it is not impossible that, like Yiṣchâk 'Isaac,' Yiphtâch 'Jephthah,' &c., it is a verbal form. If so, it would be the third person of the imperfect, formed by prefixing *n*, as

---

[1] Schwartz, *Sonne, Mond und Sterne*, p. 228.

[2] In G. Rawlinson's *History of Herodotus*, I. 490 *et seq.* One might also think of the Arabic nafara 'to fly.' The Sun is a *fugitive*, as has been already shown.

[3] Lenormant, *Premières Civilisations*, II. 21.

[4] On the primary signification of the root *mrd* in Semitic, see Fried. Delitzsch, *Studien über indogerm.-semit. Wurzelverwandtschaft*, Leipzig 1873, p. 74.

in Aramaic. Schrader [1] regards this prefixed *n* in Nimrôd as a sound used for the formation of *nouns*. I will also call to mind incidentally that on Babylonian ground we meet also with the name of a god Merôd.[2] The wars of Nimrod with Abraham are not preserved in the Old Testament, but are in Agadic tradition, which has also retained from the Nimrod-myth an expression of a truly solar character; that *three hundred and fifty kings* sit before Nimrod, to serve him.[3] Similarly against Joseph, the giver of increase, the rainy sky, fight 'the *men with arrows*'[4] (ba'alê chiṣṣîm, Gen. XLIX. 23), 'who exasperate him and *shoot* and persecute him.' So again Jacob fights against Esau the *hunter*. It is always the battle of the sky of Night and Clouds against the Sun, who sends his arrows to repel the invader. One somewhat more complicated mythological conception having reference to the arrows of the sun is found on Hebrew ground. The sun and the moon stand still, and then go in the direction of the arrows which were sent off before them. This view is known to poetry, except that there it is Jahveh who shoots the arrows, so that the sun and moon

> Walk to the light of thy (Jahveh's) arrows,
> To the brightness of the glitter of thy spear.—*Hab.* III. 11.

The rays of the moon also are here designated arrows.

Esau is a hairy man, Jacob a smooth man (Gen. XXVII. 11). '*The first came out red, quite like a hairy mantle*'

---

[1] *Die Keilinschriften und das Alte Testament*, p. 17, and *Die assyr.-babyl. Keilinschriften*, p. 212. Compare Merx, *Grammatica Syriaca*, p. 201.

[2] Levy, *Phönizische Studien*, pt. II. p. 24.

[3] Adolf Jellinek, *Bêth ham-midrâsh*, V. 40; see supra, p. 32.

[4] I am fully aware that in Hebrew poetry arrows are frequently, indeed most frequently, to be understood of lightning. 'He sends out his arrows and scatters them; lightnings in great number and discomfits them' (Ps. XVIII. 15 [14]). But the arrows of Joseph's adversaries must from the very nature of the myth be rays of the sun. If the hunter is the Sun, then the rays can only be something which the hunter in that ancient time used for shooting. Mythology is not the product of a well-thought-out consistent system, and so nothing is more likely than that two different things should be treated in the same way by virtue of some feature common to both. Thus the solar ray and the lightning are the same in mythology—an Arrow.

(XXV. 25). For the present we will put the redness aside, and pay particular attention to the element of hairiness. Long locks of hair and a long beard are mythological attributes of the Sun. The Sun's rays are compared with locks or hairs on the face or head of the Sun.

Helios is called by the Greeks the *yellow-haired*; and in Greek poetry *χρυσοκόμης* or *ἀκερσοκόμης* is a frequent epithet of solar gods and heroes. A Latin poet also calls the sun's rays *Crines Phoebi.*[1] In an American legend the Sun-god Bocsika is introduced as an old man with a long beard; the Viracochaya of the Peruvians, the Quetzalcoatl of the Toltecs, the Coxcox of the Chichimecs, solar figures all of them, possess this strongly emphasized characteristic of the long beard.[2] Indeed, this feature is sometimes ascribed in popular fancy to historical personages, as e.g. to Julius Caesar, who was imagined to have been born with long hair; and his name was popularly explained from this circumstance—*caesaries.*

We must here consider a point in the history of Art, which occupied archeologists about the years 1820–30, and especially the meritorious numismatist Ekhel. I refer to the representation of Janus as *biceps, vultu uno barbato, altero imberbi,* which some regarded as the old traditional conception of Janus, while others thought it comparatively modern; the question of age is, however, not a question of principle at all.[3] In any case it may be assumed as probable that this picture of the two-headed 'Opener,'[4] is not an accidental idea, devoid of all mythical

---

[1] See a fuller description in Schwartz, *Sonne, Mond und Sterne,* pp. 218–220.

[2] J. G. Müller, *Geschichte der amerikanischen Urreligionen,* p. 429.

[3] See this question treated and its literature cited in Creuzer, *Symbolik und Mythologie,* 3rd ed., I. 57.

[4] For the description of the Sun as an Opener, I am enabled to insert a supplementary datum, borrowed from a book which was published when p. 97 of the present work (to which I refer back) was already printed. In a cuneiform Hymn to Samas, the Sun-god, he is addressed thus:

O Samas! from the back of the heavens thou hast come forth:
The barrier of the shining heavens thou hast opened;
Yea the gate of the heavens thou hast opened.

(German translation of George Smith's *Chaldean Account of Genesis,* with

import; but that on the contrary, the two bearded and beardless representations of the Sun-god express two points in the Sun's life; he appears in the morning and evening (as 'Opener' and 'Closer,' *Janus Patulcius* and *Janus Clusius*) with smooth, beardless face, i.e. without powerful rays, but in the middle of the day with a large beard and hairy face.[1]

When the Sun sets and leaves his place to the darkness, or when the powerful summer sun is succeeded by the weak rays of the winter sun, then Samson's long locks,[2] in which alone his strength lies, are cut off through the treachery of his deceitful concubine Delilah, the 'languishing,[3] languid,' according to the meaning of the name (Delîlâ).[4] The Beaming Apollo, moreover, is called the Unshaven; and Minos cannot conquer the solar hero Nisos, till the latter loses his golden hair.[5]

It is then clear what the description of Esau as a man born hairy in contradistinction to the smooth Jacob denotes—the same as the epithet îsh ba'al sê'âr 'hairy man'

additions by Dr. Fr. Delitzsch, Leipzig, 1876.) The passage quoted is one of Delitzsch's additions, p. 284. I think this Hymn is a remarkable illustration of our hypothesis that Yiphtâch, 'the Opener,' is a linguistic description of the Sun.

[1] I owe to the kindness of my honoured friend Dr. Hampel, Custos of the archeological section of the Hungarian National Museum, the verification of a reference in the *Bulletino dell' Instituto di Correspondenza Archeologica*, 1853, p. 150, to a stone which exhibits the same representation of the head of Janus as the coin in question, viz.: 'una testa doppia, di cui una facie è barbata, l'altra giovanile.'

[2] See *Naphtali*, discussed in § 14 of this Chapter; p. 178.

[3] Compare *Sol languidus* (Lucretius, *De rerum nat.*, V. 726).

[4] The Arabian historians transfer the entire Biblical story of Samson (Arabic Shamsûn), to the time of the Mulûk al-ṭawâ'if; and in their narrative the hero fights against Rûm [i.e. the Greek Empire at Constantinople]; for the jawbone of an ass is substituted that of a camel. See Ibn al-Athîr al-Ta'rîch al-kâmil, Bûlâḳ edition, I. 146.

[5] Schwartz, *Ursprung der Mythologie*, p. 144, where Sif and Loki of the Scandinavian mythology are also mentioned. The hairiness of the solar heroes has been translated into an ethnographical peculiarity in modern Greek popular legends. Bernhard Schmidt (*Das Volksleben der Neugriechen*, I. 206) says, 'In Zante I encountered the idea that the entire power of the ancient Greeks lay in three hairs on the breast, and vanished if these were cut off, but returned when the hairs grew again.'

(2 Kings I. 8) in the description of Elijah: the rays of the sun, whose mythical representative Esau is. It is a more difficult question whether the solar character of this hero is capable of proof from his name. If, not to have recourse to non-Hebraic languages, we derive 'Êsâv from the Hebrew verb 'âsâ 'to do, accomplish,' and explain it as the 'Accomplisher, Worker,' or the like, then this description of a solar hero is suitable enough for a legend of civilisation, which sees in the sun the power that brings to perfection the corn and fruit, and produces in human society a legally secured condition of social life, in short, the Perfecting Agent. But such a description is less consonant with the sense possible to the ancient myth, in which the ideas and conceptions just mentioned were not yet developed. If then the name 'Êsâv cannot be etymologically explained in the spirit of the oldest mythical circle of ideas, we are necessarily driven to conjecture that the appellation does not belong to the oldest stratum of the materials of Hebrew legends, but was introduced by a legend of civilisation. This conjecture appears all the more probable when we remember that Jacob's hostile brother in the Bible itself bears another name besides Esau, much more expressive and suited to the earliest period of the formation of legends; namely, Edôm 'the Red.' In later times, when the original signification of the myths was entirely forgotten, these two names Esau and Edom were found in the story of the brothers' quarrel, as appellations of the brother with whom Jacob fights. Attempts were made to harmonise them; and the name 'the Red' was connected with the *red* pottage (Gen. XXV. 30), as well as with the more characteristic feature belonging to the old mythic stage, that the hostile brother was admônî, 'of a reddish colour.' But the name Esau also can be rescued for the old myth, if we connect this name with the Arabic a'tha 'hairy,' which is etymologically related to the name Esau.[1] Thus the name

[1] See Ewald, *History of Israel*, I. 345, note 1.

Esau would come in contact with the above-discussed mythic characteristic of the Solar hero, that he is an îsh sê'âr, a hairy man.[1] In the Phenician mythology the antagonist of Usov (whom those who do not utterly reject the authenticity of the statements of Sanchuniathon identify with Esau) lives in tents and is called Shâmîn-rûm 'the high heaven,'[2] i.e. the dark night-sky. The identity of the conceptions *Abh-râm* and *Ya'akôbh* would find further confirmation here. We are led to a different series of solar characteristics by the name Edôm, an unquestionably ancient designation of the Solar hero. We will consider together the names Edôm and Lâbhân, both appellations of hostile brothers of the Night-Sky. But before we begin this, I will mention another contest of Jacob's, to which the original writer devotes only a few lines: 'Then Jacob remained behind alone; and there wrestled a man with him until the morning rose. And he saw that he could not do anything to him, so he knocked his thigh-socket, and Jacob's thigh-socket was dislocated in wrestling with him. And he said, Let me go, for the morning has risen' (Gen. XXXII. 25–27 [24–26]). Thus Jacob fights with a man who cannot conquer him, but whom he must let off at the rise of the morning. This is the Dawn, who wrestles with the end of the night, and in the end breaks loose, so as to go up to the sky. The Night is a *limping* figure (ver. 32 [31]). This again is a feature in the myth of the hero of darkness, which we meet with also in classical mythology, e.g. in Hermes, κυλλοποδύων.[3] It probably indicates the opposite to the swiftness and the rapid never-ceasing course of the day, the sun and the dawn.

§ 11. Jacob is pursued and made to fight by the *Red* and by the *White*. Both words are designations of the

---

[1] In Gen. XXVII. 11, the received punctuation is îsh sâ'îr.—Tr.

[2] Compare Tiele, *Vergel. Geschied.* p. 447.

[3] Schwartz, *Ursprung der Mythologie*, p. 146; see above, p. 34.

same thing, *i.e.* the Sun. It strikes us as very strange that the myth should call the same object now red, now white. To appreciate this fact, we must think of the various stages which the sense of colour has to pass through in old times, until it is fully developed. Even in much later times we come across extraordinary fluctuations of language on Semitic ground in the designation of colours for solar phenomena. As the demonstration of this fact appears important to our present subject and things in connexion with it, the reader will excuse me for pausing longer than usual at this point and taking some excursions from the centre of our investigations. The names of colours were in ancient times very vague; the primitive man could not elevate himself to make any sharply defined distinction and classification of colours. *Red* and *white* are therefore here not exactly red and white, according to our modern distinction of these colours, but rather *light* or *bright-coloured*. It is a great merit of the late Lazarus Geiger, too early called home, to have most clearly exhibited this phase of the history of the development of ideas and their expression in language, and illustrated it with the light of psychology and comparative philology.[1] His ingenious researches have raised to a certainty the theory that the capacity for distinguishing colours has arisen, both in the individual and in the whole race, in the course of history, through gradual general development; that its beginning follows very late after the beginnings of other intellectual capacities; and that, even after man had grasped the distinction of different classes of colour, the *fixing* of his conceptions of colour made very slow progress, so that he often attributes first one and then another colour to the same object. The shading-off of colours, when once understood, has yet been fixed in the human mind with such difficulty, that

---

[1] *Zur Entwickelungsgeschichte der Menschheit*, pp. 45-60.—*Ursprung und Entwickelung der menschlichen Sprache und Vernunft*, Bd. II. book 3.—Compare Lazarus, *Leben der Seele*, II. 80; *ibid.* p. 185 note.

we find in many languages the most helpless wavering in the use of names of colours. As this phenomenon, important in man's mental development, is no less so in relation to the origin and the understanding of the elements of myths, we will pause over Geiger's disquisitions, to consider still further the fluctuating nature of the designations of colour in language, and especially to notice how far from clear and unsullied a reflexion impressions of colour cast on language, their natural medium of expression. We will however stay in the neighbourhood of the proper subject of investigation, and bring only Semitic words under consideration. Let us pick out the designations of Gold in this field. We cannot say in general terms of the Semitic languages that in the designation of gold and silver they do not express the optical difference between them, as a scholiast remarks in reference to Homer; for the appellations both of gold as *brilliant*, *shimmering*, and of silver as *pale*, prove that at least the different shine of the two metals was observed at the stage of the formation of language.[1] Far less definite, however, than this distinction of the two according to the general impression made on the sight, is the designation of the sensation made by each separately. The appellations of gold in Hebrew, Aramaic and Arabic, zâhâbh, dahabhâ, d̲ahab, denote *brilliant* in general; whereas the Assyrian and Phenician[2] word for gold, ḥuraṣu (which is the same as the Hebrew chârûṣ), expresses no optical sensation.[3] The

[1] For *Silver* the three North-Semitic languages, Assyrian, Aramaic, and Hebrew, have the same word, and in so far 'form a strict union,' as Schrader says, in opposition to the South-Semitic languages, which employ other words for the designation of this metal.' *Keilinschriften und das A. T.*, p. 46.

[2] Chârûṣ = gold has in recent times been frequently met with on Phenician territory, e.g. in the Inscription of Idalion published by Euting, II. 1, in the Inscription of Gebal (De Vogüé in the *Journal asiat.* 1875, I. 327), and in an unpublished Carthaginian Inscription (Derenbourg in *Journal asiat.* 1875, I. 336).

[3] The consideration of the Hebrew cheres 'Sun' might suggest that both it and the old word for gold (chârûṣ), composed of possibly related sounds, both originated in the notion of *shining*.

former appellations describe an optical sensation; but no definite colour-sensation. Indeed, even a late Arabic poet says of gold: al-ḏahab al-nârî,[1] 'the *fire-like* gold,' which, if a description of colour, is a very vague one. Ru'bâ b. al-'Ajjâj, an Arabic poet living in the second century of the Hijrâ, says: [2]

Hal yanfa'unî kaḏabun sichtîtu * au fiḍḍatun au dahabun kibrîtu ?
Will a great lie save me ? * or silver, or *sulphur-gold*?

Here gold and sulphur are compared together as similar, at all events in colour, for colour is the only possible *tertium comparationis* between them; and in fact we also find in Arabic the expression 'yellow sulphur, as if it were gold' (kibrît aṣfar ka'annahu ḏahab).[3] I lay particular stress upon this, because a common phrase among the Arabs is, al-kibrît al-aḥmar 'red sulphur,' to denote a peculiar person, one without his equal, inasmuch as there is no red sulphur. Now gold, of all things, is commonly used both in the later literature and in popular speech with the epithet *red* (al-ḏahab al-aḥmar). This phrase, as Osiander has proved,[4] occurs also in Ḥimyaric, and passed from Arabic into Persian and Turkish (in Persian zeri surch; in Turkish ḳizil altyn), and is used especially when minted gold is opposed to silver coins. The former is *red* money, the latter *white*: e.g. wa-mala'tum aydîkum min al-ḏahab al-aḥmar wal-fiḍḍâ al-beyḍâ 'you have filled your hands with *red gold* and *white silver*;' [5] dihhezâr dînâr zeri surch, 'ten thousand dînârs of *red gold*.' [6] In a very noteworthy essay, Belin has shown with reference to Turkish that in the Ottoman Empire the metal

---

[1] Al-Maḳḳarî, *Analectes*, etc., Leyden edition, I. 369. 3.

[2] Al-Jauharî, s.r. *kbr*.

[3] Yâḳût, *Geogr. Dictionary*, II. 609. 8.

[4] *Zur himjarischen Alterthumskunde*, in *Zeitsch. der D. M. G.*, 1865, XIX. 247. Compare Halévy, *Etudes sabéennes*, in *Journal asiat.*, 1874, II. 523.

[5] Pseudowâḳidî, ed. Nassau Lees, p. 181. 6.

[6] *Hist. de l'économie politique en Turquie*, in *Journal asiat.*, 1864, I. 421. Compare also Sprenger, *Alte Geographie Arabiens*, p. 56.

money is divided into *white*, 'aḳ,' and *red*, 'ḳizil';[1] and in Egypt at the present day the silver piaster is called abyaḍ 'white,' to distinguish it from the copper money *chorde*. Mu'âwiyyâ said to Ṣa'ṣa'â, 'Thou Red one;' and he answered, 'Gold is red.'[2] Thus we see that *red* has become the constant designation of the colour of gold. Now in what harmony does this stand with the above-quoted designation, 'sulphur-coloured gold,' when we consider at the same time the proverbial kibrît aḥmar 'red sulphur'?

Ethiopic designates gold, not by a derivative of the root 'ḏhb,' like the other languages of the same stock, but by the word waraḳ. We cannot decide *a priori* whether in its origin this word expresses a colour-sensation or not. In Arabic also we find waraḳ or wariḳ in a similar signification, and I can scarcely believe that it must be thrown out of the original treasury of the Arabic vocabulary. Von Kremer classifies it with the Arabic words borrowed from the Persian stock, and refers it to the Huzwâresh *warg*.[3] In old time it was equivalent to 'property, goods.'[4] The poet Suḥeym, an elder contemporary of Moḥammed, says in a little poem, 'The poems of the slave of the Banû-l-Ḥasḥâs on the day of competition are worth as much as noble birth and waraḳ (property);[5] and in some of the traditional sayings of Moḥammed a collateral form of the same word, riḳâ, denotes 'money.'[6] The Arabic lexicographers give the signification of both forms as al-darâhim al-maḍrûbâ 'stamped coins,' drachmas. In the more general signification we find waraḳ used by Abû Nuwâs in a poem of youth or rather childhood. The poet Ibn Munâdir, finding little Abû Nuwâs leaning against a pillar in the mosque, took a great fancy to him, and addressed an erotic poem to him; upon which the

---

[1] The use of *black* should also be noticed; dirhem saudâ and kara ġurush.

[2] In *al-Tha'âlibî* in the *Zeitsch. der D. M. G.*, 1854, VII. 505.

[3] *Culturgeschichtliche Streifzüge*, p. xi.

[4] Compare *Aġânî*, III. 90. 10. Fada'a bichâzinihi wa-ḳâla kam fî beyt mâlî faḳâla lahu min al-waraḳ w-al-'ayn baḳîyyatun.

[5] Thorbecke, *Antarah, ein vorislamischer Dichter*, Leipzig 1867, p. 41.

[6] al-Ḥarîrî, Paris edition, 2nd ed., p. 467.

boy extemporised the following verses, and wrote them on the back of the letter:

You write me a letter of praise without any waraḳ (present);
　　That is like a house built on a foundation of reeds;
But I should think it much pleasanter than your eulogy on me,
　　If you would send me a pair of black shoes and a fine dress.
If you are willing, do get me a waraḳ (present): if you do so
　　I shall not turn you away.[1]

We see clearly from this example how general the meaning of waraḳ is in Arabic; even a pair of shoes and a dress are included in it. It is, however, probable that the word, which certainly comes from the south of Arabia, originally denoted specially *gold*, but being supplanted in this narrow sense by ḏahab in ordinary Arabic, was applied first to gold-money, then to money generally (even of silver), and lastly by a further generalisation to goods and objects of value of all kinds. Its South-Arabic origin is also confirmed by the fact that it occurs in Himyarite,[2] beside ḏahab and kethem; and there is no reason for supposing, with Halévy, that it denotes specially *de l'or en feuilles*, contrasted with *de l'or en poudre*.[3] On the other hand, it must be noticed that the root waraḳ in the Semitic languages designates a *colour*, either *green* or *yellow*, and that it is probably owing to this circumstance that gold is in Ethiopic called waraḳ. But this word of colour itself is very fluctuating. Whilst in Ethiopic it designates the colour of gold, in Hebrew it gives a name to *grass* (yereḳ), and similarly in Arabic the green leaves are called waraḳ, notwithstanding which its diminutive urayyiḳ[4] (from auraḳ) denotes a *dark brown* camel; in irḳân it returns again to the notion *yellow* or *reddish*. The Hebrew of the Talmûd and the Targûm employs yârôḳ (which in Biblical Hebrew is mostly used for *green*, but sometimes of a pale face for *yellow*, e.g. yêrâḳôn 'jaundice') chiefly for a green colour, of vegetables

---

[1] *Kitâb al-aǧânî*, XVII. p. 11.
[2] M. A. Levy in *Zeitschr. der D. M. G.*, 1870, XXIV. p, 191.
[3] Halévy, *ibid.* p. 539.
[4] Freytag points this word urayḳ.—Tr.

and precious stones;[1] nevertheless, we find in the Talmûd (Bab. Nedârîm, 32. a) hôriḳân bezâhâbh 'he made it yârôḳ with gold,' i.e. made it yellow, gilded it. We have in Ps. LXVIII. 14 [13] yeraḳraḳ chârûṣ, *flavedo auri*. There is a noteworthy passage in Berêshîth rabbâ (sect. 4 near the end), in which the various colours of the sky are mentioned: red, black, white, and also yârôḳ.

The above remarks show how little consistency and distinctness there is in the relation of the names derived from colour to the various types of colour. The same result is reached when we inquire, with what designations of colour other objects are combined. For we find almost everywhere the greatest fluctuation, whether we consider the etymological value of the names themselves, or study the adjectives attached to them. In the most favourable cases only the class of colour--light or dark—is observed; but within the class nothing definite is found. Arabic especially is a field offering abundant matter for observation and demonstration, on which the excellent labours of Lazarus Geiger might be corroborated, completed and extended; but I cannot undertake such a task at this place. We will now limit our observations to the point which has to be established here: the views of colour which were attached to day and night, the sunny sky and the night-sky, the grey of the morning and the red of the evening.

In the Vedas, when day and night, sun and darkness, are opposed to each other, the one is designated *red*, the other *black*. 'The gods have made the night and the dawn of different hue, and given them *black* and *red* colours' (Rigveda, I. 73. 7). 'The *red* mother of the *red* calf comes; the *black* leaves his place to her' (Rigveda, I. 113. 2). 'The dawn comes forward, driving off *black night*' (Rigveda, I. 92. 5: compare VI. 64. 3).[2] In Hebrew

[1] J. Levy, *Chaldäisches Wörterbuch*, I. 345.

[2] 'The Sun had long since in the lap
Of Thetis taken out his nap;
And, like a lobster boil'd, the Morn
From black to red began to turn'—

—says *Hudibras*, canto II.

poetry we find no similar case, in which the opposite colours of the antagonistic forces are thus clearly set against one another. Indeed, we do not even find that a separate colour-epithet is given to each. Still it seems certain that at least Night was brought into connexion with the colour black;[1] otherwise a sentence such as 'Darker than Blackness (châshakh mish-shechôr) is their form' (Lam. IV. 8) would be impossible. We may infer from this that the notions of chôshekh 'Darkness' and shechôr 'Blackness' were closely connected together. This is in Arabic one of the commonest combinations. The dark night is sometimes called al-leyl al-ḥâlik—a word denoting the deepest shade of blackness. To the same class also belongs ad'aj (in leyl ad'aj 'black night'), another adjective denoting *black*. Chudârîyya is an Arabic word which denotes both *raven*[2] and *night* (one cannot help thinking of the Hebrew 'erebh 'evening' and 'ôrêbh 'raven'). The verb iktaḥal is used of Night: 'She has coloured herself with the black dye[3] al-kuḥl, e.g. wa-l-ẓalâm iḏa-ktaḥal (Rom. of 'Antar, VI. 53. 12). Poetry gives the same evidence as language itself. As in other literatures, so in Arabic, darkness is the term of comparison for everything black. The black hero of the best loved Arabic popular romançe is pictured as 'black as the colour of darkness, riding on a horse which resembles the darkness of night' (aswad kalaun al-ẓalâm 'ala jawâd min al-cheyl yaḥkî ẓalâm al-leyl: Rom. of 'Antar, IV. 183. 14). This is the source of a poetic figure much used by Arabic poets in application to a mistress with light features and dark hair. So Bekr b. al-Naṭṭâḥ says (Ḥamâsâ, p. 566): 'She is as white as if she were herself the brilliant noon-

[1] In the Babyl. Talmûd, Yômâ 28. b, the falling of the shades of night is described as the time when meshacharê kôthâlê 'the walls are black.'

[2] Called by Freytag an *eagle*.—Tr.

[3] In Harîrî (Paris edition, 2nd ed.), p. 644. 4, we read of the Dawn: ḥîna naṣal chiḏâb al-ẓalâm 'when the dye of darkness was washed off.' The Arabic word here used for 'dye' is generally employed of gay colours, e.g. al-ḥinnâ; but it is self-evident that here only al-kuḥl can be meant.

day-sky, as if her *black* hair were the *night* which darkens it.' The black hero 'Antar, contrasting his own colour and that of his beloved 'Ablâ, compares himself regularly with the night, and her with the dawn (e.g. 'Antar, VII. 136 penult.). She herself once addressed him thus, 'Go, in the name of God, thou colour of night' (sir fî âmâni-llâhi yâ laun al-duja, VI. 162. 4), and he often repeats the idea that his colour and that of night are the same. Thus (XVIII. 66. 12):

In akun yâ 'Ablata 'abdan aswadâ * fasawâdu-l-leyli min ba'ḍi ṣifâtî
Wafachârî annanî yauma-l-liḳâ'i * yachḍa'u-ṣ-ṣubḥu liseyfî wa-ḳanâtî.

Though I am, 'Ablâ, a black slave,
And the blackness of night is one of my qualities,
Yet it is my boast that on the day of encounter
The Dawn bows before my bow and spear.

As a black man is compared to night, so, inversely, the latter is likened to a black gipsy. Abû-l-'Alâ al-Ma'arrî, who is remarkable for accurate pictures of nature, says of the sky dazzling with stars, 'This night is a Gipsy's bride, decked out with pearls:' [1]

Leylatî hâḏihi 'arûsun min az-zan- * ji 'aleyhâ ḳalâ'idu min jumâni.[2]

On another occasion the same poet (II. 106. 4) compares the night to black *ink*:

Katabnâ wa-a'rabnâ bi-ḥibrin min ad-duja * suṭûra-s-sura fî ẓahri beyḍâ'a balḳa'i.

And one of the most ordinary descriptions of *darkening* is that 'Night put on her *black* adornments.' [3] From all this it is seen that it is perfectly usual and matter-of-course

[1] In Persian black hair is called mû i-Zengî 'Gipsies' hair,' and zulf-i-Hindu, 'Indian hair,' i.e. black like an Indian's (e.g. Rückert, *Grammatik, Poetik und Rhetorik der Perser*, p. 287). So in the well-known verse of Ḥafiẓ, in which the poet gives away all Bochara and Samarkand for the black mole (bechâl-i-Hinduwesh, 'Indian mole') of his Turkish boy (Dîwân Râ, no. 8. v. 1; ed. Rosenzweig, I. 24).

[2] *Saḳt-al-zand*, I. 91. 7.

[3] E.g. *Romance of 'Antar*, VII. 115. line 4 from below: wa-kasa-l-leylu ḥullat al-sawâd.

to associate Night with the colour *Black*.[1] Indeed, by the Black the poet understands *par excellence* Night. Abû-l-'Alâ al-Ma'arrî, the poet so frequently quoted in this section, says at one place (*ibid.* I. 131. 2): 'The *Black* one, whose father is unknown to men, has shrouded me in clothes from himself (i.e. in black or dark ones).' Nevertheless, we can convince ourselves here too, that even this point of the conception of colour is not devoid of fluctuation. For the blackness of night is not nearly so distinct a conception as ours when we speak of a black night. On the contrary, it is not yet separated from the general category of *dark colour*, to which green and blue also belong. When the land of the Banû Madhij was visited with drought, the tribe sent out three explorers (ruwwâd, from the singular râ'id), to look for suitable pasturage. One of them says in his report in praise of the splendid green meadows of the land he recommends, that the surface of the land is *like night*, so green is it.[2] Al-Afwah, a Preislamite Arabic poet and sage,[3] in a verse quoted by the lexicographer al-Jauharî (under the root *sds*), associates Night with the colour of *sudûs*. So also Abû Nucheylâ,[4] a later poet who lived under the Abbasid dynasty as their laureate, says 'Put on as thy shirt Night, black and dark like the colour of *sundus*':

Waddari'î jilbâba leylin daḥmasi * aswada dâjin mithli launi-s-sundusi.[5]

Another anonymous poet, or rather verse-monger, says

---

1 Varro treats it as self-evident that 'black' is the most suitable epithet for Night, and is thereby tempted to a very curious etymology in his work *De ratione vocabulorum*. He explains the word *fur* 'thief' by saying that in the old Latin *fur-vum* was equivalent to 'black,' and thieves practise their dark deeds at night. 'Sed in posteriore ejusdem libri parte docuit (scil. Varro) furem ex eo dictum quod veteres Romani furvum atrum appellaverint: at fures per noctem quae atra sit facilius furentur' (Aulus Gellius, *Noctes Atticae*, I. 18. 3–6).

2 Opuscula arabica, ed. W. Wright, Leyden 1859, p. 30. 11; compare p. 31. 12.

3 *Aġânî*, XI. 44.

4 *Ibid.*, XVIII. 139.

5 Ibn al-Sikkît, p. 344.

in the same sense 'Among the nights a dark night, when the sky is like the colour of *sundus*':

Waleylatin min-al-layâlî ḥindisi * launu ḥawâshîhâ kalauni-s-sundusi.[1]

But sudûs and sundus denote a garment the colour of which is regularly mentioned as achḍar 'greenish.' So, e.g., twice in the Ḳorân (Sûr. XVIII. 30, LXXVI. 21), where the joys and delights of Paradise are described, *green sundus garments* are promised to the faithful; and similarly in a tradition mentioned by al-Ġazâli[2] we find it said of men who become brethren in God, 'Their beauty shines like the sun, and they are clothed in *green sundus garments*' (wa-'aleyhim thiâb sundus chuḍr).

But this uncertainty of the colour which is associated with the Night is far less prominent than the fluctuation which prevails when the colour of the Day has to be described. In the former case, with a few exceptions based on the impression which a certain peculiar night may have made on the mind of the speaker or poet, black is by far the prevailing colour. Not so with the colour-distinctions of the solar phenomena. Here usage wavers among three colours, which are usually connected with the various stages of the Sun himself: *golden-yellow*, *red*, and *white*. The greatest definiteness is found to exist with reference to the first. It refers mostly to the dawn and sunset. In Aramaic the early morning is ṣafrâ. Etymologically this word is capable of many explanations which justify the above-expounded mythical conceptions of the dawn. It may be explained, as the soundest lexicographers on Semitic ground do explain it,[3] to denote *curled locks of hair*, or *one who springs, leaps*. Both explanations take us back to mythic attributes of the morning-sun; in the second we see the morning-sun springing up to heaven from behind the hills like a bird (ṣippôr). But I believe that the word ṣafrâ is related to aṣfar, a colour-name in

---

[1] Ibn al-Sikkît, p. 345.

[2] *Iḥyâ 'ulûm al-dîn*, II. 148.

[3] Gesenius, *Thesaurus*, p. 1183.

Arabic, which, though like all such it has an extremely vague signification, and may even mean *nigredo*, prevailingly indicates a golden-yellow colour. Now while the Aramaic ṣafrâ is exclusively the morning-sun (compare Ἠὼς κροκόπεπλος, Iliad, VIII. 1, and μελάμπεπλος of the night), in Arabic the colour-word in question is prevailingly applied to the evening-sun: 'Until upon him came the end of the day, and the Sun put on the garment of yellowness' (ila an atâ 'aleyhi âchir al-nahâr wa-labisat al-shams ḥullat al-iṣfirâr, Rom. of 'Antar, VI. 244. 1). Another example, in which the succession of time comes out with still greater clearness, is: 'They had defeated al-No'mân at noon; then they took rest till the Sun put on the garment of yellowness, and towards evening dust appeared before them' (wa-kânû ḳad sabaḳû al-No'mân bi-niṣf al-nahâr wa-achadû râḥâ ḥatta labisat al-shams ḥullat al-iṣfirâr wa-'ind al-masâ ṭala' 'aleyhim ġobâr, Rom. of 'Antar, VI. 35. 2). It is remarkable that in Egyptian the setting sun is said to throw out rays of *tahen*—a metal distinguished for its saffron colour, which is frequently contrasted with the colour red.[1] Chabas finds this contrast to constitute a difficulty in the comparison with the setting sun. Semitic analogies, however, show that the association of saffron colour with the sun, especially the evening-sun, is not confined to Egyptian. No case on Arabic ground is as yet known to me in which this yellowish colour, al-iṣfirâr, is attributed to any other stage of the sun's course except the evening. But there is the word aṣbaḥ (from ṣubḥ 'the early morning') 'morning-coloured,' used of the lion, which is said to denote a colour near to aṣfar.[2] At all events, the Aramaic ṣafrâ and the Arabic usage teach us that a yellow colour is in

---

[1] Chabas, *Etudes sur l'antiquité historique d'après les sources égyptiennes*, etc. 2nd edition, Paris 1873, p. 34, where the article by Le Page Renouf is referred to.

[2] Ibn al-Sikkît, p. 193, whom I follow as a reliable ancient authority; al-Jauharî and Freytag after him understand aṣbaḥ somewhat differently.

Semitic an attribute of both the morning- and the evening-sun. It is very different with the two other colours, white and red. There we meet with greater fluctuations. Sometimes the morning-sun is described as white, in comparison with the sun of the advanced day; sometimes the former is bright red and the latter white :

Ka'anna sana-l-fajreyni lammâ tawâlayâ * damu'l-achaweyni za'farâni wa-ayda'î.
Afâḍa 'ala tâlihima-ṣ-ṣubḥu mâ'ahu * fagayyara min ishrâḳi aḥmara mushba'i.

As if the light of the two daybreaks when they follow one after the other
Were the blood of the two brothers saffron and red.
The dawn poured its waters over the latter,
And changed into white its deep red.[1]

At its very first appearance the morning-dawn is of saffron colour, then a bright red comes, and the further the day advances, the whiter it becomes. The two daybreaks (al-fajrân), as the scholiast observes on this passage, are al-kâḏib wa-l-ṣâdiḳ—the *lying* or supposed one, which precedes the true dawn, and the latter itself. The very poet, however, from whom I quote this fragment, at another place exactly inverts the order of colour: representing the white or grey colour as appearing first, and then passing into the reddish or saffron. In a poem to a friend, in which he gives a beautiful description of night, he brings forward Night as in love with the stars. But she grows old—

Thumma shâba-d-duja wa-châfa min al-haj- * ri fagaṭṭa-l-mashîba bi-z-za'farâni.

And Night grew grey, and feared the desertion [of her lover, the starry heaven]:
So she dipped her grey hair into saffron.

[1] Abû-l-'Alâ, II. 107. 3–4.

[2] *Saḳt al-zand*, I. 93. 1. These ideas of the relations of colours are found expressed with characteristic energy by the eccentric Persian poet Abû Isḥâḳ Ḥallâjî; he says, 'When the Sun in the blue vault turns his cheek into yellow, it makes me think of saffron-coloured viands on an azure dish' (Rückert, *Grammatik, Poetik und Rhetorik der Perser*, p. 126). The conception of turning grey combines that of both colours—the white appearing beside the black. According to *Aġânî*, II. 41. 7; those clouds which combine the two colours are called shîb 'grey' (al-saḥâ'ib allatî fîhâ sawâd wa-bayâḍ).

The idea that the poet intends to express here is, that Night at its latter end becomes grey, when the grey morning begins to appear, and that to preserve the appearance of youth and be still acceptable to her lover she must put on red paint. But even the brightness of the sun by day (ḍiâ al-nahâr) is compared by the same poet to the grey hairs of an old man (II. 226. 2), as is also the brightness of the stars:[1]

Ra'âhâ salîlu ṭ-ṭîni wa-sh-sheybu shâmilun * lahâ bith-thureyyâ wâ-s-simâkeyni wa-l-wazni.[2]

He that was brought out of clay [Adam] saw it [the world], when its hair was all grey,
With the Pleiades, the two Fishes and the Balance.

We find the same figure, of which we have seen Abû-l-'Alâ to be so fond, used by Abû-l-Ḥasan 'Alî b. Isḥâḳ al-Waddânî, a Maġreb [North African] poet, who says of the morning: 'It is like the greyness which spreads itself over the black hair of youth (the black night):'

Dâna-ṣ-ṣabâḥu wa-lâ ata wa-ka'annahu * sheybun aṭalla 'ala sawâdi shibâbî.[3]

So, inversely, when the hair grows grey it is said 'The dark night is lighted.'[4]

From all these cases it may be gathered that the progress of the sun from the dawn to the full day is treated sometimes as a transition from a whitish to a reddish colour, sometimes as the reverse. Sometimes the redness of morning begins, and turns into white; sometimes the greyness, which passes into red.[5] But both conceptions are also found combined in a single idea: thus, for instance, al-'Arjî the poet says:

---

[1] I will mention here that according to al-Ġazâlî (*Iḥjâ*, IV. 433) the stars have various colours, some tending towards red, others towards white, others towards leaden: wa-tadabbar 'adad kawâkibihâ wachtilâf alwânihâ faba'ḍuhâ tamîl ila-l-ḥumrâ wa-ba'ḍuhâ ila-l-bayâḍ wa-ba'ḍuhâ ila launi-r-ruṣâṣ.

[2] Abû-l-'Alâ, I. 195. 1.

[3] In Yâḳût, IV. 911. 7.

[4] Ḥarîrî's *Maḳâmâs*, p. 675. 7: Istanâra-l-leyl al-bahîm.

[5] See Excursus H.

Bâtâ bi-an'âmi leylatin ḥatta badâ * subḥun talawwaḥa ka-l-aǵarri-l-ashkari.

They both passed a joyous night, until began
The morning to appear, like a red horse with white forehead-spot (ǵurrâ).[1]

Some already-cited examples have enabled us to observe that when day is contrasted with night, it is done by calling the night black and the day white. To the former instances I will now add another for clearness' sake: 'Till the whiteness of the day became black' (ḥatta 'âda bayâḍ al-nahâr sawâdan, Rom. of 'Antar, XXV. 5. 4). The attribute *white*, applied to the sun of the advanced day, is especially clear in a passage which I must not omit to mention. The poet al-Mutanabbî says:

Azûruhum wa-sawâdu-l-leyli yashfa'unî * wa-anthanî wa-bayâḍu-ṣ-ṣubḥi yuǵrî bî.

I visit them when the *blackness of the night* aids me;
And I retire when the *whiteness of the morning* drives me away.

A critic[2] remarks on this passage that the writer ought to have spoken of the *day* rather than of the *whiteness of the morning*, as the rhetorical law of al-muḳâbalâ 'antithesis' demands as the opposite to Night not Dawn, but Day. Thus 'the whiteness of day' would be better. Another passage with the antithesis is contained in Ḥarîrî: 'The white day becomes black' (iswadda-l-yaum al-abyaḍ).[3] This use of language is characteristically exemplified in the expression sirnâ bayâḍa jauminâ wa-sawâda leylatinâ, 'we travelled night and day' (literally, 'we travelled during the whiteness of our day and the blackness of our night,' Aġânî, II. 74. 20). But apart from any antithesis, the white colour is attributed to the light of the morning and the day: falamma-rtafa'at al-shams fabyâḍḍat, 'after the sun had risen high and *become white*,' is said in a tradition.[4] In the Romance of 'Antar (XXIV. 111. 3), a horse is thus described: 'he was

[1] *Aġânî*, I. 158. 23. [2] al-Anṭâḳi, *Tazyîn al-aswâḳ*, etc., p. 405.
[3] *Maḳâmâs*, p. 128; cf. Mehren, *Rhetorik der Araber*, p. 99.
[4] al-Buchârî, IX. 35.

white in colour, as if he were the day when it breaks, or the moon [1] when it shines with full beams' (wa-hua abyaḍ al-laun ka'annahu al-ṣabâḥ iḏa-nfajar wa-l-ḳamar iḏâ badar).

On Assyrian ground also we discover the idea of the *whiteness* of the sun, expressed, not indeed by a word directly signifying a colour, but yet by an epithet which is undoubtedly founded upon this idea. In the lyrical poem, called by Schrader 'The Assyrian Royal Psalm' (line 29), a land with a *silver sky*,[2] i.e. with a bright shining sunny sky, is desired for the king. So here the bright sunny sky is represented as of silver colour. On the other hand, Ḥomar^{m}, the name of a Himyarite god,[3] has perhaps a solar meaning, equivalent to the Arabic aḥmar 'Red;' at all events, the fancy that he may be a sort of Bacchus (chamr 'wine') sounds improbable. In Hebrew literature we find no direct indications of the colours which were associated with the sun: an indirect indication is afforded by the passage in Is. XXIV. 23, where it is said that 'the sun grows pale and the moon red.'[4] In the Talmûd literature, however, we find an incidental discussion of the colour of the sun; to which one of the Excursus is devoted.[5]

I have paused long on the ideas held of the Sun with reference to colour, longer than is consistent with the symmetry of my book, and have especially brought up many examples from the Arabic language, celebrated for its wealth of synonyms and epithets—all with the object of giving probability to my ideas on the mythical character of Esau or Edom and Laban, Jacob's two hostile kinsmen.

---

[1] The notion of the white colour of the moon is also the foundation of one of the Hebrew names of the moon. In the verse Ẓabyatun admâ'u mithla-l-hilâlî 'a gazelle red like the new moon' (*Aġânî*, VI. 122. 21) the moon is treated as red. But in the appellation al-layâli al-bîḍ 'white nights,' by which are meant nights illumined throughout by the moon, the moonshine is associated with a white colour.

[2] *Die Höllenfahrt der Istar*, p. 75.

[3] Halévy, *ibid.*, p. 556.

[4] See Excursus I.

[5] See Excursus K.

We have seen that the sun is called *white* quite as frequently as *red*;[1] now is it not certain beyond a doubt that the two foes of Jacob the Night-sky, namely Edom the red and Laban the white, are only names for the Sun, formed by the Hebrew myth on the ground of the sun's colour? The war of darkness and the stormy sky against the red or white sunny sky is described in the rich language of Mythology, which has devoted such multifarious appellations to this struggle, as a strife of one who follows on the heel of his brother, against the white and the red. Here we will return to a point which was anticipated in the Third Section of this chapter; I mean the fact that the mythic feature which, with other solar characteristics, has fastened itself on the description of David, a perfectly historical person, that he was admônî 'reddish,' belongs to the same group of mythic ideas. It is a bit of solar myth: 'He is red, and of excellent sight and good eyes' (1 Sam. XVI. 12).

Thus the mythical appellations Jacob, Edom, and Laban appear to be cleared up, and the features belonging to them have discovered to us the nocturnal character of the first-named and the solar of the two latter personages. I have confined myself to the most essential point, the statement of the fact and the identification of the mythic figures in the centre of the story. If we were to use the collateral points also as mythic matter, more abundant results might be attained. But we must limit ourselves to an investigation of the main features, since in the present position of mythological inquiry it would be difficult

---

[1] Among the Arabic names of the sun, we find the curious appellation al-jaunâ (Ibn al-Sikkît, p. 324), a word of colour, which belongs to the aḍdâd of the Arabic philologians, i.e. words with contradictory signification, and may denote either white or black (see Redslob, *Die arab. Wörter mit entgegengesetzter Bedentung*, Göttingen 1873, p. 27). Al-jaunâ is especially the setting sun, e.g. lâ âtîhi ḥatta taġîb al-jaunâ, 'I cannot come to him till the jaunâ sets;' and the setting sun is well described by a colour-word which, by its faculty of standing for either white or black, answers to the transition from sunshine to darkness.

and dangerous to try to pick out with any confidence from the epic descriptions in the Bible all that belongs to the original myth. It might, for instance, be urged that Jacob is endowed with a *deceitful* character, since he cheats the one of his blessing and his birthright, and the other of his sheep (Hermes), and this might be treated as characteristic of the *night*, as the figures of the night-sky are credited elsewhere with a thievish nature. 'Like thieves,' said the ancient Indian singer, 'so the nights stole away with their stars, that Sûrya might become visible' (Rigveda, I. 50. 2).

In a legend of the Palatinate the *King of the Night* residing at the Ice-sea *stole* the Sun;[1] Rachel steals the household-gods of her father Laban (Gen. XXXI. 19); and Jacob himself, as the Scripture expresses it, *steals* the heart of Laban the Aramean, not telling him of his intention to fly (v. 20).

> Now wrapt in mantle, like a thief, the Night is seen,
> She covers o'er her silver-studded raiment's sheen.

says Arany, in his 'Gipsies of Nagy-Ida'[2] (Canto I. v. 21).

But what I have hitherto explained is only one side of Jacob's mythical characteristics: we have seen against whom he fought. But Jacob did not only fight: he loved also, loved with tenderness and self-abnegation. He wooed, he married; and the history of his children takes up a considerable portion of the Book of Genesis. The loves of the Night-sky, the names of his wives whom he gained by conquest, and of the children that came out of his loins, must be an important part of the Myth of the Night-sky; and we should be accomplishing our task very imperfectly if we refused to enter on the consideration of these figures of Hebrew mythology.

---

[1] Communicated by Henne Am Rhyn, *Deutsche Volkssagen* &c., p. 219. no. 427.

[2] *Nagyidai Czigányok.* In the original Hungarian:

> Most az Éj fölvette tolvajköpönyegét,
> Eltakará azzal pitykés öltözetét.

§ 12. Let us turn first to his women. He has both wives and so-called concubines. In my opinion this distinction belongs to the original form of the myth; and some explanation of its significancy must be given at the outset. There is another already-discussed name of the night-sky, Abhrâm, with which are associated both a legitimate wife Sârâ, and a concubine Hâgâr; and in the latter we discovered the mythical bearer of a solar name, 'the Flying one.' This circumstance leads to the discovery that, whilst the concubines in mythical phraseology are figures of *opposite* nature to their master, like Hagar a solar figure to Abram the dark sky, the names of the legitimate wives represent figures homogeneous to the nature of the husband. This is the case preeminently with Sarah, Abram's wife. The name signifies *Princess, Lady*, the Princess of the Heaven, the Moon, the Queen who rules over the great army of the night-sky (ṣebhâ hash-shâmayîm). Another name of the moon in Hebrew mythology is probably Milkâ (the wife of Abraham's brother Nahor, Gen. XI. 29), i.e. 'the Queen'—not expressly *wife*, but grammatically the feminine form of Melekh (Abhî-melekh) 'King' (the Sun), like Ashêrâ (Moon) from Âshêr (Sun), or Lebhânâ (Moon) from Lâbhân (Sun). 'Queen or Princess of Heaven' is a very frequent name for the Moon.[1] We learn most remarkable facts from the Chaldee-Babylonian series of deities, which, though not old enough to be a myth, must, like every theogony, have sprung from mythology misunderstood. In this system, in which the deities are arranged in male and female triads, so that there is always a male deity parallel to the goddess of the female triad who stands at the same spot, Sîn (the Moon) and Gula of the male triad are balanced respectively by 'the highest Princess' and by Malkît 'the Queen' in the female; and these are only Sarah and Milcah again. Istar also is described as

[1] On *Regina coeli*, see Jablonski, *Opuscula*, II. 54 *et seq.* (ed. Te Water).

Princess (sarrat) of heaven;[1] which is probably connected with the fact that this goddess of the Assyrian Pantheon, who is commonly compared to Venus, in later times became a moon-goddess.[2] Sir H. Rawlinson says that Μισσαρή in Damascius may be cognate with the Assyrian Sheruha or Sheruya, the wife of Asshûr, and signify 'the Queen.'[3] And as it is the *stars* over which the Queen of the night-sky bears sway, she is *siderum regina* in Horace (*Carmen saeculare*, v. 35).[4] Even in the latest times the Hebrews called the moon the 'Queen of Heaven' (melekheth hash-shâmayîm, Jer. VII. 18), and paid her divine honours in this character at the time of the Captivity. The Hebrew women who had migrated to Egypt answered the Prophet who warned them: 'As to the word that thou has spoken unto us in the name of Jahveh, we do not listen to thee; for we shall certainly do all the things that have gone forth from our own mouth; burning incense to the *Queen of Heaven*, and pouring libations to her as we have done, we and our fathers, our kings and princes, in the cities of Judah and the streets of Jerusalem, and were filled with food and were happy and saw no evil; whereas ever since we have ceased to burn incense to the *Queen of Heaven* and pour libations to her, we have wanted everything, and been consumed by sword and famine. And when we were burning incense to the Queen of Heaven and pouring libations to her, was it *without our men* that we made cakes for her, to receive her image, and poured libations to her?' (Jer. XLIV. 16–19). This reply leads us to infer that the moon-worship in Judah was specially attractive to the women and allowed by the men, and was not a mere secondary religious act, but a prominent worship of the first rank; yet a worship which, considering the prevailingly solar character of the religion of an

[1] In Fox Talbot, quoted by Schrader, *Die Höllenfahrt der Istar*, p. 98.
[2] *Zeitchr. d. D. M. G.*, 1873, XXVII. p. 404.
[3] G. Rawlinson, *History of Herodotus*, App. B. I., Essay X. (I. 484).
[4] Schwartz, *Sonne, Mond und Sterne*, 269, 274.

agricultural people, was then kept up chiefly by the women as the relic of an ancient nomadic age. What was the antiquity of this lunar worship among the Hebrews, is testified (as has long been known) by the part played by Mount Sinai in the history of Hebrew religion. For this geographical name is doubtless related to *Sin*, one of the Semitic names of the moon. The mountain must in ancient times have been consecrated to the Moon.[1] The beginning of the Hebrew religion, which, as we shall see, was connected with the phenomena of the night-sky. germinated first during the residence in Egypt on the foundation of an ancient myth. The recollection of this occasioned them to call the part of Egypt which they had long inhabited ereṣ Sînîm 'Moonland' (Is. XLIX. 12). Obviously the lunar worship of Nomads stands in connexion with the prominent position occupied by the figures of the night-sky in their mythology. When, through that psychological process which results in the decay of the life of the myth and the rise of a religious view of the world, the mythic elements become religion, then the Moon is not believed to possess those deleterious qualities of which the later legends of the American nations are full, but is rather regarded as the source of blessing and success. The Hebrews called the most fruitful place in their new country, the 'City of the Palms,' formerly delightful, though now a very cheerless hole, by a name denoting *Moon-city*—Yerêchô (Jericho). An analogous system of nomenclature is mentioned by Ḥamzâ of Iṣpahân, a Persian who wrote in Arabic, who says in his *Kitâb al-muwâzanâ* that, because the moon is the cause of an abundant supply of water and of rain, the names of the most fruitful places in Persia are compounded with the word *mâh* 'moon:' e.g. Mâhidînâr, Mâhishereryârân, Mâhikârân, Mâhiharûm &c.[2] For, in the opinion of the

[1] See especially Osiander in the *Zeitsch. d. D. M. G.*, 1865, XIX. 242 *et seq.*
[2] In Yâḳût, IV. 406.

Iranians the growth of plants depends on the influence of the moon.[1] The Arabic language still shows clearly the mythical connexion between the moon and good pasture,[2] in the fact that the same word, which as a noun, al-ḳamar, signifies moon, as a verb, ḳamara, expresses the notion *multus fuit* (de aqua et pabulo), and ḳamir means *multa* aqua.

The nomadic Hebrews called Sarah, the Princess of Heaven,[3] i.e. of the night-sky, Abram's legitimate wife. The same relation between wife and concubine comes out with still greater distinctness in the case of Jacob, Abram's synonym. His legitimate wives are Leah and Rachel; to the latter he is bound by the tenderest love—a love which in the view of the Biblical writer became the ideal of self-sacrificing conjugal affection. Both their names are homogeneous to Jacob's mythical character, and the bearers of these mythical appellations are figures of the dark sky of night and clouds. It will be regarded by serious investigators as no mere chance that the word

---

1 The constant epithet 'holding the seed of bulls' brings to view the idea that the influence of the moon produces fertility in cattle (Spiegel, *Die heiligen Schriften der Parsen* [in German], III. xxi.). According to Yasht, VII. 5, it is the moon 'that produces verdure, that produces good things.' Compare *Catullus*, XXXII (XXXIV) v. 17–20, where the poet apostrophises the Moon—

> Tu cursu, Dea, menstruo
> Metiens iter annuum,
> Rustica agricolae bonis
>   Tecta frugibus exples.

2 This connexion is also clear in the Hottentot mythology. Heizi Eibib, which means moon, is there the name of the man to whom grave-tumuli are consecrated, and who is addressed in prayer for good sport and numerous herds (Waitz, *Anthropologie der Naturvölker*, II. 324).

3 Max Müller's view (*Introduction to the Science of Religion*, p. 184), 'When Jeremiah speaks of the Queen of Heaven, this can only be meant for Astarte or Baaltis,' is correct only if Baaltis be identified with the Moon. The correctness of this identification, which was first asserted by Philo Byblius, and has been conceded by the older interpreters Grotius and Lyra, and by many modern ones, is very probable; for the name Baaltis stands in the same relation to Ba'al (Sun) as Milkâ to Melekh, Lebhânâ to Lâbhân, and Ashêrâ to Âshêr. Tiele also (*Vergelijkende Geschiedenis*, p. 512) says the same as Müller.

Lê'â in its origin signifies the same as Delîlâ, namely, *languida, defatigata*, the *Languishing, Weary, Weak*—the setting Sun that has finished its day's work, or rather the time when there is no longer any sun, but the Night, who cuts off from her long-haired lover or bridegroom the locks (*crines Phoebi*) in which his whole force resides; the Night, which robs the Sun of his splendid rays, and causes him to fall powerless to the ground and lie blind on the battle-field. Even in a product of the Jewish literature of a later age the expression chấlâsh 'weak, debilitated' is used of the setting sun. 'He is like a hero who goes forth strong and returns home powerless; thus the sun at his rising is a mighty hero, and at his setting a *weakling*.'[1] Nothing similar is connected with the name Lê'â; yet it is clear that this name is an appellation of the setting sun or the advancing night, when we read: we'ênê Lê'â rakkôth 'the eyes of Leah were weak' (Gen. XXIX. 17).[2] How closely the ideas 'End' (here that of the day) and 'Weariness' hang together in Semitic, we see clearly in the Aramaic word shilhâ, shilhê 'end,' which is developed out of the Shaph'êl form of the root lehî (the Hebrew lâ'â, whence the name Lê'â), which denotes 'to be wearied.'[3] The name Râchêl is still clearer and less ambiguous. It signifies 'Sheep.' When the ancients raised their eyes to heaven and saw grey clouds slowly driving over the celestial fields, they discovered there the same as our children see when in their innocent imaginations they find figures of hills and animals in the sky. Men who form myths stand in this respect on the same intellectual stage as our children. How finely has Angelo de Gubernatis, in the introduction to his most original work 'Zoological

[1] Midrâsh Shôchêr Ṭôbh on Ps. XIX. 7.

[2] The contrast of Leah's weak eyes to Rachel's beauty belongs not to the mythic stage, but to the epic description.

[3] There is no reason to separate the word shilhê from the Shaph'êl shalhî, as Levy does in his *Chald. Wörterbuch*, II. 481; compare Reggio in the Hebrew journal *Ozar Nechmad*, I. 122.

Mythology,' attached his profound explanations of the old animal-mythology, which are based upon a sympathetic poetical feeling after the sentiments of a mythic age, to vivid memories of that early age in which the enquirer after myths himself looked up to heaven and *made* myths! Moreover, what the primitive humanity that created myths and the children of our advanced modern age read in the picture-book of nature,[1] is still found there by people who, although they no longer make myths, yet excel us in immediate observation of nature. The sandhills and downs of the Sahara are variously called by the natives kelb 'Dog,' kebsh 'Ram,' or chashm el-kelb or chashm el-kebsh 'Dog's nose' or 'Ram's nose.'[2] But it is chiefly the clouds that gave so much food to fancy. On Arabic ground we can refer to a treatise by Abû Bekr ibn Dureyd, a linguist of an early age known to every Arabist, on the 'Description of the Rain and the Cloud,' which the learned Professor William Wright has published in a useful collection. In this treatise many a vivid picture is to be found which exhibits the continual working of the old mythic views.[3] Even a modern literature nearer to us may be quoted; for who knows not the classical passage in Shakespeare, where Polonius makes observations on the forms of the clouds—a series of mythical observations, which the same poet allows another of his heroes to condense into a mythological *résumé*:

> Sometime we see a cloud that's dragonish;
> A vapour sometime like a bear or lion,
> A tower'd citadel, a pendent rock,
> A forked mountain, or blue promontory
> With trees upon 't, that nod unto the world,
> And mock our eyes with air.
>
> *Antony and Cleopatra*, IV. 14.

If the sky is a pasture, it is most natural to see in the

---

[1] See *Zeitschr. für Völkerpsychologie und Sprachwissenschaft*, 1869, VI. 237, 252.

[2] Rohlfs, *Quer durch Afrika*, I. 204.

[3] *Opuscula Arabica*, pp. 16–39.

clouds beasts feeding there. So the nomad Arab sees in the clouds herds of camels,[1] and calls a small herd of twenty or thirty camels by the same name by which he describes a broken-off fragment of cloud—al-ṣirmâ. The poet Abû Ḥibâl calls a rain-cloud dalûḥ, i.e. 'a heavily laden camel;' [2] and according to the Arabian philologist al-Tebrîzî a cloud accompanied by thunder and lightning is called al-ḥannânâ 'the bellowing,' because the ancient Arabs compared a thundering cloud[3] to a camel that breaks out into loud bellowing from painful desire to reach home.[4] How full of meaning is the myth that lies hidden behind this expression ḥannânâ! The camel on a journey has gone far away from home, longs to be back again, and bellows with terrible pain: it is the Thunder.[5] And this myth was not confined to the Arabs; we find a slight trace of it among the later Jews, in the Talmûd. When it thundered, they said, 'The clouds groan.' Achâ b. Ja'aḳôbh describes meteorological phenomena in the following words: 'The lightning sparkles, *the clouds groan* (menahamîn 'anânê), and the rain comes' (Berâkhôth, fol. 59. a). This mythical conception is only a variation of the more general view that thunder is a *lion's roaring* (Job XXXVII. 4; shâ'ag is used specially of the lion), out of which grew the roaring of Jahveh, mentioned in many passages of prophecy and poetry—a result of the monotheistic transformation of mythical ideas. In Arabic hamhama is used both of the lion's roaring and of thunder; and so also zamjara. In the work of Ibn Dureyd

---

[1] E.g. *Ḥamâsâ*, p. 609, v. 6: *Nâbiġâ*, VI. v. 9. [2] *Ḥamâsâ*, p. 391, v. 2.

[3] Commentary on *Ḥamâsâ, ibid.*

[4] The Arabian poet Ibn Mayyâdâ, in a description of the lightning (*Aġânî*, II. 120. 9), says 'it lights up the piled-up cloud, which is like a herd of camels, at the head of which those that long for their home cry out with pain: yuḍî'u ṣabîran min saḥâbin ka'annahu * hijânun arannat lil-ḥanîni nawâzi'uh.

[5] The ancient Arabs understood that the thunder and lightning were caused by the clouds whence they issued. Many passages might be quoted in support of this, but Lebîd Mu'allaḳâ v. 4, 5, is sufficient. Ḥanna (to sigh, to groan with desire) is therefore equivalent to 'to thunder,' e.g. *Aġânî*, XIII. 32. 8. ḳad ra'adat samâ'uhu wa-baraḳat wa-ḥannat warjaḥannat.

already quoted an Arab says of a thunder-cloud, 'Its thunders groan like camels longing to get home (ṭirâb), and roar like raging lions.'[1]

The Arab saw in the clouds a herd of camels, in a single cloud a single camel.[2] The ostrich, which is a favourite term of comparison in Arabic poetry, is also seen by them in the clouds. Zuheyr b. 'Urwâ says of a little cloud visible behind a larger one, that it was an ostrich hung up by the feet (ka'anna-r-rabâba duweyna-s-saḥâbi * na'âmun tu'allaḳu bi-l-arjuli).[3] From the Hebrew mythology we have the similar conception of the cloud as a *sheep*, as Râchêl. She is the legitimate wife of the dark, nocturnal or overclouded sky. When the cloud let fall its wet burden in drizzling rain upon the earth, the primitive Hebrews said 'Rachel is weeping for her children'—a phrase preserved from an age of mythic ideas, which was retained to a late age in a very different sense.[4] For as the Arab regarded the thunder as the cloud's cry of pain, so the Hebrew could see in the rain Rachel's tears. Even up to the present day the Arabs say of the rain: 'The sky weeps, the clouds weep;'[5] and the idea was not strange to the Greek, who spoke of the 'Tears of Zeus.'[6] In the Romance of 'Antar, XXV. 58. 4, it is said of the rain:

The gloomy heaven weeps with tears, that stream in constant flow
Out from the eye of a rainful cloud.

The poet Ibn Muṭeyr says most beautifully of the weeping sky: 'The cloud smiles at the lighting up (of the lightning), and weeps from the corners of her eyes, the moisture of which is not excited by splinters (sticking in the eye); and

---

[1] See W. Wright, *Opuscula Arabica*, p. 20. 10; 21. 7.
[2] *Ibid.*, p. 29. 2.
[3] *Kitâb al-Aġânî*, XIX. 157. 1.
[4] Jeremiah XXXI. 15, Matth. II. 18.
[5] Compare al-Sherbînî Hezz al-ḳuḥûf, etc., lithographed Alexandria, p. 253. The Arabs also said of the red evening-sky that 'it wept bloody tears' (al-Maḳrîzî, *al-Chiṭaṭ*, Bûlâk edition, I. 430).
[6] Clemens Alex. *Strom.* V. 571.

without either joy or grief she combines laughing and weeping.'[1] Rachel has a favourite son called Yôsêph (Joseph). This name signifies: 'He multiplies,' or, from the explanation already given, 'The Multiplier.' He is called in a hymn addressed to him, 'The blessing of the heaven above, the blessing of the flood that lies below, the blessing of the (female) breasts and of the womb' (Gen. XLIX. 25). Can we doubt that this is the Rain, which multiplies—the blessing from above, which lies below in floods of water, the rain which mythologically was so often regarded as the nutritive milk of the milked cows of the clouds?[2] And probably the old Arabic idol called Zâ'idatu,[3] i.e. 'the Multiplieress,' has the same mythological signification as the synonymous term Joseph in Hebrew, and may therefore be regarded as a goddess of Rain. Can the least doubt be felt, that 'the Multiplier,' the son of the cloud, must be the rain, as wine is called the daughter of the grape,[4] and the fruit the son of the tree,[5] and as bread is called in Arabic jâbiru-bnu ḥabbata, like 'Strengthener, son of Mrs. Grain?'[6] Moreover, while these latter views are natural, but not spread abroad everywhere, the idea that the rain is the child of the cloud is universal. We meet it among the Greeks, for Pindar sings:

---

[1] See Nöldeke's *Beiträge zur altarab. Poesie*, p. 34.

[2] In mythology the clouds are also called udders. See Mannhardt, *German Mythenf.*, pp. 176–188; so in Arabic, Ibn Muṭeyr apud Nöldeke l. c.

[3] Ibn Dureyd, *Kitâb al-ishtiḳaḳ*, ed. Wüstenfeld, pp. 13, 14.

[4] Ibnat al-'inab, in the celebrated wine-song of Wâlid b. Yazîd (*Aġânî*, VI. 110. 5). Wine is well known to be called in Hebrew 'Blood of the grape,' dam 'ênâbh (*Deut.* XXXII. 14); compare the Persian chôni rûz in Waṣṣâf ed. Hammer, p. 138. 6: shahzâdegân bâ yekdiger chôni rûz chordend.

[5] In Siamese luk mei is 'son of the tree, fruit' (Steinthal, *Charakteristik*, p. 150); compare Midrâsh rabbâ Leviticus, sect 7, where 'children of the tree' are spoken of, châlaḳtâ khâbhôd la'êṣîm bishebhîl benêhem. The pearl is called by Waṣṣâf, p, 180. 15, zâdei yem 'son of the sea.' A curious mythological relationship is found in the Polynesian system; the year, a daughter of the first pair, combined with her own father to produce the months, and the children of the latter are the days (Gerland, *Anthropologie der Naturvölker*, VI. 233).

[6] Fleischer in the *Zeitschr. d. D. M. G.*, 1853, VII. 502 note.

. . . ἔστιν δ' οὐρανίων ὑδάτων
ὀμβρίων, παίδων Νεφέλας (*Olymp.* XI. 2, 3),—

just like the Arabs. The poet Moḥammed b. 'Abd al-Malik said, when a violent shower of rain delayed the arrival of his friend al-Ḥasan b. Wahab, 'I know not how to express my complaint against one heaven which keeps back from me another heaven (the friend), unless indeed I utter curse and blessing together: Let *the former become childless*, and the latter live long.'[1] The cloudy heaven was to lose his children—i.e. the rain was to cease.

Lastu adrî mâ ḏâ aḳûlu wa-ashkû * min samâ'in ta'ûḳunî 'an samâ'i
Ġayra annî ad'û 'ala tilka bi-th-thuk- * lî wa-ad'û lihâḏihi bi-l-baḳâ'i.

It is this 'Multiplier, Son of the Cloud,' alone who can bring aid when the earth is visited by long drought and famine. The *multiplying* Rain gives back to the parched earth her fertility and procures nourishment for starving mankind. This simple idea is formed from the mythic base into the story of the famine in Egypt and Joseph's aid in allaying it. The myth itself, while it lived, was general, not bound by time or place, limited neither geographically or chronologically. When no longer understood and when lost to human consciousness, it became a locally defined legend, belonging to a certain historical period. This is the same experience which meets us in most of the myths of Hellenic Heroes. The Sun, which daily assails with an iron club and slays the monsters of darkness and the storms, when personified as Herakles does his deeds in a small place in Hellas, Nemea or Lerna. While Joseph imparts fertility to the parched earth, and in his character of 'Multiplier' delivers it from the curse which rested on it, the prophetic hero, in whom we have already detected some solar features, does the opposite. Elijah, who ascends to heaven on a fiery chariot

[1] *Aġânî*, XX. 54. 16.

with a fiery horse, the 'hairy man,' curses the soil of the Hebrew land in the time of Ahab (again a localising and chronological limitation of what the myth had told in general terms without such limitation) with drought, want of rain, and unfruitfulness; he is the cause of a fearful famine (1 Kings XVII. 1).

The 'Multiplier' has also severe contests to sustain. The most celebrated of them is that which he maintains against her who loves him dearly, whose name is preserved to us only in legendary tradition—Zalîchâ, the 'Swift-marching.'[1] We know her already. He flies from the temptress, but *leaves his cloak in her hand* (Gen. XXXIX. 12). This feature, which seems to us only accessory, may have been an important element of the original myth. We shall see further on, that the figures of the night-sky or the dark sky generally are provided with a covering or cloak, with which they cover over the earth or the sun, and thus produce darkness. It is a different battle that he fights against his brothers, the 'Possessors of arrows,' i.e. the sun-rays, which shoot at the rain-cloud and try to drive it off. Joseph's persecution by his own brothers and expulsion to Egypt is only the other side of the Egyptian myth of Osiris and Typhon and the Phenician myth of Adonis; the solar hero being in the latter cases, and the rain-hero in the former case, the object of persecution. While the sarcophagus of Osiris starts from Egypt on its travels, and lands at Byblos on the Phenician coast, Joseph when sold goes in the opposite direction from Canaan to Egypt. Both these myths became local legends, one in Egypt, the other in Canaan; consequently the direction of the wandering is modified in conformity with the locality.

From the battle of the rainy sky against the solar

[1] Arabic tradition knows another name besides Zalîchâ for this person. In al-Ṭabarî her name is given as Râ'îl; see Ouseley, *Travels in various Countries of the East*, London 1819, I. 74; also in al-Beyḍâwî's *Anwâr al-tanzîl*, ed. Fleischer, I. 456-8.

heroes with their arrows our myth makes the Rainbow to arise: just as the lightning was called 'the Arrow of God,' so the rainbow was in later times described as the 'Bow of God' (ḳashtî, Gen. IX. 13). The later legend of civilisation gives to the rainbow a foundation which is quite foreign to mythology. In mythology the rainbow appears to be attributed to Joseph, who, when overcome and driven off the field by the 'Possessors of arrows,' is after all not totally defeated, for 'his bow abode in strength' (Gen. XLIX. 24). This expression indicates the following conception. When the rain-cloud was driven from its place by the solar heroes, he fixed his bow in the sky, to be ready for a future fight. Thus in the Hebrew myth the rainbow is a bow belonging to the hero of storms. We find the same idea in the Arabic mythology. Besides other names, the rainbow bears that of ḳausu Ḳuzaḥa, 'the bow of Ḳuzaḥ' (who has been proved so be a storm-hero); and it may be gathered from some passages which Tuch has incidentally brought together in his Treatise on Sinaitic Inscriptions,[1] that Ḳuzaḥ shoots his arrows of lightning during the storms from this same bow, which after the conclusion of the battle appears in the sky. In the same Hebrew hymn which contains the above mention of the Bow, ebhen Yisrâ'êl 'the Stone of Israel' is named. Perhaps I am not at fault in conjecturing that the Stone here has a solar signification, and is used of the Sun which after the victory over Joseph appears on the firmament. We know from Schwartz's [2] demonstrations, which Kuhn has recently confirmed in his academical treatise on the stages of development in the formation of Myths, that in mythical language the sun and other luminous bodies are called 'stones.' To the same mythic cycle belongs the circumstance that

---

[1] *Zeitschr. d. D. M. G.* 1849, III. 200. See above p. 73. *et seq.*

[2] *Sonne, Mond und Sterne*, pp. 1. *et seq.*

David slays his giant-foe by casting stones. And tradition[1] says that Cain killed Abel by throwing stones. But on the whole we find in the above-quoted hymn (called Jacob's) only slight hints that can be claimed for the mythic period; for the remains of primeval hymns like that fragment were in later times so overgrown with matter derived from historical circumstances, that we must be content if we can discover what were the points of view and conceptions chiefly represented by these fragments. The reason why it is so difficult to reconstruct the old mythic view of the Hebrews concerning the Rainbow, obviously lies in the fact that it was supplanted by a later theological explanation (Gen. IX. 12–17). It is curious that the reason assigned in this later passage for the origin of the Rainbow was not able to obtain general credence, and that even Christian popular legends frequently appear to flow from ancient mythic conceptions. I will only mention an instance given by Bernhard Schmidt—the Christians in Zante call the rainbow 'the girdle, or the bow of the Virgin, *τὸ ζώναρι, τὸ τόξο τῆς παναγίας*.[2]

§ 13. Now while Jacob's lawful wives are mythical figures homogeneous to himself, as we have seen, his collateral wives, the two concubines Zilpah and Bilhah represent figures of the ancient myth standing in a position of opposition to Jacob. The mythical character of Zilpah has been already determined, in the Seventh Section of this chapter. For this determination we had no other resource but the etymology of the name, no mythical matter having been preserved concerning this mythical figure. The case is reversed when we enquire into the meaning of Bilhah. The resource of etymology abandons us here; for, even if we assume that the abstract idea represented

---

[1] Weil, *Biblische Legenden der Muselmänner*, p. 39. *Zeitschrift d. D. M. G.*, 1861, XV. 86.

[2] *Das Volksleben der Neugriechen*, Leipzig 1871, I. 36.

by the name must here be understood in a participial sense (Bilhâ = 'the Trembling, Terrified'), yet, in the want of analogous cases, the signification of the name brings us to no track worth pursuing. But, on the other hand, we fortunately have a material myth (as opposed to a mere name), relating to Bilhah: 'Reuben went and lay with Bilhah his father's concubine' (Gen. XXXV. 22).

The transition from one aspect of nature to another is not always regarded by the myth from the point of view of a battle, in which the vanishing aspect is represented by the conquered and the approaching one by the conqueror. The myth speaks equally frequently of love and union, i.e. of sexual connexion. The vanishing aspect disappears in that which immediately follows: they become one, as man and wife. In the myths of sexual union, the mythical feature that the two figures one of which follows the other are brother and sister, father and daughter, or mother and son, is sometimes disregarded. We had an example of this in the Hebrew myth of the union of Shechem with Dinah. This is very frequent in Aryan mythology; and it is sufficient to refer to the part of Max Müller's essay which deals with this subject.[1] There is a very fine myth of this kind, preserved in a work ascribed to Plutarch, *De fluviorum et montium nominibus* (IV. 3). It is there said with reference to the Ganges, 'Near it is situated the mountain *Anatole*, or the Rising,' so called for the following reason: 'Helios saw the maiden Anaxibia dancing there, and was seized with violent love for her. No longer able to control his passion, he pursued her with desire to force her to yield to his desire. The maiden, surrounded on every side, escaped into the temple of Artemis Orthia on the mountain Koryphe, and was lost to the eyes of her pursuer. He, following after, and unable to overtake his beloved, went

---

[1] *Chips,* &c. vol. II., the latter part of 'Comparative Mythology,' and *Lectures on the Science of Language,* Second Series, Lecture IX. 'The Mythology of the Greeks.'—Tr.

up to the same mountain grieving. Therefore the natives call the mountain Anatole or 'Sun-uprising,' as Kaemarus narrates in the tenth book of his 'Indian Affairs.'[1] Here, where the sunrise is not even the result of a union, but very characteristically that of disappointed love, Helios is no relative whatever of the Dawn, any more than Shechem of Dinah, or Abimelech, the later Sun-god (Melekh, compare Abhîba'al and Ba'al), of Rebekah, whom he loves (Gen. XXVI), or of Sarah, 'Moon,' whom he takes to himself (Gen. XX). However, the view which we shall encounter in the myth of Lot, that the lovers or united couples are blood-relations, brother and sister, or parent and child, is more prevalent. The idea of a son in love with his mother is quite general in Asiatic mythology, as Lenormant proves: in the old Babylonian mythology Dâzî, the Hebrew Tammûz, is lover of his mother Istar, &c.;[2] among the Egyptians Amôn is called the husband of his mother Neith; and among the Hindus Pûshan is described as both his sister's lover and his mother's husband. When after long darkness a mysterious Twilight slowly advanced, followed by the Dawn with ever-increasing rapidity, the Aryan said, 'Prajâpati loves his own daughter Ushas and forces her,' or 'Indra seduces Ahalyâ the Night,' or forms a union with his mother Dahanâ.[3] To the same class Sarah also seems to belong, as she is not only wife but also sister of Abram. Reuben marries Bilhah, his mother, or more correctly his father's wife. Reuben is a figure homogeneous to Jacob, and therefore belongs to the night, as we discover most certainly from the circumstance that in the battle of the 'Possessors of arrows' against Joseph he is on the side of the latter and tries to save him, while Judah, a solar man, proposes to sell Joseph (Gen.

[1] Plutarchi *Fragmenta et Spuria*, ed. Fr. Dübner, in F. Didot's Collection, Paris 1855, p. 83.

[2] *Lettres assyriologiques et épigraphiques*, Paris 1872, II. fifth letter.

[3] Müller, *History of Sanskrit Literature*, p. 530; *Chips*, &c., II. 163 *et seq.*; Fiske, *Myths*, p. 113.

XXXVII. 21, 26). In a myth such sympathy indicates that the subject and object of it are at all events not hostile figures: we have already seen this in the relations between Isaac and Esau and between Rebekah and Jacob. However, Reuben here seems not to be the night in general, but the twilight which forms the beginning and the end of the night, if we attach weight to the fact that Reuben is Jacob's son. Though unimportant and not even necessary for the appreciation of the myth, this is very probable. The Sun is the mother of the Twilight, for the twilight proceeds from the sun. So when at the end of the night the morning-darkness gives way to the sun or dawn and disappears in them, Reuben and Bilhah are united. Whatever part the twilight may play here, it is at least clear that this myth speaks of the union of Night with its mother Day: when Night gives place to Day, from whose womb it was born but yesterday, then the myth says 'Reuben is marrying his mother.'

§ 14. But before we continue the chapter on love and sexual union, the materials of which are mainly drawn from the history of Jacob's family, it is desirable to insert some remarks on the mythological significance of that family. Our mythological observation leads to the following result. From its first commencement the myth speaks of *twelve children* of Jacob, i.e. of the dark night-sky. These children, on whose names the myth lays no stress, can hardly be anything else than the shining troop which has its home in the night-sky—the Moon and the Eleven Stars (comp. Gen. XXXVII. 9, achad 'âsâr kôkhâbhîm). These are Jacob's children, though in a different sense from that in which Isaac is the son of Abraham, or Joseph the son of Rachel. In these latter instances the conception of a parental and filial relation was the result of the impression produced upon the creators of myths by constant succession; in the case of Jacob's sons it is only meant that the eleven stars and the moon together form the Family of the

Night-sky. This conception having once been grasped, there was nothing to hinder creators of myths from speaking of a son of Jacob who did not belong to that Family. And if there were a myth which said that Jacob fought with his son, as is said of Abraham, then we could not seek such a son in the family of stars which fills Jacob's house. It is a general rule which must never be lost out of sight in the investigation of myths, that mythology does not present a *system*, whose separate elements are comprehensive results, or abstractions from *continuous* observation of nature. What is told in the myth expresses how each *single* observation affects the mind of man. Hence the various modes in which the myth speaks of a phenomenon; viewing it from various positions, it constantly changes the names, and recognises different relations. Whoever finds contradictions in all this must not turn against the interpreter and reconstructor of the myth, but against the mind of man itself which created myths: his dispute lies with the latter, not with the method of mythological science.

Jacob's twelve sons, who are mentioned by name in the document in Genesis, can hardly have had their separate existence acknowledged at so early an age as that of the myth which comprised them under the general name of the twelve sons of the starry sky. Fathers of tribes with twelve or thirteen children (even in the numeration of Jacob's children this uncertainty of number occurs) are frequently met with in Biblical genealogies, e.g. Joktan, Nahor, and Ishmael. The same tendency towards the number twelve is encountered in genealogies in other parts of the world. In the Ojibwa legend Getube has twelve children, of whom the eldest is called Mujekewis, and the youngest, who obtains great power and successfully repels the evil spirits, Wa-jeeg-e-wa-kon-ay.[1] At a later time, when a harmonising of the legendary matter, not

[1] Schoolcraft, *Historical and Statistical Information respecting the History, Condition and Prospects of the Indian Tribes*, 1851, II. 136.

from a set purpose, but from the acknowledged tendency of the human mind to bridge over contradictions, was going on, then a desire was felt to know the names of the twelve sons. When mythic consciousness and the stage when the mind was self-impelled to mythic conception were long passed, and the real meaning of names connected by mythology with certain deeds was no longer known, twelve such names, most of which had no longer any meaning, were taken at random and called Jacob's twelve sons. Thus were obtained twelve names to answer the general proposition, 'The Twelve form the Family of Jacob.' Among these names there are true sons of Jacob, i.e. some who are declared by the myth itself to be so: here the genealogical narrator employed data derived from the myth. Next, there are some among them whom the myth treats not as sons of Jacob but as sons of his wives. For we must not forget that when Joseph is said to be son of Rachel, the myth does not trouble itself to ask who the father was. The conception that 'the Rain is the son of the Cloud,' which is expounded in the mythic description of Joseph's birth, is not the result of any consideration of the names of the two parents who gave life to him; but the myth-former, seeing the cloud heavy with rain and observing the rain dripping from its lap, combined these two impressions and said, 'The Cloud has borne the Rain.' The later genealogical story could then easily find a father for the children of Zilpah, Rachel and others, in him whom the myth introduces as husband of those female figures.

Other Hebrew tribes have names totally free from any mythical character, and ethnographical (Judah) or geographical in nature. The last especially must of course have originated after the conquest of Canaan, since they are connected with geographical peculiarities of that land. One of these is Ephraim, whose name we shall see in the Fourth Section of the Eighth Chapter to be derived from the name of the town Ephrathah; another is Benjamin.

The name Bin-yâmîn is associated with the division of the land, and signifies *Son of the right side.* The tribe was probably so called by the leading tribe of Judah, on whose right side Benjamin was his next neighbour.[1] Yet myths have attached themselves even to these geographical and ethnographical names, as they have to many historical ones. Concerning some no mythical features have been preserved, which is most to be regretted in the case of Gad. This name occurs in a later age with a religious signification (Is. LXV. 11), and would doubtless yield much instruction if a fuller myth gave us insight into its original meaning and connexion. Gad is commonly held to be the so-called Star of Fortune (Jupiter); but it is difficult to determine whether Gad's sons, when they were called his sons, were put into connexion with the Star. If they were, we should have a case analogous to the Arabic appellation 'Daughters of the star al-Ṭârik' (see above, p. 57). As some Arabian tribes call themselves 'Sons of the Rain' (benû mâ al-samâ), &c. so the Hebrew tribes, at the time when the myth still lived in the understanding of all, took names from the mythical figures, one calling itself 'Sons of the Longhaired,' another 'Sons of the Multiplier' &c. I think I cannot be wrong in assuming this nomenclature of the tribes to be older than the assignation of names to each of Jacob's twelve sons. When the names of tribes had long been in existence, they were brought forward to serve as names for Jacob's sons; and thus they laid the foundation of the genealogical tradition which traces the people of Israel to its first father Jacob, and thence goes back to his father and to Abraham.[2]

---

[1] See Geiger, *Jüd. Zeitschrift für Wissenschaft und Leben*, vol. VIII. p. 285. Breslau 1869.

[2] Kuenen (in his *Religion of Israel*, I. 111 in the translation) expresses the opinion that only the degree of mutual relationship between the fathers of tribes was a later idea: that, e.g. the less noble tribes were called sons of Jacob's slave-girls, and those that were bound together by closer fraternal feelings were regarded as sons of the same mother. Compare now also Zunz, *Gesammelte Schriften*, Berlin 1875, I. 268.

But the mythical matter transmitted to us concerning the twelve who are introduced as the sons of Jacob, independently of what we have already discussed, is very little. Some names resist any reasonable etymology, or at least any etymology consonant with the character of mythical appellations. Still, even from these scanty materials we can pick out some single points that seem worthy of preservation as relics of the old Hebrew mythology. If the investigation of this subject is to be successfully pushed further than I can pretend to do in this treatise, the accurate enquirer will have especially to adduce the forty-ninth chapter of Genesis, known as 'Jacob's Blessing,' from which I have already borrowed materials. In this ancient piece I am convinced that many fragments of *hymns* are contained which originally had for their subject those mythical figures to which in their present form as *blessings* they refer. We have in this fragment a sort of Hebrew Veda before our eyes.

Those figures among Jacob's sons, of whom I venture to treat,[1] so far as there are means available have a solar character, with the exception of those which we have already recognised to be figures of the sky of night and clouds, and of one other figure (Levi) in which we shall discover something antagonistic to solarism. Zebhûlûn was seen even by Gesenius to mean the *Round, Globular*. Though we cannot find any analogous expression as a name for the sun, it must be acknowledged to be a very natural one. I believe that Zebhûlûn designates the sun at the end of its course when its red ball appears on the horizon of the sea. Anyone who has had the opportunity

[1] There still remain some names whose etymological explanation is difficult, as Re'ûbhên and Shim'ôn. Yissâsekhâr (Issachar) translated literally might be 'the Day-labourer,' certainly a fitting designation for the Sun, expressing how he does his day's work, like a day-labourer. Yet I cannot look upon that as a mythical description, because it would be an unpardonable anachronism to suppose that that primeval age when myths were created would speak of day-labourers, especially after the fashion in which the idea is expressed by the word Yissâ-sekhâr, 'he takes up his *wages*.'

of admiring a sunset at the sea-side, will understand why people living there should call the setting sun *globular*; for its true globular form is especially perceptible and striking in such localities. That the name Zebhûlûn owes its origin to such considerations is evident from the language of the Hymn to Zebulun: 'he rests at the edge of the sea' (lechôph yammîm yishkôn, Gen. XLIX. 13); and this verse (especially in yishkôn) further confirms what was said on p. 116. Naphtâlî (from the root *ptl*, 'to twine, twist,' whence pâthîl 'thread'), is 'he of the plaited locks of hair.' The Hymn calls him 'a hind let loose' (ayyâlâ shelûchâ, ver. 21), which is decisive for the solar meaning of Naphtâlî with the locks of hair. For the Semites call the Dawn a *hind*—the Hebrews ayyeleth hash-shachar 'the Hind of the Dawn' (Ps. XXII. 1), the Arabs al-ġazâlâ.[1] Even the Talmûd seeks and finds the reason for the identification of the Dawn with a Hind;[2] and another ancient Jewish-Arabic philologist, Moses ben Ezra, in his book on Poetry, also recognised the connexion of this appellation in Hebrew and in Arabic.[3] Accordingly, we must think of a solar interpretation when we read that among the furniture of the ancient Ka'bâ at Mekka, besides various idols, there were *golden Gazelles*, which were carried off and buried by the Jurhumites, but found again by 'Abd-al-Muṭṭalib in the well Zemzem.[4] The mythical description of the rising sun as a hind or gazelle is explained by the animal's horns; for the myth which regards the

[1] Which according to al-Damîrî, *Ḥayât al-ḥaywân*, Bûlâķ 1274, II. 219, is used only of the rising sun; we can say ṭala'at al-ġazâlâ 'the gazelle rises,' but not ġarabat 'he sets.' Abû Sa'îd al-Rustamî the poet (in Behâ al-Dîn al-'Âmilî, *Keshkûl*, p. 164. 13) carries out the mythological figure still further, using the verb naṭaḥa 'to butt,' said of horned beasts. Describing a fine building, he says tanâṭaḥa ķarna-sh-shamsi min sharafâtihi, that 'as to splendour it butts in rivalry with the sun'—as if the palace and the sun were knocking their horns together.

[2] *Babyl. Tract. Yômâ*, fol. 29. a: 'As the hind's horns branch out to every side, so also the light of dawn spreads out to all sides.'

[3] *Journal asiatique*, 1861, II. 437.

[4] Caussin de Perceval, *Essai sur l'histoire des Arabes avant l'Islamisme*, I. 260.

Sun's rays sometimes as arrows, sometimes as locks of hair, also treats them sometimes as horns. For this reason the Hebrew language has only one word to denote 'horn' and 'ray of light,' viz., ḳeren; and for the same reason Moses, who received many features of the solar myth, as Steinthal has pertinently proved in his treatise on the Story of Prometheus,[1] was imagined provided with horns, i.e., with beaming countenance (Ex. XXXIV. 29, 30, 35), a symbol which sacred art has preserved only too faithfully. In the Edda the point of the horn of Heimdall (the sun) is fixed in Niflheim (abode of cloud), i.e. the rays of the sun come forth out of darkness. The glyptic representation of the Assyrian god Bêl in the Louvre is adorned with a tiara surrounded by a row of ox-horns. In the Accadian mythology the name of the goddess Ninka-si, 'the Lady of the horned face,' as Lenormant translates it, has undoubtedly a solar character.[2] The same is the case with the Egyptian Isis: Τὸ γὰρ τῆς Ἴσιος ἄγαλμα ἐὸν γυναικήϊον βούκερων ἐστι κατάπερ Ἕλληνες τὴν Ἰοῦν γράφουσι, says Herodotus (II. 41). Lucian, the frivolous scoffer at everything religious, expresses his surprise to Zeus why he is represented with ram's horns;[3] to which he makes Zeus reply by referring to a mystery into which the uninitiated cannot penetrate.[4] In a word, Naphtali of the long locks, Naphtali the swift hind, is certainly identical with the 'Hind of the Dawn.'

Whether the name Yehûdâ (Judah) belongs to mythology, or was an early ethnical name before tradition introduced it as that of a Patriarch, is difficult to determine. If the name Yehûdâ could be referred to an etymon which

---

[1] Given in the Appendix to this work.

[2] Lenormant, *La Magie chez les Chaldèens*, Paris 1874, p. 140. In the decadence of magic, however, the horns, which are connected with magic, are used even outside the cycle of solar gods; e.g. 'On voit Bin la tête surmontée de la tiare royale armée de cornes de taureau, les épaules munies de quatre grandes ailes, etc.,' *ibid.* p. 50. Here the horns are for butting, not to symbolise rays. However, in this particular case of Bin the mythical meaning is not very clear. As he is sometimes called 'the southern sun over 'Elâm,' *ibid.* p. 121, the horns in the passage quoted may have something to do with his solar character.

[3] *Deorum Concilium*, 10.

[4] See Herodotus, II. 42, IV. 181.

exhibited a solar signification, we should decide for the former alternative, on account of the solar characteristics which are attached to the name. The most plausible etymological explanation would be 'the Splendid,' or (on account of the feminine termination â, added to the passive participle with an abstract force) 'Splendour.' But if the second alternative be correct, and the name Yehûdâ had from the first only an ethnographical force, then, as in the case of other names not belonging to primeval myths, we must suppose that the solar myths, in company with which we find these historical names, were attached to them in later times.

It is a true solar legend[1] that Judah forms a sexual connexion with Tamar. The latter name denotes 'Fruit;' and the myth of her union with Judah expresses the fact that the autumn-sun pours its rays over the fruits of the trees and fields. Thus the Hebrew agriculturist may have said at harvest-time, when the hot rays of the sun rapidly ripened the fruits: and he may at such a time, especially with reference to the vintage, have addressed to the autumn sun 'Yehûdâ' the hymn which is contained in the so-called *Jacob's Blessing* for Judah (Gen. XLIX. 11-13):

He binds to the vine his foal,
To the wine-tree his ass's young one.
He washes in wine his clothes,
And in blood of the vine his covering.
Reddish is his eye from wine,
And white his teeth from milk.

This is a truly mythic picture of the Sun, pairing at vintage-time with the Vine. The red eyes and white teeth need no further discussion after what has been said in § 11 of this chapter. But a few words are needed in explanation of what is said of the ass and foal. It is

[1] We will not claim any importance for the fact that in Sanchuniathon's account of the sacrifice of Isaac the name Jeûd is given instead of Isaac; consequently if Jeûd be identical with the Hebrew Jehûdâ, the fact that Jeûd is here equivalent to Isaac would prove the solar character of Jehûdâ.

sufficient to point to the fact that the reddish-brown ass is one of the animals used in the old mythology to designate the sun.[1] The point of resemblance must be sought in the *reddish* colour; and hence in the Semitic languages the ass is called the *Red* (Hebrew chamôr, 'ass'; Arabic aḥmar, 'red').[2] It is probably in consequence of the solar significance of the ass, that Shechem's father is named 'the Ass' (Hamor; and in Arabic 'Ass' is a very frequent personal name),[3] and Issachar is described as a bony ass. Therefore to say, as is said in our hymn, that the foal and the colt are bound to the vine is equivalent to saying that 'the Sun forms a connexion with the Vine;' it is only a different view of the myth of the connexion of Judah with Tamar. This connexion of the Sun and the Fruit, which is the fundamental thought of the myth of Judah and Tamar, was developed with the aid of other elements into the later form found in the story in Gen. XXXVIII. The same myth was also attached to figures of the historical age in the legend of Amnon and Tamar (2 Sam. XIII. 1–20). David's son Amnon loves his sister Tamar; and keeping her near him to wait upon him under the pretence of being ill, takes the opportunity to ravish her. Here the myth of the love of the Sun for the Fruit has been transferred to Amnon, a perfect unmythical personage. But Tamar is here quite the same as the personage whose connexion with Judah is described in Genesis; although in the legend of Amnon and Tamar it is Amnon who pursues Tamar, whereas in that of Judah and Tamar the

---

[1] Angelo de Gubernatis, in his *Zoological Mythology*, is peculiarly indefinite on the mythological significance of this animal; compare Pleyte, *La Religion des Pré-Israelites*, Leyden 1865, p. 151, where much useful information will be found on the worship of the Ass.

[2] See Gesenius, *Thesaurus*, pp. 494 and 1163.

[3] On the Arabic proper name *Ḥimâr*, Yâḳût, II. 362, may be consulted; cf. Ibn Dureyd, *Kitâb al-ishtiḳâḳ*, p. 4. The Arabic proper name Misḥal is also connected with the Ass; it alludes to the screeching of the wild-ass; see *Tebrîzî's Scholia to the Ḥamâsâ*, p. 200 penult. Compare *al-Meydânî*, II. 98: akfar min Ḥimâr.

intriguer and seducer is Tamar. When people in ancient times perceived the fruit of the tree gradually change its colour till the autumn-sun shone on it, after which it fell down ripe, they saw in this a love-affair between the Sun and Fruit, which ended with their union. We have here, therefore, to do with that phrase of mythology in which men, as agriculturists, but still standing on the myth-creating stage of intellectual life, speak of vegetation and its causes in terms which later, at the religious stage, will give rise to dualistic religious ideas. Different from the Iranian religious dualism, which sets up two mutually hostile powers, this dualism will put side by side two factors of the course of vegetation (see above, p. 15). This kind of dualism is met with very frequently in the Semitic—especially North and Middle Semitic—religions. Indeed, were we to investigate closely the legends and love-stories which fill the history of the Arabic nation and tribes before Islâm, we should probably discover mythological matter turned into history, which would possess great similarity with the legend of Judah and Tamar. We will select here one only of these stories, which has preserved transparently enough its mythical character. On the mountains Ṣafâ and Marwâ, which still play a part in the pilgrimage to Mekka, there formerly stood two idols named Isâf and Nâ'ilâ, who were said to have been two persons of Jurhum who having committed improprieties in the Ka'bâ were turned into stone in punishment for desecration of the holy place[1]—which, be it incidentally observed, is no rare offence in modern times. It need scarcely be observed that this conformation of the story is due to a distinct Mohammedan tendency imparted to it, and that

[1] *Ḳazwînî*, ed. Wüstenfeld, I. 77, II. 166. I must also just refer to the story of Muṭ'im, as told in Yâḳût, IV. 565, and mention that Muṭ'im 'he who gives food' is likewise the name of an ancient Arabian idol. Even Krehl, in his work on the *Preislamite Religion of the Arabs*, p. 61, attempted to explain mythologically the story of Isâf and Nâ'ilâ, interpreting the latter name as 'she who kisses.'

the interpreter of the myth has to regard only the germ of the story—the sexual union of Nâ'ilâ with Isâf. Now the mere translation of these words give us to understand the meaning of the myth. Isâf means *solum sterile, unfruitful ground*, and Nâ'ilâ, *she who presents* (a *nomen agentis* from nâla 'to present'). No deep acquaintance with Arabic literature is necessary to convince one that the latter name may be simply an epithet of the Rain, which the Arabs can as readily call the Giver as they compare a liberal giver with the rain (compare geshem nedâbhôth, Ps. LXVIII. 10 [9]). Thus the liberal Rain unites with the unfruitful Ground and encourages vegetation. Out of this, as out of most unions of this sort, sexual licence was evolved at a later time.

The names of Judah's sons, Perez and Zerah,[1] are solar: the latter denoting 'the Shining one,' who comes into the world with a red thread on his hand, and the former 'he who breaks forth.' This name is founded on the same idea as is present in the German *Tagesanbruch*,[2] the Hungarian *Hajnalhasadás*, i.e. 'the breaking through of the dawn'[3] (exactly the same as Perez), the Arabic, fajar (especially infajar al-ṣubḥ or infajar al-fatak̤ 'erupit aurora').[4] The dawn breaks through, or rather tears asunder, the veil of darkness and breaks forth out of it.

After this survey of the solar figures found among Jacob's sons, we will conclude this section with the consideration of another mythical name belonging to the class of designations of Jacob's sons which is connected with the dark sky of clouds and night. This is *Levi*. If we contemplate this name unbiassed by the etymological explanation of it given in the Bible (from lâvâ 'to cleave

---

[1] Pharez and Zarah in the English Bible, derived through the LXX. from the pausal forms Pâreṣ and Zârach.—Tr.

[2] And English *Daybreak*.—Tr.

[3] From Hajnal 'dawn,' and hasadás, abstract substantive from root hasad 'to split, tear open.'—Tr.

[4] Abû Nuwâs says of the dawn, maftûk̤-ul-adîmi, *Yâk̤ut*, III. 697. 22.

to'), I think we shall not be inclined to doubt that Lêvî bears the same relation to the serpent's name livyâthân, as another serpent's name nâchâsh bears to the enlarged form nechushtân, which is given as the name of the brazen serpent broken in pieces by King Hezekiah (2 Kings XVIII. 4). The name certainly does not denote 'brazen;' for an image is more naturally named from the object it represents than from the matter of which it is made. And the form livyâthân necessarily presupposes a simpler form, from which it could be derived by the addition of the termination âthân (or only ân, if we suppose the original word to have passed through the feminine form livyat), as nechushtân necessitates the preexistence of the simpler nâchâsh. If we have in English a word *earthly*, then, even if no word *earth* actually existed at the time in the language, we could with perfect justice assert *a priori* that the word *earth* must have once existed, in order to make the formation of *earthly* possible. Similarly the existence of the form livyâthân justifies the assumption of a simple noun-form, as the basis of that derivative enlarged by suffixes.

Now fortunately this simple form is preserved to us in the name Lêvî, and we may therefore unhesitatingly affirm that Levi means 'Serpent.' Mythology speaks of a serpent that devours the sun, of a Storm-Serpent, which the Sun assails with his rays; they are the serpents, dragons and monsters with whom the Solar heroes of the Aryan mythology wage their contests, which Herakles even in his cradle crushes and afterwards overpowers at Lerna and Nemea; the same, which sometimes, on the other hand, keep their ground and come forth victorious from the battle with the Sun, when the Sun, repulsed by a boisterous Storm, is forced to abandon the celestial battle-field.

A serpent on the way,
An adder on the path,
That bites the horse's heels,
So that the rider falls backwards,

(Gen. XLIX. 17), they are called in the Hebrew hymn of the battle of the Rain-serpent with the Sun-horse.[1] It is this same serpent that bears a 'fiery flying serpent' (sârâph me'ôphêph, Is. XIV. 29), i.e. the Lightning; that in common with the lightning is called the 'Flying Serpent' (nâchâsh bârîach, Is. XXVII. 1), for whose conqueror the Sun, the monotheistic ideas of later times substituted Jahveh 'who with his might lashes the sea, and who with his intelligence pierces the monster (Rahab); by whose breath the heaven becomes bright, whose hand has stabbed the *flying serpent'* (Job XXVI. 12, 13). The hissing of this flying Serpent is said in an American myth to be the Thunder; and the Lightning is called by the Algonquins an immense serpent, which God spat out.[2] The Rain itself is regarded in mythology as a serpent; the columns of water which fall in a serpentine course to the earth are called the 'Crooked Serpent' (nâchâsh 'aḳallâthôn). The flying Lightning, the crooked Serpent (both livyâthân), and the great Monster in the sea, which tries to devour the Sun when he sinks into the sea in the evening, are assailed by the Sun, and the monotheistic prophet transfers the attack upon them to Jahveh (Is. XXVII. 1; compare Ps. LXXVI. 4 [3]). It is to be noted that, in speaking of night and storms, even the later poetry uses the expression that they 'bite, wound,' because the Serpent of darkness and tempest bites and hurts the Sun. 'I said, Surely the darkness will bite me (yeshûphênî), and the night [will bite] the light near me' (Ps. CXXXIX. 11); and so of the storm (Job IX. 17). Everywhere here the verb is used which is employed in Gen. III. 15 to denote that the serpent wounds the heel of the man. In

[1] This hymn is applied to Dan, to whom it is quite unsuitable, as Dan has a solar character. We are tempted to conjecture that it originally referred to a non-solar figure, perhaps actually to Levi, whose name is synonymous with nâchâsh 'serpent.' This is the more probable, because no separate section of Jacob's Blessing is devoted to this son, and in the only words relating to him he is coupled with Simeon.

[2] See *Zeitsch. für Völkerpsychologie &c.*, 1871, VII. 307.

these passages of poetry, therefore, we find an echo of the myth which declares that the Serpent of the storm, when victorious, bites, wounds, or even swallows down the hero of the Sun. We encounter the Rain described still more clearly as a serpent in the sacred literature of the Parsees, in the first chapter of the Vendidâd, verse 2, where it is said that Ahuramazdao created Airyana-vaêjô to be the best of all lands, whilst in opposition to his act the Deadly Aegrô mainyus created the 'flowing serpent' (azhim raoidhitem) and the snow. Professor Haug was the discoverer of this explanation of the *azhim raoidhitem*;[1] nevertheless he translates it 'a powerful serpent,' as he thinks that the word 'flowing' can be only understood of the ejection of the venom, or of the writer's remembrance of a warm spring which may have existed in the land Airyana-vaêjô. It is a very obvious conjecture that the *flowing* serpent means the Rain; the more so because it is mentioned in conjunction with Snow.[2] The last shoots of this mythological conception are discovered in the system of the Ophites, in which the serpent represents a *moist substance*.[3]

Levi (with Simeon, whose etymological value is no longer determinable), is introduced in the Hebrew myth (Gen. XXXIV.) as the slayer of Chamôr 'the Ass' and Shekem (see above, p. 125). Of the same two brothers it is said in the fragments of hymns already quoted, sometimes that 'for their amusement they destroyed the bull' (XLIX. 6)—the horned solar animal whose horns (rays) the storm-serpents eradicate ('iḳḳerû). It is at the same time perfectly clear in this interpretation that no difficulty at all resides in what is always troubling the expounders of these passages—in the fact, namely, that these brothers

---

[1] The first chapter of the *Vendidâd* translated and explained, in Bunsen's *Egypt's Place* &c. III. 494 *et seq.*

[2] As raoidhitem may also signify 'running' (root rudh = to flow and to run), a 'running snake,' literally the same as nâchâsh bârîach, might be meant.

[3] Möller, *Kosmogonie*, p. 193.

are said in the hymn (or Blessing) to have killed a bull (shôr), whilst no mention is made in the narrative of any such act.

§ 15. In the Biblical story of the family of Jacob we have met with a few of those myths of Love which the Aryan mythology developed in such variety and richness. One of the best known myths of this kind is the story of Oedipus and Jokaste. The king of Thebes received a sad oracle, declaring that he would be exposed to serious danger from a son who would be born to him by his wife Jokaste. He therefore exposed Oedipus, his new-born son; and the latter, having been marvellously saved from death and educated at Corinth, travelled to Thebes when grown to manhood, but killed his father on the way. Arrived at Thebes, he delivered the city from the terror of the Sphinx, and was proclaimed king, after which he married his mother Jokaste. When he received information of the two horrible crimes that he had unconsciously committed, the murder of his father and the incest with his mother, in despair he put out his own eyes and came to a tragic end. Everyone knows this celebrated Hellenic story, which in the Oedipus-Tragedy was worked out powerfully in its ethical bearings so as to excite the emotions and touch the heart.

Oedipus kills his father, marries his mother, and dies, a blind and worn-out old man. The hero of the Sun murders the father who begot him—the Darkness; he shares his bed with his mother—the Evening-glow, from whose womb (in the character of the Morning-glow) he had been born; he dies *blind*—the Sun sets. We have seen above that the setting sun loses the bright light of its eyes.[1]

What a universal act of the human mind, and how

---

[1] Max Müller, *Chips* &c., II. 164; Fiske, *Myths* &c., p. 113. On the blinding, see p. 109 *et seq.*

little affected by ethnological distinctions, the production of myths is, and what agreement is consequently discovered in the direction taken by this myth-formation among the most dissimilar peoples and races of the earth, will be most strikingly brought home to us by the discovery that this very myth of marriage with a mother occurs among the Hebrews just as much as among the Aryans. We have already seen that Reuben marries his father's wife Bilhah. We observe that in the Hebrew myth the hero of Darkness occupies the central position, whereas in the Hellenic it is the Solar hero who shares his mother's bed. But while the myth of Reuben and Bilhah is only mentioned quite shortly in the Old Testament, there is another myth which has grown into a long story in the Biblical narrative—that of Lot's daughters. But before we pass to this, I wish to call attention to a concurrence which I believe has never yet been noticed, but which may excite to further meditations. The whole story of Oedipus, quite in the form in which we find it among the Hellenes, occurs also as an *Arabic tradition*, without change except in the persons. One of the many Nimrods which the Arabic legend seized upon (six Namâridâ 'Nimrods' are commonly reckoned),[1] son of Kena'an and Salchâ, is the Oedipus of the Arabic story. In consequence of an intimidating prophecy, he is exposed by his parents, that he may die and not be a source of danger to his father. But he is miraculously suckled by a tigress (whence his name Nimrûd is said to be derived, for nimr is 'tiger' in Arabic), and subsequently brought up by the inhabitants of a neighbouring village. When grown to manhood he contrives to bring together a great army, and becomes involved in a war against his father Kena'an, whom he slays in the decisive battle. He marches in triumph into his capital, and marries his mother Salchâ. Thus the outlines of the Oedipus-story have been attached to the solar

[1] See al-Damîrî, *Ḥayât al-heyvân*, I. 70.

hero of the Semites, Nimrod the hunter. The story is told at full length in the long introduction to the Romance of 'Antar (I. 13 *seq.*), and I leave it to readers competent to judge, to decide between two possibilities. Either the Arabs borrowed from the Greeks and simply took to themselves this version of the Oedipus-story; in this case the remarkable fact of such a transference would provoke a searching enquiry into the middle points between Greece and Arabia, which made it possible to borrow mythology, and also into the extent and nature of such borrowings. Or we may assume that the story was independently and gradually formed by the Arabs without external influence, so that the elements of the Arabian as of the Greek story reach back, to the primeval age of the creation of myths, and that with the Arabs also it was originally a myth of the war of the Sun with the Night, and his union with the Evening-glow. The latter view is favoured by the circumstance that in the Arabian version the story of Oedipus putting out his eyes is wanting—a feature which would certainly have been taken if the Arabian story were only a borrowed one. But the above-mentioned questions ought to be investigated before any decision in favour of one of these possibilities can be arrived at, however inclined I may be from personal feeling towards the assumption of borrowing.[1]

The story of Lot and his daughters as told in Genesis in one of the Biblical passages most notorious for its obscenity; let us see, however, what appears to have been its original meaning. When the aged Lôṭ and his family were saved from the Divine judgment on Sodom and Gomorrha, which converted those cities into a sea of bitumen, he left his wife behind him, converted into a pillar of salt, at a point of the coast of the Dead Sea, which is still shown to credulous travellers, and lived in a cave with his two unmarried daughters. These made

[1] See Excursus L.

their old father drunk in two successive nights, and perpetrated with him an act of unchastity which is to us almost unmentionable (Gen. XIX. 30–38). But the science of Mythology has often saved the honour and moral worth of primitive humanity by restoring the original mythological meaning of many a story; and so here we shall be able to prove that the Lôṭ-story, in the form in which we have received it, is only the tradition of the myth of the Sun and the Night, the understanding of which was lost in a later unmythological generation. Through the clever succession of ideas suggested by the solar theory, the science of Mythology on Aryan ground at one blow caused the ideal heights of Olympus to tower in their original purity above the endless chain of scandalous acts which mythology misunderstood attributed to the immoral inhabitants of the mountain of the Gods; and the method which guides us in these studies will aim at the same result on the domain of Hebrew mythology.

We return to Lôṭ. This name (formed from the root lûṭ 'to cover') denotes 'he who covers.' 'Darkness *covers* the earth, and clouds the nations' (Is. LX. 2). 'For I did not shrink before the Darkness, when thick darkness *covered* (everything) before my face' (Job XXIII. 17). 'Thou hast pressed us down to the dwelling-place of the sea-monsters, and *covered* us *over* with deep shadow' (Ps. XLIV. 20 [19]). The Semitic designations of darkness are mostly formed from roots denoting 'to cover': so e.g. 'alâṭâ in Hebrew, 'ishâ in Arabic;[1] and the most prominent Semitic word for Night, layil, laylâ, etymologically means only something that *covers*.[2] In Aryan languages also, the Sanskrit Varuṇa and the Greek *οὔρανος*, which denote the overclouded sky, are formed from the root *var* 'to cover,' in opposition to the bright day-sky, Mitra.[3] Keeping on Semitic ground, we find in Arabic copious illustrations of this

[1] Connected with ġashiya 'to veil.'

[2] See Gesenius, *Thesaurus*, p. 749.

[3] Max Müller, *Chips* &c., II. 68.

conception. The words ġashiya, damasa, ġatha, saja, etc. (compare ġardaḳat al-leyl, ta'aṭṭam al-leyl), combine the notions of Darkness and Covering-up. Accordingly the coming on of night is expressed by janna al-ẓalâm, literally 'the darkness has covered up' (e.g. Romance of 'Antar, V. 80. 3); and for the simple words 'of an evening,' or 'at night,' the Arabic expression is taḥt al-leyl 'under the night,'[1] or fuller taḥt astâr al-ẓalâm 'under the veils of the night' ('Antar, X. 70, 1); and the Night is above the day, 'aleyhâ.'[2] The Night is a garment or carpet spread out over the Day. 'It is he,' it is said in the Ḳorân (Sûr. XXV. v. 49), 'who made the Night as a garment or veil for you.' 'We have made the Night as a clothing' (Sûr. LXXVIII. v. 10).[3] The Arabic poet Abû-l-'Alâ al-Ma'arrî uses the most palpable expression for this conception of the darkness of night. Describing his swift camels, on which he traversed great distances at Night, he says (I. 131. v. 4) 'in their swift course they tore the mantle of night,' i.e. they ran so quickly that they unrolled the garment which covers the surface of the earth at night. On this conception of the nature of Night I believe a peculiar expression in the Arabic language to be based. In the old classical Arabic, nights which either have no moonshine at all, or have none at the beginning and only a little quite at the end, are called layâlin dur'un; and when a verb is required, adra'a al-shahr is said. This adra'a is unquestionably a denominative verb from dir', which signifies a 'breast-plate,' or a breast-covering of any sort. The Arabic expressions just quoted are founded on the idea that the breast (al-ṣadr), i.e. the upper side, the first part, of such nights is dark, covered by a garment, so that only the uncovered lower side or end is visible. In the cosmogony of Mo-

---

[1] Arsala achâhu Sheybûb taḥt al-leyl, '*Antar*, VI. 102. 9.

[2] *Ḥamâsâ*, p. 566. v. 2.

[3] Libâsan, compare Sûr. VII. v. 52; XIII. v. 3; yuġshî-l-leyla-n-nahâra.

hammedan legends, Night is represented as a *curtain*, ḥijâb.[1]

The clothing of the Night is of black colour, leylâ ḥâlikat al-jilbâb, as is said in Arabic,[2] (compare μελάμπεπλος νύξ[3]), a 'pitchy mantle,' as Shakespeare says,

> The day begins to break, and night is fled
> Whose pitchy mantle overveil'd the earth.
> *King Henry VI.* First Part, II. 2.[4]

And in Arabic poetry also we meet with night described as a 'pitchy mantle.' For the poet Abû-l-Shibl says in a remarkable elegy[5]:

> Shamsun ka'anna-ẓ-ẓalâma albasahâ * thauban min-az-zifti au min-al-ḳîrî
> A sun, as if darkness had clothed him
> With a garment of resin or pitch.

The darker the Night, the thicker is the black cloak with which it is provided. Even modern languages have expressions like *thick* darkness (Hungarian *vastag setétség*); in Arabic a very dark night is called a night with a heavy covering, leyl murjahinn.[6]

The name Lôṭ, accordingly, signifies, like the Hellenic female forms Kalyke, Kalypso (from καλύπτω), the *Covering Night*. It is very significant of the Night that the Greek figures are represented as weaving clothes for the Thunderer:[7] they weave the cloak with which they cover over the world when they spread darkness over it. Surely

---

[1] In *Yâḳût*, I. 24. 2.

[2] Ḥarîrî, p. 162, 2nd ed.; compare the Commentary, in which particular stress is laid on the act of covering up: li'annahu yuġaṭṭî mâ fîhî. Compare al-Meydânî, II. 112. 23: al-leyl yuwârî ḥaḍanan.

[3] Eur. *Ion*, v. 1150; it is also called ποικίλον ἔνδυμα ἔχουσα, and in Aeschylus, *Prom.* v. 24 ποικιλείμων νύξ, from the gay robe of stars.

[4] Compare *King Richard II.*, III. 2. 'The cloak of night being pluck'd from off their backs.'

[5] *Kitâb al-aġânî*, III. 28. 24.

[6] I quote also a passage from the Uigur language: 'The creation tore its black shirt,' *i.e.* the day has dawned: Vámbéry, *Kudatku Bilik*, p. 218; compare p. 70, 'I have put off the cloak of darkness;' p. 219, 'The daughter of the west spreads out her carpet.'

[7] Max Müller, *Chips*, &c., II. 83. Schwartz, *Ursprung d. Mythologie*, p. 245.

no one will after all this doubt that the name Lot is a designation of the Covering Night. Should this be still doubtful, perhaps the following fact from the domain of the Arabic language may bring conviction. Everyone knows the Arabic word kâfir, at least in its usual meaning of Infidel. Even the earlier Arabian philologians, who, notwithstanding frequent amusing whims and hobbies, often exhibit a fine feeling and very sober judgment as to etymology, said that this word received the meaning Infidel only through the dogmatism of Islâm, that it originally denoted the *Coverer*, and that the transition of meaning was founded on the idea that the Infidel covers up God's omnipotence. Similarly in Hebrew the verb kâphar is said of God when he *forgives* (i.e. covers) the sins of men; in Arabic ġafar.[1] In Arabic the Unthankful is also a kâfir, a 'Coverer,' since he *covers* the blessings he has received: and in late Hebrew he is similarly termed kephûy ṭôbhâ 'one who covers up the good.'[2] In short, the kâfir is properly the Coverer. Now the darkness of night is called kâfir by old Arabian poets. We have already (in the Tenth Section of this chapter, p. 134), quoted for another purpose the verse of the poet of the tribe Mâzin: 'The Shining one stretches his right hand towards him who *covers up*,' where the latter is kâfir, the Night. The celebrated poet Lebîd, too, says in his prize-poem (Mu'allaḳâ, v. 65): 'Until the stars stretch out their hands towards the kâfir, and the weaknesses of the boundaries are covered over by their darkness,'

Ḥatta iḏâ alḳat yadan fî kâfirin * wa'ajanna 'aurâti-th-thuġûri ẓalâmuhâ.

And the poet al-Ḥumeyd says, 'They (the camels) go to water before the breaking of the morning, whilst the son of splendour (the dawn) is still *hiding in the cloak*,' i.e. before it is yet day,

Fawaradat ḳabla-nbilâji-l-fajri * wabnu ḏukâ'a *kâminun fî kafri*.[3]

---

[1] al-Beyḍâwî's Commentary on the *Ḳorân*, I. 19. 21 *et seq.* Abû-l-Baḳâ, *Kulliât*, p. 305.

[2] See Excursus G.

[3] Ibn al-Sikkît, p. 322.

A very witty use of the application of the epithet *kâfir* to the Night is make by the poet Behâ al-Dîn Zuheyr. He would fain prolong the duration of the night, which passes away far too soon for all the pleasures that it brings him in the midst of a merry circle, and so he says: 'To me is due from thee the reward of a Champion of the Faith [in battle against the infidels], if it is true that Night is a *kâfir* (an infidel, properly a 'coverer'),

Lî fîka ajru mujâhidin * in ṣaḥḥa anna-l-leyla kâfir.[1]

As the Darkness of night is what covers over and hides, so on the other hand the Dawn, or the Sun in general, is that which uncovers and discloses. We have met with this conception before in the case of Noah (p. 131). In Arabic safara or asfara is said of the *uncovering* of any concealed object, and the same words are used of the breaking-forth of the morning sun. There is no doubt that this latter usage is deduced from the signification 'to reveal, uncover;' the instance quoted in the lexicons, 'The night which removes the cover from the morning of the Friday' (yusfir 'an), i.e. which precedes Friday, shews by the preposition *'an* that 'to uncover' is the fundamental signification. Thus the Arabic etymologists whom I mentioned in a former work[2] may be right in a certain sense in tracing back most of the derivations of the root safar to this sense. But in Egyptian and in the Arabic

[1] *The Poetical Works* of Behâ-ed-Dîn Zoheir of Egypt. By E. H. Palmer, Cambridge 1876, I. 108. 7. It is impossible to quote this edition without an expression of admiration for the perfection to which Arabic typography has been brought in England in this magnificent Oriental work, the production of which redounds to the imperishable credit of the University of Cambridge. It may be pronounced one of the most beautiful Oriental books that have ever been printed in Europe; and the learning of the editor worthily rivals the technical get-up of the creations of the soul of one of the most tasteful poets of Islâm, the study of which will contribute not a little to save the honour of the poetry of the Arabs. Here first we make the acquaintance of a poet who gives us something better than monotonous descriptions of camels and deserts, and may even be regarded as superior in charm to al-Mutanabbî.

[2] *Beiträge zur Geschichte der Sprachgelehrsamkeit bei den Arabern*, no. I, in the *Sitzungsberichte der kais. Akademie der Wissenschaften*, Vienna 1871, Jan. p. 222 *et seq.*; or in the reprint p. 18 *et seq.*

of the desert the word al-sufrâ denotes the Sunset, the reason of which is by no means clear.[1] No doubt can now be entertained that our Lot is identical with his namesake the Arabic Kâfir the Concealer, the Covering Night. Now we can consider the myth. 'The daughters of Night form a sexual connexion with their father.' When the evening glow, which is a daughter of the Night (for, as we have seen, the myth identifies the morning and the evening glow), unites with the shades of night and becomes darker and dimmer, so as at length to lose itself in the night, the myth-creators said, 'The daughters of Lot, the Coverer, are going to bed with their father.' From the bright, lively character, which the myth must have attributed to the Glow in comparison with the dark, heavy Night, they would naturally regard the aged Lot as the victim of an intrigue of his lustful daughters; whereas in the Aryan myth it is Prajâpati who uses force against his daughter Ushas. The names of Lot's daughters are not given in the Old Testament; but we know them from another source. The Arabic legend in which the story of Lot, communicated by Jews, likewise finds a place, tells us their names. It is scarcely credible that these are pure inventions of the Arabs; it is much more probable that they received them, as they did much else, from the traditions of the Jews. But the Jewish tradition itself has lost the names, as it has lost much else that was not written down. In the Arabic statements, however, there occur such various versions of the names as to show clearly that they are instances of the corruption by which foreign names are constantly ruined beyond recognition in Arabic manuscripts. One version gives Rayya as the name of the elder, Zoġar as that of the younger (see Yâķût, II. 933. 22, 934. 16); and from the latter a town is said to be named, which is mentioned in some ancient Arabic poems. Ibn Badrûn (ed. Dozy,

1 Wallin's articles in the *Zeitsch. d. D. M. G.*, 1851, V. 17; but see above p. 43.

p. 8) calls them something like Rasha and Ra'ûsha (or Ra'vasha?); Mas'ûdî (*Prairies d'or*, II. 193) Zaha and Ra'va. Among these differing forms, every one of which is probably based on a corrupt text, Zaha is the only one that may confirm the solar character of Lot's daughters in the myth. But I think the myth of Lot is clear enough in itself to dispense with any such problematic confirmation.

If the conception of Kerûbhîm (Cherubim) is native to the Hebrews, and not borrowed at a later period from foreign parts—a question which must be regarded as still an open one—then we may find here also the *Coverer* (compare kerûbh has-sôkhêkh 'the cherub that covereth,' Ezek. XXVIII. 14), the covering cloud; and hence may be derived the function of concealing and covering which was given to the cherubim in the later ceremonial, as also their connexion with the curtains.[1] 'Jahveh rides on the Cherub,' says one of the later religious poets (2 Sam. XXII. 11), 'and appears on the wings of the wind; he makes darkness round about him, tents, collections of water, gloomy clouds.' Here the dark overclouded rainy sky is described; and when Jahveh sends rain over the earth, he rides on the Cherub, and 'mists are beneath his feet,' and the dust which he turns up while riding, forms the shechâḳîm (properly the dust), the overcast sky. Jahveh is described in other passages also as riding on clouds (Is. XIX. 1). Accordingly kerûbh would originally denote the covering cloud, and whatever is connected with the Cherubim in later theological conceptions would be a transformation of ancient mythological ideas.[2] Now the root *krb* is used in Himyarite inscriptions in titles of kings, as Mukrib Saba, or Tobba' kerîb, i.e. as Von Kremer explains them,[3] '*Protector* of Saba,' '*Protecting*

---

[1] See Vatke, *Biblische Theologie*, p. 327, and Gesenius, *Thesaurus*, p. 711, where importance is attached to this.

[2] The conception of Cherubim penetrated even into Mohammedan regions, e.g. Ḥâfiẓ, ed. Rosenzweig, III. 526 *penult.*, chalweti kerrûbiân 'âlem-i-ḳuds.

[3] *Ueber die südarabische Sage*, Leipzig 1866, p. 27.

Tobbaʿ.' This is easily explained by the fact that in the Semitic languages words signifying 'to protect' are often derived from the fundamental idea of 'covering.' 'The Cherubim spread forth their wings' (1 Kings VIII. 7), i.e. they cover. To spread out the wings (kenâphayîm) over some one is in Biblical language the usual expression for the protection which is allotted to him. In Arabic the same word (kanaf) signifies not only a bird's wing, but also concealment, shade (compare Ps. XCI. 1–4), and protection.[1]

The opinion that the Cherubim were borrowed from foreign parts is accordingly much less probable than that which maintains that they originated with the Hebrews;[2] and the latter view receives further support from the fact that the Cherubim can be easily fitted without any violence into the system of Hebrew mythology. It is again supported by the connexion between Cherubim and Seraphim, the latter of which are originally Hebrew. This connexion agrees moreover with the results of our mythological researches. As Kerûbh as 'Coverer' belongs to the dark cloudy sky, so the Serâphîm must be a mythological conception pertaining to the same series, if we adopt the correct interpretation of them as *Dragons*,[3] and remember the mythological meaning of serpents and dragons (*supra*, p. 27, 184, *sq.*). It then becomes probable that the theological significance of Cherubim and Seraphim belongs to the remains of the very earliest form of Hebrew religion, and approximates to the facts of which I shall speak at Chapter VI. § 5, pp. 224, 5.

[1] See Gesenius, *Thesaurus*, p. 697.
[2] See Dillmann, in Schenkel's *Bibellexikon*, I. 511.
[3] *Ibid.*, V. 284.

CHAPTER VI.

THE MYTH OF CIVILISATION AND THE FIRST SHAPING OF HEBREW RELIGION.

§ 1. In close connexion with that stage of development of the myth-producing faculty which is inaugurated by the beginnings of agricultural life, is found a natural consequence of the solar myth among agriculturists—the Myth of Civilisation.

We have seen that the advance in civilisation from the nomad life to the agricultural stage is accompanied by that inversion of the direction of the myth which puts the Sun in the foreground and allows a tone favourable to him to prevail in it, whereas at the nomad stage it was the night-sky and the phenomena of nature connected with it that engrossed the sympathy of the formers of myths. Now here we again encounter a remarkable phenomenon. No intricate psychological foundation or historical demonstration is required to prove that our own stage of civilisation—and not ours alone—is intellectually qualified to compare itself either with a lower stage through which it has long since passed, or with a higher which is now only beginning to be aimed at by our best spirits,—so as to estimate its value from the point of view given us by our social system. For let two different stages of civilisation, social systems or conditions be brought before any man's observation so that he notes their essential difference, and the perception of this difference will awaken an impulse to measure them off against one another and form a judgment on the perfection of the one and the insufficiency of the other. And not only does the man who has reached the higher stage feel himself impelled to compare his new condition with that of those who remain behind on the less perfect stage already passed by him; but also those who stand on the lower stage, but are acquainted with the altered mode of life of others, contemplate the advanced stage and set off its value against that of the stage on which they still stand. Thus we have seen above that huntsmen and fishermen have their ideas about agricultural life. Still he who has reached the higher stage will be more generally impelled to such meditations than those who still stand on the lower. When the question has arisen in his mind, it must finally culminate in the enquiry, What was the origin or who was the author of the great advance which procures for him such advantages over one who stands lower? It is true, the agriculturist is not always conscious that his stage of civilisation is the result of an *advance* at all; for in many nations there exists no consciousness that any less perfect stage preceded that of the agriculturist. But this consciousness is not a necessary condition of the raising of the question; the mere observation of the *difference* between the two stages of civilisation suffices to prompt it. And it will come more and more into the foreground when the gradual progress within the limits of the agricultural stage has advanced so far as to develop the social consequences of the new state in all their fulness. Social order and laws are non-existent for the nomad, who has not yet formed for himself any permanent social system. At his stage they are not merely superfluous, but even in a certain sense inconceivable. The wranglings, the objects of which are chiefly wells and pastures, are settled and composed, not by laws and rights established once for all, but by strength of arm, or between disputants of peaceful disposition by separation: 'And their arose strife between the herdsmen of Abram's cattle and the herdsmen of Lot's cattle. And Abram said to Lot, Let there be no strife, I pray thee, between me and thee, between my herdsmen and thy herdsmen; for we are brethren. Is not the whole land before thee? Separate thyself, I pray thee, from me: if thou goest to the left hand, then I will go to the right; or if thou goest to the right hand, then I will go to the left' (Gen. XIII. 7–9).[1] And on occasion of a dispute about a well, Abimelech said to Isaac: 'Go from us; for thou art much mightier than we. And Isaac departed thence, and pitched his tent in the valley of Gerar, and dwelt there' (Gen. XXVI. 16, 17). Arts, manufactures and other occupations are inconceivable at this stage; for the wants of the nomad are so limited that the conditions of his existence are satisfied by his tents, herds, and pasture-ground.

The answer which the agriculturist gives to the question about the origin of the arts and manufactures, of social order and law, all of them products of agricultural life, is what we call the Myth of Civilisation. This Myth of Civilisation, which we encounter among the most various nations, refers the authorship of the advanced and refined state of civilisation to the *Solar figures* of the myth, which, to the prejudice of the figures of the dark sky, are brought into the foreground by the human mind on its advance to agriculture. It is therefore a spontaneous act of the human mind that is made the cause of a series of phenomena, of which it is itself really the result.

The Greek and Roman mythology abounds with data verifying the Solar character of the stories of the origin of civilisation and morals. Arts and manufactures are constantly brought into connexion with mythical names which are recognised by comparative philologists as designations of the Sun. Not only the musician but the

---

[1] An interesting Arabic parallel to this occurs in Yâķût, III. 496. Thaķîf and al-Nacha', who with their herds were migrating together, determine to separate: 'So one said to the other: Assuredly this land can never support both me and thee. If thou goest to the west, then I will go to the east; and if I go to the west, then do thou go to the east. Then said Thaķîf, Well, I will choose the west. Then said al-Nacha', Then I go to the east.' *Ibid.*, p. 498, occurs an equally curious arrangement between two nomad tribes.

smith of Olympus are Solar figures; so also the first navigator and founder of cities. The right understanding of Mythology was long hindered by the so-called Euhemeristic system, which assumed that the gods of mythology, and especially of the Greek and Roman mythology (for scarcely any others were sufficiently known to be considered), were only great benefactors of humanity, who after their death were rewarded by divine honours; and this system has been maintained till the present day. The Myth of Civilisation consequently had to be fitted into the frame of this convenient system. It was said that posterity had from mere *Gratitude* raised the inventor of the arts to the throne of deity. Petrarch says, 'We know that the founders of some arts after their death were rewarded by divine honours, rather from grateful than from pious feelings . . . Thus Apollo was made a god through his lyre, Apollo and Aesculapius through medicine, Saturn, Liber and Ceres through agriculture, Vulcan through his smithy.'[1] This mode of regarding the subject was not only upheld from Euhemerus down to Petrarch, but exerted its influence on the interpretation of the ancient stories even to our own times.

However, the consideration of the store of legends of humanity in general, as far as they are brought under our ken, collected and analysed according to their historical and psychological truths, teaches us that the founder of all the order and morality which result from the more civilised agricultural life is, in the language of the old stories, the Sun. The so-called Myths of Civilisation are always put into connexion with the Sun, or with some of the copious synonyms which mythology gives to the Sun.

---

[1] *De vita solit.* I. 10. Inventores artium quarundam post mortem divinitatis honore cultos audivimus, grate quidem potius quam pie. Nulla enim est pietas hominis qua Deus offenditur, sed erga memoriam de humano genere bene meritorum inconsulta gratitudo mortalium, humanis honoribus non contenta, usque ad sacrilegas processit ineptias. Hinc Apollinem cithara, hinc eundem ipsum atque Aesculapium medicina, Saturnum, Liberumque et Cererem agricultura, Vulcanum fabrica deos fecit.

These myths must exist in every nation which has won its upward way from nomadism to agriculture, or from tribal life to society. As soon as the agriculturist began to use the ploughshare, he could not but observe the difference between his life and that of the nomad, who fixed his tent-plugs in the earth at a different place from day to day, moving from pasture to pasture, whilst he himself had the control of permanent dwellings, protected by definite unalterable laws, and lived a life of regularity, yet full of enjoyment and variety, strongly contrasting with the Bedawî's monotonous independence. Then, when the source of this difference was sought, all the advance was attributed to the Sun, as the author and encourager of agriculture and inventor of the more refined arts and enjoyments of life. Moreover, the connexion which the Myth of Civilisation establishes between the Founder of cities and the Wolf, as e.g. between Romulus and a she-wolf who suckled him, has lately been explained by Prof. Sepp through the signification given to the wolf in the solar myth—with perfect justice, though perhaps going rather too far in the elaboration of details.[1] Like Apollo, Osiris also is *γεωργίας εὑρετὴς*, *Μουσῶν μαθητής*, 'Inventor of agriculture and teacher of the arts;'[2] and in this point the myths of nations quite distinct in race agree. A few examples taken from sources wide apart will make this clear.

One of the Solar heroes of the Persian myth of civilisation is Jemshîd, whose character can scarcely be doubtful to the mythologist, after the consentaneous characteristics with which the epic poet Firdôsî and the historian Mirchond fill up the description of his life.[3] His very name indicates clearly enough a solar signification; and

---

[1] *Ausland*, 1875, p. 219 *et seq.*

[2] Sir G. Wilkinson on *Herodotus*, II. 79, note 5.

[3] Even Herder compared together these two sources of information on the story of Jemshîd, in the Appendix to vol. I. of his writings on Philosophy and History.

to this must be added the fact that he combines many characteristics of the solar supporters of the Myth of Civilisation. He first gives to Irân, till then savage, the benefits of civilisation. He is the first builder of cities, the inventor of the fine arts, especially of music, navigation (which belongs especially to the solar myth, as we have seen), and, as Mirchond explains at length, of the cultivation of the vine—an Iranian Noah. He divides the whole nation into four classes: Scribes, Warriors, Agriculturists, and Artists. Thus it is he who puts an end to the nomadic tribal life. In this breaking up into castes not the slightest trace is discoverable of any notice of pastoral life; on the contrary, in the story of Jemshîd as worked out by the later narrator, probably in close agreement with the still living mythical tradition, especial weight is laid on *Agriculture.* The solar chronology is also due to Jemshîd. Mirchond says: 'As often as the Chosrev of the stars, the Sun, took away the royal robe of rays from the fish's tail and threw it on the neck of the ram, Jemshîd appointed an assemblage of the great and noble at the foot of the throne. He instituted all the appliances of pleasure, and spread out the carpet of joy, and called the day Neurûz.' The Prometheus-side of the Jemshîd-story is surprising. The Persian hero of civilisation, like the Greek, is chastised and hurled down by God for his presumption; his fall is occasioned by *Zohak*, who conquers him, *from whose shoulders dragons grow up* (the dragons of the Storm and the Night). After a fall of a hundred years he appears on the coast of the Chinese sea. The Sun is devoured by the monster waiting for him at the bottom of the sea, but afterwards rises again out of the sea, like Jonah in the Hebrew myth.

If now we turn from ancient Irân to the American tribes, we find the Myth of Civilisation take the same direction. There also the origin of morals, law and order is attributed to the Sun. I quote one of the numerous myths of civilisation from J. G. Müller, who deserves great credit for his work on American religions, which makes American mythology known in Germany. It is the myth of civilisation belonging to the Muyscas, inhabitants of the Terra Firma in the plain of Bogotà, who tell as follows of the commencement of civilisation among themselves: 'In the earliest times, before the moon was, the high plain of Cundinamarca was closed in and the pass of Tequendama not yet opened. Then the Muyscas people were savage, without agriculture, without religion, without morals, without civil rule. Then there appeared *a bearded old man who came from the East*, who had three names, Bochica, Nenequetheba, and Zuhé, and was represented as having three heads. He taught the savages to wear clothes, to till the land, to worship the gods, to form states. His wife had also three names, Huythaca, Chia, Yubecayguaya. She was dazzlingly beautiful, but so malicious that she plotted to destroy all her husband's salutary undertakings. And she actually succeeded by secret magic arts, in causing the Funzha (now Rio Bogotà), the river of the country, to rise to such a height as to overwhelm the whole high plain with flood. Only a minority of the inhabitants were able to escape to the summits of the mountains. But then the just wrath of Bochica was kindled; he drove the wicked woman off the earth for ever, and changed her into the Moon. Since then there has been a moon. And to get rid of the troubles of the earth, Bochica made an opening in the wall of rock, and allowed the water to run off by the majestic waterfall of Tequendama, 570 feet high. When the land was thus dried, the people that were left were called to civilisation, and the Solar worship was introduced, with a sacerdotal order, periodical feasts, sacrifices and pilgrimages. At the head of the state Bochica set a secular and a sacerdotal chief, settled the chronology, and after a life of two thousand years at length withdrew, bearing the name Idacanzas.' [1]

[1] *Geschichte der Amerikanischen Urreligionen*, Basle 1867, p. 423. This myth of civilisation is given also by Tylor, *Primitive Culture*, I. 318 *et seq.*

So much for the Myth of Civilisation. It is certainly wrong to try to find matter of history in these stories of civilisation, and, with Markham, Rivero, and Tschudi, to see in Bochica and the other bearded heroes of civilisation belonging to American mythology 'missionaries of the worship of Brahma, of Buddha, and probably of other sects.'[1] My readers will surely perceive the perverseness of such a proceeding. J. G. Müller himself recognised the Sun in Bochica, the civiliser of the Muyscas; but he did not find out all the mythological relations which determine his solar character. The most important of these is the circumstance that Bochica is 'a bearded old man, who came from the East.' Here then, as in other American myths, the Sun's rays are regarded as the long white beard of the old man of the sun, in the same sense in which they appear elsewhere under the form of *locks* of hair (see supra, p. 137). And as in Egyptian the rising sun has a different name from the setting, and the same distinction of name is stamped upon the Hebrew myth also (Leah and Delilah on the one side, and Dinah, Zilpah, Asher, etc. on the other), so in the myth of the Muyscas the three names of the Sun refer to his various positions at rising, noon, and setting, which probably played a part in the ancient myth of the Muyscas. The corresponding three faces of the Sun express the same idea that produced the myth of the two of Janus (see p. 137); with the difference that the American myth notices three phases of the Sun, and the Roman only two. The Sun is opposed by the Moon, the sky of day is engaged in an everlasting war with the sky of night. The circumstance that the moon causes the flood exactly agrees with the American conception, which connects water with the moon.[2] The moon also is provided with three names in our American myth, and these three

[1] See Dr. Robert Hartmann, *Die Nigritier: eine anthropologisch-ethnologische Monographie*, Berlin 1876, Thl. I. p. 176.

[2] Brinton, *Myths of the New World*, New York 1868, p. 130.

names have the same signification as the three of the Sun, i.e. the conception that each of the varying phases of the moon is itself an independent object. Dr. Anton Henne, a Swiss mythologist, first considered the meaning of the three visible forms of the moon (as contrasted with the four astronomical phases) in mythology, especially German, and cited some parallels from classical mythology.[1] Now although this feature of the triple form of the moon is undoubtedly expressed in many myths, among others in the American one under review, yet Henne-Am-Rhyn seems to go rather too far, in referring the many variations of the German story of the three spinning girls and so forth to this mythical idea. Many of these variants bear the undeniable impress of a mythical description of the setting Sun's or the Night's battle with the bright Sun of day; especially that in which one of the Sisters is quite white, the second half-white and half-black, and the third *blind.* Unquestionably the Sun of day is the quite white sister; the Sun shortly before setting the half-white and half-black; and the Night the blind one (see supra, pp. 109–10).[2] The solar character of the princess Märthöll (no. 586, Henne-Am-Rhyn), *who is as beautiful as the sun, and can only weep golden tears* (see Excursus E), can escape no one.

The moon-lit sky of night appears in the Myth of Civilisation averse to all the blessings which the Sun grants to the agriculturist. In this character it appears frequently, especially in the American mythology;[3] whereas in the Oriental the connexion between the moon and water suggests the idea that the moon produces

---

[1] Otto Henne-Am-Rhyn, *Die deutsche Volkssage, etc.*, p. 281 *et seq.*

[2] *Ibid.*, p. 285, the author says on the other hand: 'The blind sister is of course always the invisible new moon, the half-black and half-white the half moon, the quite white the full moon.'

[3] See Hellwald, *Ueber Gynäkokratie im alten Amerika,* third art. in *Ausland* for 1871, no. 44, p. 1158. In the language of the Algonkins the ideas Night, Death, Cold, Sleep, Water, and Moon are expressed by one and the same word.

fertility and freshness in the soil (see supra, p. 160). In the Voguls' story of civilisation, a small fragment of which, from the collections made by Antony Reguly, is contained in the important work of the Hungarian Academician Paul Hunfalvy on the 'Country and People of the Voguls,' [1] *Kulyater* is the builder of the first city. The solar character of Kulyater cannot be doubted, if the following portion of the Vogul story be taken into consideration: 'He dwelt in a house locked with seven iron locks. Tarom was angry with him, and seized him by one foot, and he fell into the heart of the foaming sea.' This is the sunset. The reason why the Founder of Cities (whom the Vogul reckons among the evil spirits and regards as the originator of death [2]) appears here in an unfavourable light is the same as that which we shall discover for the tone of dislike which the Hebrew story adopts towards the agriculturist Cain. Till they became Russified the Voguls remained prevailingly a hunting people, and their myths did not rise to the elevation of the view of the world possessed by agriculturists. The Vogul story of the Creation [3] reflects exactly the ideas of a hunting and fishing people; it speaks only of the chase and of catching fish.

Now we have seen that the Myth of Civilisation expresses the same idea in nations of the most different races. Even in the Japanese myths of civilisation, published by the learned Japanese Dira Kittao,[4] a thoroughly solar character is evident. Manufactures and arts, social order and law are always attributed to the Sun as author, not only by Aryans, but even by the still unclassified

[1] *A vogul föld és nép, Reguly Antal hagyományaiból*, Pest 1864, p. 139.

[2] In the Hottentot story it is the Hare (on his solar significance see supra p. 118) that is represented as the origin of death, in opposition to the Moon (Waitz, *Anthropologie der Naturvölker*, II. 342).

[3] See the article 'Une genèse vogule,' in Ujfalvy's *Revue de Philologie*, Paris 1874, livr. 1. The original text and a Hungarian translation are given by P. Hunfalvy in his lately quoted work, p. 119–134.

[4] *Ausland*, 1875, p. 951 *et seqq.*

American tribes. If the knowledge of the American languages were more advanced than it is in our time, and if the mutual relations of those languages were not 'exceedingly perplexing, for the same reason as those presented by the Polynesian and African dialects, and in a yet higher degree,'[1] we might gain some understanding of the origin of the many proper names which we encounter in the above myth and in the other members of the copious American mythology; and this would lead us to a far more accurate idea of their origin and life than is possible with petrified myths of civilisation. Nevertheless, before we part from them, we will still just notice that the introduction of social laws, political constitutions and religious institutions such as are ascribed in the Muyscas' myth to the Sun himself as an old man, is frequently attributed to the *sons of the Sun.* There is no need to prove that in such stories the sons of the Sun are identical with their father the Sun. So e.g. Orpheus, son of the Sun, calls into cities men living a savage life in the forests, and urges them to a more civilised life. Again, the Indian legislator Vaivasuta is son of the Sun. And, not to neglect again here American mythology, the two sons of the Sun, Manco Copac and Mama Oello, are brought forward in the Peruvian myth of civilisation as teachers of civilisation. There is no reason whatever to identify Mama Oello with the Moon, as J. G. Müller does;[2] and it would even run counter to the very nature of the Myth of Civilisation. For, as we saw in the previously cited American myth, the Moon is the very power that paralyses the work of the Sun in introducing civilisation and law. To this place belongs also the idea, which is found in many nations, that the founders of their legislation and religion were born from virgins, made to conceive by the Sun's rays.[3] This

[1] Whitney, *Language and the Study of Language*, London 1867, p. 346.

[2] *Amerikanische Urreligionen*, p. 305.

[3] Waitz, l.c. I. 464 *note.* Among other examples Waitz quotes this: 'In Mexico Huitzlipochtli, was born of a woman who took to her bosom a feather-

element of the solar myth still operates in a story told by the Persian poet Ferîd al-Dîn 'Aṭṭâr, who introduces a maiden's dream as follows: 'Then the Christian maiden saw in a dream that a Sun *fell into her lap*, opened his mouth and said, etc.[1]'

§ 2. The sources of the ancient Hebrew mythology have preserved no less considerable remains of the Hebrew people's myth of civilisation; and it moves in the same direction as has been indicated above. The invention of arts and manufactures, morals, law, and social order, is attributed to Solar figures. Especially noteworthy in this connexion is the fourth chapter of Genesis, where mention is made of the beginning of the building of cities, and of the invention of agricultural and of musical instruments; and the ninth chapter of the same book, in which the first commencement of social order secured by law is related. All this is attached to names of which other mythical features besides those concerning civilisation are recorded, features which point to their solar significance, and serve to fill up the story of the civilising activity of their bearers.

But the Solar figures are authors not of manufactures and civil order only: the human race itself has the Sun as its author, through whose children mankind is propagated. The name Âdâm, Abû-l-bashar 'father of all flesh,' as the Arabs call him, is, as is obvious at a glance, a solar appellation 'the Red'; etymologically the same word as Edôm. When the Hebrew story of civilisation derives the human race from the Red one, it does the

---

ball is a solar designation, is not easily determined.' In connexion with it I will only mention that Shakspeare in one passage calls the sun a 'burning crest.'

> But even this night,—whose black contagious breath
> Already smokes about the burning crest
> Of the old, feeble, and day-wearied sun,—
> Even this ill night, your breathing shall expire.—*King John*, V. 4.

[1] Manṭiḳ al-ṭeyr, ed. Garcin de Tassy, p. 58 (from a communication of my friend Dr. W. Bacher).

same as the Greeks when they call the mother of mankind Pyrrha 'the Red.'[1] The Hebrews call the mother of mankind Chawwâ (Eve) 'the mother of all that lives' (Gen. III. 29),[2] i.e, 'the Circulating' (in Arabic ḥawa V), a name of the Sun, the feminine synonym of Zebhûlûn 'the Round;' a very ancient appellation of the Sun, the traces of which we meet also in the Vedas, where (Rig-veda, I. 174. 5) the Sun is called a Wheel, or, as he frequently is in other passages, a Chariot. This is based not only on the conception of the Horses of the Sun drawing his chariot, but on the original conception of this chariot, as consisting of a single wheel or of a cylinder on a sloping plain, as Lazarus Geiger has admirably demonstrated.[3]

It is also to be considered that the mythological genealogy of the Hebrews makes the world to be peopled by the descendants of Cain, children of the Sun, and that a second progenitor of the human race, Noah, is likewise a solar figure. We must here of course disregard the late Seth-genealogy, at the time of the drawing up of which even the minimum of mythical conception necessary to the working-out of the Myth of Civilisation had already vanished. It is not impossible that originally two or even more now forgotten versions of the myth of population existed—one which called the first father of the human race Adam, and another which attached the propagation of mankind to the name Noah, and that then, by the interposition of the story of the Flood which made the whole human race perish, the two versions grew into harmony with one another in the popular mind. But

---

[1] By the Red the Sun is surely unquestionably to be understood, and not, as Max Müller says (*Introduction to the Science of Religion*, p. 64), the Earth.

[2] It should at the same time be noticed that in Arabic, in which, as in Hebrew, men are usually called banû Adam, the expression banû Ḥawwâ'a (sons of Eve) also occurs; *e.g.* in a verse of the Kumeyt (*Aġânî*, XV. 124; wa-cheyru banî Ḥawwâ'a), in a poem of Abû-l-'Alâ al-Ma'arrî, I. 96. 1, of al-Murtaḍî in the *Keshkûl* of al-'Âmilî, p. 169.

[3] *Ursprung der menschlichen Sprache und Vernunft*, II. 42.

in any case it is certain that the Hebrews made Solar figures the ancestors of mankind.

Thus among the Hebrews also it was the Solar myth that answered the question concerning the primeval origin of agricultural civilisation; and thus was completed the picture of what modern interpreters love to call the 'Origins.' It is this side of the formation of legends which maintains its life and productiveness longest among men. For there is always a latent instinct and powerful impulse in the mind of man to cancel all notes of interrogation, and to gain and to give intelligence on the origin of all that surrounds him. We well know how many stories are current in the mouth of the people, stories of comparatively modern origin, which have for their subject the rise of rivers, mountains and institutions. How charming are the Hungarian stories invented to explain the origin of the two great rivers which traverse that beautiful country! and who knows not into what petty details this impulse of the human mind pushes its way? It treats nothing as a matter of course and as sufficiently explained by the mere fact of its existence; it finds everywhere a Why and a How, that must be answered. It not only seeks reasons of existence, and dives into cosmogonies, for the overpowering universe of the world and the grander features of it, mountains and seas; but even what distinguishes one being from another—the ox's horns and the camel's short ears, the lion's mane and the black stripes on the ass's back—it cannot leave unexplained. It is the same noble instinct that created the fables on the origin of things, and that encourages the grand discoveries of the truths of natural history: the instinct that impels us to understand aright all that lies around us.

It may be affirmed that among the Semites this impulse to explain the origins of things maintained its longest existence as a living power productive of stories. Even on the subjects on which the Biblical accounts gave information, men did not rest satisfied with these accounts, but allowed free and unlimited scope to stories.[1] A large part, indeed almost the whole, of the Arabian answers to questions concerning the Origins, is a Postislamic product of popular story. All that the Arabs learned on the subject from tradition or from stories still in process of formation was collected in works entitled Kutub al-awâ'il, or 'Libri Principiorum.' The best known and widest circulated of these, is the Kitâb al-awâ'il, written by Jelâl al-Dîn al-Suyûṭî, a voluminous writer of the tenth Mohammedan century, a part of which was published by Professor Richard Gosche, with an instructive introduction on literary history.[2] In former times it was so extensively circulated in the East that a revised version was also prepared, which was everywhere copied even before the clean copy (tabyîḍ) was made.[3] But several hundred years before al-Suyûṭî, an Andalusian scholar, Tâj al-Dîn b. Ḥammûyâ al-Sarachshî (born A. H. 576) had written a work in eight volumes on the Origins of Things; and I believe that this work, of which the classic historian of the Moors in Spain[4] gives an account, is the most extensive of its kind. In the above-quoted work, Gosche maintains the view that the whole Sêpher tôledôth, which is familiar to us as one of the original elements of which the composite Book of Genesis consists, was mainly concerned with these 'Origins,' and is the Hebrew representative of the copious Awâ'il literature of the Arabs. But we cannot admit this, when we consider that this book of sources, to judge from its known fragments, has rather a genealogical character, and, though containing

[1] See Excursus M.

[2] *Die Kitâb al-awâ'il der Araber*, Halle 1867; congratulatory article on occasion of the meeting of the German Oriental Society at Halle.

[3] I know this work (entitled Muḥâḍarat al-awâ'il wa-musâmarat al-awâchir) from a manuscript of it in the public Viceregal Library at Cairo. In the catalogue of the year 1289, p. 92 *antepenult*, it is erroneously entered with the title Muchtaṣar al-awâ'il wal-awâchir.

[4] al-Makkarî, *Analectes de l'historie et de la littérature des Arabes d'Espagne*, II. 69. The awâ'il are there called uṣûl al-ashyâ.

the myths of civilisation, does not embrace the cosmogony, which is of a decidedly later origin. Therefore, if we must at any price find an analogy in Arabic literature to the Sêpher tôledôth, we ought rather to look to the many works composing the copious genealogical literature of the Arabs, called Kutub al-ansâb.[1]

§ 3. In regard to the Hebrew myths of civilisation we must pay attention to another circumstance; to do which we must again go back to what has been said above on the phases of development of the myths. In determining the amount of mythical matter which was worked out in any period of development of human civilisation, we must not, as was fully explained above, start from the materials and the elements employed in the myths in question, so much as from the direction or tendency of the myth and the general ideas which prevail in it. But yet this view requires some qualification, insofar as the designation of some human occupation is employed in the phraseology of the myth. I mention this with especial reference to the name Ḳayin (Cain), which denotes Smith.[2] It is obvious that this manufacture must have already existed in society before such a name could come to be employed in a myth. But, on the other hand, the myth of the war of the Sun with the Cloud or the Wind cannot have so recent an origin. We must accordingly concede to the Myth of Civilisation an influence upon the form of the mythic matter—an influence which not only produced an alteration in the tendency of the myth, but also introduced new names and figures, which, as is evident from the linguistic meaning of the names themselves, arose at the stage of conscious civilisation. The story of the murder of Abel belongs, no doubt, to the primitive myths which were already formed at the nomadic stage; a solar name

---

1 A general view of this literature can now be obtained from Ibn al-Nedîm's *Fihrist*.

2 The name Yissâ-sekhâr (Issachar) must also fall under our consideration here, if we treat it as a Solar name (Day-labourer). See supra, p. 177.

must have been given to his murderer, just as in the dialectic variant of Hebhel (Abel), namely, Yâbhâl (Jabal), his father Lemekh (Lemech) is named as the murderer. Later, at the stage of the Myth of Civilisation, the murderer of Abel is called Ḳayin (Cain), the smith and inventor of agricultural implements, whose name is indeed also a solar appellation, but one that already belonged to the Myth of Civilisation. The same case occurs in the story of Jacob. Originally, in the nomadic myth, Jacob's hostile brother was called Edôm, the Red, the Sun. For this name the Myth of Civilisation substituted 'Êsâv (if we explain this as the Worker, the Accomplisher; see p. 139);—again a name which is essentially solar, but could arise only with the Myth of Civilisation.

In this wise the Myth of Civilisation, starting from the general ideas of the agriculturist, opened a wider circle of vision in the notions held of the Sun, and with the new enlarged circle created new names for the Sun, which then drove into obscurity some older appellations belonging to the primitive form of the myth.

§ 4. Before we conclude our diagnosis of the Myth of Civilisation, we will cast a momentary glance at the forms in which this group of myths shows itself in other Semitic nations. The founder of civilisation in the Assyrian and Babylonian myth is the Oannes of Berosus. '*During the daytime* Oannes held intercourse with men, taught them sciences and arts, the building of cities and temples, laws and the introduction of the measurement of planes; further, he showed them how to sow and reap: in a word, he instructed them in everything necessary to social life, so that after his time they had nothing new to learn.' In a word, Oannes is the teacher of civilisation and inventor of all art and sciences, all law and order. That this founder of civilisation has a solar character, like similar heroes in all other nations, is shown in the very next words of Berosus: '*But when the Sun set, Oannes fell into the sea, where he used to pass the night.*' Here evidently only the Sun can be meant, who in the evening dips into the sea, and comes forth again in the morning and passes the day on the dry land in the company of men. He is half fish half man, and in this respect identical with the Canaanitish Dâgôn, whose name denotes 'Fish.' Dâgôn also is, with the Assyrians as well as with the Canaanites, the god of fertility of the soil and founder of civilisation. He is 'Inventor of the plough, distributor of grain, protector of the cornfield;' and in Assyria we find him represented with his head covered by a *horned* cap.[1] The combination of the two characters is to be explained, not by supposing that the idea of the god of fertility was connected with that of the rapid propagation of the fish, but by the solar meaning given in mythology to the fish. It must not be overlooked that in this connexion the fish is always spoken of as *rising out of the water*—like the Sun, who, having passed the night in the water, issues forth again in the morning.

We see the same also in the extant Phenician myth of civilisation, which is narrated by the Sanchuniathon of Philo Herennius. Perverted and spoiled as the stories of the Phenicians may have been by the pen of the Greek author, who contemplated Phenician mythology through the medium of the Greek cosmogony, corrupted and Hellenised as the proper names especially are, yet these pieces of information are undoubtedly based on real stories which were current among the Phenicians. It is a pity to lavish on them so much profound thought and symbolising combination as has been done by Bunsen, Movers and many other scholars; but, on the other hand, it is an equal mistake to condemn the entire mass as a useless forgery and declare it unworthy of attention in investigating Phenician antiquity. The real task is

[1] See Duncker, *Geschichte des Alterthums*, 1874, I. 206, 266.

rather to penetrate the bewildering labyrinth of misunderstandings to the simple and original. The confirmation given in the last few years by the cuneiform inscriptions to the *Babylonica*, which are referred to the reports of Berosus, ought to moderate any extreme scepticism on the subject of the Phenician affairs which are quoted from Sanchuniathon, Mochus and others.

The Phenician Cosmogony of Philo Herennius says that Chrysoros, who as the Opener, Navigator, and Smith has already appeared to us (pp. 98–9) to have a Solar character, was the progenitor of Ἄγρος or Ἀγροτής and Ἀγρύηρος, and says of these, 'From them are derived the agriculturists and those who hunt with dogs. These latter are also called Ἀλῆται, or Wanderers to and fro. From them are derived Ἄμυνος and Μάγος, who taught men how to found villages and feed herds.' This is only the Myth of Civilisation of the agriculturist again, which everywhere brings the commencement of agriculture, the foundation of cities and civilisation, into connexion with the Sun. As from Cain is descended Enoch, whose name is attached to the first city in the world, so from Chrysoros, the Phenician Cain, are derived those who first adapted their places of sojourn to the requirements of settled dwellings. In a word, the genealogy only asserts that the Sun occasions the choice of fixed dwellings and consequently of agricultural life. But the fact that the hunting and nomadic life[1] is introduced together with the origin of agriculture, and that the first commencement of the one is put into combination with the founders of the other, occasions some difficulty, which cannot be simply denied and put aside. Now it is certainly possible that the Myth of Civilisation among the Phenicians, in whose neighbourhood alongside of agricultural life nomadic life also was in full force—for their view extended over all Palestine and the valley

[1] Can the Semitic ôhel 'Tent of the Nomads' be concealed in the word Ἀλήτης?

of the Jordan—referred the origin even of the latter mode of life to the Sun, as the founder of all social life. But it is also possible that what Philo asserts on a Phenician authority concerning nomads and hunters is founded on a misunderstanding of the original information. For the sons of Chrysoros, the Sun, were evidently described as hunters and wanderers. Now *Hunter* and *Wanderer* are, as we have seen, attributes of the Sun, who shoots his rays at the monster of the storm, and is 'a fugitive and a vagabond,' engaged in a migration from east to west. Cain is an exile and wanderer, but not a nomad. But through misunderstanding the Solar hunter and wanderer may have been converted into the founder of the hunting and nomadic life. Even Bunsen, though starting from a different point of view and influenced by other considerations, designated this very passage as a perversion of the Phenician account, perpetrated by Philo and perfectly in accord with the system followed by him.[1] The original Phenician account must, no doubt, have been different.

§ 5. Although Cain and Esau cannot possibly have been incorporated with the old Hebrew mythology till the myth of the origin of civilisation was unfolded, yet they retain the mischievous and hostile character which the nomadic myth always assigns to solar figures. This fact illustrates the general observation which I made above (see p. 81) with especial reference to the Hebrews and Arabs—that in many nations the consciousness of an advance in passing on to the agricultural life is never aroused, or only very late, and that they rather regard this advance as retrogression and look back on the nomadic state as a more perfect one. Among the Hebrews, accordingly, the heroes of civilising agriculture, with the exception of Noah, take a position in the myth far less influential than similar heroes in other nations. The sympathetic light in which Noah was regarded is closely

[1] *Egypt's Place in Universal History*, IV. 223.

connected with his position in the story of the Deluge, which was added at a very late period to the Hebrew series of stories.

To understand this fact, however, we must cast another glance at the oldest stage of Hebrew Religion, at which religion had not yet fully shaken itself free from mythology, but was closely united with it, and only beginning to have a separate form. Whatever be the psychological factors that produce the religious tendency in man—an attitude of the soul which can no longer be treated as congenital,—it must be regarded as established and certain that the psychological process of the origin of religion, a process influenced only in its most advanced stages by ethical and esthetic forces, is in the first instance developed out of the older mental activity which resulted in the creation of myths. After the exhaustion of the mental activity that forms myths, which is equivalent to the disappearance both of mythical productiveness and of vivid understanding of myths, men have no longer any consciousness of what may be called the etymology of the myth. Then the mythical figures begin to be individualised; and parallel with this process runs the linguistic phenomenon that polyonymy disappears and all the phases of meaning previously expressed by separate names are combined in one or a few. The various synonyms for Sun, Darkness, etc., which existed in the myth, lose their significance; the different names for these natural phenomena, in each of which one feature or element of them was expressed in language, succumb to one single name, which then comprises in itself all their features and elements. The names Helios and Shemesh take the place of all other designations created in myths for the phenomenon of the Sun. These other designations, e.g. on Hebrew ground Jephthah, Asher, Edom and others, forfeit the signification which they originally had when myths were formed, and instead thereof are individualised. These names become personal names, and the stories of which they are the subjects become events of society. Thus from physical stories arise stories of gods and heroes; thus the nomenclature of the Sun and the Darkness produces a host of names of gods and heroes. For the personages who are thus imagined are powerful celestials, and the forgotten processes of which the myth spoke preserve for some time their heavenly scene of action.

This process of transformation of myths is inevitable, because bound up with the laws of development of the human mind and human speech; at a certain stage of the development of mind and language, the myth must become theology. But the process is gradual, so that the commencing stages of theological development do not break loose at once from the mythical consciousness, and the latter loses its colour gradually before it disappears altogether. A stage of this kind, at which Myth is turning into Religion, is most clearly exhibited by the Myth of Civilisation. Some bit of divine nature or peculiar personality always cleaves to the hero of civilisation; and some such myths actually live long unimpaired after the greater number have been metamorphosed into theology or religion. Thus, for instance, among the Hebrews the origin of religion is to be traced in its germ as far back as the nomadic age. Even at that stage, though of course towards the end of it, we observe the Hebrew myth of the beneficent sky of night and rain turning into religion. For a searching investigation of the religion of the nomadic Hebrews proves the object of their veneration to have been the dark overcast sky, connected (where it is not distinctly declared) with mythical figures of undoubtedly nocturnal character. I must briefly refer to what was indicated above (pp. 72, 73) of the worship of the night-sky and the rain among the Arabs. The religious stage of the nomadic Hebrews is still to be recognised in the reminiscences, transmitted by theocratic historians, of that age, which was to them a forty years' wandering in the desert preceding the conquest of Palestine. To the same stock, as sources for the reconstruction of this religious stage, belong also some accounts contained in the Prophetical books; and they cannot but be considered historically credible—of course in the sense in which such reminiscences must be critically estimated as sources of history. For it is certain that such recollections lived on a very long time in the nations of antiquity, and that, if the special tendency of the reporter be stripped off, they may yield objective matter of history.

The most important datum of this kind is the question of the Prophet of Tekoa, which refers to a great expanse of history—a passage which has spurred many learned men to attempt ingenious interpretations.[1]

> Did ye offer unto me sacrifices and offerings in the desert forty years, O house of Israel? Did ye bear the huts [read Sukkôth] of your king, and Kiyyûn (Chiun) your idol, the star [read kôkhâbh], your god whom ye had made to yourselves? (Amos V. 25, 26.)

It is evident from this important passage that the nomadic Hebrews worshipped their god or gods by huts, and that one among the objects of their worship was a Star, let alone what star Kiyyûn may be, whether identical with the Arabic keyvân, or some other. Thus, so far as we can infer from the Prophet's word, their divine worship was paid to the night-sky. The nomad looks on the night-sky as a pasture where the herdsman (for the mythical figures of the night-sky are mostly regarded by him as herdsmen) lets his cattle feed; and it is easy to conceive that at the theological stage he venerates in huts the mythical figure now converted into a god, ascribing to him the same dwelling which he occupies on high in the sky. The most important feast of the nomadic Hebrews was the Feast of Sukkôth, or Tabernacles, which probably

---

[1] Besides German scholars, Dutch orientalists and historians of religion especially have written very ably on the passage in Amos; the latest of whom, Tiele, in his *Vergelijkende Geschiedenis*, pp. 539 *et seq.*, mentions in a note the most prominent Dutch labours on the subject.

stands in close connexion with these Sukkôth of a god, and at the agricultural stage became a Harvest-feast. But even at that stage the connexion of the feast with nomadic life and the past nomadism of the nation itself, lived long in its memory (see Lev. XXIII. 43). That which they worshipped in the huts was not the Sun,[1] the bright sky of day, but kôkhâbh, a Star, doubtless no particular star, but only the starry heaven in general. For the rain, the most beneficent element to the nomad, was identified with the stars, i.e. with the sky at night. In the view of the ancient Arabs there were also Hyades in the starry heaven; we meet in poetry with the expression marâbî' al-nujûm 'spring rain of the stars' (*Mu'allaḳâ* of Lebîd, v. 4). A familiar phrase in the speech of the nomadic Arabs is 'the stars have brought rain.'[2] Moḥammed forbids the Moslims to express their common idea of the origin of the rain by their usual phrase muṭirnâ binau' kaḏâ 'we have received rain from such and such a star,' though he allows the connexion of the rain with the stars, and only insists on the recognition of Allâh as first cause, while the nau' is the immediate origin.[3] Similarly the Mohammedan Arabs were forbidden to call the rainbow the bow of the Thunder-god Ḳozaḥ.[4] The dew, also, has a connexion with the anwâ' 'stars' (plural of nau'). It is not without interest to find

---

[1] No weight must be attached to the word malkekhem 'your king,' in which many have tried to find a datum for the high antiquity of the worship of Moloch by the Hebrews; for the suffix shows that the word cannot be taken as Môlekh, the name of a god. And the worship of that God appears everywhere as one borrowed from the Canaanites.

[2] *E.g.* in the following fragment of a poem: 'We lived in Chaffân in company with a people, may God give them rain by the constellation of the Fishes (saḳâhum Allâh min al-nau' nau' al-simâkeyn), then may a constellation give them abundant water (farawwâhum nau'), [a constellation] whose shining spreads light abroad' (in Freytag, *Darstellung der arabischen Verskunst*, p. 253).

[3] See Lane in the *Zeitschr. d. D. M. G.*, 1849, III. 97. Krehl, *Vorislamische Religion der Araber*, p. 9.

[4] *Yâḳût*, IV. 85. 19. *Tâj al-'ârûs*, II. 209.

this view in a Jewish-Arabic writer of the middle ages.[1] The worship of the kôkhâbh 'star' by the Hebrew nomads must therefore have a special connexion with the rain. Ancient mankind did not distinguish between the cloudless sky which grows dark at night, and the sky gloomy with clouds and rain by day (see supra, p. 42). He notices the darkness only, not the various times of day or night at which it occurs. Hence a sunless sky in general is treated as bringing rain. To show what connexion he imagined to subsist between the *huts* (sukkôth) and the rainy sky, I will quote a verse of a hymn to Jahveh, attributed to David, and said to have been sung on his deliverance from the power of Saul:

> He made darkness round about him into *huts* (Sukkôth), collections of water, clouds of the sky. (2 Sam. XXII. 12.)

The various reading for the expression chashrath mayim 'collections of water,' which is preserved in Ps. XVIII. 12, where this hymn is given in a somewhat corrupt and less original form, deserves attention nevertheless. The words are cheshekhath mayim 'darkness of water' or 'rain-bringing darkness.'

The more we study the information preserved to us on the religion of the nomadic Hebrews, the stronger is our conviction that it consisted in a veneration of the sky of clouds and rain, and was developed immediately from the elements of the nomadic myth. We read that in the desert God went before the Hebrews *as* a pillar of cloud by day and *as* a pillar of fire by night, and showed them the way (Ex. XIII. 21);[2] that he *as a pillar of cloud* came between the pursued Hebrews and the pursuing Egyptians (Ex. XIV. 19, 20) by night (for the day breaks soon after, Ex. XIV. 24); that he appeared to Aaron and Miriam in the pillar of cloud (Num. XII. 5); that, as the

---

[1] Sa'adia, who translates Job XXXVIII. 28, eglê ṭâl 'store-houses of dew,' by the Arabic anwâ' 'stars,' Gesenius, *Thesaurus*, p. 21.

[2] See Num. XIV. 14, where before the two pillars are mentioned it is only said that the *cloud* stood over them.

later psalmists, preserving the theological phraseology of ancient times, say (Ps. XCIX. 7), he speaks with his Prophet as a pillar of cloud. But what need is there to enumerate all the passages which speak of the God of the wandering Hebrews in connexion with the pillar of cloud, and describe his turning away as the retreat of the cloud, or to show that the cloud was retained in the popular tradition of a later monotheistical age as kebhôd Yahwe 'the glory of Jahveh?'[1] It at least appears from them that the nomadic Hebrews attached their religious veneration to the Cloud; of which one of the latest relics is preserved in the name 'Ananyâ (Ananias), i.e. 'Cloud-God,' and another in the phrase that God 'rides upon a cloud.' Another feature of the nomadic religion is expressed in al-Damîrî's words that 'the ancient Arabs paid divine honours to a white lamb, and when the wolf came and devoured the lamb, they chose another lamb to receive the same honours.'[2] From what was said above (p. 165) with reference to Rachel, it is not difficult to perceive that this white lamb is only a bright cloud like a lamb. This deification of clouds is also found elsewhere. The people of Bonny on the west coast of Africa comprise their idea of the Deity in the name Shûr or the cloudy sky;[3] and if the learned Italian Assyriologist Felix Finzi[4] is right, we find among the chief gods of the Assyrians the Cloud, which looks like a relic of the ancient time, when instead of the solar powers the Assyrians deemed those of the dark sky worthy of their worship. This scholar wishes to explain the Assyrian divine name Anu as etymologically identical with the Hebrew 'Ânân 'cloud' which certainly well suits the two epithets of the deity, 'Lord of Darkness'

---

[1] For Hebraists I note that I take the בּ be in be'ammûd 'ânân as *Beth essentiae*.

[2] *Ḥayât al-ḥaywân*, II. 52.

[3] Bastian, *Geographische und ethnographische Bilder*, p. 169, and some passages in books of African travel quoted by Waitz, *Anthropologie der Naturvölker*, II. 169.

[4] *Ricerche per lo studio dell' antichità assira*, Turin 1872, p. 467.

and 'Gatherer of Shades.'[1] In this case, however, the identity of Anu with the Oannes of Berosus could not be maintained, as the solar character of Oannes is undoubted; but this identification rests on a very slender base, and leads to no better understanding either of Anu or of Oannes.

With the worship of the Clouds is naturally united that of the Rain, which we find deified by many primitive nations. We find this, for instance, in the Akra people or the Gold Coast of West Africa. They express the question 'Will it rain?' by the words 'Will God come?'[2] Among the heathen of the tribe of Baghirmi in Central Africa, with whom Dr. Nachtigall, lately returned from that region, has made us acquainted, the name Deity is identical with the designation of Storm.[3] In the language of the Wamasai in Eastern Africa the feminine noun Aï (with the article Engaï) has the two significations God and Rain.[4] This deification of rain and storm is moreover identical with Serpent-worship, wherever the latter occurs. For the adoration of the Serpent and Dragon is derived from the mythical conception which regarded rain as a 'fluid serpent' (see supra, p. 186); and wherever it is met with at a more advanced stage of civilisation it is a residuum from that stage at which men knew no more beneficent power than the dark overcast sky, the rain, the dragon that opposes the sun Bêl. The Egyptian and Indian theological ideas of the serpent are examples of such residua of the ancient nomadic views. Where a solar worship has grown up, either the old conception of the beneficent serpent continues to exist alongside of the new views, without being understood or harmonised with these, or else the defeat of the Serpent by the victory of

---

[1] Tiele, *Vergelijkende Geschiedenis*, p. 301, however, calls this last epithet 'much too general to draw any conclusion from.'

[2] Lazarus Geiger, *Ursprung und Entwickelung der menschlichen Sprach und Vernunft*, I. 346.

[3] In Petermann's *Geogr. Mittheilungen*, 1874, XX. 330, pt. 9.

[4] K. Andree, *Forschungsreisen etc* II. 362.

the Sun becomes a feature of the new religion, and the Serpent appears as a hostile figure. So, for instance, in Persia and elsewhere. Max Müller actually opposes the very method of Comparative Mythology which he himself introduced and maintained so brilliantly, when he declares 'There is an Aryan, there is a Semitic, there is a Turanian, there is an African serpent, and who but an evolutionist would dare to say that all these conceptions came from one and the same original source, that they are all held together by one traditional chain?'[1] No doubt this single chain of tradition is a perfectly unscientific assumption, but none the less does the same original source serve as origin of serpent-worship everywhere, namely, the old mythical conception; and the varieties of view that we meet are to be classified not according to ethnological races, but by historical stages of civilisation. Certainly we shall at length have to cease seeking a motive for the worship of the Serpent where the symbolical school have persistently sought it even to the most recent times—in the 'Conception of the deep wisdom of the serpent and of the mystic powers which are said to belong to its nature.' The Serpent-worship as a form of religion is a further development of the mythical expressions which describe the rain as a serpent, made when these expressions had become unintelligible; in the same way as the worship of crocodiles, cats, etc., are traced back to a solar myth, the meaning of which had been forgotten.[2] The apparently mutually contradictory significations which are attached to the serpent in the myth and the worship must be traced back, not to opposite views held by different races, but to varying modes of understanding the myth, which might all emanate from the idea of the serpent. How often in the mythology of one and the same people we find the same object employed for the apperception of most different, or even opposite, things!

---

[1] *The Academy*, 1874, p. 548, col. 2.

[2] See Excursus D.

The adoration of the Serpent is also demonstrable of the Hebrews when nomadising in the desert; for only in this sense can the Brazen Serpent be understood, the adoration of which was commenced by the Hebrews of the desert and continued to the latest times (Num. XXI. 9, 2 Kings XVIII. 4). It also deserves notice that that Hebrew tribe which had from the earliest times the care of religious affairs and provided the worship called itself 'Sons of the Serpent,' Benê Lêvî[1] (see supra, p. 183), and that it was these who fell upon their compatriots when on the exodus from Egypt they were about to introduce a solar element into their religion by the adoration of the Golden Calf.[2] It was the Sons of Levi, the priests of the ancient religion of the nomads, who defended conservatism, and would not allow the solar bull-worship to raise its head.[3]

Accordingly, the tribal designation 'Sons of the Serpent' belongs to the long list of such names which are derived from animals.[4] Lubbock and Tylor, especially, have put this species of tribal nomenclature into connexion with the so-called Totemism; but in any case it is natural to assume that the original relation of the animal to the origin of the tribe or nation which claims it as its ancestor is purely mythological.

§ 6. Thus, then, the most ancient religion of the Hebrews in the desert was derived immediately from the myths of the nomads. To complete the above exposition, it is now only needful to refer to the traces of Lunar worship, which were treated in a previous chapter (pp. 158–160).

---

[1] Accordingly this appellation belongs to the same category as those which are noticed above, p. 175. In genealogical notes elsewhere also the Serpent occurs as ancestor; I need only mention the case which stands nearest to our subject in prehistoric Arabia—that of al-Af'a b. al-Af'a, 'the Viper,' head of a branch of the people of Jurhum, Ibn 'Abdûn, p. 71 *et seq.*

[2] On the solar significance of the Bull-worship see Kuenen, *Religion of Israel*, I. 236 *et seq.*

[3] I believe the historical narrative in Ex. XXXII. 26–29 is to be taken in this sense. It is solar worship that is forcing its way into the strictly nomadic religion of the Hebrews, and the Levites are guardians of the nomadic religion.

[4] See Bastian in the *Zeitschr. für Völkerpsychologie*, 1868, V. 153.

Not till after the entrance into Palestine, i.e. after the transition from nomadic wanderings in the desert to a settled agricultural life, does Solar worship appear among the Hebrews, chiefly in the northern part of the land; but even there it is only introduced in imitation of the rites of the neighbouring Canaanitish tribes, which, having been long settled in Palestine as agriculturists, had formed a complete solar ritual. The Hebrews brought no such system into the conquered land; on the contrary, their religion was, as we have seen, of a purely nomadic character, having its centre in the adoration of the dark sky of night. That it was so is evident also from the fact that the solar worship employed by the Egyptians had no attraction for the people of Israel during their residence in that country. Accordingly in this point the Hebrews were radically different from other tribes that had immigrated into Egypt, which are generally comprised under the common name Hyksôs. For in some of these tribes a fully developed solar form of religion, including even the wildest excesses of the service of Moloch, is found to have been adopted even as early as their residence in Egypt.[1]

The objects of the adoration of the nomadic Hebrews were the cloudy sky and the rainy sky.[2] But not only was direct worship addressed to the Cloud and the Rain; their will was also regarded as a revelation of destiny, and consulted. At first any nomad would look to the Cloud and the Serpent, to learn what the gods wished; but at a later time such knowledge generally becomes the property of certain persons—perhaps originally a sort of Rain-makers, like the Mganga in Eastern Africa. The persons among the Hebrews who understood this revelation and could exert influence by magic on the higher powers were the me'ônenîm and menachashîm, the

[1] Ebers, *Aegypten und die Bücher Moses*, I. 245 *et seq.*

[2] On the adoration of the night-sky a passage of the Midrâsh should be consulted (Mechiltâ, ed. Friedmann, fol. 68 a), in which the possibility of a demûth chôshekh 'an idol of Darkness,' is assumed.

'Observers of Clouds and Serpents,' as mentioned regularly together (Deut. XVIII. 10). In the same book of law in which the adoration of the seʿîrîm is strictly prohibited, it is also forbidden to observe clouds and serpents (Lev. XIX. 26). I am well aware that the connexion of these two verbs with the words for cloud and serpent is denied by some authorities of note;[1] but the objections raised in reference to the first at least lead to the establishment of nothing more tenable.

Still there is another question which ought to come under our notice here, the answer to which shall form the conclusion of this chapter. When the nomad Hebrew's Myth of the victory of the night-sky over the day-sky, or of the unjust violence to which the dark sky falls a victim, was converted into a nomadic Religion, in which the mythical figures were individualised and adored as great powers; was not adoration then addressed to the *names* which had been assigned to the night-sky in the myth of the nomads? In other words, were not the deities themselves called Abram, Jacob, etc., just as among the Aryans the mythical figures when converted into gods were called by the same names as they had in the myth? For it was mainly the appellations becoming unintelligible that occasioned the process of transformation, and so it would be expected that in the resulting religion these names would occupy the centre. It is, indeed, the consequence which we should necessarily infer *a priori* from all that has been said. We should infer that those names of the sky of night and rain, of which the myth of the nomad was chiefly composed, at the theological stage became names of theological meaning. Yet this does not appear at all clearly in the Old Testament books. The reason is, that most of the historical books belonging to the Bible are coloured by a theocratic concep-

[1] Most recently by Ewald, *Die Lehre der Bibel von Gott*, I. 234 *et seq.* On the purpose and importance of the interpretation of winds and clouds among the Babylonians, see Lenormant, *La divination et la science des présages chez les Chaldéens*, Paris 1875, pp. 64–68.

tion, and as literary works are advanced even beyond that stage of the national mind at which the mythical figures were converted into *Ancestors*. For not only religion, but history also, is formed out of myths at a certain stage of their development. But the mythical names really belonged first to theological nomenclature before they became historical, as names of Ancestors. This is proved by the fact, which has been mentioned already for another purpose, on which Dozy, in his book on Jewish-Arabic Religious History, has with excellent tact laid emphasis,[1] that none of these mythical names occurs as a human name in the whole course of ancient history, and even in modern history not till late,[2] any more than an Indian would be named Sûrya, Ushas or Dahanâ, or a Roman Jupiter or Saturn, or a Greek Herakles or Aphrodite. This proves that the mythical names of the Hebrew nomads possessed a superhuman significance before they became historical names.

Yet there is still a fact belonging to the latest age which shows that the memory of a former connexion of theological ideas with the names Abram and Jacob had not even then altogether vanished. The great Prophet of the Hebrew people in the Babylonian Captivity, whose name is unknown to us only that we may admire the more his noble soaring spirit, cries in a prayer to Jahveh:

> For thou [Jahveh] art our Father;
> Abraham knew us not,
> And Israel [Jacob] acknowledged us not;
> Thou, Jahveh, art our Father,
> Our Redeemer, whose name was from eternity.—Is. LXIII. 16.

It is obvious that here the names of Abraham and Jacob are *opposed* to that of Jahveh. Therefore it is Jahveh, not Abraham; Jahveh, not Jacob! Jahveh is the omniscient redeemer and protector of the people Israel; the others take no care of it. Can we read in this opposition of names anything else but that the writer wishes to con-

[1] *De Izraelieten te Mekka*, Haarlem 1864, p. 29.
[2] See my remark in the *Zeitschr. d. D. M. G.*, 1874, XXVIII. 309.

trast the idea of a God recognised as the only true with the memory of something different, which ages ago passed for divine, but is unworthy of adoration now, when the Prophet brings forward the *omniscience* of Jahveh as an irrefragable argument for the exclusiveness of his divinity? I think not. And it is not stated without a purpose that Jahveh is the redeemer of the Hebrew nation 'from eternity' (mê'ôlâm), i.e. even from that age in which to the popular mind Abraham and Jacob towered over the range of humanity into the sphere of the gods. We ought further to notice the change of the names Abhrâm and Ya'aḳôbh into Abhrâhâm and Yisrâ'êl (Gen. XVII. 5; XXXII. 29 [28]). The motive alleged for the change of Abhrâm 'High Father' is, that the historical character of the patriarch as Ancestor may be brought into the foreground: 'for I have made thee father of multitudes of nations.' To Jacob the later *ethnographical* name of the people is given. Thus the memory of that to which the ancient Hebrews had paid divine honours was to be suppressed as a thought of something divine but hostile to Jahveh; and its place was to be occupied by the memory of the *Ancestors* of the nation, in which character the Patriarchs are warmly commended to the people by this very prophet (LI. 1, 2). We must next explain what was the impulse that drove the Hebrews to form out of the nomenclature of their ancient myth the names of their ancestors, or in other words to translate a considerable portion of their mythological phraseology into ethnological.

CHAPTER VII.

INFLUENCE OF THE AWAKING NATIONAL IDEA ON THE TRANSFORMATION OF THE HEBREW MYTH.

§ 1. THE nomadic stage of the Hebrew tribes reached its end at the moment when a large part of them gained a land for themselves on the right bank of the river Yardên (Jordan); and that is the true beginning of the History of the Hebrews. Nomadism holds in itself nothing essential to the world's history. Hence the nomadic age of most great nations fades away into the vague, and there are at most separate and unimportant reminiscences by each tribe of its 'days of battle,' which give the historian any fixed points for the construction of his picture. There is scarcely any other nomad people that has had greater vicissitudes in its changeful life than the Arabic tribes: yet they scarcely afford any fixed points when we try to survey their history. For it is not tied to any definite limited soil; no geographical unity runs throughout it. A true national history is inseparable from one country, which in peace presents the conditions necessary for the development of civilisation, and in war offers an object for the enthusiasm of assailants and defenders. There can be no history without a definite land to which the events of history cling. The nomad cares less for a particular territory than for his goods and chattels, when he goes to war.[1] The Desert, and the roamer who roves over its

[1] Palgrave gives an excellent picture of this state, in his *Central and Eastern Arabia*, I. 34: 'The Bedouin does not fight for his home, he has none; nor for his country, that is anywhere; nor for his honour, he never heard of it; nor for his religion, he owns and cares for none. His only object in war is . . . the desire to get such a one's horse or camel into his own possession, etc.'

broad surface, have no history proper. Only isolated vague memories, such as can attach themselves to a great geographical territory, are at our command as points of support for the history of the Hebrew nomads. Their proper history begins with the conquest of Canaan. This conquest was by no means, as is still often assumed, a program of political reorganisation, long nourished in the mind of the people. On the contrary, the fact that we find the tribes on coming from Egypt (whence it cannot be seriously doubted that they came) engaged in roaming about on the left side of the Jordan before they entered Palestine, proves that the Hebrews did not dream of the prospect of exchanging their nomadic life for one in towns. In case they had any such intention, a way from Egypt to Palestine was always open to the people, independently of the route by sea, which could scarcely be thought of from the want of means and adequate preparation. They would have traversed the northern part of the desert al-Tîh, aiming directly at Hebron, on nearly the same track as that taken by the Patriarch's family according to the Biblical narrative in going from Canaan to Egypt. The theocratic historian himself finds a difficulty here, and ascribes to Moses strategic reasons for adopting another course: 'And Elôhîm led them not by the [regular] road to the land of the Philistines, because it is near; for, thought Elôhîm, [there is danger] lest the people should repent when they see war, and return to Egypt' (Ex. XIII. 17).

But the fact is really that on leaving Egypt the people wished to continue in their old mode of life, roving from desert to desert, seeking out one pasture after another; they were indifferent to the cultivated side of the Jordan, and chose by preference the wild eastern side, that is to this day the scene of that restless Beduin life which runs continuously from the bank of the Euphrates to the Sherra mountains. Nomadism is the most conservative life imaginable. For hundreds and thousands of years this plain has been occupied by the same tribes, alternately binding themselves for mutual support against a common foe—often even in modern times the townsmen, and quarrelling among themselves on the slightest provocation. A perfectly new tribe entering from other parts would have great difficulty in holding its ground there; and there is no wonder that the nomadic Hebrews in the desert east of the Jordan were driven by constant struggles further and further to the north, and, having at last discovered their self-protection to be impossible there, resolved to cross the Jordan and try their fortune in the towns. Another circumstance pressed this decision upon them. The further they pushed northwards, the nearer they came to the great northern power which stopped further advance. Great kingdoms whose territories are bounded by deserts have never left these deserts and their inhabitants alone, but have always been diligently engaged in the subjection of the desert tribes: it was so ages ago, and is so still. The wars of the Grand Turk against the Beduin-tribes in Syria, Palestine and Arabia, those of the North-African powers against the nomadic tribes which form their boundaries, are historical continuations of political events of the very oldest times. The remark of Manetho, the Egyptian priest and historian, is therefore very good: 'According to the agreement they travelled from Egypt through the desert to Syria with their whole households and possessions, not less than 240,000 souls. But in fear of the Empire of the Assyrians—for these were then masters of Asia—they built a city in the land now called Judea, etc.[1]

Here comes that remarkable turning-point in the life of the Hebrew people—the abandonment of nomadic life and transition to the civilised life of towns. The passage of the Jordan marks this turning-point. That river is still the boundary-line of two stages of civilisation, nomad-life and town-life. Not the entire mass of the

---

[1] Josephus, *Contra Apionem*, I. 14.

nation submitted to these changes; we know that a large portion of it, remaining at a half-nomadic stage, declared itself averse to the removal, and preferred to stay on the left bank of the Jordan, which is the Nomad's paradise—a plain blessed with splendid pasture and fine woods, of which the Bedawî even now says 'Thou wilt find no land like Belkâ.' The Biblical document gives the exact name of the portion of the people which resisted the transition to town-life; they are described as the sons of Reuben, the sons of Gad, and a part of the tribe of Manasseh. We have no right to decide how much historical truth there is in the contract between the two sections of the nation, by which the larger only gave its consent to the practice of cattle-breeding east of the Jordan by the smaller on condition that the latter would render all possible service to their martial brethren at the conquest (Num. XXXII). Enough that after many long-protracted struggles with the people of the land the advancing Hebrews got a large part of Canaan into their power. The details and the chronology of these wars lie outside my present scheme. The history of the civilisation of the Hebrews in Canaan has here to be considered only on one side—with reference to the history of Religion. In the previous chapter we left the nomadic people wandering in the desert, and worshipping those beneficent powers which provide the nomad with his conditions of life and protect him from the scorching heat so hostile to wanderers—the Rain, his mother the Cloud, and the luminous smile of the cloud, the Lightning. The commencement of religion does not kill off the whole myth at one blow. For the mental activity required for the creation and propagation of myths does not cease when polyonomy vanishes, but only has its full vivaciousness abridged by that process of language. But the process goes on very gradually; on domains not yet fully attacked by it, accordingly, the telling of myths continues for long. One part may remain when another has been converted into religion. Now the law described in Chapter IV. would require, that, after settlement in towns and adoption of agricultural life, the part of the Hebrew myth which was not yet turned into religion should be subject to a development corresponding to the transition from nomadic to agricultural life, by which the solar figures, the victors over Darkness and Storm, take up the position of honour and sympathy always accorded to them by the agriculturist.

§ 2. Here, however, we have to notice a peculiarity of Hebrew development resulting from the occupation of Canaan.

Politically, the Hebrew nation on settling in Canaan had power to annihilate a few small tribes which before the occupation had held the middle of the land. But they brought with them a minimum of civilisation and mental endowments, and intellectually had nothing to oppose to the long-established civilisation of the old inhabitants,[1] and especially of the neighbouring Phenicians, who even then were the ancient occupiers of a great historical position. In mercantile and industrial respects, especially, they were very dependent on that nation, which was the chief bearer of the commerce and industry of antiquity.[2] How should the Hebrews have risen above such dependence? for the Phenicians exerted a powerful intellectual influence not only upon the mentally inferior tribes of Canaan, but also upon the western nations with which they held intercourse; as in recent times Ewald has again strongly asserted.[3] Notwithstanding the contradiction of some scholars who depreciate Phenician civilisation,[4] this seems to be tolerably well established.

---

[1] See Duncker, *Geschichte des Alterthums*, 1874, I. 253.

[2] In Ezek. XXVII. 17, the wares, the export of which made the Hebrews dependent on the Phenicians, are enumerated in detail.

[3] *Die Vorurtheile über das alte und neue Morgenland*, in *Abhandl. der königl. Gesellsch. der Wissensch.*, Gottingen 1872, XVII. 98.

[4] So *e.g.* Jas. Fergusson, *Rude Stone Monuments*, p. 38; Mommsen, *History of Rome*, 1868, II. 18 *et seq.*

There is a phenomenon which has been repeated countless times in the history of the world. A conquered people intellectually superior to its conquerors may, any political dependence notwithstanding, enforce its intellectual preeminence by assimilating to itself the nation which has succeeded to its dominion. The political victor has no power to incorporate the mind of the subjugated, if the latter possesses a higher civilisation than his own. For example, the Hyksôs, who were strong enough to annihilate the rule of the Egyptians in the Delta, could found no independent civilisation in the conquered land, but made the Egyptian culture entirely their own. And when the Aztecs, or more strictly the second horde of the Chichimecs (Northmen), coming from Aztlan and California, overwhelmed Anahuac in the twelfth century, and subjugated the Toltecs, a people which had already attained a certain degree of civilisation, it was again the conquered that imparted their culture to the conquerors. All the elements of civilisation—arts, manners, rights, usages, writing, etc.—which the Spanish conquerors found existing among the Aztecs, had been received by them from the conquered Toltecs, to whose intellectual influence they were forced to accommodate themselves, not having anything more potent of their own to impart.[1] The same is seen in China, first in the tenth and again in the seventeenth century. The victorious Khitem dynasty, as later the Manchu dynasty, which still holds the sceptre of the Middle Kingdom, could only accept and advance the native civilisation and the peculiarities of the old Chinese nation. And who can help thinking of the often-quoted instance of the Franks as conquerors of Gaul? And the relation of the Normans to the population of France conquered by them is most curious. The conquerors lost their mother-tongue in favour of the French, took to

---

[1] Lenormant, *Essai sur la propagation de l'Alphabet phénicien dans l'ancien monde*, ed. 2, Paris 1875, I. p. 25.

themselves French institutions, laws and customs, and actually transplanted subsequently the French language to England.[1] The same phenomenon is also encountered on the domain of Religion.[2] For the Phenicians, to whom we recur, it was the easier to establish their system, as they came as conquerors to places where they found a population intellectually inferior to themselves. When by the foundation of Carthage they gained an establishment in Northern Africa, they exerted an influence on the Libyans which almost suppressed everything native. 'Phenician civilisation prevailed in Libya just as Greek in Asia Minor and Syria after Alexander's campaigns, if not with equal force. At the courts of the nomad Sheikhs Phenician was spoken and written, and the civilised native tribes took the Phenician alphabet for their languages; but it was neither the spirit of the Phenicians nor the policy of Carthage to Phenicise them entirely.'[3] But this very Phenician language, which as bearer of a higher civilisation suppressed the language of surrounding tribes and the civilisation connected with them, had in its turn to step into the background. A civilisation of superior force and intensity, the Arabian, assailed it, and put the Arabic language of the conquerors of North Africa in the place of that of the Carthaginian colonies. Renan is wrong in asserting, 'L'arabe n'absorba que les dialectes qui lui étaient congénères, tels que le syriaque, le chaldéen, le samaritain. Partout ailleurs, il ne put effacer les idiomes établis.'[4] We will not here enter on an enquiry, to what extent Arabic in the middle ages and in modern times has supplanted other idioms. But two considerations must be suggested in answer to Renan's thesis.

The first is, that it is difficult to see what power

---

[1] W. D. Whitney, *Language and the Study of Language*, London 1867 p. 169; cf. F. von Hellwald, *Culturgeschichte*, p. 154.

[2] Hellwald, *ibid.*, p. 482.

[3] Movers, *Die Phönizier*, II. 2. 439 *et seq.*

[4] *Histoire générale des langues sémitiques*, p. 200.

a relationship of language like that between Arabic and Phenician can possess to cause the weaker civilisation connected with one of the languages in question to be supplanted by the stronger civilisation belonging to the other; when the relationship is so remote as to be clearly understood only by linguists, and neither known to ordinary people speaking either tongue, nor even instinctively felt by the popular mind (if any such instinct can be allowed in psychology). Indeed Semitic philologists themselves, even with the knowledge of one or more of the Semitic dialects besides their mother-tongue, arrived comparatively late at acknowledgment of this relationship.[1] It is easy to understand how within the bounds of the Arabic tongue the Northern dialect supplanted the Southern, when the Northern tribes, especially that of Kureysh, gained the political and social hegemony over Arabia, and their dialect was written down and introduced into literature. Here, to say nothing of political and religious causes, the extraordinary similarity of the two shades of the Arabic language, of which the commonest Arab could not but be conscious, made the suppression of the one in favour of the other easy; we have frequent opportunities of observing the same in the dialects of European languages. But it is not so easy to conceive that a relationship in language which is only to be discovered by learned research can promote the process of suppression of dialects. To the Arab, Syriac is as foreign as French or any perfectly strange tongue. Botrus al-Bustâni, an eminent savant at Beyrût, the compiler of a dictionary of his native language and active editor of several Arabic journals, had no fewer difficulties to overcome when he devoted himself to the study of the Syriac language in the Maronite convents of Lebanon, than when he learned English by intercourse with Dr. Van Dijk at the American Protestant Mission; perhaps even greater, as in the latter case mouth-to-

[1] See my *Studien über Tanchûm Jeruschalmi*, Leipzig 1870, p. 12.

mouth intercourse removed many difficulties. A Maronite priest at Damascus assured me that the acquisition of the Italian language gave him but few hard nuts to crack, whilst in the language of his Syriac Church he could not get further than the elements which were indispensable to his office. The Fin found no special difficulty in becoming Swedish, because Swedish is a Teutonic and Finnish a Ugrian language. In Hungary, during a long subjection to the Turks, Turkish had no appreciable effect on the language, except in lending a few words, although Hungarian and Turkish belong to one and the same group of languages. Hence when one language ousts another, it is not their relationship, but solely the superiority of the one people in intellect and matters of culture that determines the result.

The second answer to Renan is that it is historically untrue that Arabic could conquer only cognate idioms, but elsewhere had no power to oust the native tongues. Where is the Coptic now? a once powerful language having no connexion with Arabic, the vernacular use of which in Egypt was totally annihilated by the Arabic. The dialects of the Negro countries are beginning to give place more and more to the Arabic, and their ultimate defeat in the contest with that language will be hastened by the advances of the power of the Viceroy over the equatorial regions.

This is the great struggle for existence on the domain of Mind—a struggle which the Hebrews, with the small amount of culture that they brought to Canaan, could not sustain, nor even attempt, against the settled population and the neighbouring powerful Canaanites of the coast. On this a basis could be found for a hypothesis which has never had any other foundation of the least firmness. It is now revived by Professor J. G. Müller of Basle.[1] The Hebrews, we are told, originally spoke a

[1] *Die Semiten in ihrem Verhältniss zu Chamiten und Japheiten*, Basel 1872, p. 134.

different language not connected with that of Canaan; but, not being able to bring it into general use in their new country, gave it up, and took over from the Canaanites the language that we call Hebrew, which really possesses a far more palpable similarity to all known relics of the old idioms of Canaan than is the case with languages which though connected, are intrinsically distinct. And assuredly the consideration of the lately found Moabitish monument, the column of victory of King Mesha, which shows us a form of language perfectly intelligible by the aid of the Hebrew grammar and the Hebrew lexicon, and an historical style indistinguishable from that of the Hebrews, involuntarily suggests the thought that we ought to speak rather of identity than of connexion of languages. Even the Phenician language, though not, as many erroneously suppose, absolutely identical with Hebrew, nor even so near to it as the more Southern language of Moab, exhibits a far closer relationship with the latter than is generally found between different languages of the same family.[1] Phenician was certainly not an idiom unintelligible to the Hebrews; and indeed a Hebrew prophet even calls his mother-tongue the 'language of Canaan' (sephath Kena'an, Is. XIX. 18). The idea that the Hebrews changed their language in Canaan possesses, indeed, no high degree of probability, especially in so extreme and violent a form as is given to it by J. G. Müller—least of all for us, inasmuch as the nomadic myth of the Hebrews, which was created quite independently of Canaan, never contains any but Hebrew names. But in matters of culture and manners, in which the Hebrews, only just working their way up out of the nomadic stage, still held a very primitive position at their entrance into Canaan, they were most certainly influenced by the con-

[1] This question will be found very satisfactorily discussed in Stade's article '*Erneute Prüfung des zwischen dem Phönicischen und Hebräischen bestehenden Verwandtschaftsverhältnisses*,' in the *Morgenländische Forschungen*, Leipzig 1875, pp. 169–232.

quered original inhabitants and by their powerful neighbours. These influences were immediately perceptible in the form given to Religion and to social and political institutions. The Hebrews did not possess sufficient resistant force of mind to work the solar elements of *their own* myth into a religion suitable to an agricultural people, and had no strength to repel the Canaanitish Solar religion, which must have been already long growing into completeness from an old Canaanitish Solar myth; they could not accept the challenge, but yielded. With general notions of religion they also adopted its forms and institutes—the Temples, which bear the same relation to the Sukkôth used for Divine worship as the fixed house of the townsman to the hut of the nomad; the High places;[1] the sacred Trees and Woods; the Human Sacrifices; the Priesthood, whose relation to the Sons of Levi among the nomads again resembles that of a powerful dynasty to the family of a Bedawî Sheikh; the Ritual of Sacrifice, and much besides. With the religion and religious institutions of the Canaanites, their religious terminology was also naturalised among the Hebrews. The Phenician title of the Priest, Kôhên—*Κοίης* (Hellenised from *Κοίην*) *ἱερεὺς Καβείρων ὁ καθαίρων φονέα · οἱ δὲ κοής* (Hesychius) —became among the Hebrews also the official name of the public sacrificers; and the fact that a derivative verb was formed from it proves it to have become completely naturalised in ordinary speech.[2] The extant monuments of the sacrificial ritual of the Phenicians, viz., the so-called Sacrificial Tablet of Marseilles, discovered in 1845, and the Carthaginian Sacrificial documents published more

---

[1] See Merx, *Archiv. f. wissensch. Erforsch. d. A. T.* pt. 1. 1867, p. 108.

[2] In late Aramaised Hebrew we find the feminine kehantâ (=kôheneth) for a Priest's Wife, equivalent to êsheth kôhên; see Levy, *Chald. Wörterb.* I. 356 *a*. It comes thence to be used in a general signification, of an honest, irreproachable woman, in opposition to pundâkîth, properly an innkeeper, in *Mishnâ Yebhâmôth*, XVI. 7.

recently by Davis,[1] place before our eyes much the same as we have in part of the Book of Leviticus; and it is to be assumed that, although, after the profound investigations of Graf[2] and Zunz,[3] the Post-Captivity origin of that book is impressed with increasing urgency on our conviction, still the Sacrificial laws contained in it are only a codification of older regulations which arose and were in force in sacerdotal circles at the time of the Hebrew dominion in Canaan, but were not, and ought not to be, known to the people, as they referred only to priestly functions. It would be inconceivable that a regular sacrificial worship could exist without such arrangements and fixed ritual. Among the Carthaginians the contents of these sacrificial tables, with the ordinances and apportionments to be found on them, had *canonical* validity, and were not occasional or arbitrary orders. That this is so, is to be inferred from the fact that the sacrificial tariff discovered by Davis in the ruins of Carthage exhibits only an abridged edition of the Marseilles Tablet, which also was derived from Carthage.[4]

Not only religious, but also social and political institutions were introduced from the Phenicians into the public life of the Hebrews. How else could a nation passing suddenly without political experience from nomadic to civil life produce those institutions without which a nation can neither constitute itself as a state nor continue to exist? Thus we find among the Hebrews from the beginning the Shôpheṭîm (Judges), who are known as

---

[1] See Ernst Meier's essay on the former in *Zeitsch. d. D. M. G.*, 1865, XIX., and Nathan Davis, *Carthage and her remains*, London 1861.

[2] *Die geschichtlichen Bücher des A. T.*, Leipzig 1866.

[3] *Bibelkritisches*, in the *Zeitsch. d. D. M. G.*, 1873, XXVII. 682–89, especially the theses 22–26. Zunz appears to have laboured independently of Graf, but arrives at almost the same results.

[4] Bargès, who has earned great credit for his elucidation of the Marseilles table in several writings, disputes the authenticity of the inscription discovered by Davis (*Examen d'une nouvelle inscription phénicienne découverte récemment dans les ruines de Carthage et analogue à celle de Marseille.* Paris 1868).

Suffetes of the Carthaginians from Livy and the Inscriptions. It must be assumed that, although this institution is not distinctly proved to have existed in the mother-country, its root is to be sought there; which harmonises well with the highly developed civic constitution of the Phenicians. To draw an inference from the institutions of the colonies to those of the mother-country must here, as in other cases also, be treated as perfectly justifiable. Let it be remembered that we should have no knowledge even of the elaborate system of priests and sacrifices among the Phenicians, but for two remarkable monuments of antiquity: the Tablets of Marseilles and of Carthage. On one of the most important elements of Phenician religious life, therefore, information is only to be found in the colonies; and the same must certainly be true of social and political questions. In the present case it is sure to be allowable, as the official name Shôphêṭ is found in a Greek translation used of Tyre and Sidon. It must not indeed be supposed that the Shôpheṭîm of the Hebrews can be placed exactly beside the Phenician Suffetes. Whilst the latter is a permanent dignity and a fixed institution, the Shôpheṭîm of the Hebrews are not so much officials as a sort of *duces ex virtute*, 'who might come and go without any alteration in the legal bases of the state,' as Ewald says.[1] But if we have to allow that the Hebrew Shôpheṭîm are not holders of so fixed an office as their namesakes in Phenicia, but were only guerilla-chiefs in times of pressure of war, yet Phenician influence cannot be denied, when we see that, just when the nomadic tribal divisions were beginning to grow very loose and to make way for town-life, these chiefs were called by a name identical with the official name of certain Phenician dignitaries of rather different character. It is evident from this that the Hebrews regarded their provisional chiefs as equivalents of these Phenician officers

[1] *History of Israel*, II. 360.

of state; they apperceived them, so to speak, by an idea derived from Phenicia. But, on the other hand, this view of the influence of the Shôpheṭîm rests on the picture of their actions given in the 'Book of Judges.' Now it must not be forgotten that many of these Judges' names are mythical (as Samson, Jephthah, Gideon), used to fill up a period which to posterity was a mere blank with no historical contents, except the bare fact of a continuous contest with the Philistines. This historical frame, as we shall soon see, is filled with myths, which, when re-interpreted in a national sense, yield a supply of national heroes, who then can be introduced as Shôpheṭîm. But the harmonising of national stories was not pushed to a sufficient degree of continuity to form a foundation for a fixed historical picture. It is therefore better, in forming our judgment on the dignity of the so-called Judges, to allow ourselves to be determined more by the name Shôpheṭîm itself than by the nature of the nationalised myths attached to it. Grätz[1] has quite recently renewed the attempt to render doubtful the existence of the Shôpheṭîm-institution among the Hebrews, and especially combated any connexion of the Shôpheṭîm with the Punic Suffetes; and in this the judgment of the most competent professional authorities is on his side. But, not to speak of his view of the Shôpheṭîm as representatives of an institution, he sets up a linguistic conjecture which arouses many a doubt. For it requires strong etymological imagination to deny to the Hebrew word shâphaṭ the signification *judicare*. Sober Biblical students and philologists will not be imposed on by the passages quoted by Grätz in justification and support of his conjecture. Not to mention other passages, compare only the words of Is. I. 17, 23 with the passages of Scripture which, Grätz says, speak of rushing up to the aid of 'oppressed or injured persons, widows and orphans.' The word rîbh

[1] *Geschichte der Juden*, Leipzig 1874, I. 407 *et seq.*

is not calculated to support this conjecture. But, that the Shôphetîm, though not hereditary nor even paid officers of state (as no one would pretend they were), were yet certainly heads of the state, appointed by the voice of the people, is proved by the mere fact that the Shôphêṭ was regarded in the same light as the Melekh, as a species of the same genus. So e.g. in Judges IX. 6, 16, where the instalment of a Shôphêṭ is denoted by hamlîkh, and Judges XVII. 6, XVIII. 1, XXI. 25, where the interregnum between one Shôphêṭ and the next is described as a time 'in which no melekh (king) reigned over Israel, and every one could do what was right in his own eyes.' And the consideration of the word Shôphêṭ itself leads to the conviction that the office was an institution suggested by Phenician custom. For it is found in no other Semitic language in the same signification as in these two dialects of Canaan.[1] The Samaritan, in which Shâphaṭ is also found,[2] scarcely requires separate mention. So the Hebrews, as was so often the case, must have borrowed the term shôphêṭ, together with the corresponding institution, from their cultivated neighbours; for it cannot be assumed that the expression for an idea implying so advanced a stage of civilisation as Judge had its origin in the primeval age of ethnological community between Hebrews and Canaanites. And later, when the Hebrews began to appreciate the institution of Kingship, as existing in many neighbouring nations,[3] and wished to be ruled by kings, the theocratic historian himself describes this innovation as borrowed, making the people say to the prophet Samuel, 'Give us a King to judge us, as all the

---

[1] See Stade's exhaustive exposition in the *Morgenländische Forschungen*, p. 197. But I cannot share the opinion of my respected friend, that the Hebrews could borrow nothing from the Phenicians because the two nations passed through a completely distinct religious and political development.

[2] *Shefaṭ-'Adad* in Nabatean, quoted by Ernst Meier in *Zeitsch. d. D. M. G.* 1873, XVII. 609, is also problematical.

[3] Duncker, *Geschichte des Alterthums*, I. 371.

nations [have a king], that we also may be like all the nations, and that our king may judge us and go out before us and fight our battles' (1 Sam. VIII. 5, 20). Even concerning the political subjection of the tribes of Canaan, it has long been perceived that this was by no means so complete as is commonly supposed, but that the Canaanitish element in the centre of the Hebrew dominion was powerful enough[1] to nourish exterior religious or civilising influences. A somewhat later didactic poet exclaims, 'They did not destroy the nations which Jahveh told them [to destroy]; but mixed with the nations and learned their works' (Ps. CVI. 34 *seq.*). To this time belongs the naturalisation of theological terms and consequently of theological conceptions, for the independent working out of which the Hebrews had not passed through the necessary historical experience and continuous religious stages, but in which the history of the religion of the Canaanites found its natural result. At the time when the nomadic nation of the Hebrews entered Canaan, it first, so to speak, produced out of the ancient myth the first elements of a religion; we cannot speak of a *system* of religion existing in that age. In the Canaanitish peoples, on the other hand, a systematical religion had already been formed. Even independently of the preponderating spiritual influence of the native population, it was particularly natural to the Hebrews to attach themselves to their system, as community of language familiarised them with much of the religious terminology of the Canaanites. Ever since the Hebrews had by their own efforts begun to have any religious ideas, they called every power which they regarded as divine Êl and Shadday 'the Powerful;' and as these Powers (which they also called Elôhîm, i.e. 'the Worshipped' or 'the Feared') were seen by them on the dark sky, Êl was also called 'Elyôn 'the Highest'

[1] The data belonging to this subject are lucidly brought together in Kuenen's *Religion of Israel*, I. 182.

(a synonym of Abh-râm). To the Hebrews these names were not yet exclusively theological, *termini technici* of religion. Religion itself had not yet grown so stiff and fixed as to have taken from such names their appellative character: and that of Elôhîm and ʻElyôn continued to the latest times. But with the Canaanites even at that early age these ancient Semitic expressions had been already employed long enough in a theological sense to take the step which converted them into a religious terminology. Many synonyms of the terms in question are found among the Phenicians as religious terms, and among the Hebrews (when the words are equally native there) in a completely appellative sense, e.g. Baʻal 'Lord,' Kabbîr 'Great, Powerful.'

This community of language greatly promoted the introduction of Canaanitish religion among the Hebrews. Although the above-mentioned names impressed the Hebrews differently, being not yet limited to a specially religious signification, yet the knowledge of their meaning as words, which was native to the Hebrews, promoted the acquisition of the ritual attached to them by the Canaanites. Thus it came to pass that besides Êl, Elôhîm, ʻElyôn, Shadday, even Baʻal received worship from the Hebrews in Canaan, of which the Biblical documents often speak (and he is not likely to have been the only divine person borrowed from the Phenicians), and that those names which had previously begun to assume a religious sense were, by intellectual as well as practical intercourse with the Canaanites, filled with the force they had to the Canaanites. It is therefore the exact opposite of the real state of things to call the Elôhîm-idea specially Hebrew, and make Jahveism Canaanitish, as some Dutch theologians do. It is equally impossible to suppose the names themselves to have been unknown till then to the Hebrews, as J. G. Müller infers in connexion with his ethnological hypothesis.[1] The names, as component parts

[1] *Semiten, Chamiten und Japhetiten*, p. 160 *et seq.*

of the language, are the property of Canaanites and Hebrews alike; only their theological employment and the worship founded upon them are to be regarded as Canaanitish. But it is especially this employment of the names which has to be considered in relation to the History of Civilisation.

Thus we see how the Hebrews in Canaan learned much as to religion as well as to politics from the conquered neighbouring aborigines. The religious ideas produced on the nomadic stage from the nomadic mythology were wiped away, and only a few relics of the old nomadic religion remained to a late age, either actual residues or mere memories. Spiritually poor, the nation was handed over to the powerful influence of the already formed culture of Canaan, and thus condemned to mere receptivity. Accordingly, they never had an opportunity of further developing their myths on the agricultural stage and converting them into elements of a religion. Hence comes the remarkable fact that from this point the myths of the Hebrews cease to grow, in the way in which those of the Aryan nations grew. Only a small cycle of myths of the Sun and of Civilisation were formed at this time; and the regular advance of the Mythical to the Religious was arrested by that religious influence which pressed in with full force from outside. The most complete and rounded-off solar myth extant in Hebrew is that of Shimshôn (Samson), a cycle of mythical conceptions fully comparable with the Greek myth of Herakles. But Samson never got so far as to be admitted, like Herakles, into the society of the gods. Those who say that mythologists have converted Samson to a *deus solaris* make a malicious perversion of the truth, merely because they set themselves against any mythological investigation on Semitic ground.[1] Whilst the Hebrews were thus taking in from the Canaan-

[1] Equally exaggerated on the other side, however, is Tiele's view (*Vergelijk. Geschied.*, p. 182), treating the story of Samson as borrowed from the Canaanites. See also Duncker, *l.c.* II. 65.

ites things quite new to them, by which the regular further growth of their own was arrested, a considerable portion of their own store of legends must naturally have been starved out. For whatever ceases to grow, falls into slow decay, and at last disappears and leaves no sign behind. Here is discovered the origin of the defectiveness and fragmentary nature which strikes us in reconstructing the old Hebrew myths, when compared with the richness and variety of the Aryan myths among those nations which have passed through all stages of civilisation regularly and without obstruction or perverting influence from foreign forces.

The Myth is converted either into Religion or into History; the figures of the myth become either Gods and god-born Heroes, or Ancestors of the nation to which the myth belonged. What part of the myth cannot be converted, or has not been converted, into religion, and what has ceased to be religious without ceasing to exist in the popular mind, is converted into history; for all that remains in the human consciousness as a living portion of it must have a distinct impress; no meaningless vegetating is possible. Nothing is without an impressed form; when an old impress has lost its meaning, a new one is made. It is these new impressions that keep the elements of the ancient myth alive in the mind of the people far beyond the mythical age. Among the Hebrews this new force worked more powerfully than elsewhere in changing the form and impress of the still living elements of the myth, converting almost all myth into history.[1] This result was attained with the cooperation of an important factor in the History of Civilisation, which also determined

[1] This fact, moreover, refutes Buckle's thesis (assuming the very opposite course of development), which makes history to be the earlier, and to be subsequently degraded to 'a mythology full of marvels.' This thesis has been estimated at its true value by Hermann Cohen in an article entitled *Die dichterische Plantasie und der Mechanismus des Bewusstseins*, in the *Zeitsch. für Völkerpsychologie etc.*, 1869, VI. 186-193.

the *direction* which the myth should take in being transformed into history. We must now consider this factor.

§ 3. Though the Hebrews were intellectually dependent on the older inhabitants of Canaan, and had to take up a receptive position towards them in matters of civilisation and religion, it was nevertheless inevitable that a strong antagonism should grow up between the two sides. The Hebrews edged themselves in like an unbidden guest into the midst of the Canaanitish system of tribes. As they could gain their political position in that system only by conquest and repression, so also they could maintain, protect, and confirm it only by continuous defensive wars. We find Philistines, Moabites, and Edomites the constant deadly foes of the existence of the Hebrew state, and the history of Israel in Canaan is filled up with incessant struggles of greater or less magnitude, in which the Hebrews, themselves scarcely settled in a home, were forced to engage against the repressed old inhabitants on the one hand, and the menaced neighbouring peoples on the other. Moreover, the nomadic characteristic, still preserved by the Hebrews, of faithfully maintaining the memory of their national individuality, could not be entirely obscured by their new spiritual life, which was only borrowed from strangers, especially as the constant wars in which they were necessarily involved against those strangers were calculated to heighten and confirm it. Indeed, the spirit of tribe and race, the repelling and exclusive tendency which characterised the Canaanitish peoples,[1] nourished in the Hebrews the desire to insist on the enforcement and development of individuality on their side too. This exclusiveness, this consciousness of individual peculiarity which lived in the mind of the people, could not now find expression in religion. When even modern Biblical criticism, coming

[1] Mommsen, *l.c.* book III. chap I.

into the inheritance of a conception which obtained acceptance from religious animosity, still continues to insist on the 'National God of the Hebrews,' it commits a decided error, at least in reference to the age of which we are now speaking, and especially with regard to the Elôhîm. The consciousness of national peculiarity could not, at this stage of religion among the Hebrews, find any expression on the domain of religion. Yet it must perforce gain expression somewhere, and could not do so anywhere except on a domain on which the most original impress of their own mind was still visible--in the myths, insofar as they were not yet swept away by foreign influence.

The awaking of National Consciousness plays a very prominent part in the history of the development of the Myth. From the moment when in ancient times this idea began to fill the soul of a great national community, it seized on and transformed the whole material of which its mythology was made. The fact that this noble consciousness gives a distinct direction of its own to everything that fills the human soul, is another proof of its power to transform the spiritual life. In modern times the kindling of national self-consciousness, advanced by the arousing of spiritual opposition to foreign influences which had previously repressed national individuality, causes the production of documents to prove the awakening of this national opposition, documents which belong to the best part of literature and intellectual labour. Similarly, in ancient times before literature, this consciousness of opposition impressed its image especially on the myth, and made that subservient to its purpose. And on considering the relation of the myth to the idea of nationality, we see on many sides, how closely and inseparably the two are connected together, how the idea operates to transform the myth, and how it needs the myth as a support; for the myth, going back to the earliest times, confers on the new idea something like an historical title, and gives a broad basis to the intenseness of its force by furnishing a justification of it. Hence it comes to pass that nations which have preserved no great stock of original myths on which the awakened national consciousness could fall back, instinctively create similar stories, and this even in relatively modern times, in which a system of religion hardened into crystal on every side, combined with the corresponding stage of intellectual development, would leave no room for the revival of mythical activity. Of this there are two noteworthy instances, one in the middle ages (the twelfth or thirteenth century), the other in this century. The Cymry of Wales, becoming alive to the opposition in nationality between themselves and the English, felt the need of finding a justification of this opposition in the oldest prehistoric times. It was then first suggested to them that they were descendants of the ancient renowned Celtic nation; and to keep alive this Celtic national pride they introduced an institution of New Druids, a sort of secret society like the Freemasons. The New Druids, like the old ones, taught a sort of national religion, which however, the people having long become Christian and preserved no independent national traditions, they had mostly to invent themselves. Thus arose the so-called Celtic mythology of the god Hu and the goddess Ceridolu, etc., mere poetical fictions, which never lived in popular belief.[1] The other instance is furnished by the Hungarian national literature of the time when, to revive the 'ancient glory,' Andrew Horváth and Michael Vörösmarty created new myths, mythic figures and a national epic, in place of the mere fragments remaining of the old Hungarian cycle of myths, with the view of reviving national feeling and consciousness in their fellow countrymen. And a few of these new creations have in a course of a few decads of years penetrated so deep into the national mind as to be treated as

---

[1] Holtzmann, *Deutsche Mythologie*, p. 28.

something primitive and aboriginal; so e.g. Hadúr, the god of war, etc.[1]

Far more organic and natural is the effect produced by the national sentiment and national opposition on the form of the myth wherever copious mythic materials exist, which it can influence and transform. The entire contents of the myths—the mythological figures and all that is told of them—are apperceived by the national movement and receive from it a new interpretation. This may be seen clearly in the case of the old Persian myth, mentioned briefly above (pp. 15, 16), where I showed that all that it told of the contests and mutual relations of the Sun and Night was, at the stage of the rising national consciousness, converted into contests between Îrân and Tûrân—the heroes of mythology became national heroes, the victorious Sun became a victorious helper and saviour of the nation, and the malicious intriguing Darkness the cunning hero of the hostile people. This national interpretation of the myth is only another side of the process which resulted in individualising the mythical figures and created personalities of theological significance. I have already insisted on the fact that another set of the mythical figures when converted into individuals assume an historical character. This comes to pass in various ways: either the myth which is turned into history first passes through the stage of religion, and then becomes history; or secondly, the historical transformation is effected in immediate sequence upon the old mythological stage; or lastly, the mythological figures assume a meaning which is at the same time both religious and historical, like the Greek Heroes. On the development of the Hebrew myth also the awakening of the national spirit exercised a great influence. The consciousness of national individuality gave a new direction to all the ideas of the Hebrews, and so also to their mythology. Among the Greeks and Indians the

---

[1] Paul Gyulai, *Vörösmarty élete* [Life of Vörösmarty], Pest 1866, p. 49 *et seq.*

chief figures of mythology—not to speak of occasional localisation—preserved a cosmopolitan character; for Zeus, Indra, and others have no special national character. But the figures of the Hebrew myths at this period became the national progenitors of the Hebrew people, and the mythology itself the national primeval history of the Hebrews before their settlement in the land of Canaan. Abhrâm, the 'High Father,' is converted into Abhrâhâm, the abh hamôn gôyîm, 'Father of a mass of Nations,' and at the same time into hâ-'Ibhrî, 'the Hebrew' (Gen. XVII. 4, 5, XIV. 13); and all other figures of the myth are made to subserve the national idea. On the one hand, they are eager to have documentary proof of their nation's noble origin and glorious past; on the other, they nourish a feeling of opposition towards other nationalities, on which they cast shame. The nation of Edom receives Esau as ancestor: and the reminiscence of nomadic conceptions which draws their sympathy towards Jacob, the persecuted brother, and turns with antipathy away from the red solar hunter, is again revived in the service of the formation of a national myth which paints Esau in the most repulsive colours. The old mythological incest of Lot's daughters is made the cause of the origin of two Canaanitish tribes, the Ammonites and the Moabites.[1] The Philistines also are dragged through this story-making process of national antagonism. The primeval heavenly 'Father-King' Abimelek, who conceives a warm love for the wife of the Morning-sky and thinks to carry her off, is made a king of the Philistines, and Shechem, the Early Morning, the seducer of Dinah, is converted into a prince of the Hivvites. In the story of Dinah, as given in Genesis, we have an especially eloquent testimony to the national animosity to which this conversion of the myth owes its origin. This aspect of the story has been very fully proved by a Dutch scholar, Dr. Oort. It exhibits in the people newly awakened to national self-consciousness a

---

[1] See Excursus N.

tendency to abominate all connexion with the Canaanites, and introduces as representatives or types of this tendency the brothers Simeon and Levi, the zealots for the purity of the Hebrew family.[1] Thus we see that the national treatment of the myth is not merely of the nature of narrative, but at the same time also instructive or didactic. Ham, the unworthy son who reveals the nakedness of the solar hero, is regarded as the defiler of his father and made the ancestor of all the Canaanites, and visited by his father's curse. 'And Noah awoke from his wine and learned what his youngest son had done to him. And he said, Cursed be Canaan, let him be a slave of slaves to his brethren. And he said, Blessed be Jahveh, the God of Shem, and let Canaan be a slave to them' (Gen. IX. 24–26). We see that the national passion turns especially on Canaan: for the story makes the offended father curse, not the offender Ham, but Canaan, who is in the ethnographical genealogy only his grandson. It is impossible to be blind to the factors which are concealed behind such a conception. In the case of Esau too, the national story makes him choose his wives from the daughters of Canaan, to whom Isaac, the patriarch of the Hebrews, and Rebekah the mother of the tribe, strongly object (Gen. XXVII. 46, XXVIII. 1, 6, 8); so much so that the mother would rather die than that her favourite son Jacob should also take one of them to wife, and the father repeatedly urges on him to have nothing to do with that people. On this very occasion it is mentioned with emphasis that Esau is identical with Edom, or according to another version is the father of Edom (Gen. XXXVI. 1, 43).

The national pride of a people roused to a consciousness of its worth must be strengthened by the memories of national heroes, and find nourishment and life in such memories; and this impulse works with a revived force even in later times, in which historical reminiscences of the olden time are beginning to fade. The Hebrew

---

[1] *Godgeleerde Bijdragen*, 1866, p. 983 *et seq.* With him Kuenen agrees, *The Religion of Israel*, I. 311 *et seq.*

people found heroes even in some mythical figures; they were turned into Hebrew national heroes, and their celestial contest became a national war against the Philistines, and was removed to the age of the Shôphețîm or Judges, which was in memory connected with the hardest struggles and fiercest wars against the Philistines. The blinded Shimshôn, Samson, the setting sun robbed of his locks and his eyesight, is brought forward as a victim of the perfidious cunning of the Canaanites. The Goat Yâ'êl (Jael), and the Lightning Bârâķ, the Smasher Gide'ôn, mere mythical expressions (clearly exhibited as such by Steinthal), are sent to battle against the Philistines; and the attractive part of the handsome ruddy sharp-eyed youth who slays the monster of darkness by throwing stones, is assigned as a piece of biography to the historical hero-king David, who slays the Philistine giant Goliath in single combat, and delivers the Hebrew people from their dangerous enemy.[1] From the last example we see that, besides mythical figures becoming historic personages in the service of the national idea, historical figures also may receive biographical features proper to mythic heroes. Not only are the figures of the myth converted into historical ones by assigning to them a part in historical events, but events of mythology are shifted into historical times by fastening them on to historical persons.

The entire materials of legend are clothed in a national garb. The Hebrews in Canaan retained the nomadic tribe-divisions. Every tribe was provided with an ancestor, and every one of these ancestors was made a son of Jacob, who was at the same time identified with Israel. The twelve stars of the nightly sky descended upon the new people of Canaan, and took on themselves the duties of Eponymi. The history of each of these

[1] Like the Hungarian national hero Nicolas Toldi, who overcomes the Czech (Bohemian) hero in single combat.

fathers of tribes became the tribe's historical reminiscence. The national passion, the revived consciousness of individuality, blew the glimmering sparks of story-building into a clear flame, and determined the direction or tendency of the stories. The history of this epoch suggests a motive for the prevailingly *national* development of the Hebrew materials of legend. Hence it comes to pass that the individualised figures of the Hebrew myth appear as national ancestors and fathers of tribes, some as fathers of the Hebrew people with a negative spirit of exclusiveness towards everything foreign, some as fathers of the hostile tribes, combating the ancestors of the Hebrews. Thus the ancestors reflect in a dim primitive age their own fortunes and relation to the tribes of Canaan. The same psychological process which in later time caused the Agadic interpreters to declare the principle: ma'asê âbhôth sîmân lebhânîm 'the deeds of the Patriarchs are types for their descendants,'[1] was, inverted, the creative cause of the legends of the fathers and their doings.

In such wise did the Hebrew people find expression for the consciousness of their individuality, which they might easily have utterly lost in their spiritual dependence upon their neighbours; namely, in a new interpretation of their ancient myths. When they were becoming quite Canaanitish through what they borrowed from others in religion and culture, their whole soul was again electrified, and a new spirit aroused by the feeling of self dependence confirmed by severe contests. What it could not put into the religion, which it was powerless to create of itself, it put into a glorious series of poetical legends. These expressed both the national consciousness on the one hand, and the national passionateness on the other; and it may be assumed that with the progress of animosities the tone of the legends increased in bitterness. I adduced above the development of the Persian national

---

[1] Compare *Genesis rabbâ*, § 48.

legend as an instance showing how a national legend grows out of a myth. At the close of this chapter I will again revert to the same region of legend, to show how national animosity can operate in transforming old materials down to the latest times, in which new legends can scarcely be still created. Firdôsî gives the national legends of the contests with Tûrân, formed from the myths. But the lately roused antagonism of the Persians to the Arabs, who had become the dominant power and were extinguishing Iranism, also finds expression in the form which he imparts to the legends. On reading his description of the behaviour of the Arabian ambassadors at the court of Ferîdûn, we observe that the legend here takes a tone of hostility to the Arabs, and criticises the dark side of the Arabian national character; and the sufferings of Irej, the ancestor of the Iranians, are intended to be a type of the subjugation and vicissitudes of the Iranian race. Selm himself (the Shem of the Shâhnâmeh in relation to Îrân and Tûrân) is represented as malicious, passionate, and intriguing.[1]

[1] See *Shâhnâmeh* (ed. Mohl), p. 124. vv. 121–29 and pp. 139–40, etc.

CHAPTER VIII.

COMMENCEMENT OF MONOTHEISM AND THE DIFFERENTIATION OF THE MYTHS.

§ I. We have seen a new feeling aroused in the breast of the Hebrews, and gaining such force and intensity as to fill their souls with a new thought and impart spiritual significance and direction to their political life.

In the history of the world there sometimes appear nations endowed with very small power of influencing the outside world, and whose intellectual mission is quite subjective, or, if we prefer so to call it, negative, insofar as their entire historical life is taken up by the realisation of the endeavour not to fall victims to some foreign intellect bearing down upon them from the outside, but to preserve their individual being, their peculiarity, their nationality, not merely in an ethnological but in an historical sense also.

The Hebrew nation was preserved from the state of intellectual passivity by the aroused consciousness of national individuality. The consciousness of individuality awoke, and as soon as it was fully roused, there began that section of the life of the nation which was distinguished by a peculiar productiveness on the domain of ideas. The influences received from outside could be neither extinguished nor cancelled, seeing that to them was mainly due the formation of the mind of the nation; but the national consciousness had now introduced a new condition of further civilisation, which caused these foreign elements to be dealt with in a peculiar and independent way. No doubt a long time was needed to allow the results of this national reaction to strike root in the soul of the nation; but we shall see that a true Hebraism was formed by slow progress out of Canaanism, until at last the choicest and noblest minds of the nation seized upon the idea which gave full expression to the principle of nationality and freed it from the last traces of Canaanitish influence.

§ 2. The consequences of the national reaction are exhibited in the first representatives of the house of David, in the history of the Hebrew nation and in the desire of political unity to put an end to the old disunion and give strength against the Canaanites. The religious and political centralisation, which forms the program of David and Solomon, was the first and most forcible expression of the roused national spirit. I will leave the political arrangements on one side; for although they certainly come within the range of the general description which I have to give of the character of the period, yet the nature of these studies urges me more to consider the forces which act on the history of religion. With reference to this I must prefix some almost self-evident remarks on the relation of Polytheism to Monotheism: self-evident I say, yet even now still doubted and disputed, because on this subject even the least prejudiced inquirers on questions of antiquity and the history of ancient civilisation still use words in accordance with the old traditional system.[1] The idea that a Monotheistic instinct is inherent in a certain race or certain nations is refuted by historical facts so far as relates to the Semites, the consideration of whose psychological condition had suggested the opinion, and has also been exhibited as generally untenable by Steinthal's and Max

---

[1] Hartung, in the first part of his *Religion und Mythologie der Griechen*, contradicts himself again and again on this subject. At first he makes monotheism precede all development of religion (p. 3), then he sees nothing religious at all in monotheism (p. 28), and next the growth of religion proceeds from polytheism to monotheism, not the reverse way (p. 32).

Müller's psychological criticism of the meaning of instinct. But equally untrue is the idea of an original Monotheism, which later in history dissolved into Polytheism. This idea, which moreover identified the original monotheism with that of the Bible, prevailed almost universally in former times. Recently Rougemont, a French ethnologist, has endeavoured, in his work 'Le Peuple Primitif' (1855), to find a basis for it by supposing Polytheism to have sprung out of the original Monotheism through the medium of Pantheism by reason of a superfluity of religious life and over-richness in poetical inspiration.[1] Of course many theological systems endeavour to maintain this position; but also scholars who are but little influenced by theological prepossessions sometimes support it in their special provinces of study, having recourse to methods of deduction inspired mainly by an obsolete mysticism. So, for example, the sound scholar François Lenormant assumes that in Egypt Polytheism grew out of an original Monotheism by the process expressed in the following words: 'L'idée de Dieu se confondit avec les manifestations de sa puissance; ses attributs et ses qualités furent personnifiés en une foule d'agents secondaires distribués dans une ordre hiérarchique, concourant à l'organisation générale du monde et à la conservation des êtres.'[2] This is the old story of the separation of the notion of a single god, given by an alleged primeval revelation, into its parts and factors! Another renowned investigator of Assyrian and Babylonian antiquity, Jules Oppert, also, speaks of a common monotheistic groundwork of all human religion.[3] But from the nature of the case, and in accordance with the laws of development of the human mind which can be deduced from experience, the fact is the very reverse. The history of the development of religion, modified of course in accordance

[1] Waitz, *Anthropologie der Naturvölker*, I. 363 *note*.
[2] *La Magie chez les Chaldéens*, p. 72.
[3] *Annales de la Philosophie chrétienne*, an 1858, p. 260.

with our more educated conception of its origin, appears in the main to be what old Hume asserted of it in his 'Natural History of Religion:' 'It seems certain, that, according to the natural progress of human thought, the ignorant multitude must first entertain some groveling and familiar notion of superior powers, before they stretch their conception to that perfect Being, who bestowed order on the whole frame of nature. We may as reasonably imagine, that men inhabited palaces before huts and cottages, or studied geometry before agriculture, as assert that the Deity appeared to them a pure spirit, omniscient, omnipotent, and omnipresent, before he was apprehended to be a powerful though limited being, with human passions and appetites, limbs and organs. *The mind rises gradually from inferior to superior.*'[1] This becomes still surer when we remember that religion begins where mythology, from the elements of which theistic religion takes its rise, ceases to live. For as these elements are always very numerous, it is not possible but that every religion must begin with a multitude of divine figures, i.e. with Polytheism. For it is impossible to point to any mythology which has to do with only one single name; yet from such a one alone could a monotheistic religion spring directly. Accordingly Polytheism is the historical *prius* of Monotheism, which can never exhibit itself except as historically evolved out of Polytheism. The

[1] *Essays, Moral, Political and Literary*, ed. Green and Grose, vol. II. p. 311; compare Buckle's *History of Civilisation in England*, in 3 vols. vol. I. p. 251; Pfleiderer, *Die Religion und ihre Geschichte*, II. 17. Before Hume the view that Polytheism was a degradation of a previous Monotheism was generally admitted. But Hume's exposition did not put an end to this radically false idea. Creuzer's great work, *Symbolik und Mythologie der alten Völker, besonders der Griechen*, is based on this false assumption, and Schelling's Philosophy of Religion starts from the same premiss. And many able English scholars still speak again and again of the degradation of the primeval Monotheism into Polytheism. Not only one-sided theologians start from this axiom; Gladstone's mythological system, in his *Studies on Homer and the Homeric Age*, and *Juventus Mundi* is founded upon it, all progress in history philology and mythology notwithstanding.

brilliant company of Olympian gods is therefore older than the first stirring of monotheistic feeling among the Greeks. Those who invert the historical order transfer to the religious condition of primitive humanity that which is only postulated by their own mind, and ascribe to the primeval man a religious tendency which in themselves was the result of laborious abstract speculations.

But all the contents of the human mind, like those of the material world, are subject to a constant evolution, or progressive change of form into something more perfect; and so Polytheism has an inherent tendency to further development, being indeed itself the result of a similar development of mythology. This tendency paves the way for the approach of Monotheism; for this it is to which the polytheistic stages of religion tend in their further development. We may see in the human mind, equally on a large and on a small scale, the inclination to the unification of whatever is similar in kind though hitherto divided into many individuals; abstraction and formation of general ideas are the climax of his power of thought. So is it in politics, and so also in the conception of nature.

The same unifying mental action, operating on the development of religion, creates in Polytheism an active tendency towards Monotheism. Even in those ethnological races for whom, in contradistinction to the Semitic race, Renan vindicates a polytheistic instinct, this tendency is active; and in any sphere which exhibits a complete and finished chain of religious evolution, we always find at the beginning Polytheism and at the end the Unitarian idea of God, whether in the form of Pantheistic Monism or of abstract personal Monotheism; whether coupled with the ideas of the Transcendency, or that of the Immanency, of God; whether excited by religious contemplation and absorption as with the Hebrew prophets, or by philosophical speculation as with the Greek sages. A mode of transition from Polytheism to Monotheism is found in the religious system which, while assuming a multitude of gods, distinguishes one of them as the most powerful, as the ruler not only of the world, but of the company of gods also. This system, to which Homer's conception of Zeus as πατὴρ ἀνδρῶν τε θεῶν τε belongs, possesses quite as much of Monotheism as of Polytheism, and expresses powerfully the monotheistic inclination concealed in Polytheism. Max Müller justly makes a distinction between Monotheism and Henotheism. A penetrating investigation of the Greek and the Indian literatures, the chief representatives of what Renan calls the polytheistic instinct, would prove the gradual formation of strata of monotheistic transformation, which attached themselves to Aryan polytheism and drew it in the monotheistic direction. Classical philologians have not neglected the study of the religious spirit on this subject, which prevails in the Greek tragedians and historians, not to mention the philosophical writers.

We have noted two kinds of impulse which usually promote a monotheistic revolution from Polytheism: religious absorption and contemplation on the one hand, and philosophical speculation on the other. Another powerful force must be mentioned in this connexion—the form of political institutions. This also exercises no small influence on the formation of the idea of God. If man has ascribed to the Deity the attribute of might and sovereignty, which is very natural to him, he will then apply to the gods the idea of power which he has gained by experience of human rulers, and will estimate their power according to the quality which he perceives every day in his earthly sovereigns; for the picture of these forms his sole conception of beings endowed with might and dominion. Only in the Immortals, he extends into infinity whatever he observes in his earthly rulers as something finite; since that which excites religious feeling in man is the impulse 'to advance beyond what is given him, beyond what he finds existing, and to push forward from the limited to the illimitable and absolutely perfect.' But this advance beyond what we have here is more than 'in itself a valuation of what we have, a measuring of it against the infinite,' as Steinthal admirably describes it in his fine lecture on 'Myth and Religion.'[1] It also connects the valuation of the infinite, and the quality attributed to it, with what we have here and know from daily experience. Hence the tendency of religious ideas is directly dependent on the ideas which are embodied in political and social life. Thus it was said by so early a writer as Aristotle, 'that all men say that the gods are under regal rule, because they themselves, some even now, and others in ancient times, have been so ruled; for men conceive not only the forms but the lives also of the gods as similar to their own.'[2] And similarly Schelling says, briefly, 'It seems hardly necessary to point out how closely magisterial power, legislature, morals, and even occupations are bound up with conceptions of the gods in all nations.'[3] What, for instance, are the inhabitants of the Hellenic Olympus? A powerful and conscious Aristocracy, at the head of which stands the most powerful among them—not all-powerful, for he is dependent on a mightier Fate, which prevents his accomplishing all that his will has determined, and

---

[1] In Virchow and Holtzendorff's *Sammlung gemeinverständlicher wissenschaftlicher Vorträge*, 1870, Heft 97, p. 20.

[2] *Polit.* I. 1. 7: καὶ τοὺς θεοὺς δὲ διὰ τοῦτο πάντες φασὶ βασιλεύεσθαι, ὅτι καὶ αὐτοὶ, οἱ μὲν ἔτι καὶ νῦν, οἱ δὲ τὸ ἀρχαῖον ἐβασιλεύοντο· ὥσπερ δὲ καὶ τὰ εἴδη ἑαυτοῖς ἀφομοιοῦσιν οἱ ἄνθρωποι, οὕτω καὶ τοὺς βίους τῶν θεῶν. Waitz, *Anthropologie der Naturvölker*, I. 466, says: 'Considering the multitude of superhuman beings, it is certainly very natural to follow the analogy of human relations, which is often carried out with great consistency, and to assume gradations of power among them, one being regarded as the first and highest of all. But this idea may easily be rendered unfruitful through the very analogy which suggested it, because in human society the power and repute of individuals are frequently changing.' But even this fact is not unfruitful with regard to religion; for on this analogy a world of gods with a head liable to change may be imagined.

[3] Schelling's *Sämmtliche Werke* (Cotta's edition, 1856), II. Abth. I. 52 (*Einleitung in die Philosophie der Mythologie*).

even on the surrounding aristocracy of the other gods, who once bound their powerful ruler! He owes his dominion to this very aristocracy: when Zeus had gained the victory over the Titans, says Hesiod,[1] the gods offered him the supreme rule (ὤτρυνον βασιλευέμεν ἠδὲ ἀνάσσειν), and when he had entered upon it, he distributed offices and dignities among his electors (ὁ δὲ τοῖσιν ἐΰ διεδάσσατο τιμάς). Are these different circumstances from those of the aristocratic republics of Greece?—is the relation of Zeus to the subordinate gods unlike that of the εἷς κοίρανος to the members of the aristocracy who are subject to his command, but yet possess a considerable influence over him? Turning from the classical Hellenes to the boisterous Bedâwî, of Arabia, we discover a conception of God under the very same point of view. A great investigator of Arabia observes: 'Nor did I ever meet, among the genuine nomade tribes, with any individual who took a more spiritual view, whether of the Deity, of the soul of man, or of any other disembodied being soever. *God is for them a chief* [a Nomad Sheikh!] . . ., somewhat more powerful of course than their own headman, or even than Ṭelâl himself, but in other respects of much the same style and character.'[2] If we turn our thoughts to a religious system of most recent origin, our experience is still the same. To the inhabitants of the Salt-Lake City in America, God is the President of immortal beings. 'The employment of familiar political ideas, or application of political figures to theocratic ends, as in speaking of the Presidency of God, colonies, eligibility, race, is a natural and obvious device.'[3] This, however, must rather be referred to apperception than to symbolism.

In a despotic state the conception of God must take a different direction, because the apperception of the notion of dominion and power is essentially different. This

[1] *Theogon.* vv. 882–85.
[2] Palgrave, *Central and Eastern Arabia*, I. 33.
[3] Von Holtzendorff in the *Zeitsch. für Völkerpsychologie etc.*, 1868, V. 378.

may be observed not only in nations of high culture, but even in tribes living in a state of nature, on a comparison of their religious and political conditions; though in the latter case we have not the means of pursuing the analogy with the same certainty. But, by way of illustration, I will refer to a comparison of the political condition of the Negro tribes which incline to a monotheistic view of religion with those of the polytheistic Polynesians.[1] Molina, too, found in Chili that the god Pillan's government of the world agrees exactly with the Araucanian political system, and concludes with the observation, 'These ideas are certainly very rude; but it must be acknowledged that the Araucanians are not the only people who have regulated the things of heaven by those of the earth.'[2] But we will now stay on the firmer ground of civilised nations. Let us take, for instance, the great Assyrian empire. One powerful ruler, endowed with unlimited authority, at whose commands great and small, high-born and slave, bend the knee, to whose arbitrary will almost the whole of Western Asia is subject, guides the destinies of his colossal empire, independent of men. After him follow the Viceroys of the separate provinces, Satraps, and a host of officials of court and state with accurately defined powers and in distinct order of rank. Whoever honours them and is obedient to them, only honours in them the King of kings, and exhibits his obedience to the all-powerful lord. Thus it was at the flourishing period of this immense empire; and to this political system corresponds exactly the religious idea, which grew up parallel with the growth of the empire from small beginnings. At the head of many subordinate gods stands the 'God of gods,' to whom all the sacrifices and expressions of homage offered to the

---

1 Waitz, *l.c.* II. 126 *et seq.* and especially pp. 167, 439, on the religion and politics of the Negroes, and Gerland in the sixth volume of the same work (*passim*) on similar institutions among the Polynesians.

2 In Tylor, *Primitive Culture*, II. 306.

subordinate, so to speak, satrap-gods, are indirectly presented. He is adored in the temples built in honour of his subordinates (see supra, p. 122). He is the 'God of Armies,' just as the King of kings is 'Lord of Armies.' In a word, we have to do with a form of religion that combines absolute monarchy with Polytheism. And is it surprising, considering the influence exercised by the mighty Assyrian empire on Western Asia, the nations of which it surpassed in manners and culture, that this form of religion became the prevailing tone of theology throughout the region?

Thus, while political division promotes in religion Polytheism, political unity and centralisation help the monotheistic development to break forth. As, when the political system is centralised, individuals only contribute to form a united political organism, and lose their personality in special functions which make each different from the other, so the idea of one common god arises and prevails over the many local deities, who are then subordinated to the former as their supreme Lord.

In the Hebrew nation likewise it was the political centralisation which established itself in the epoch distinguished by the names of David and Solomon, which at the same time conduced to the confirmation of Monotheism. It cannot be known for certain what sort of worship it was that was practised at various places in the land beside the so-called 'Ark of the Covenant' (arôn hab-berîth), before David removed the Ark to the political centre, and Solomon erected the magnificent Temple, of which the Books of Kings and the Chronicles give so elaborate an architectural description. But it must be assumed that the monotheistic working-out of the Elôhîm-idea in the Hebrew nation coincided with the centralising movement, that is with the period when the king directed the religious sentiment of the whole people to Jerusalem. This religious development again became powerful and was greatly encouraged by the newly strengthened National spirit, the influence of which on the spiritual life of the people was traced in the preceding chapter. For since the Hebrew nation was conscious of occupying a position of strict alienation from the tribes among and near which it dwelt, the exclusive tendency and negative character of this consciousness clung also to its conception of God, and thus it formed the idea of One God, who was the divine opposite to the gods of the nations, corresponding to the idea of the Hebrew nation as a nation opposed to the other nations. So long as the nation had no living consciousness of its national separation, and had not advanced to the point of saying 'I am something quite different from you,' no reason was forthcoming why the Hebrews should hold a negative position towards the objects of worship of other peoples; and they were, in fact, quite dependent on the latter, and receptive in temper. But having once risen to a consciousness of their own individuality, they regarded their own God exclusively as the Existing one, and denied the existence of the gods of nations towards which it acknowledged a national opposition. The germs of this religious development, so favourable to Monotheism, are bound up with the rise of a strong national consciousness; but the latter would not alone avail to create Monotheism at one blow; it only stimulates and encourages, but has need of other psychical and historical coefficients. Eduard Hartmann, who, in his recent work on the Philosophy of Religion, justly insists on the influence of the idea of nationality upon the growth of Monotheism, calls attention to another stage in the relation of the nation to the gods of strange peoples—that at which the strange gods are looked on as *usurpers*. Speaking of the three phases of development of Hebrew monotheism, he says:[1] 'With the increase of national feeling, their pride in their God was heightened. From the moment when they raised him to the position of

---

[1] *Die Religion der Zukunft*, Berlin 1874, p. 102.

sole creator of heaven and earth, they could not but regard the dominion of other gods on the earth created by Jehovah as usurped, and could only hope for the honour of their own God that ultimately the peoples would turn to him and adore him as the highest God, the only creator of the world. But then the progressive development of Monotheism went further, to the point of not merely regarding the strange gods as usurpers beside Jehovah, but of declaring them to be *false* gods.' What is the exact meaning of this view of *usurping* gods in the growth of Monotheism? In the growth of religions there is no stage at which certain divine persons are acknowledged as powerful and influential on the fate of the world or of a nation, and yet treated as possessing *illegitimate* power and *influence.* Their power might be unjustly exercised, but never illegitimate. The existence of gods is identified with their legitimacy. The conquest of some gods by others, which is told in theogonies and mythologies, is not explained by supposing one of the contending powers to have usurped his power, but by regarding the conquered as weaker than the conquering one.

This monotheistic development was very gradual, and passed through many stages in unfolding itself out of Polytheism. People spoke of the 'God of the Elôhîms of Israel' (Êl elôhê Yisrâ'êl), without giving any account as to who these Elôhîms were and what were their names. Whatever may be said, the plural form Elôhîm itself, the interpretation of which as *pluralis majestatis* belongs to the stage of pure Monotheism, decidedly indicates that a plural conception was inherent in this word. Such expressions, created by polytheistic imagination, were retained at the monotheistic stages, Like the myth, they lost their original signification, and were used by zealous monotheists without any idea of the Polytheism which had created them and been expressed by them. This Monotheism comes to light in the monotheistic turn which was given to the name Elôhîm; and the stronger the national life, and the intenser the national sentiment grew, so much more eagerly did the people grasp this Elôhîm-idea as a national one, entirely ignoring the fact that the name was not its exclusive property. At the conclusion of the national development the Elohistic monotheism attained perfection; but from the very beginning the mind of the nation lived in the conviction that 'Elôhîm was not like the Elôhîms of the nations.' The monotheistic turn given to the word is distinctly impressed on the form hâ-Elôhîm = ὁ Θεός, which is related to Elôhîm exactly as among Mohammedans Allâh to Ilâh. An important part in the encouragement of this monotheistic development was played by the Levitical priesthood, which conducted the centralised worship; as also by those inspired men of action who appeared as teachers and monitors in the early days of the monarchy, precursors of the later great Prophets, harbingers of the epoch of the *Prophètes écrivains*, as Renan correctly calls them.[1] The later Prophets, although when writing history they depict these precursors as completely imbued with their own intentions, did not ignore their position as precursors. Elijah and Samuel were prototypes of prophecy, in whose lives and actions the prophetic historian of a later time unfolded his own program; but even they are endowed with infirmities foreign to later Jahveism; and these faults are characterised as such. A prophet of the Postexilian period, in which a history of the growth of Jahveism as reconciled with the law (tôrâ), with Moses as law-giving prophet at the head, was already brought into notice, regarded Elijah as the precursor of the 'great and dreadful day of Jahveh.' Malachi, namely (III. 22, 23 [IV. 4, 5]), one of the chief representatives of the reconciliation effected between the two opposites, Sacerdotalism and Jahveism, exhorts the people to remember the Tôrâ of Moses, and in the same breath speaks of Elijah, the

---

[1] *Histoire générale etc.*, p. 131.

chief member of the old school of prophecy, as precursor of the great day of Jahveh. These are two reminiscences, valuable in a religious sense to the prophet of the Post-exilian period.[1] However gradual may have been the full development of Monotheism among the Hebrews, on a consideration of the chronology it is impossible to deny that it had a far more rapid course there than elsewhere. This rapidity of revolution is expressed very significantly in the monotheistic turn given to the word Elôhîm, which looks as if (to use mathematical language) the separate Elôahs had been added up and put in a bracket to represent a Divine Unity, adequate to the sudden national unity produced out of political divisions only just composed.

Thus the awakened idea of Nationality left its impress also on the domain of religion. But it is now quite intelligible that the religious expression thereby introduced, possessed an obvious defect, inasmuch as it bore on its front a contradiction which no mere National sentiment could get rid of, the word Elôhîm being common to the Hebrews and the Canaanites. This contradiction gave the first stimulus to the creation of the word 'Jahveh,' the specially Hebrew term. The origin of this Divine name may therefore be most probably assigned to this period, as a necessary result of the religious element of the idea of Nationality. An agricultural people could very easily grasp the idea of God as an idea of 'him who makes to be, who produces;' and it is not impossible that this appellation had its first origin at the time of the formation of a myth of civilisation, and passed from a primitive solar to a later religious significance. But during this whole period Jahveh remained a mere word, a *flatus oris*, an Elôhîm connected with the nation. No deeper meaning, distinguishing Jahveh from the Canaanitish Elôhîm, was as yet attached to the word; that belongs to a later age, that of the Prophets. Moreover, the name itself did not

[1] Thus this much-discussed verse contains no prophecy, but a recollection of the phases of the growth of religion in past times.

at first force its way deep into the soul of the whole people, but remained as something external,—a Divine name, identical with hâ-Elôhîm, and implying no more. Fights, such as the Prophets fought, first created the Jahveh-religion in opposition to Elohism. Accordingly, it will be best to lay no stress on the existence of the Name before the point at which it obtains a religious significance and begins to be filled with its lofty conception.

§ 3. At the same time with the monotheistic idea there arose a multitude of religious views, which necessarily had an influence on the development of the myths into history. And insofar as the Hebraisation of the Elôhîm-idea confirmed, and even became the centre of the consciousness of nationality, the conversion of the myths into national history, of which the previous chapter treated, naturally received a peculiarly religious tone.

Here we see the germ of that theocratic character which people take a pleasure in introducing into the earliest history of the Hebrews, but which unquestionably presupposes a high development of the Elôhîm-idea. The theocratic system is a league between the religious and the national ideas. As the myths were transformed in the preceding period into national history, so now in this Elohistic time, their interpretation in a national sense is supplemented by a theocratic aim, which again imprints a new stamp on the old mythology, and exhibits the thoughts and feelings of the Hebrews in richer measure than before. Those legendary figures which at the time of National aspiration became Patriarchs or forefathers of the Hebrew nation, now enter the service of the theocratic or religious idea, and become pious servants and favourites of God. Mythical events and contests which in the national period were converted into national history of primeval times, now take a liturgical or religious turn. Not till now could the question, why Abraham was willing to kill Isaac, arise distinctly in the mind. And the answer was at hand: he did it at the command of Elôhîm—he *sacrificed*, for he was Elôhîm's faithful servant, capable of sacrifice. The other Patriarchs also become pious, God-fearing individuals; their adventures and lives become types of Elohistic piety, as they had previously been made types of the history of the nation. The political idea also, *i.e.* the conviction that it was necessary for the Hebrew nation to possess the territory which they called their own, is carried back to the patriarchal age in the repeated promises of Elôhîm to the Patriarchs that their descendants should possess themselves of the land of Canaan. This was the highest, the religious sanction of the National idea; and this conception the most prominent factor in the production of the direction imparted at this time to the stories of the Patriarchs. The national legends had only aimed at proving by documents the noble ancestry of the Hebrew nation and the high antiquity of their antagonism to the nations who subsequently were their enemies; and endeavoured to demonstrate that the national character and the national preeminence of the Hebrews were founded in the earliest times, and could be fully justified from the history of their ancestors. In this later religious and theocratic epoch, on the other hand, there is infused into the legends a tendency to transform the ancestors into *religious* prototypes and individuals in whom the ancient preference of Elôhîm for the Hebrew nation could be exhibited, and the truth established that this preference of Elôhîm was a primeval distinction which advantageously marked off the Hebrews from the other nations of Canaan.

This accordingly determines the form impressed on the myths, which had already suffered several modifications, by the rise of a religious and theocratic course of ideas; and I deem it unnecessary to exhibit in detail every portion of the matter constituting the Hebrew legendary lore in which this stratum of development is observable. Scarcely any part of the stories of the Patriarchs is free from this new force of development, and we should have to reproduce them all in their fullest extent to give a collection of examples of what has been said. It must, however, be added, that this impulse to the further development of the legends is not confined to those relating to Canaan. The same impulse draws the history of the Hebrews in Egypt also into the sphere of its operation. For, independently of the fact, that the conception of the residence of the Hebrews in the land of the Pharaohs receives a theocratic modification, the later mutual relation of the Hebrew and the Egyptian nations is prefigured in the patriarchal story, and gains a prototype in the relation of Abraham to Pharaoh. A famine in Canaan obliges Abraham to move into Egypt; and this journey is made the reason why 'Jahveh plagued Pharaoh and his house with great plagues' (Gen. XII. 17), until 'Pharaoh gave an order to some men concerning him, and they escorted away Abraham and his wife, and all who belonged to him' (v. 20). This foreshadowing of later historical events and the insertion of them into the body of old stories is, as we see, an important factor in the development of Hebrew stories. Each epoch works into the old legendary matter whatever preeminently occupies the mind of the age, in such a manner as to indicate the intellectual attitude and tendency of the later time.

§ 4. There is still another feature of the development of legends to be mentioned—one which is closely bound up with an important alteration of the political institutions of the Hebrew nation. This feature, though nearly connected with the National transformation of the legends, historically belongs to the age with which we have to do in this chapter. This stage of development of the legends may best be termed the *Differentiation* of the National Legends.

The political and religious centralisation, which formed the program of the first two representatives of the Davidical dynasty, and which bound the highest power in the state to one city, Jerusalem, as a geographical centre, and to one family, as the visible representative of that power, did not meet with unmixed applause everywhere. Jerusalem lies close to the southern limit of the Hebrew territory. If the South came to the front, the northern parts of the kingdom might be deprived of all influence on affairs of state and religion. The inhabitants of the northern district were practically condemned to be only bearers of the burdens, imposed on the subjects of the kingdom through the luxury growing up in the centre of monarchy and of religion; for very little enjoyment of, or pride in, this splendour could fall to their share. And then the religious centralisation took all importance and influence from the sanctuaries and places of assembly in the North, which before the centralisation were spread over the whole kingdom in due proportion. Nothing, therefore, could be more natural than the reaction in the North, which spread after the death of Solomon under his weak successor, and ended with the division of the kingdom. The history of this division and the circumstances connected with it are sufficiently well known from the Old Testament narrative (1 Kings XII.), in which no essential element is devoid of historical credibility. All of it is a natural consequence of the then condition of the Hebrew kingdom. Now it is very intelligible that in the northern district, the centralising and theocratic spirit, which was at bottom the reason of the political secession, could not find an entrance, and that therefore the northern district remained at the Elohistic stage as it was before an advance had been made to pure Monotheism—in relation to religion scarcely yet separated from Canaanism, but with respect to nationality sharing the common Hebrew sentiment. Accordingly, in the spiritual development of the Northern kingdom, the theocratic interpretation of the past ages of the nation, excited by the centralising movement, is not merely treated as unimportant, but positively does not appear at all. This, of course, is true not only of the spiritual condition of the northern Hebrews after the secession, but of their spiritual life during the whole period of the formation of the theocratic spirit in the South. For the very fact that the Northerns possessed little knowledge of and no inclination for this tendency, then all-powerful in the commonwealth, gave an impetus to the secessionistic aspirations, which under the strong rule of Solomon had no opportunity of declaring themselves, but burst out all the more forcibly and persistently at the commencement of a feebler reign. But while the theocratic spirit, so peculiar to the Southern kingdom, forms a distinction between the characters of the North and of the South, intense national consciousness and national opposition to the Canaanites is common to both. This feeling grew up equally in both of them. But even in respect to this, the political separation naturally produced its consequences. Nationality is very closely tied to political unity. The abstract idea of nationality becomes illusory if there is no united state in which it appears in a concrete form. The consciousness of national oneness is enfeebled, if the political state does not coincide with the nation in a single idea. Hence we see how eager nations divided into separate political states are for a struggle for union, when once their national consciousness wakes out of sleep. On the other hand, in states formed by a union of peoples of various nationalities, we observe a certainly justifiable endeavour, on the part of the strongest and therefore ruling nationality, to inoculate the weaker ones with its own national sentiment, and thereby produce a common feeling of unity.

The political separation of the Northern region from the centralised Hebrew state, produced a remarkable and very important alteration in the sense of nationality hitherto worked out in common. The political opposition between North and South encouraged also the recognition of a difference in their common genealogy. As the general Hebrew idea of nationality found nourishment in the store of legends, so also the consciousness of this secondary difference sought justification in the mythology. This sense of difference came to light more clearly in the northern Hebrews than in the southern. The former wrote the name Joseph on their banner, and derived themselves directly from that son of the common ancestor, and in opposition to the southerns laid more and more stress on this special feature of their origin; moreover, it was not so much Joseph that concerned them as Ephraim, who is named a son of Joseph. We must not forget that this name Ephraim has only a secondary origin. For when the national purpose of the story was once drafted in the mind of the people, it was developed in details in a most independent fashion. The biography of the ancestors was worked out exhaustively; that to which the existing legendary matter offered no suggestion or occasion was supplied by the restless activity of the popular sentiment. In various places in Canaan sepulchral caves had been pointed out from the earliest times—or rather caves which were employed for sepulture; for it is pretty certain that they were originally intended rather for the living than for the dead. Now could anything be simpler than to imagine the bones of ancestors to have been placed there, and to bind to these places the sacred piety which was felt by an enthusiastic nation for venerated progenitors? It is generally known that such an origin of traditions relating to graves is not uncommon in the history of civilisation and religion. Saints' graves have as many interpretations fastened on them as feast-days and popular festivals. Hebron was a place suitable for this treatment, and so popular tradition placed there the bones of the Patriarchs and their wives, and attached the general national piety to the place. Accordingly King David acted in sympathy with the lately aroused national enthusiasm, when he chose Hebron for his residence (2 Sam. II. 1, 11). And the popular belief concerning the graves of the Patriarchs was so firmly fixed in the soul of the nation as to become in later generations a meeting-point of the piety of three religions towards their sacred antiquity. Mohammedans, Jews, and Christians vie with each other in the adorations which they lavish on the 'Double Cave' at Hebron. Mohammedans, who place the prophet Ibrâhîm al-Chalîl higher than either Jews or Christians, have done more for the authenticity of the graves of the Patriarchs at Hebron than either of the older religions, from which they received the tradition concerning them. I know of no literary work emanating from Christians or Jews, written in defence of the authenticity of this cave. Conviction was left to faith and piety rather than to historical certainty. But it was a Mohammedan—not even an Arab, but a Persian—that undertook this task. 'Alî b. Ja'far al-Râzî wrote a book entitled al-musfir lil-ḳulûb 'an ṣiḥḥat ḳabr Ibrâhîm Isḥâḳ wa-Ya'ḳûb 'Enlightener of hearts concerning the correctness of the grave of Abraham, Isaac and Jacob.' Ibn Baṭûṭâ of Maġreb (North-Western Africa), a great Mohammedan traveller, who made a pilgrimage to al-Chalîl (Hebron), quotes largely from this book on occasion of his description of the Graves of the Patriarchs.[1] But popular tradition has preserved far more recollections of graves of Patriarchs and Prophets than Scripture, and Mohammedan tradition considerably more than Jewish. This testifies eloquently how incomplete stories are felt to be as long as they can tell only of events and persons without connecting everything with a definite locality. Popular tradition always feels the want of topographical completion, as long as it can give no distinct account of the places where the events of which it speaks took place, where its

[1] *Voyages d'Ibn Batoutah,* I. 115 *et seq.* The jealousy with which the Mohammedans for a long time forbad Christians and Jews to visit the graves of the Patriarchs only began at the year 664 A.H. 'L'an 664 Bibars défendit aux chrétiens et aux juifs d'entrer dans le temple de Hébron; avant cette époque ils y allaient librement, moyennant une rétribution' (Quatremère, *Mémoire géogr. et hist. sur l'Égypte,* Paris 1841, II. 224).

favourite heroes lived and worked, where they were cradled and where they slept their last sleep. This impulse was felt in ancient times, and produced the localisation of myths. Accordingly, the Mohammedan popular tradition knows of the grave of Adam on the mountain Abû Ḳubeys,[1] of that of Eve at Jeddâ, of that of Cain and Abel at Ṣâliḥîyyâ, a suburb of Damascus, of that of Seth in the valley of Yahfûfâ in Antilibanus,[2] and of those of some of Jacob's sons, as of Reuben at Jahrân, a place in the south of Arabia,[3] of Asher and Naphtali at Kafarmandâ, between ʿAkkâ (Acre) and Tiberias. Even Zipporah, the wife of Moses, was a person sufficiently interesting to popular tradition to have a grave assigned to her;[4] just as Mohammedan tradition asserts the grave of Ham to be in the district of Damascus,[5] and that of the forefather of the Canaanites to be at Chörbet râs Kenʿan near Hebron,[6] and also shows that of Uriah at the edge of the desert beyond the Jordan.[7] The Mohammedans took interest also in the grave of Aaron, and it was from them that the Jews received the local tradition relating to it.[8] But it also happens not unfrequently, that popular tradition allows one and the same patriarch or prophet to be buried at several places, often far distant from each other. Various countries take a pride in possessing the last remains of venerated persons, and vie with each other for this privilege. Even so established a tradition as that which placed the graves of the Patriarchs at Hebron, and was especially firm with regard to Abraham (al-Chalîl), is not so irremovable but that it could be localised somewhere else also. The district of Damascus has its tradition of Abraham, and the village of Berze its cave with

[1] Ibn Ḳuteybâ, *Handbuch der Geschichte*, ed. Wüstenfeld, p. 10.
[2] Burton and Drake, *Unexplored Syria*, London 1872, I. 33.
[3] Yâḳût, *Muʿjam*, IV. 291. 11 *et seq.* [4] *Ibid.*, p. 438. 16.
[5] Burton and Drake, *l.c.* p. 35.
[6] Rosen in *Zeitsch. d. D. M. G.*, XI. 59. [7] Yâḳût, III. 720. 3.
[8] Zunz, *Geogr. Literatur der Juden*, no. 109, *Gesammelte Schriften*, I. 191.

Abraham's grave.[1] The most noteworthy instance of the kind is the grave of Moses himself. It is well known that the Bible has nothing definite to say of the place of interment of this prophet; and hence in the Jewish popular tradition the prevailing idea is that it is impossible to discover the place where rest the bones of the Prophet with whom the origin of religion is so closely connected—the very same thing as the Sunnite Mohammedans assert of the grave of 'Alî.[2] 'And he (Jahveh) buried him[3] in the valley in the land of Moab, opposite Beth-Peor, and *no man has known his grave up to the present day'* (Deut. XXXIV. 6). The little Pesiḳtâ thinks the purpose of this was 'that the Israelites might not pay divine honours to his grave, and raise a sanctuary at it, and also that the heathen should not desecrate the place by idolatry and abominations.' It is at least certain that, as appears from the Biblical words just cited, the grave of Moses was imagined to be in the valley and beyond the Jordan; for the Prophet had never crossed the river. It may also probably have been in the region thus indicated in the Bible, that, according to an assertion in the older Midrâsh on Deuteronomy, a Roman Emperor—a royal precursor of the Palestine Exploration Society—sent explorers to find the grave, in vain: 'The government of the Imperial house sent people out with the order, Go and see where Moses' grave is. So they went and searched above, and they saw something below; so they went down again, and saw it above. So they divided themselves, and again those above saw it below and those below saw it above.'[4] Islâm, how-

---

[1] Alfred von Kremer, *Mittelsyrien und Damaskus*, Vienna 1853, p. 118.

[2] al-Damîrî, *Ḥayât al-ḥaywân*, I. 59: ''Alî is the earliest Imâm whose burial-place is not known. It is said that before his death he ordered it to be kept secret, knowing that the sons of Umayya would attain to power, and that his grave would not then be safe from desecration. Nevertheless, his grave is shown at various places.'

[3] Or 'And *they* buried him' (LXX. ἔθαψαν), as it is understood by many excellent scholars.—Tr.

[4] Siphrê debhê Rabh, ed. M. Friedmann, Vienna 1864, § 357 and note 42 of the editor.

ever, possesses the grave of Moses at several places. The best known place is the hill Nebî Mûsa, a very beautiful eminence in a romantic situation, well worth visiting by a slight but fatiguing dêtour from the road from Jerusalem to the Dead Sea; not much visited by pilgrims now on account of its inconvenient position. Here, in the centre of a ruined compound, is to be seen the grave of the Prophet, a great sarcophagus, the carpet covering which bears an inscription informing us of its venerable contents. Thus this grave is not in the valley, but on a hill; not beyond the Jordan, but on the Jerusalem side. But also an old mosque at Damascus was said, at all events six hundred years ago, to contain the sepulchral monument of Moses;[1] and his grave is also said to be on a hill called Hôreb, three days' journey from Moḳḳa.[2]

For Aaron's burial-place Mohammedan tradition has assigned two places, one about where it would be looked for according to the Biblical account,[3] and the other, which is chiefly visited as Aaron's Grave, on the hill Ohod.[4] This last position has been brought into connexion with a legend of Moses and Aaron staying in the Hedjaz.[5] An Arabic savant, 'Abd-al-Ġanî al-Nâbulsî, finds an occasion, in his book of Travels, to notice the circumstance that the grave of the same Patriarch is shown at numerous places.[6] Sometimes an inscription is found at *every one* of these burial-places. But such inscriptions are not made with *mala fides* by mere deceivers of the people. They are only the written expression of what lives in popular belief; and when inscriptions occur at various places referring to the grave of the same

[1] Yâḳût, II. 589. 21.

[2] Sepp, *Jerusalem und das Heilige Land*, II. 245.

[3] *Ṭûr Hârûn*, Yâḳût, III. 559; Ḳazwînî, I. 168; see Burckhardt in Gesenius, *Thesaurus*, p. 392.

[4] *Zeitsch. d. D. M. G.*, 1862, XVI. 688.

[5] Burton, *Personal Narrative etc.*, 1st ed. II. 117, or 2nd ed. I. 331.

[6] *Zeitsch. d. D. M. G.*, *l.c.* p. 656. On duplicates in Mohammedan and Christian traditions about graves, see Sepp's article on Samaria and Sichem, (*Ausland*, 1875, pp. 470–72).

prophet, the reason is that the local popular tradition of each of those places happened to be reduced to writing.[1] An interesting example of this is the grave of the Prophet of the nation of 'Ad, the disappearance of which—an unsolved ethnological riddle—occasioned the rise of the Mohammedan legend of the prophet Hûd. The grave of this prophet is shown both at Damascus[2] and in the region of Ẓafâr in the south of Arabia, the scene of his activity. Ibn Baṭûṭâ, who visited both tombs, reports that both were marked with an inscription in the following words: 'This is the grave of Hûd, son of 'Âbir: the most excellent prayers and greetings for him!'[3]

The grave of Rachel is also marked out by tradition, which puts it in the neighbourhood of Ephrâth, subsequently and still called Bêth-lechem (Beth-lehem). This sepulchre is to the present day the object of pilgrimage to the adherents of three religions. The myth calls Joseph the son of Rachel, and we know of Ephrayîm (Ephraim) as son of Joseph. Now the name Ephrayîm seems to belong to the period of the differentiation of the national legends, and to be a secondary form to Ephrâth, which passes for the burial-place of his ancestress. For we find also the derivative noun Ephrâthî, *i.e.* 'belonging to Ephrâth,' in the two senses 'a man from the place Ephrâth' and 'a descendant of Ephraim;' and Ephraim himself is called Ephrâthâ in a passage in the Psalms.[4] The prophet Samuel and his ancestors are also said to have been

---

[1] A *mala fides* should not be assumed even in the case of inscriptions like those mentioned by Procopius, *De Bello Vandalico*, V. 2. 13; see Munk's *Palestina*, German translation by Levy, p. 193, note 5. They are everywhere old legendary popular traditions, which in later time become fixed by an inscription. From such inscriptions we must distinguish fictitious sepulchral monuments, in which the intention to delude is manifest, *e.g.* the inscription on the graves of Eldad and Medad, on which see Zunz, *l.c.* no. 43, p. 167. On Jewish accounts of the burial-places of the ancients Zunz, *l.c.* pp. 182 and 210, should be consulted.

[2] Sepp, *l.c.*, II. 269.

[3] *Voyages*, I. 205, II. 203. A brief list of graves of prophets which are shown at Tiberias and some other places is given in Yâḳût, III. 512.

[4] See Gesenius, *Thesaurus*, p. 141.

Ephrâthî-men (1 Sam. I. 1).[1] This identity between the name of the burial-place of Joseph's mother and the name of his son is probably not accidental, but produced under the influence of the national tendencies of the North; and the reaction of the spirit of the South may have suppressed the old name of the place and substituted the modern Bêth-lechem. Now in my view the name Ephrayîm was originally not a personal but a national name. After the separation the Northern Hebrews called themselves 'those belonging to Ephrâth.' For the word Ephrayîm has the form of a plural of a so-called *relative* adjective (Arabic *nisbâ*), derived from Ephrâth by throwing off the feminine formative syllable *ath* and attaching the new formative syllable directly to the base of the word. Of this Semitic mode of formation the Arabic gives a good instance; there the feminine ending of the proper name (*t*) is regularly cast off in forming the *nisbâ*, and the relative termination is attached to the body of the word: e.g. from Baṣrat^{un} not Baṣratî but Baṣrî, 'a man of Basrâ.' In Hebrew, the feminine termination is cast off when it appears in the shortened form *â*; *e.g.* Yehûdâ (Judah), whence Yehûdî; Timnâ, whence Timnî. But an instance occurs in which even the termination *th* is cast off before the formation of the relative. Instead of Kerêthî, the form generally used in the phrase hak-Kerêthî wehap-Pelêthî 'the Kerethites and the Pelethites,' the form Kârî is found (2 Sam. XX. 23 Kethîbh); the *th*[2] being discarded, and the vowel of the first syllable lengthened by way of compensation (*productio suppletoria*). I

[1] If this means that he belonged to the tribe of Ephraim, it is easy to understand why the author of the Chronicle (1 Chr. IV. 18 *et seq.*) claims him for the tribe of Levi, when we consider the generally acknowledged Levitical tendency of that late book of history. It would appear to one holding Levitical sentiments impossible that a man who is said to have often offered sacrifices (1 Sam. IX. 13), and to have served in the sanctuary of Shiloh under the High-priest Eli, should have been anything but a Levite.

[2] Consequently the discarded ת th must be regarded as an inflexion, and shows us that the word has no connexion with Crete.

assume the same formation in the present case (though the regular *Ephrâthî* is also used), the termination of the relative adjective being attached directly to the base Ephr, after the rejection of the *th*. We know further that the idiom of the Northern part of the region covered by the Hebrew language contained much that is generally called Aramaism. The Aramaic relative adjectives are formed in *ay*, and they are occasionally met with in Hebrew also;[1] Ephray, forming the plural Ephrayîm, is an instance. This latter form accordingly signifies 'those belonging to Ephrâth,' and is the national name of the Hebrews of the North, used afterwards as a designation of their ancestor. Many instances of a similar proceeding occur in the Biblical genealogies.

Thus the Northern Hebrews possess national memories connecting them with Joseph-Ephraim. It is therefore quite natural that, as the national difference which parted the Northern from the Southern people became more evident, vivid and acknowledged, the mind of the former was more occupied with the cycle of stories about the person and adventures of Joseph. The existing mass of stories offered abundant opportunity for this, and more productive matter could scarcely be imagined than the story of the hatred of the brethren towards Joseph, the Patriarch of the North. The Northerns consequently seized this portion of the Patriarchal history, and worked it out in the interest of their national separatism, always contriving to let the supremacy of Joseph above Judah clearly appear. They take pleasure in representing Judah crouching in the dust before Joseph the ruler, and owing his life entirely to the will of the generous brother, towards whom he had formerly borne such bitter ill-will. Joseph is brought forward with satisfaction and pride as the brother whom the aged father treated with the greatest favour and distinction, and whose life alone was able to

[1] Ewald, *Ausführl. Lehrb. d. hebr. Sprache*, § 164. c; *Grammar* transl. Nicholson, § 343 end.

revive his fainting spirits; while Joseph's mother was the only woman whom the Patriarch really loved, whereas the Southerns were descended partly from the ugly Leah, Judah's mother, who became Jacob's wife only by deceit and craft, and partly from slaves.

National stories are created by the awaking consciousness of opposition; and, as we have seen, they transfer to primeval times the national spirit of opposition, which is an affair of the present, and ascribe a reflex of it to the respective ancestors. This is the spirit of the stories of Joseph, worked out by the Northern in opposition to the Southern Hebrews. The enmity of the two Hebrew kingdoms is transferred to the earliest times, and prefigured in the picture of the relation between Joseph and his brethren. The chief portions of this mass of Northern stories which were reduced to writing at a later time, and thus fixed in a definite form, were contained in the ancient document distinguished by most critics as the 'Book of Uprightness' (Sêpher hay-Yâshâr).[1]

I must here refer to a very ingenious theory concerning the matter in hand, which was propounded not long ago by A. Bernstein.[2] He imagines the differentiation of the mass of Hebrew stories to have been such that the story of Abraham, the Patriarch of Hebron, belongs to the Southern kingdom, whilst that of Jacob, the Patriarch of Beth-el, was produced by the political tendencies of the Northern realm. Before these more recent stories he supposes the oldest of the Patriarchal stories, which was connected with the worship at Beer-sheba, to have existed, but to have been afterwards obscured by the later legend about Abraham. Bernstein leaves these stories of political tendency to fight it out together, and entangles them in the antagonism between North and South, until at

[1] Aug. Knobel, *Die Bücher Numeri, Deuteronomium und Josua*, p. 544. On the Northern origin of this book most candid Biblical critics are agreed.

[2] *Ursprung der Sagen von Abraham, Isak und Jakob.* Kritische Untersuchung von A. Bernstein. Berlin 1871.

last after the disappearance of the opposition they become common property and are blended together. Althóugh from what has been said there appears to be no question but that in the treatment of the legendary matter, the political situation was no insignificant factor, yet it is impossible to set up the three Patriarchs as products of mere political tendencies. For we have proved that the origin of their names goes back to the very earliest age when myths were first created. No doubt this or that feature in the *tout ensemble* of the story took a different character according as it was handed down by the inhabitants of the Northern or of the Southern kingdom; and sensible interpreters have long paid particular attention to these differences. But the names are not later *inventions* or fictions; they are primeval, and among the oldest elements of the Hebrew language; and, similarly, the most prominent features of the stories, derived from the ancient myth, are free from all that national or political tendency which attached itself in much later times to the ancient material.

§ 5. In general the Northern kingdom, in which no theocratic tendency seized on and transformed the existing mass of stories, held the legends, which were guided in a national direction, firmer, and felt more affection for them. Besides the Patriarchal stories, those which fill up the age of the Judges (Shôpheṭîm) gave the most scope to national pride. There the stories of the true Hebrew national heroes and their heroic battles with the Philistines are found. In respect to theocracy this whole age has little importance, and the stories were utterly incapable of a theocratic transformation. For the very aim of Hebrew theocracy was, first to prefigure the theocratic destiny of the Hebrews in the history of the primeval age, and then to show in as favourable a light as possible the beneficent revolution brought on by the house of David. But for this purpose it was essential that this period of theocratic movement should contrast advantageously with an untheocratic time, unfavourable to any such movement, and that the spirit of David's rule should be the very opposite of the preceding administrations. Consequently, the stories of the Judges suffered no theocratic transformation. But transformation and development constitute the very life of Legend, which, if not accommodated to the new current of feeling, is abandoned, and ceases to live; having in its old form no meaning to a new age.

There are unequivocal testimonies which prove that to the theocratic mind the stories of the Judges were utterly dead, and were consequently neglected by it. Two of these testimonies deserve especial mention. The Book of Chronicles (dibhrê hay-yâmîm), which we have been long accustomed to regard as a history written in a strictly sacerdotal spirit, enumerating by name all the priests, Levites, singers and door-keepers of the central sanctuary of Jerusalem, utters not a syllable respecting the entire period of the Judges, but commences the history proper at the death of Saul and accession of David. And another part of the Canon, the Book of Ruth, the object of which is to connect David's genealogy with an idyl, and which expresses the moderate theocratic ideas of the restoration, while the matter of its narrative occupies no determinate chronological position, indicates this very chronological vagueness by the words wa-yehî bîmê shephôt hash-shôpheṭîm, 'it was in the days when the Judges ruled,' *i.e.* it was once in the olden time (Ruth I. 1). The 'Judges' time' here denotes an indeterminate period, whose chronology is effaced. That period, in fact, does labour under an indefiniteness which almost baffles the chronologist, and the Biblical Canon itself could only be drawn up by leaving an excessively lax connexion between the three periods—the occupation of Canaan by the Hebrews, the monarchy after David, and the untheocratic period lying between the two.

But the Northern spirit was strongly attracted to the period of the Judges and the stories belonging to it, since it felt itself to be the continuator of the homogeneous spirit of the history of the times before David; and thus literature is indebted to an author belonging to the Northern kingdom for the ground-work of the Book of Judges.[1] Thus then was accomplished the division of the mass of legends of the Hebrews.

---

[1] As the drawing up of the Canon belongs to an age in which the antagonism between North and South had ceased to exist, the literary prŏducts of the North which were still preserved from old times obtained a place in it, though always brought into harmony with the all-pervading theocratic character by occasional interpolated modifications of sentiment.

CHAPTER IX.

PROPHETISM AND THE JAHVEH-RELIGION.

§ 1. The most brilliant point in the history of Hebrew Religion is distinguished by an ingenious original idea, imported by the Hebrews into the development of religion —a single thought, yet in itself sufficient to secure for that short history a permanent place on the pages of universal history. The idea of Jahveh is what I allude to.[1]

To the question, when this idea was born, the sublimity of which exerted so powerful and irresistible an influence over the noblest minds, it can only be answered that we labour in vain if we try to find the exact point of time of its origin. As the Nile, to which those who have been cradled on its banks ascribe a great magic force, cannot be easily traced to its source, so with the idea of Jahveh: we do not see it spring into life, we only see it after its creation, and observe how it works and kindles new spiritual life in the souls of those who acknowledge it. The Mohammedan idea of Allâh is the only one which may perhaps vie with the sublimity of that of Jahveh;

---

[1] With respect to the originality and the specifically Hebrew character of the notion of Jahveh, I consider the most correct assertion yet made to be what Ewald declared in reference to the alleged Phenician Divine name Jah; for when we examine the passages and the data on which Movers' and Bunsen's opposite view is based, their apocryphal nature strikes us at the first glance. This is especially true (to mention one case only) of the passage of Lydus, *De mens.* IV. 38. 14: Οἱ Χαλδαῖοι τὸν θεὸν ΙΑΩ λέγουσιν . . . τῇ Φοινίκων γλώσσῃ καὶ ΣΑΒΑΩΘ δὲ πολλαχοῦ λέγεται κτλ. (See Bunsen, *Egypt's Place in Universal History*, vol. IV. p. 193). As to the occurrence of the name Jahveh in the Assyrian theology there is not yet sufficient certainty. Eberhard Schrader, who refers to it, imagines the name to be borrowed from the Hebrew (*Die Keilinschriften und das Alte Testament*, p. 4).

yet even that is far from occupying so lofty an eminence of religious thought as the idea of Jahveh.

If, translating the word Jahveh into a modern European language, we say that he is the one who 'Brings to be,' produces and works out Being, we do not in the most distant manner indicate the fulness of meaning which is embodied in that religious technical term. To appreciate it, a sympathising soul must be absorbed in all that the Prophets bring into connexion with the expression Jahveh. Shall I translate all that these inspired men declare of Jahveh? I should have to interpret the entire prophetic literature of the Hebrews, and yet should produce only a pale reflex of all the splendour which envelops Jahveh with glory in the speeches of the Prophets.

I have mentioned the Mohammedan idea of Allâh. Although etymologically identical with Elôhîm, that name may afford a parallel to the Hebrew idea of Jahveh, not only in its essence and meaning, but also in its history. It was not unknown as a technical religious expression to the Arabs before the time of Moḥammed. To the Pre-islamite or heathen system of Arabic theology, which had its centre in the sanctuary at Mekka, the Divine name Allâh was familiar. But with what a new meaning did the preaching of the epileptic huckster of Mekka inform it! Through the gospel of the Arabian Prophet Allâh became something quite new. Yet even in this respect Jahveh appears still grander. For, while the Mohammedan idea of God clings close to the etymological signification of the word Allâh, insisting primarily on might and unlimited omnipotence, in the Hebrew Prophets' idea of Jahveh the name becomes a mere accident and accessory, and the true meaning presses with its full weight in a direction quite distinct from the signification and etymology of the word, which was formed in an earlier age. I have already declared my opinion as to the period in which the Divine name Jahveh may have emerged into notice among the people (p. 272), and the impulse which produced it. We can also demonstrate the existence of the name after that period from many proper names which are compounded with the name Jahveh, either full or abbreviated (into Jâhû or Jâ), that name forming either the first or the second member of the compound. From the fact that such names occur in the Northern as well as in the Southern kingdom, it is also evident that the name Jahveh itself had been formed before the separation.[1] On the other hand, we ought not to infer too much from the early occurrence of such names in the canonical books. For, in the first place, not every Jô- at the beginning of proper names is an abbreviation of the Divine name; if our knowledge of the ancient forms of Hebrew speech could be extended, this Jô- would probably in many cases be degraded into the first syllable of a verb, as has been shown by M. Levy to be probably the case in the name Yô'êl (Joel);[2] secondly, it must be remembered that there is a possibility that many of these names received a Jahveistic colouring only from the theocratic writers. The possibility of this is seen in the fact that even the name Yôsêph, in which the first syllable has nothing to do with Yahveh, once occurs in the form Yehôsêph (Ps. LXXXI. 6 [5]),[3] and still more clearly in the conversion of the name Hôshêa' into Yehôshûa' (Joshua), which the Biblical narrator certainly refers to a very high antiquity (Num. XIII. 16).[4] But at all events, we must not seek the

[1] To this may be added that the Moabite Stone speaks of the vessels of Jahveh which king Mesha carried off as plunder from the Northern kingdom (line 18). Kuenen goes too far in finding a connexion between the worship of Jahveh in the Northern kingdom and the figures of bulls (*Religion of Israel*, I. 74 *et seq*).

[2] In the article *Ueber die nabathäischen Inschriften von Petra, Hauran u. s. w.*, in the *Zeitsch. d. D. M. G.*, 1860, XIV. 410.

[3] This must not be placed in the same category with cases in which the insertion of can be explained phonologically (Ewald, *Ausführliches Lehrb. der hebr. Spr.* § 192. *c*; *Böttcher*, I. 286). See the Agadic explanation of this, which I have quoted in the *Zeitsch. d. D. M. G.*, 1872, XXVI. 769.

[4] The changes of name mentioned in 2 Kings XXIII. 34, XXIV. 17, should also be considered here. It is not probable that these changes were ordered by the Kings of Egypt and of Babylon; for in that case the names received in

origin of the name Jahveh outside the Hebrew circle, and endeavour to explain it from foreign elements, as those did who used to see in Jov-is a namesake of Jahveh,[1] and even went to China to find the origin;[2] and as is still done by some in the interest of Egyptian antiquity, who find in the Egyptian *nuk pu nuk*, 'ego qui ego,' the prototype of the Hebrew Ehye asher ehye 'I am who I am.' But the identification of the Egyptian with the Hebrew formula was recently justly attacked by Tiele,[3] who, however, at the same time, has a private hypothesis of his own on the origin of this idea of God. After proving it to be neither Egyptian, nor Canaanitish, nor Aryan, he refers its origin to the Kenites; supposing the Hebrews to have borrowed the idea of Jahveh from that desert tribe, then to have forgotten it in Canaan, and subsequently to have made it their own again, when the Prophets had revived its use.

---

exchange would have been quite different, Egyptian and Babylonian respectively in form (compare Dan. I. 7). The change of Elyâḳîm into Yehôyâḳîm is especially noticeable, for it is a direct alteration of an Elohistic into a Jahveistic name. Such a change is usually the simple consequence of a religious revolution, as is seen in other cases. Thus, e.g. King Amenophis IV., when he directs his fanaticism against the worship of Ammon, and places that of Aten in the foreground, changes his Ammonic name into *Shu en Aten*, 'the light of the solar orb.' See Brugsch, *L'histoire d'Égypte* (1st ed.), I. 119, and Lenormant, *Premières civilisations*, I. 211. Of Moḥammed also we are told that he altered those portions of his followers' names which savoured of idolatry, substituting monotheistic terms; thus one 'Abd 'Amr had his name changed to 'Abd al-Raḥmân (Wüstenfeld, *Register zu den genealogischen Tabellen*, p. 27). The pious philologian al-Aṣma'î always calls the heathen Arabic poet Imru-l-Ḳeys, Imru Allâh, changing the name of the heathen god Ḳeys into the monotheistic Allâh (Guidi on Ibn Hishâmi's *Commentary etc.*, Leipzig 1874, p. XXI.).

[1] As Pope in the Universal Prayer: 'Father of all: . . . Jehovah, Jove, or Lord!'—Tr.

[2] For instance Strauss, in the *Zeitsch. d. D. M. G.*, 1869, XXIII. 473. But not only Jahveh, but even Elôhîm was brought from China. The glory of publishing this eccentric idea to the world belongs to M. Adolphe Saïsset, who wrote a whole book, entitled *Dieu et son homonyme*, Paris 1867, to prove very thoroughly that the Elôhîm of Genesis was really—the Emperor of China! The book is 317 octavo pages long.

[3] *Vergelijkende Geschiedenis*, pp. 555, 561.

But whatever be the origin of the word Jahveh as a technical term of theology, the living and working idea of Jahveh was first introduced into the circle of Hebrew thought by the Prophets. For this reason I have not discussed Jahveism till now; which will be approved by all who see that we cannot speak of ideas as existing and living until they appear as factors in the history of human thought. What means the *existence* of an idea (as I would say to those who fancy the Jahveh-idea to have been originally the property of a separate caste), if it lives in the brain or the heart of a few individuals, without exercising any force or influence on the world beyond? Could we say of electricity that it exists in nature, if we did not see it interfere as a factor in the life of nature? So the Jahveistic idea must be held to commence its life only when it begins to act upon the spiritual life of the nation. To have caused this is one of the most perennial leaves in the crown of glory won by the Prophets.

I cannot imagine that any of my readers are ignorant of the nature of the labours of the Hebrew Prophets, and therefore we need not here specially characterise their work. By Prophets we do not of course mean those soothsayers, or as they were called Seers (chôze, rô'e), whom we meet with in the period preceding that of the Prophets, and also later [1]—to whom the young man could apply in confident expectation of finding lost property, when his father had sent him to look for his lost asses; nor do we mean those wonder-workers whose occupation was to suspend and interrupt the regular order of nature for special purposes and for a certain time; nor those who, before the priesthood had become a closed institution, occasionally attended to the sacrifices offered to Elôhîm. We mean those men who, when the people had exhausted all the inspiration which they could derive from the idea

[1] To this group belongs, on Arabian ground (besides the well-known 'arrâf and kâhin), the muḥaddath 'the well-informed;' on whom see De Sacy's *Commentary on Ḥarîrî*, 2nd ed., p. 686.

of Elôhîm, came forward as new representatives of the idealism, the inspiration and the waning conception of nationality, which they now announced in a still higher degree, and as preachers of the ideal in a nation in which 'from the sole of the foot up to the head there was no soundness, but wounds, and stripes, and raw sores, which were not pressed out nor bound up nor softened with ointment,' whose 'princes'—themselves 'rulers of Sodom' over a 'people of Gomorrah'—'were dissolute, partners of thieves, all loving bribes and running after rewards, who judged not the orphan nor let the cause of widows come unto them;' 'who built up Zion with blood and Jerusalem with iniquity,' in which 'the heads judged for bribes, and the priests taught for hire, and the prophets practised magic for silver,' and which 'drew down guilt with cords of lies and sin as with the rope of a cart;' and who 'called evil good and good evil, made darkness light and light darkness, made the bitter sweet and the sweet bitter' (Is. I. 6, 10, 23, Mic. III. 10, 11, Is. V. 18, 20).

Into such a depth of immorality and carelessness was the Hebrew nation plunged by an institution which had grown up out of the Hierarchy. Centralisation of worship, formality, lip-service and a so-called piety quite mechanical, which are incapable of promoting either high idealism or morality of thought, and indeed discourage both, but which are well able to kill the most elevated soul, to cover the warmest temperament with a thick crust of ice, and to blunt the noblest heart,—these grew up at the bidding and after the pattern of the priests. A rude service of sacrifices, which brought down the idea of God more and more to the level of the senses, converted Mount Zion into a shambles, while the shameless practices of sacerdotal speculators turned the central sanctuary of Jerusalem, in the words of Isaiah, the noblest hater of that corrupt caste, into a 'den of robbers.'

The Prophets knew their enemies, and perceived the

roots of all the prevailing evil which gave life to the flourishing tree of immorality. They determined to dig up the tree and to clear away its roots. In the very front row stood the priesthood and the bloody service, upon which they turned with all the inextinguishable fanaticism of their noble passion. But the matter could not end here. The national enthusiasm which had been aroused in an earlier period, proved to be but a transient straw-fire; no noble element of that enthusiasm remained to help a new elevation of sentiment. For, independently of the corruptions of the priesthood, the political tendencies of the nation were such as to aid in slowly but surely undermining the idea of nationality. A tiny people, jammed in between great powers on the north and south, and itself nourishing vain desires of political power far above its capabilities and sufficient to wear it out, torn asunder as it was by internal dissensions,—such a people was constantly driven to seek alliance with those great powers. But these alliances soon put out the national fire which had blazed up for a short time in the temper of the people. The consciousness of being thrown on the protection of strangers kills the feeling of independent individuality. Moreover foreign, and especially Canaanitish, manners, were more and more naturalised at the courts of Hebrew kings; the kings connected themselves by marriage with adjacent courts, and the ladies obtained increased liberty for foreign habits in the midst of the Hebrews. The Canaanitish worships were again received in the capital, and soon obliterated whatever power and stimulus the Hebraised idea of Elôhîm still possessed in the direction of national elevation. It is an historical fact that the decline of nations begins when, instead of developing the elements and powers inherent in themselves, they carelessly throw up their own characteristics and yield themselves up without resistance to possibly more refined but foreign influences. What Cicero's father said of the Hellenised Romans is very instructive on this point, that the better a Roman knew Greek the less he was worth.[1]

The Prophets were not philosophers of culture; they did not start from great principles abstracted from the study of experience, in pondering the course of the world; but conviction and enthusiasm lived in them. They were bad politicians, but unsurpassable representatives of the idea of Nationality. An experienced statesman of that age would have refrained from censuring the alliance with foreign powers; that was the only chance left to the Hebrew nation of adding a few hours of existence to those already counted. But the Prophets lash this political experiment at every step, and say that only the moral awakening cf the nation can bring about a possibility of saving its political existence. 'Ephraim delights in wind and pursues east-wind, while he daily perpetrates more lies and oppression, and they make covenant with Assyria, and oil is carried to Egypt,' says Hosea (XII. 2 [1]), to the Northern kingdom. At the very last hour Jeremiah (II. 18) treats fraternisation with the foreigners as equivalent to abandoning Jahveh: 'What hast thou to do with the road to Egypt to drink of the water of the Shîchôr [Nile]? and what hast thou to do with the road to Assyria to drink of the water of the River [Euphrates]?' They were the purest and most ideal representatives of national individuality and independence. We are here especially interested in one point relating to the history of Religion —the Prophets' mode of dealing with the two Divine names Elôhîm and Jahveh.

§ 2. It is well known that the Hebrew idea of God finds expression in the canonical Biblical literature in two distinct ways: in the direction of Elôhîm and in that of Jahveh. Each grasps the idea of God, and tries to use it for the instruction of the people, in its peculiar fashion. The Jahveistic school, which is identical with Prophetism,

[1] Mommsen, *History of Rome*, edition of 1868, III. 446 *et seq.*

is opposed to the Elohistic, and avoids the employment of Elôhîm as a proper name of God; it treats Elôhîm as merely a universal generic name for Deity, but not as the proper name of the One God. We can easily convince ourselves of this by contemplating the collections of speeches of the Prophets, and the fundamental part of Deuteronomy, which stands nearer to the prophetic spirit than any other part of the Pentateuch. Here we have prevailingly only 'Jehovah my (thy, our, Israel's) Elôhîm,' but these expressions are often abandoned for the simple hâ-Elôhîm, which is regarded as a proper name completely covering the name Jahveh.[1] But in prophetical books in which the Elohistic appellations occur here and there as proper names of the Deity, these cannot from their rare occurrence serve as a counterpoise to the extensive use of the name Jahveh. Their use can only be regarded as a reference to the past, in presence of the then modern view of the Deity. The immediate question, which still remains open after the results gained by the critical school, in establishing the mutual relation of the two Divine names, may be formulated thus: Whence comes it and what is the reason that the Prophets occupy a position of repulsion towards the theological validity of the idea of Elôhîm?

This antipathy is easily explicable and quite natural from the religious and national position of the Prophets. We have already seen that the idea of Elôhîm, if not actually borrowed, was at least confirmed by outside influences, and that the Hebrews held it in common with the Canaanites. And the consequences of its not having grown up in Hebrew soil were exhibited in its further development, when, after the idea of nationality had spent its short-lived flames, the Hebraised idea of God,

---

[1] This is meant only as a general assertion, and is the general impression left by the Prophetical books. There are, in this as in other respects, various grades perceptible between the different Prophets. The prophetical Jahveistic idea is not so powerful and exclusive in all as in the Babylonian Isaiah.

allied with the equally borrowed sacerdotal institution, generated those immoral religious practices which are characteristic of the Canaanitish decadence. Moreover, the fact that this theological conception was originally borrowed and not native, was the very thing calculated to make it offensive to the Prophets; and their antipathy to it caused them to tie their religious view of the world, their moral convictions, nay their whole God-loving soul, to a name which had hitherto remained in the background, but which was now brought forward by their genius to the front rank, and became the bearer of all that they thought and felt concerning God.

In this sense, the Prophets were creators of Jahveism. The word Jahveh had previously been a meaningless breath, a *flatus oris*, as I said before. Now first it became an active power, as the expression of opposition to the existing evil, the centre of the new aspiration preached by the Prophets. Consequently, it is not the word and its meaning that have the chief import here, but the civilising power associated with the word, its force working on minds. This is not the only instance in which a watch-word has had an influence far beyond that which was natural to it as a mere word; so that its original signification has become a matter of indifference. In the word Jahveh the National feature is the essential one.

§ 3. In connexion with this we must not forget that the Prophets have a very living conception of a Creator when they speak of Jahveh, and that most of the words existing in Hebrew for the idea of Creating, are employed most frequently by the Prophets and especially by the Babylonian Isaiah. Great stress is laid on the 'Creation of Israel.' Jahveh is the Creator of the Hebrew people. It is also undeniable that the Prophets occupied themselves with finding a metaphysical definition of the idea of Jahveh, and discovered a precisely expressed definition in the well-known Ehye asher ehye, 'I am he who I am,'

They lay stress on the *unchangeableness* of Jahveh: he is eternally unchangeable. But it must, on the other hand, be borne in mind that the recognition of Jahveh cannot have started from this sort of metaphysical speculation, which does not, on this or on any other subject, naturally spring up till a later stage of development of the original idea. The metaphysical foundation of the idea of Jahveh must be subject to this rule, and therefore the sentence Ehye asher ehye 'I am who I am,' must be assigned to a later time, when Jahveism was already fully formed. Thus then it is the Prophet Malachi, living late after the Captivity, who expresses the sense of this formula in more ordinary language by the words 'For I Jahveh change not' (III. 6). Another expression of the same idea is used frequently by the Babylonian Prophet—the words anî hû 'I am He,' where the pronoun hû does not refer back to anything mentioned before (Is. XLIII. 10, XLVI. 4, XLVIII. 12). The second of these passages especially shows that the formula anî hû expresses most emphatically the eternal unchangeableness of Jahveh:

Hearken unto me, O house of Jacob,
And all the remnant of the house of Israel,
Ye that are carried from the belly,
Or lifted up from the womb,
Even to old age *I am He.*

And so the last passage has 'I am He, I am the first, I am the last.'

We have this anî hû in a fuller form in the Song of Moses (Deut. XXXII. 39), as anî anî hû, and the former is probably an abbreviation of the latter. But the latter is itself grammatically only a mode of expressing by pronouns what Ehye asher ehye expresses by verbs.[1] Now the Song of Moses and the Blessing of Moses, which is connected with it, are easily proved by an examination of their contents to move in much the same prophetical circle of ideas, except indeed that these ideas are already mingled with views which prevailed later, at the time of

[1] 'I am I' (hû being equivalent to the verb *to be*) = 'I am who I am.'—Tr.

the compromise. To mention a few examples: the assertion that Jahveh made and established Israel (vv. 6, 15), but that Israel forgot him that made him (v. 18), the exhortation to the people to remember the days of old (v. 7), and the reference to the Tôrâ appointed by Moses (XXXIII. 4), vividly recal the speeches of the second Isaiah (XLIV. 2, LI. 13, XLVI. 9 etc.) and Malachi (III. 22 [IV. 4]). Besides these passages, Deut. XXXII. 2 may be compared with Is. LV. 10 and Job XXIX. 22 *et seq.*; v. 16 (where the idols are called zârîm 'strangers') with Jer. II. 25, III. 13, Is. XLIII. 12; v. 17 with Jer. XXIII. 23 (in both which the strange gods are called 'gods from near'). If the reading êsh dâth in the Blessing of Moses v. 2 is correct, the word dâth points to a society accessible to Persian words; and the passage in Deut. XXXII. 39, where the doctrine of the resurrection of the dead is mentioned as a recognised article of faith,[1] confirms this impression. Thus also the anî anî hû[2] which occurs in this passage, compared with anî hû which is used by the second Isaiah, is a proof that metaphysical speculation on the idea of Jahveh arose only in the latest period of the development of Prophetism.

§ 4. In the time of the earlier Prophets, however, the chief weight of the Jahveistic confession was given to national and moral ideas.

The assertion which it is usual to insist upon, that Jahveh was the National God of the Hebrews, is therefore true in a certain degree. It is not true that the Prophets could conceive as the Familiar spirit of a handful of Hebrews that infinite Idea towards which their deepest desire and love was directed, which was to them the

---

[1] See Kuenen, *Religion of Israel*, III. 41.

[2] Bunsen must be named as the writer who lays the most stress on the importance of this anî anî hû, bringing this formula into connexion with the metaphysical definition of the idea of Jahveh (*God in History*, I. p. 74 *et seq.*). Lessing's 'Nur euer Er heisst Er' (only *your* He is called He, *Nathan der Weise*, I. 4) is with justice adduced by Bunsen.

impersonation of that pure holiness which is the end of the Prophets' ethics, and which in their eyes represents the infinite sublimity after which the prophetic spirit nobly strove. But it is true that in the view of the Prophets, the Hebrews were the first to understand Jahveh, and that the extension of this understanding over all mankind is the ideal of Prophetism as it affects the world's history. If any one questions this cosmopolitan side of the Jahveistic theology, he will probably be cured of his error by impartially reading the speeches of the Próphets of all the various phases of prophecy; *e.g.* for the earlier time Is. II. 2–4, words which are almost literally repeated by Micah IV—a proof how deeply rooted in the mind of the Prophets was the conviction there expressed,—and for a later age, Is. LXVI. 18, 19. This great Prophet of the Captivity addresses mankind in general: 'Hearken to me, ye islands, and attend, ye nations from afar' (Is. XLIX. 1); and another Prophet of Israel in Babylonia, who speaks of a common festival of all mankind, knows of no Canaanites in the house of Jahveh (Zech. XIV. 16, 17). This cosmopolitan character of Jahveism is most precisely defined by a somewhat earlier Prophet, Zephaniah (III. 9, 10). No doubt it is true that in recognition of Jahveh the Prophets regard the Hebrew nation as the centre, and Mount Zion as the source of the streams of water which is henceforth to fill the whole earth 'as water covers the bed of the sea' (Is. XI. 9); and also that they treat Jahveh's love of mankind as if the lion's share of it would accrue to his own people. But on the other side it is equally true that, after the extension of the idea of Jahveh over the world, which the Prophets lay down as the ultimate and highest aim of spiritual effort, the prophetical view regards all nations of the earth, even Egypt and Assyria, as equal before Jahveh, the common God of them all. 'In that day shall Israel be third in alliance with Egypt and Assyria, a blessing in the middle of the earth, whom

Jahveh of hosts has blessed, saying Blessed be my people Egypt, and the work of my hands Assyria, and mine inheritance Israel' (Is. XIX. 24, 25). It is, therefore, especially in reference to the then present time, at which ideals were only beginning to be framed by this free outlook to the future, that the distinctively National character of the idea of Jahveh is emphasised. This is very natural, since it was by national impulses that the Prophets were roused into enthusiasm for Jahveh; for that enthusiasm, as I have previously urged, was produced by an intense antipathy to the foreign elements which confronted them chiefly in the idea of Elôhîm, common to Israel and Canaan, and including all the abominations of the Canaanitish worship, and all the laxity of manners introduced from foreign parts into the higher ranks of society. With the Canaanites dissolute forms of worship were results naturally developed out of the previous history of their religion, and could be traced backwards to their origin in Mythology. Being such, they could not have so ruinous an influence on morals and character as among the Hebrews, who seized on the immorality as such, without having had any share in the previous historical stages which led to it. If for *unbelief* we substitute *absence of historical preparation*, the correct observation made by Constant on Roman Polytheism is applicable to this case also: that indecent rites may be practised by a religious nation without detriment to purity of heart; but if unbelief takes hold of the nation, such rites are the cause and the pretext for the most revolting corruption.[1]

The idea of Jahveh, therefore, according to the intention of the Prophets, was to stimulate a return to National enthusiasm; and the zeal against the spreading vice and immorality is directed more against the foreign character of the vice than against the immorality itself. 'O house of Jacob,' says Isaiah (II. 5–7), in close contact with the

[1] B. Constant de Rebecque, *Du Polythéisme Romain*, II. 102, quoted by Buckle, *Civilisation*, II. 303.

speech in which he anticipates the moral redemption of mankind through beating their swords into scythes and their spears into ploughshares, 'come ye! we will walk in the light of Jahveh. For thou hast forsaken thine own people, O house of Jacob, because they (*i.e.* the members of that house) are full of divination [1] and soothsayers, like the Philistines, and join hands (*i.e.* contract friendship) with the children of strangers, and their land was filled with silver and gold, and there was no end of their treasures, and their land was filled with horses and there was no end of their chariots.' In these words we see unequivocally how the 'light of Jahveh' is contrasted with foreign customs. It ought to be observed that in Deuteronomy, the book which stands nearer than any other part of the Pentateuch to the Prophets' views on the world and religion, the collecting of much silver and gold and horses [2] is censured (XVII. 16 *sq.*), in fear lest the people should be denationalised thereby and inclined towards the 'foreign,' which in Deuteronomy always means Egypt.

Many scholars hold the utterly incorrect view that the idea of Jahveh was, even from the Egyptian age before the Exodus, the property of a few *élites*, either Levitical priests or Prophets; a sort of esoteric religion, into which no uninitiated could pry, and from which Prophetism grew up. If this view were as correct as it is impossible, considering the circumstances of the development of Hebrew religion, we should still have to consider the first appearance of the idea of Jahveh quite independently of any such secret society. And it must also be borne in mind that Egypt was to the Hebrews a 'House of slaves' (bêth 'abhâdîm), as the Bible says (Ex. XIII. 3 etc.), not a Theological College. In Egypt they appropriated very

---

[1] It is best to read with Gesenius miḳḳesem for miḳḳedem.

[2] Hosea XIV. 4 [3] must also be noted, where the alliance with Assyria is condemned in the words 'Asshur will not save us; we shall not ride on horses.' See also Zech. IX. 10, X. 5, Micah V. 9 [10].

few religious ideas. Were it otherwise, we should assuredly not have to wait till after the Babylonian Captivity to find the belief in immortality among them. It is also a special characteristic of the Prophetic Jahveism, that it insists that this idea was destined to be universally recognised in the Hebrew nation itself; and this contributes to the sublimity of the prophetic conception. In contrast to the secret society cautiously locking up its mystic knowledge, how grand looks a free corporation, whose hopes are concentrated on the idea that at that time 'I [Jahveh] will pour out my spirit upon all flesh, and your sons and daughters will prophesy, and upon your slaves and handmaids I will pour out my spirit in those days;' 'and all thy sons will be disciples of Jahveh;' 'and they shall all know me, from the least to the greatest of them,' etc. (Joel III. 1 *sq.* [28 *sq.*], Is. LIV. 13, Jer. XXXI. 34).

It is almost self-evident that to the national enthusiasm of the Prophets the political difference between the Northern and the Southern Hebrews scarcely exists. The Prophets extended their influence over the North as well as over the South; and Hosea especially addresses his exhortation to both kingdoms, mentioning Judah in the first division of his verses constructed in parallelism, and Ephraim in the second. The Prophets even announce the reunion of the two sections of the Hebrew state.[1] The Northern kingdom was naturally much farther removed from the religious ideas of the Prophets than the Southern. The hierarchy of Jerusalem, which grew out of a sort of theocratic system, might at least exhibit some appreciation of the preaching of Jahveism; some trace of monotheistic Elohism still existed there, but was quite foreign to the North. The persecution of the Prophets was accordingly much more violent and indiscriminate in the Ephraimite country than in the South, where however it was not absent. The story of the Prophet Elijah

[1] See Ezek. XXXVII. 15–28.

(Êlîyâhû 'My God is Jahveh'), as given in the Book of Kings, is intended to depict the furious persecution of the preachers of Jahveh. Elijah is a typical Jahveist, placed by the prophetical writer who conceived him at a time before true Prophetism was in existence among the Hebrews. As the Prophet painted the character of the 'Servant of Jahveh' ('ebhed Yahve) for the future, as a type of human perfection, so Elijah serves for a similar type in the past. The representatives of Jahveism succeeded in making the person of Elijah so popular as to attract to himself various remnants of ancient myths, as we saw in a previous chapter. But at bottom Elijah is nothing but a type of the persecutions to which Jahveism was exposed in the Northern kingdom on the part of the rulers and priests. The prophetical historians, fond as they are of painting historical personages of the Hebrew nation in colours borrowed from the ideal of Jahveism, are also no less addicted to drawing up descriptions of lives which are typical of Prophetism. Such a life is that of the prophet Samuel, who is regarded as founder of the Schools of the Prophets, and consequently of Prophetism itself. The portraiture of his character, as opponent of an untheocratic monarchy, of the king who showed himself deficient in national feeling by sparing the Amalekite chief, and of a corrupt priesthood, is only a program of Hebrew Prophetism, clothed in a biographical dress and expressing the Prophets' sentiments in speeches, When the inevitable catastrophe came, and the Northern kingdom fell first, and the subsequent overthrow of the Southern kingdom put an end to all Hebrew independence, the Jahveists, the most earnest representatives of the idea of Hebrew nationality, accompanied the people into captivity. Then first began the time when the Jahveistic ideas bloomed most freely and were taken up with greatest enthusiasm. In the Captivity prophetic thoughts soared to their highest point in the speeches of that immortal prophet whose name is unknown, the so-called Second Isaiah. But we find there also representatives of the sacerdotal formal religion—not, indeed, of the coarse sacerdotalism of Jerusalem, for that was impossible without the central temple, bloody offerings, and political independence—but of a certain direction of religious thought. For, at the very time when idealistic Jahveism had worked itself up to the doctrine of the 'historical vocation of the people,' these were exciting the people's hopes by visions, speaking of the architectural proportions of the new temple that was to be built, and drawing up arrangements for priests and sacrifices. Yet even this school was considerably penetrated by Jahveism; it tacitly appropriated the positive teaching of the Prophets, without, however, entirely giving up the positive part of the sacerdotal system. Thus, far from the Temple of Jerusalem, on the banks of the Chaboras, a compromise was effected between the Prophetic and the Sacerdotal schools. This held sway over the hearts of the Hebrews in the Captivity, and formed the mental and religious basis of the Hebrew commonwealth at its restoration. It finds its first expression in the Book of Ezekiel, which announces itself, and probably correctly, as produced in the Captivity.[1] The first beginnings of this compromise appeared before the destruction of the Kingdom of Judah, under a king who had equal respect for Priests and Prophets, and allowed himself to be influenced in religious matters by both equally. The mark of this tendency to sink all differences between Sacerdotalism and Prophetism is impressed on the Book of Deuteronomy, which appeared at that time. This cannot be called a defeat of the prophetical tendencies. It is not the destiny of ideals to be realised in their native form and natural regardlessness of social and physical obstacles; they are victorious if they succeed in forcing an entrance into their former oppo-

[1] See on the other side Zunz in the *Zeitsch. d. D. M. G.*, 1873, p. 688, thesis 14 *et seq.*

nents' sphere of view, and modifying that in their own way. Now from the nature of the case, where a compromise is made, especially a compromise like the one before us, not settled and concluded by regular negotiation, but consisting of an unconsciously performed balancing of opposing energies, such a settlement is very fluctuating, and leaves open the possibility of a gradual leaning towards one or the other of the two opposite principles. We discover this fluctuation in the self-effected compromise when we contemplate two books of the Pentateuch, between the composition of which lies the whole catastrophe of the Captivity, the first throes and afterpains of which urged the completion of the compromise by bringing home the necessity of the cooperation of all the spiritual factors of human life: Leviticus and Deuteronomy. Both these books combine together sacerdotal worship and Jahveism; neither of them gives a direct negative to either of these originally contrary factors. In both books we find both elements represented, only with the difference that Leviticus sounds an eminently sacerdotal, and Deuteronomy a prevailing prophetic and Jahveistic tone. Both stand on the level of Jahveism, without however disdaining sacerdotal worship and sacrifice. In the prophetical Books of Haggai, Zechariah, and Malachi, and in the postexilian interpolations occurring in that of the Babylonian Isaiah, the various stages of the compromise may also be studied. Observe, for instance, the endeavour of Haggai (II. 11–15) to employ the sacerdotal Law (tôrâ) in a Jahveistic sense by a moral application; Zechariah's address to the High Priest (III. 3-7), in which he speaks of a purification of the restored priesthood; and especially the exhortation to the priests contained in the Book of Malachi, which enable us to form a picture of a priesthood formed on Jahveistic principles as conceived by the Prophet of the Restoration, in contrast to the priesthood of the age before the Captivity, which was the object of the passionate hatred of the Prophets.

§ 5. We have lingered over the general description of the Jahveism of the Prophets longer than the symmetry of these investigations would justify. There is now something to be said on the relation of Jahveism to the Mythology of the Hebrews.

It is to be observed on this subject that pure Jahveism, as preached by those Prophets who first formulated that ideal, had a long struggle with the conservative leanings of the people and their rulers, and that in the period before the Captivity it could not become a religious element fitted to penetrate all strata of society. Jahveism could therefore exercise but little influence on the narration of myths, *i.e.* on the mode in which myths were propagated in the mouth of the people; for only a new conception which penetrates the whole people can possibly determine and give a direction to the transformation of a myth. Moreover, Mythology was not a subject with which the Prophets felt much sympathy. Within the frame of the Puritanical Monotheism which they taught there was no suitable place for myths. Hence, also, the Prophets take so little notice of the myths of their nation (a very little is brought in by Hosea, chap. XII.); their frequent allusions to the story of the destruction of Sodom and 'Amôrâ (Gomorrah), are accounted for by the obvious parallel which they drew between those ancient cities, proverbial for their vice, and Jerusalem and Shômerôn (Samaria), together with the respective fate of each. The silence of the Prophets is no proof, although many wish to use it as such, that in their times the stories of the Patriarchs were not yet in existence; sufficient answer is afforded by the few cases in which reference is made to those stories. Their silence is much rather a proof of the power which the idea of Jahveh exerted over their souls, so filling them, that by its side the forms of Patriarchs and Heroes shrivel into insignificant persons, and the narrated events are so dwarfed that no religious elevation can be derived from them. This also explains the tone of irony assumed by the Prophet when he has occasion to allude to Patriarchs and their stories. Thus, for example, Hosea in reference to Jacob, whom he describes as deceiving his brother, as fighting against God, as subservient to women (XII. 4, 5, 13 [3, 4, 12]), and the Babylonian Isaiah in reference to Abraham, whose smallness in comparison with Jahveh he expresses (LXIII. 16). I pointed out above (pp. 229, 230), that this apparent degradation of Abraham is only directed against the remembrance of the Patriarch's divinity, and that in another passage (LI. 1 *sq.*) Abraham and Sarah are referred to as the ancestors of the Hebrew nation. To keep alive the consciousness of derivation from special ancestors was obviously not out of keeping with the National tendency of Jahveism, but rather an essential means of promoting it. In this sense the Babylonian Prophet's address should be understood: 'Hearken to me, ye that follow after righteousness and seek Jahveh! Look to the Rock, whence ye were hewn, and to the Well-hole, from which ye were dug: look to Abraham your father, and to Sarah that bore you!' (Is. LI. 1 *sq.*) In the same sense Malachi also refers to the Patriarchal age, saying, 'Is not Esau Jacob's brother? and I love Jacob, and I have hated Esau' (I. 2 *sq.*). Therefore, also, there are special forms by which the Prophets address the nation, such as 'House of Jacob,' which is excessively frequent, and 'House of Isaac' (Amos VII. 16). These forms were intended to remind them of their proper ancestry, and to keep alive the consciousness of their national peculiarity, and thus it came about that the names of ancestors were identified with the nation itself. The words Jacob and Abraham are names of the Hebrew people, in Micah VII. 20 and Is. XXIX. 22, among the earlier representatives of Prophetism: 'Thus saith Jahveh, who redeemed Abraham, concerning the house of Jacob;' 'Thou givest truth to Jacob and favour to Abraham,' *i.e.* to the Hebrew nation.

The prevailing idea, therefore, emphasised by the Prophet, is that of derivation from ancestors other than those of heathen nations. The details of the Patriarchal history are devoid of interest for him, and personages without the character of ancestors still more so. Consequently even Moses remains in the background. Not even Hosea gives his name, though he says, 'By a prophet Jahveh brought Israel up from Egypt, and by a prophet he was preserved' (XII. 14 [13]). Only in very few passages, in one early prophet, Micah (VI. 4),[1] and one of the later period, the Babylonian Isaiah (LXIII. 11 *sq.*), is the deliverance from Egypt mentioned coupled with the name of Moses. To the Exodus itself frequent reference is made, and the story of it does admirable service to the view of the theocratical vocation of the nation. But it is not till after the Captivity that the Legislator himself is brought into the foreground, in consequence of the compromise between Jahveism and the formal legality of the priesthood (Mal. III. 22 [IV. 4]).[1] Whatever of the truly mythical still lived in the memory of the people received from Jahveism a complete monotheistic transformation. Jahveh is made the conqueror of the Dragon of the Storm and of the Monsters of Darkness (see p. 27). Notice the numerous questions in the theodicy in the Book of Job, which Jahveh puts in opposition to the explanation of physical phenomena given by mythology: 'Hath the rain a father, or who begot the drops of dew? Out of whose womb came the ice, and the hoar-frost of the sky, who bore it?' (Job XXXVIII. 28 *sq.*). Such are the questions asked by the Jahveistic monotheist. Removed to this new sphere, all the myths are at once beset with denials; the monotheist's whole interpretation of

---

[1] These two passages (Mic. VI. 4 and Mal. III. 22 [IV. 4]) appears not to have been noticed by Michel Nicolas in his '*Etudes critiques sur la Bible*,' Paris 1862, I. 351, where he says of Moses, 'Son nom ne se trouve que deux fois dans les écrits des prophètes qui sont parvenus jusqu'à nous—(*Esaie*, LXIII. 12; *Jér.* XV. 1).'

nature and idea of causality lead to One only—to Jahveh; at this stage the myth is utterly overthrown. But the fact that a nation which in its primeval age formed myths, at a late period of its existence witnessed the growth of the direct negation of mythical ideas in its midst, is no reason for treating the former existence of myths as questionable.[1]

But Jahveism acknowledged the duty of reforming the subject-matter of legends, whenever a religious practice condemned by the Jahveists was supported by legendary authority. Such a practice was Human Sacrifice, which found support and justification in the story of the sacrifice of Isaac. Here, therefore, Jahveism interfered, in the manner which we had occasion to describe in the chapter on the method of investigating myths (p. 45). In this passage, even in the form in which we have it after the last revision, the will of Jahveh was manifestly introduced into the second half with a polemical purpose to oppose that of Elôhîm who in the first half demanded the sacrifice. But the case is quite different in what modern Biblical critics call the Jahveistic portions of the Pentateuch. As it is not the object of this book to write the history of the composition of the Biblical *Literature*, I cannot enter into an exposition of my views on the reduction to writing and piecing together of those literary fragments which compose the Pentateuch, including a full justification of those views. I will only briefly remark, that all the legendary literature which we now have in the Pentateuch is already more or less penetrated by Jahveism, and that only in the legal portion are a few remnants of strictly Elohistic legislation preserved. The literary form given to the mass of stories is itself the result of the compromise between the older and the Jahveistic religious tendency. Just as there are two books of law, Deuteronomy and Leviticus (to the latter of which a few

[1] I have given particular prominence to this on account of the opposite view taken by Max Müller in his *Chips*, I. 361 *et seq.*

passages of law in Exodus and Numbers must be added), both of which represent the compromise between the Sacerdotal and the Prophetical tendencies, the sacerdotal view giving the fundamental tone to the one, and the prophetical to the other, so is it also with the mass of stories. Even what are called Elohistic documents are strictly speaking Jahveistic in character, only that the name Elôhîm is admitted to be appropriate to the ancient Patriarchal age, and Jahveism is introduced as an historical event, dating from Moses. In opposition to this, another work represents the more thorough-going Jahveism. Now when the Jahveistic school came to terms with the popular religious views, and these were penetrated by the fundamental truths taught by the Prophets, the Jahveists did not disdain to get hold of the legendary matter and work it up according to their own principles. If the Patriarchs were really models of religious life, they must also have been strict Jahveists; and, therefore, these so-called Jahveistic documents describe the Patriarchs as living on completely Jahveistic ground, Eve, Lemech, and Noah as calling the Deity Jahveh, and Cain and Abel as offering sacrifices to Jahveh. As early as the time of Seth commences the general adoration of Jahveh. The historic Israel is of course to the Jahveistic writers more than to any others a ḳehal Yahve, 'adath Yahve, 'congregation, community of Jahveh.' With this principle accords all else that the exegetical school has brought together to characterise the Jahveistic narrator.[1] Moreover, in the Jahveistic writings more than in any others particular attention is paid to what is popular and national;[2] and, as would be expected from the strictly national character of Jahveism, they are distinguished by a greater and more eager zeal. I will pick out and draw attention to some terms belonging to the peculiar circle of ideas of the

[1] His fondness for humanising God by anthropomorphic expressions is the only feature, the reasons for which are not patent.

[2] See Knobel, *Die Bücher Numeri, Deuteronomium und Josua*, pp. 539, 554.

Prophets, in order to indicate the closer mutual relationship of the so-called Jahveistic documents: viz. debhar Yahve 'Word of Jahveh,' and ne'ûm Yahve 'speech of Jahveh.'[1] To anyone acquainted with the Prophetic literature it is needless to dwell on the specifically prophetic character of these two technical expressions. I call them *technical* expressions with special reference to debhar Yahve. For dâbhâr was used by the Prophets, especially those of the later times, of the speech which they proclaimed in the name of Jahveh (and in direct polemical opposition to another technical expression, massâ, Jer. XXIII. 33 *sq.*, which nevertheless occurs again in later Prophets), just as the sacerdotal school which had entered on good terms with Jahveism, when they laid stress on accordance with the Law, called instruction in the Law tôrâ. Tôrâ and Dâbhâr bear the same relation to one another as Kôhên and Nâbhî (Priest and Prophet). Jeremiah (XVIII. 18) says, 'They said, Come, we will devise devices against Jeremiah; for the Tôrâ will not be lost from the Priest, counsel from the wise, the Dâbhâr (word) from the Prophet: come, we will wound him on the tongue, and not attend to any of his words (debhârâv).' The same opposition of Tôrâ and Dâbhâr is found also in the words of a prophet of the Restoration, Zechariah VII. 12: 'They made their heart adamant, lest they should hear the Tôrâ and the Debhârîm which Jahveh of Hosts sent with his spirit by the agency of the former prophets.'[2]

How deeply the prophetic spirit after this compromise penetrated all other schools is observable in the profounder piety which thenceforth characterises Elohistic writings. We see this, for example, in the Elohistic Psalms, composed by religious singers not yet accustomed to the Prophets' name Jahveh, but who now wrote to the glory and honour of Elôhîm those sublime Songs which to this day kindle the devotion of those who wish to raise their souls

---

[1] See Knobel, *Die Bücher etc.*, p. 529.

[2] The relative clause is dependent upon *Debharîm* only.

in prayer to God. In them a spirit taught by the Prophets has penetrated the representatives of Elohism. For as regards its outward manifestation in the choice of Divine names, Elohism continues to exist even in the age of the Captivity: we meet with strictly Elohistic narratives in the accounts of the Creation and the Deluge composed at Babylon.

But we must refer to a comparatively late period the working-out of this tendency to a compromise, in which the sacerdotal view had as much share as the prophetical —a tendency which joined together in a higher unity, as Teaching (tôrâ), the Statute (chuḳḳâ) and the Prophetic word of Jahveh (dâbhâr). Consequently, the writing down of the traditions conceived in this spirit must also be assigned to a much later age than is usually done. However, we cannot speak here of any exact number of years, but only indicate in general terms periods of various classes of culture. Accurate dates can only be reached by more advanced historical knowledge on the domain of Biblical Antiquity. Perhaps this will be promoted by the constantly increasing certainty of the information to be gathered from the historical texts of the Cuneiform Inscriptions with reference to the History of Civilisation. But from the facts recognised in recent times it may with confidence be inferred that the literary activity of the Hebrews belongs in large part to the epoch of the Captivity. It should also be mentioned in this connexion that Knobel insists that the affairs of the interior of Asia were well known to his Jehovist.[1] Such knowledge cannot be the result of the contact established by the invasion. It demands closer and more friendly relations, which would make it possible to learn such facts.

All this takes us into the epoch of the Captivity. That remarkable age enriched the Hebrews' sphere of thought with many things, to which we will give our attention in the following chapter.

---

[1] See Knobel, *Die Bücher etc.*, p. 579.

CHAPTER X.

THE HEBREW MYTH IN THE BABYLONIAN CAPTIVITY.

If we limit the term *Myth* to those old sentences which the ancients used in speaking of physical changes and phenomena, then the period with which we have to do in this chapter lies outside the history of the Hebrew Myth; for the latter ceased to have any further growth to chronicle as the influence of Prophetism extended. Now, in place of the free life, organic development and gradual transformation of the myth, we have it in a final and canonical literary form, which we had to use as the only accessible source for discovering the original, and as a handle to guide us in the analytical treatment of its development. But it is not to be supposed that the parts of the Old Testament which we use as sources of knowledge on the Hebrew Myth contain the entire stock of the mythical treasures of the Hebrews, which these very fragments prove to have been very various. It must rather be assumed that in the period separating the final elaboration of these myths from their ultimate reduction to writing, a large portion of the stock was lost; which seems particularly likely, when it is considered how little importance the new religious school attached to this aspect of the Hebrew mind. Some remnants of unwritten stories have been preserved in Tradition; but the Tradition, again, has come down to us in a form which makes it difficult to discriminate the truly traditional from what belongs only to individuals (see *supra*, pp. 32, 33).

Thus the history of the Hebrew Myth after the rise of the Prophets can only be treated as a portion of the history of literature; *i.e.* it endeavours to discover the influences to which the stories were subjected during their reduction to writing. And at the outset we excluded all such investigations from the circle of our present studies.

But after the cessation of Hebrew independence the cycle of Hebrew stories received from another quarter an addition, which, though neither touching the domain of Mythology proper, nor working with elements already furnished by the Hebrew Myth, nevertheless is attached so closely to those stories which were formed by transformation of the old myths, that it ought not to be passed over in silence when we are considering the cycle of Hebrew stories.

We have already had occasion to observe the receptive tendency of the Hebrew mind, which was manifested in its contact with Canaanitish civilisation. At the first assault made by a mind superior to itself, it willingly opened its gates, and even when struggling for its national character and individuality it did not spurn the intellectual property of its antagonists. In the formation of the thought of Jahveh, and especially of the central idea of that thought, we discovered a productive genius for the first time aroused in the Hebrew people. But Jahveism came upon a nation too far gone in political impotence and dissension to be kindled even by such a spark to spiritual action. It found the nation at the very threshold of that political division which not long afterwards it had to lament beside the streams of Babylon. There the prophetic idea lived on, and indeed reached its zenith in the Babylonian Isaiah. But hieratic influences also continued to operate; and the best that the people could effect was the compromise between Jahveism and the sacerdotal tendencies represented by Ezekiel. This compromise found expression at the restoration of the

State, and gave its tone and colour to the larger portion of the Biblical literature.

The receptive tendency of the Hebrews manifested itself again prominently during the Babylonian Captivity. Here first they gained an opportunity of forming for themselves a complete and harmonious conception of the world. The influence of Canaanitish civilisation could not then be particularly powerful on the Hebrews; for that civilisation, the highest point of which was attained by the Phenicians, was quite dwarfed by the mental activity exhibited in the monuments of the Babylonian and Assyrian Empire, which we are now able to admire in all their grandeur. There the Hebrews found more to receive than some few civil, political, and religious institutions. The extensive and manifold literature which they found there could not but act on a receptive mind as a powerful stimulus; for it is not to be imagined that the nation when dragged into captivity lived so long in the Babylonian-Assyrian Empire without gaining any knowledge of its intellectual treasures. Schrader's latest publications on Assyrian poetry have enabled us to establish a striking similarity between both the course of ideas and the poetical form of a considerable portion of the Old Testament, especially of the Psalms, and those of this newly-discovered Assyrian poetry.[1] It would be a great mistake to account for this similarity by reference to a common Semitic origin in primeval times; for we can only resort to that in cases which do not go beyond the most primitive elements of intellectual life and ideas of the world, or designations of things of the external world. Conceptions of a higher and more complicated kind, as well as esthetic points, can certainly not be carried off into the mists of a prehistoric age. It is much better to keep to more real and tangible ground, and to suppose those points of contact between Hebrew

[1] See Supplement to the Augsburg *Allgemeine Zeitung* of June 19, 1874.

and Assyrian poetry which are revealed by Schrader's, Lenormant's, and George Smith's publications, to form part of the contributions made by the highly civilised Babylonians and Assyrians to the Hebrews in the course of the important period of the Captivity.

We see from this that the intellect of Babylon and Assyria exerted a more than passing influence on that of the Hebrews, not merely touching it, but entering deep into it and leaving its own impress upon it. The Assyrian poetry of the kind just mentioned stands in the same relation to that of the Hebrews as does the plain narrative of King Mesha's Inscription and of some Phenician votive tablets to the narrative texts of the Hebrews, and as does the sacrificial Tablet of Marseilles to the Hebrews' beginnings of a sacerdotal constitution. The Babylonian and Assyrian influence is of course much more extensive, pregnant and noteworthy.

The most prominent monument of this important influence is presented to us in the Biblical story of the Deluge. It was attempted long ago to discover points of contact between the respective narratives of the universal flood by the guidance of Berosus; but the only possible result of these endeavours was to encourage the old theory of an idea common to all mankind, which expressed itself in the story of a great general flood. To be sure, no obvious reason appears why this idea should force itself unbidden upon the reflexion of ancient humanity. For, with all that we know of the oldest subjects of the thought of mankind from the unquestioned results of Comparative Mythology, we must ask why the idea of an all-destroying flood, or even of a partial one confined to a limited territory, should necessarily occupy the foreground in the oldest picture of the world? In point of fact, a great number of nations are found destitute of any story of a flood. For instance, the oldest Greek mythology has no such idea; it cannot be proved to have been known to the Greeks earlier than the sixth century B.C. Whether it is indigenous and of high antiquity in India has also been doubted by distinguished scholars.[1]

On the other hand, the Cuneiform original of the Assyrian story of the Deluge, discovered by George Smith, has so much similarity, or we may rather say congruity, with the form of the story preserved in the Bible, even with respect to the raven and the dove,[2] that we are entitled to express an opinion *a priori* on these two narratives, to the effect that they point to a greater community of formation than would be the case if the community dated from the primeval Semitic age. For in that case, supposing the elements of the Deluge-story to have been so fully developed in the earliest Semitic age as we find them in the Bible and the Cuneiform Inscriptions, we must find something similar in all other Semitic nations also. It would be almost unaccountable why nothing can be traced among the Phenicians that could be placed side by side with this Deluge-story, and would be the more extraordinary if the conception of such a story took place in the age when the North-Semitic tribes were still living together.

The conclusion is accordingly almost irresistible, that the Hebrews borrowed this whole story of the Deluge from the Babylonians, and propagated it in a form resembling

---

[1] I will here cite a passage of Ibn Chaldûn, although not decisive on questions like the present: 'Know that the Persians and Indians know nothing of the Ṭûfân (deluge); some Persians say that it took place only at Babylon.' (History, vol. II.) Edward Thomas, in the *Academy*, 1875, p. 401, quotes a passage of al-Bîrûnî, in which it is said that the Indians, Chinese and Persians have no story of a Deluge, but that some say that the Persians know of a partial deluge. Burnouf believed the idea of a Deluge to be originally foreign to Indian mythology, and to have been borrowed, probably from Chaldaic sources (*Bhâgavata Purâṇa*, III. XXXI., LI.). A. Weber (in the *Indische Studien*, Heft 2, and on occasion of a critique of Nêve's writings on the Indian story of the Deluge, in the *Zeitsch. d. D. M. G.*, 1851, V. 526) declares himself in favour of the indigenousness of the Indian story, in opposition to Lassen and Roth, who agree with Burnouf.

[2] The similarities and differences of the respective stories of the Deluge are lucidly placed side by side by George Smith in *The Chaldean Account of Genesis*, p. 286 *et seq.*

the Babylonian original, even in its details and mode of expression. Moreover, Babylon is the district most of all suited to the working-out of a story of Deluge; for it is certain from Von Bohlen's and Tuch's demonstrations, that such fully developed stories of floods can only occur in nations which have in their territory rivers liable to great overflows. Consequently the region of the great twin streams of Mesopotamia is the most likely cradle for an elaborate Deluge-story.[1] A. H. Sayce, one of the most eminent English Assyriologists, in the *Theological Review* of July 1873, propounds the view that the Biblical account of the Deluge consists of two narratives: the older being Elohistic and based on a Hebrew Deluge-story, the other being placed by its side by a Jahveistic narrator in the Babylonian Captivity, and being identical with the Babylonian story preserved in the document consulted by George Smith.[2] Now, independently of the doubt as to the existence of an exclusively Hebrew Deluge-story, and of the fact that identity with the Babylonian stories has been proved of the Elohistic account also,[3] even Sayce's conception of the matter quite suffices to establish the view that the Hebrews in Babylonia at least amplified, if they did not actually construct, the Biblical story of the Deluge. It cannot be true, as Max Duncker[4] lately wrote, 'that these stories present to us an *ancient* and *common* possession of the Semitic tribes of the Euphrates and Tigris country.' We cannot assume that in those primeval, prehistoric times when the Semitic tribes, or at least the Northern group of that race, lived all together before the separation, it matters not where, they formed in common stories which presuppose a high and advanced view of the world, like the Cosmogonies and the story of

---

[1] Tuch, *Commentar über die Genesis*, 1st ed. 1838, p. 149; 2nd ed. 1871, p. 47.

[2] *Academy*, 1873, no. 77. col. 292.

[3] See *Westminster Review*, April 1875, p. 486.

[4] *Geschichte des Alterthums*, 4th ed. 1874, I. 186.

the Deluge connected therewith. At that earliest stage of human life, man labours with far simpler apperceptions than those which are requisite to form such stories. The myth in its very earliest mould, in which it is connected with the formation of language, occupies him first. But at all events, the Babylonian story received in its Hebrew transformation a purification in a monotheistic sense; or as Duncker himself appropriately adds, 'the account of the Deluge lies before us in a purer and more dignified shape in the writings of the Hebrews.'

I showed in a previous section that Noah is one of those Solar figures of which the Biblical source has still preserved some mythical features. There is no intrinsic reason why the story of the Deluge should be particularly tacked on to the person of Noah; the Assyrian tablets give Hasisadra as the name of the man saved from the flood. If the connexion of Noah with the Deluge were to be maintained at all hazards, it would be best to argue that ancient mythical traditions called him (as well as Adam) the progenitor of the human race; the other Solar figures generally assume a position hostile to the nation. The harmonising tendency, which I have already had occasion to notice, might then easily make use of Noah as hero for the story of the Deluge learned at Babylon, since here was an excellent opportunity to establish his title as ancestor of the human race. But it may be taken for granted that this use was made of Noah's name, not only at the later period when the Deluge-story was inserted in the great mass of traditional stories, but as soon as ever the Babylonian story was borrowed by the Hebrews. This is guaranteed by the Prophet of the Captivity, who calls the Deluge mê Nôach 'the water of Noah.' 'For like the water of Noah is this (thy distress) unto me, of which (water) I swore against the water of Noah coming again over the earth [Gen. VIII. 21 *et seq.*]: so do I swear against being wroth with thee and rebuking thee' (Is. LIV. 9). In Babylon, also, the Hebrews appear to have received an impulse to work out such a history of

Creation, intricate and plastically jointed, as is contained in the opening passages of Genesis. I do not mean that the cosmogony of the Babylonians was the original from which that of the Bible was copied, for in this particular matter of cosmogonies the construction of the Biblical account exhibits great individuality. But the tendency of the mind to inquire after the first beginning of both the physical and the moral order of the world was first fully roused during the residence at Babylon, so far advanced in speculations of this nature. I am confirmed in this assumption by the Babylonian story of Creation, lately discovered and edited by George Smith, which, as presented by that learned pioneer, shows great accordance with the corresponding account in Genesis.[1] It is at all events an element of the subject in hand which cannot be left unnoticed, that the notion of the bôrê and yôṣêr 'Creator' (the terms used in the cosmogony in Genesis), as an integral part of the idea of God, are first brought into common usage by the Prophets of the Captivity, especially the Babylonian Isaiah, who is particularly fond of the expression bôrê.[2] The older Prophets also know Jahveh as Creator of the world; but it is self-evident that they do not so strongly emphasise the idea, or refer to it so frequently, as for instance the Isaiah of the Captivity. Amos IV. 13, for example, says, 'For lo, he that formeth mountains and createth wind, and declareth to man what is his meditation, that maketh the dawn winged and walketh on the high places of the earth—his name is Jahveh the God of Hosts.' This passage stands in no relation whatever to the cosmogony of Genesis; indeed, in speaking of the dawn as gifted with wings (see *supra*, p. 116), it refers rather to the mythical

---

[1] *The Chaldean Account of Genesis*, pp. 60-112.

[2] Consult also Dr. Jacob Auerbach's article *Ueber den ersten Vers der Genesis* in Geiger's *Zeitsch. für Wissenschaft und Leben*, 1863, Bd. II. p. 253, who, I now see, comes very near to these ideas, but does not express them fully or clearly.

conceptions of antiquity, as also the older Isaiah frequently does. The Prophet of the Captivity, on the other hand, refers to the ideas of the cosmogony in Genesis, as is clear in Is. XL. 26, XLV. 7 (where he speaks of the Creator of light and darkness), XLII. 5, XLV. 18, especially this last passage, which refers to the banishment of the tôhû through the act of creation. By the story of creation the celebration of the Sabbath was established on entirely new grounds. Whilst in the older conception (which finds expression in the Decalogue in Deuteronomy V. 15) the Sabbath has a purely theocratic significance, and is intended to remind the Hebrews of their miraculous deliverance from Egyptian slavery after long servitude, the later version of the Decalogue (Ex. XX. 11) justifies it by referring to the history of the Creation, in which after six days of work the Creator took rest.

We cannot here enter into the question of the geographical position of the 'Êden of the Bible, nor even inquire whether the original of the idea of Eden is found in the corresponding feature of Iranian tradition; but it may be assumed that the Biblical account of Eden also arose at Babylon. It may indeed be generally presumed that the Biblical accounts of the Cosmogony and the origin of all things had not, like the matter of the old mythology, lived a long life of perhaps many thousand years in the mouths of successive generations, before the first beginnings of literary record were reached. On the contrary, we find in these parts of the Bible so artistic a perfection of description, such a harmonious roundness of narrative, that we are justified in presuming that they were not preceded by the oral concatenations of a long life of tradition, but are rather sublime imaginations which were written down soon after they were conceived in the educated circles of the nation, so as to become the common property of the whole people. There was in this a double stimulus received from the Babylonians: first, to meditate on the earliest things—the origin of the world, man, and other things of a general nature—and secondly, to produce writings on these things. The Prophets of the Hebrews at Babylon unquestionably exercised a great influence on the production of these narratives, and gladly admitted whatever tended to promote the deepening of the idea of Jahveh, as elements in their religious conception of the world. For the Prophet did not occupy a position towards the masses like the member of a corporation which opposes the people; he grew up out of the people, and raised himself above them by his individual power of thought. Yet it is easily intelligible that the Prophet, while gladly appropriating the idea of Jahveh as bôrê 'Creator,' would not set much store by the petty details of the cosmogonic imagination. The second Isaiah, the Prophet of Babylon *par excellence*, goes so far as to exhort his people, 'Record ye not beginnings, and antiquities contemplate ye not' (Is. XLIII. 18); still he does not go into open opposition to this mental tendency, and sees nothing dangerous in it—the less so, as he has himself unconsciously adopted its conclusions and often employed them in his masterly addresses.

Thus also the story of the Garden of Eden, as a supplement to the history of the Creation, was written down at Babylon, and therefore not long after the previous stories. A reference to the passage in Gen. II. 14, where the first three of the four rivers of the garden of Eden have their geographical position accurately defined, but the fourth is only mentioned by the words, 'And the fourth river is Perâth (Euphrates),' is of itself sufficient to show that those for whom the story was written must have known the Euphrates as their own river, requiring no further designation, and consequently that this must have been written on its banks. Now, although the expression 'Garden of Eden' occurs also before the Captivity (Joel II. 3), yet the Prophets of the Captivity make the first reference to that character and quality of Eden which is conspicuous in Genesis. In Joel's words only the general idea of a 'pleasure garden' appears to be connected with the name Eden. But in Ezekiel (especially frequently in Chap. XXXI.) we find the appellation 'Garden of God' used to designate Eden more fully; and in the parallelism of the members of the verse the Babylonian Isaiah (LI. 3) puts the 'Garden of Jahveh' in the succeeding member to correspond to 'Eden' in the preceding:

> He makes her desert like *Eden*,
> And her dry land like the *Garden of Jahveh.*

It is also evident from the same Prophet's words (Is. XLIII. 27), 'Thy first father sinned,' that he connected the story of the Fall with Eden, or at least that he knew the story. The mention of the doctrine of the Fall takes us to a domain which has a close connexion with the subject of this chapter. I refer to the ideas of dogmatic religion pervading the stories formed during the Captivity, which subsequently, while the canon of Scripture was being drawn up, were admitted even into those parts of Scripture whose matter dated from an earlier period, came into full life in the second Hebrew commonwealth, and continued to live in the later Jewish Synagogue. Through the growth of Persian power and Persian influence in Western Asia, where there existed many states in a condition of vassalage to Babylon, the Iranian views of religion could not but exert a great influence on the parent-state also, even before Babylon was quite overwhelmed by them through its conquest by Cyrus at the end of the Captivity of the Hebrews. Opportunity was therefore not wanting to the Hebrews to become well acquainted with the main ideas of Iranian theology; and desire was also present, as their minds were then intent upon obtaining clear views on the origin of the physical and moral order of the world, and on the chief questions concerning the 'Origins.' This influence of the Iranians on the Hebrews was exhibited not only in relation to matter, but also to forms. For there is great probability in favour of the idea, that the first suggestion to codify the sacerdotal laws of sacrifice, purification and others, came to the Hebrews from the example of the Persians.[1] One portion of these ideas has found a place in the Babylonian sections of Genesis—that which belonged to the cosmogony; others were not expressed in the Canon at all, but lived in tradition, until tradition itself was fixed in writing. This question, which would at last shed light on the details of Iranian influence on the narratives of the Pentateuch, is perversely enough not grappled with at its starting-point by many persons who labour with nervous eagerness to discover in the Iranian writings every letter of the Jewish Agâdâ, even in cases in which such a proceeding is utterly unjustifiable, and borrowing can only be suggested through the wildest guesswork. Equally perverse is the unhistorical assumption, which point-blank denies the very possibility of the Hebrews having borrowed anything from the Persians, 'among whom they never lived.'[2] Professor Spiegel, by referring to an acquaintance of Abraham with Zarathustra, has spirited the question off into the atmosphere of so distant a time that it is impossible with any regard for critical history to build upon his foundation,[3] and preferable even to adopt Volney's forgotten theory,[4] which makes the influence of Magism on the Hebrews begin with the destruction of the Northern kingdom. Others, by assuming an influence exerted by the Semites on the Iranians, and by a mistaken reverence for Hebrew antiquity, have cut away the ground from any scientific investigation of the question.[5] It is a

---

[1] This view is expounded by Kuenen in his *Religion of Israel*, II. 156.

[2] This appears to be Bunsen's opinion: *God in History*, I. 101.

[3] See Max Müller's essay *Genesis and the Zend-Avesta* (*Chips*, I. 143 *et seqq.*). The Dutch scholar Tiele occupies nearly the same position as Spiegel on this question, which he discusses fully in his book *De Godsdienst van Zarathustra*, Haarlem 1864, p. 302 *et seq.*

[4] *Les Ruines*, XX. 13. System.

[5] I must mention a third view on the concurrence of the Hebrew with the Aryan story of the primeval age; it is that which was first declared by Ewald in his *History of Israel*, I. 224 *et seqq.*, and is adopted by Lassen and Weber among the Germans, and by Burnouf and (with some hesitation) Renan among

mistaken, and anything but the right sort of reverence, when we would rather leave unknown or misunderstood a region of literature which we all love and venerate, and to which we owe most of our moral and religious ideals, than trace its elements and analyse their psychological and literary history, so as to understand the object of our love. Has Homer lost his attractiveness since we have subjected him to critical analysis, or the divine Plato forfeited any of his divinity since we have discovered some of the sources of his ideas? For the fact of Originality is not the only criterion of the admirable. Not only that which is cast in one piece from top to toe, is one whole: an alien substance which becomes a civilising agent to that in which it rests, and a patchwork which has turned out a harmonious whole, are not less admirable or perfect. Julius Braun says very justly,[1] 'There is another and indeed the highest kind of originality, which is not the beginning but the result of historical growth—the originality of mature age. We have this, when an individual or a nation has gathered up all existing means of culture, and then still possesses power to pass on beyond them and deal freely with all elements received from the past.'

Thus, then, it was quite possible for many Iranian elements to be received into the system of the literature and cosmic conceptions of the Hebrews; and we do nothing towards saving the honour of the Hebrew nationality by using force to make the Iranians pupils of the Hebrews. Karl Twesten saw the truth as to their mutual relation; and I quote his words, to show the impression made by the coincidences of Iranian and Hebrew antiquity on a sober-minded historian who considers the question free from any previous pledges to either side.

---

the French. In this view the coincidences in the respective primitive stories are to be accounted for by common prehistoric traditions which the Aryans and the Semites formed in their original common dwelling-place concerning primeval history. Renan speaks shortly on the subject in his *Histoire gén. des Langues sémitiques*, pp. 480 *et seq.*

[1] *Naturgeschichte der Sage*, I. 8.

'It cannot be pleaded that the Iranians may have borrowed from the Hebrews or drawn from the same source. For, on the one hand, these things are there an essential part of a system, whereas the Pentateuch makes no further use of them; and, on the other, they existed in times and places where, even if the possibility of a very early formation of these stories be conceded, the Hebrew theology could not possibly have any influence. The Israelites were so little known, and so rarely in contact with other nations, and the priesthoods of antiquity so exclusive, and oriental Îrân so distant, that no early influence of Mosaic doctrines on the theories of the Zend books is even conceivable. But Iranian influences on the nations of Western Asia are probable and inevitable, from the time when the Medes and Persians became the dominant powers.[1]

Such, in general terms, were the causes which yielded an increase of matter to the Hebrew store of legends during the Captivity. Through the revision and literary elaboration of the old legends in the period of the Captivity also, many Babylonian features naturally entered into the picture. I may mention Nöldeke's plausible idea (in his *Untersuchungen*), that the years and cycles of years in the Patriarchal history point to Babylon and are connected with astronomical systems. The last systematic revision of the Table of Nations (Gen. X.) may also be referred to the same time and influence. The preparation of such a survey of all known nations of the earth seems to have been possible in that ancient time only in an empire which through its wide-spread dominion had an extensive circle of view open to it in relation to geography and ethnology, and would be almost impossible within the limits of the kingdom of Judah. Although we have at the present day good reasons for treating as a mere fable the more extravagant ideas that were long current, and

[1] *Die religiösen, politischen und socialen Ideen der Asiatischen Culturvölker, etc.*, edited by M. Lazarus, Berlin 1872, p. 590.

gave rise to many lamentable prejudices, of the utter seclusion of the Hebrews in Canaan, yet their view can hardly have reached to such a distance, and, if it did, cannot have taken in such special points, as are met with in the Table of Nations. But we should exaggerate the possible influence of the connexion with the Phenicians, if with Tuch[1] we were to derive from it the ethnographical information requisite to produce that Table. And we should be applying the measure of modern expeditions to David's and Solomon's navigation—to which Mauch attributes a colonisation of Africa by Jews in connexion with the discovery of Ophir—if we were to suppose that navigation to have yielded this same geographical and ethnographical knowledge as its scientific result.

The attention of the Hebrews could not be directed to ethnographical problems on so large a scale before their residence among the confusion of nationalities in the empire of Babylon and Assyria. That period is also the first at which interest could be felt in another problem —Biblical answer to which is avowedly given at Babylon. I mean the story of the Confusion of Tongues at Babel (Babylon) in Genesis XI. 4–9.

It is not difficult to understand that the Hebrews, who in Canaan, a country of such linguistic uniformity, had no occasion to pay attention to the fact of the variety of tongues, on entering the Babylonian empire with its varying languages were naturally led to ask the question to which the eleventh chapter of Genesis offers a reply. Why, even earlier than this the Northern empire was a nation whose tongue they did not understand (Deut. XXVIII. 49),[2] 'a nation from afar, an ancient nation, a

---

[1] *Commentar zur Genesis*, 1st ed. 1838, p. 200; 2nd ed. 1871, p. 157.

[2] It should be observed that in the postexilian imitation of this sermon of castigations (now called in the Synagogue tôkhâchâ) in Lev. XXVI. 14–43, the circumstance that the people would be carried off by an enemy 'whose language they understood not' is omitted. Other points in the tôkhâchâ of Leviticus indicate that it was imagined by one who had a knowledge of the

nation from of old, a nation whose language thou knowest not, neither understandest what they say' (Jer. V. 15). Whilst even in Hesiod's time men were already called by the Greeks μέροπες 'speaking variously' (*Works and Days*, 109, 142), to the ancient Hebrew 'the whole earth was of one language and of one speech.' Now, as the impulse to ask this question arose in Babylon, the place where such a problem must force itself most irresistibly on the attention, so Babylon was found to be also the scene of the solution of the problem. It is so natural to place the origin of an event or a phenomenon at the place where it has first occurred to us or we have first perceived it. But, in fact, we find the story of the building of the Tower taking its place among the latest Cuneiform discoveries.[1] That the origin of the Table of Nations hangs together with the story of the origin of the diversity of languages is evident, not only from the inner connexion between the respective problems, but also from the fact that the Table of Nations always distinguishes the various races 'after their families, *after their tongues*, in their countries, in their nations' (Gen. X. 5, 20, 31).

The attempted etymology of Bâbhel from bâlal 'to mix,' which is tacked on to the story, is quite secondary; it is impossible to approve the notion that this etymology was itself the cause of the invention of the story that languages had their origin at Babylon. On the contrary, the essential part of the story is the origin at Babylon; the etymology is a secondary point, by which it was attempted to leave no part unexplained. People in antiquity, and even in modern times those who are more affected by a word than a thought, were fond of finding in the word a sort of reflexion of the corresponding thing. Indeed, many component parts of ancient stories owe their existence only to such false etymologies. Dido's ox-hides and their con-

---

Captivity; so e.g. the especial accentuation of residence in the land of an enemy, as in vv. 32, 36. 38, 39.

[1] George Smith, *The Chaldean Account of Genesis*, pp. 158 *et seqq.*

nexion with the founding of Carthage are only based on the Greek *byrsa*, a misunderstood modified pronunciation of the Semitic *bîrethâ* 'fortress, citadel.' The shining Apollo, born of light, is said to be born in Delos or Lycia, because the terms Apollon *Dêlios* and *Lykêgenês* were not understood. The Phenician origin of the Irish, asserted in clerical chronicles of the middle ages, only rests on a false derivation of the Irish word *fena*, pl. *fion*, 'beautiful, agreeable.' Even the savage tribes of America are misled by a false etymology to call the Michabo, the Kadmos of the Red Indians (from *michi* 'great' and *wabos* 'white'), a White Hare.[1] Falsely interpreted names of towns most frequently cause the invention of fables. How fanciful the operation of popular etymology is in the case of local names is observable in many such names when translated into another language. By the lake of Gennesereth lies Hippos, the district surrounding which was called Hippene. This word in Phenician denoted a harbour, and is found not only in Carthaginian territory as the name of the See of St. Jerome, but also as the name of places in Spain. The Hebrew chôph 'shore,' and the local names Yâphô (Jaffa) and Ḥaifâ, are unquestionably related to it. But the Greeks regarded it from a Grecian point of view, and thought it meant Horse-town. Did not they call ships sea-horses, and attribute horses to the Sea-god? Then, the Arabs directly translated this ἵππος Hippos into ḳal'at al-Ḥuṣân: ḥuṣân being *horse* in modern Arabic.[2] The Persian town Rey was made the subject of a fable, which I mention here partly because it exhibits some similarity with the subject of the 'Tower of Babel.' The Persian chroniclers relate,[3] that the old king Keykâvûs had a chariot constructed, by which, after various preparations, he intended to

[1] Fiske, *Myths and Myth-makers*, pp. 71, 154. See Tylor, *Primitive Culture*, I. 357 *et seq.*

[2] From Sepp's *Jerusalem und das heilige Land*, II. 157.

[3] In Yâḳût, *Geogr. Dictionary*, II. 893. The explanation of the name Thakîf in Yâḳût, III. 498, quite reminds one of the Old Testament way of giving etymologies of names.

ascend to heaven. But God commanded the wind to carry the king into the clouds. Arrived there, he was dashed down again, and fell into the sea of Gurgân. Keychosrau, son of Shâwush, coming to that coast, employed the same chariot to convey him to Babylon. When he came to the locality of the modern Rey, people said, bireyy âmed Keychosrau, 'on a chariot came Keychosrau.' He caused a city to be built at this place, which was called Rey, because a chariot is so called in Persian.[1]

Granting all this, it is generally only accessory features added to the main stem of the story that owe their origin to a mistaken attempt at etymologising. The existence and first origin of an entire story can scarcely be produced by an unsatisfactory etymology. With regard to the Hebrew stories, in which etymologising plays a considerable part, the same rule is, generally speaking, to be observed. There also the story is enriched in details by etymological attempts suggested later. But it is not brought into life in the first instance by this factor. On the contrary, as a connexion must be discovered between the name and the circumstances of its bearer, and the original mythical relation between them has been long lost to memory, features quite foreign to the name itself, but characteristic of the story, are sometimes brought into etymological connexion with the name and fitted on to the story. From this source emanates the striking insufficiency of many of these etymological explanations, *e.g.* of the interpretation of Abhrâhâm by Abh hâmôn 'Father of a multitude,' and Nôach (Noah) by nicham 'to comfort.' In the Hebrew Myth of Civilisation, Noah is the most prominent founder of agriculture and inventor of agricultural implements; consequently it is he that procures comfort for men against the curse imposed on the soil. This feature is not etymologically

[1] See some useful quotations in L. Löw's *Beiträge zur jüd. Alterthumskunde*, Szegedin 1875, II. 388; and very interesting references in Pott's *Wilhelm von Humboldt und die Sprachwissenschaft*, Berlin 1876, p. CIX. *et seq.*

expressed in the name Noah; but the later formation of the story about him invented a false etymology, in order to connect it with the name. The case is the same with the story of the Languages, in which Bâbhel is derived from bâlal 'to mix.' The etymology relates quite as frequently to a very subordinate feature in the story, as for instance in the interpretation of most of the names of Jacob's sons in Gen. XXIX, XXX, or in the derivation of the name Ḳayin (Cain) from ḳânâ 'to gain.' Sometimes, lastly, the etymon is given correctly, while its original relation to the person bearing the name is lost with the loss of the mythical consciousness. In such cases there frequently arises a new feature of the story. Thus, for instance, it is quite correctly affirmed that Yiṣchâḳ (Isaac) comes from ṣâchaḳ 'to laugh:' but it is no longer understood that the word designates the 'Laughing one' (the Sun), and so the laughter of the aged mother to whom the birth of a son is announced beforehand, or the laughter of other people on hearing the announcement, is introduced. In the etymology of the name Ya'aḳôbh (Jacob) both the etymon and that to which it refers ('âḳêbh 'heel') are correctly preserved, not however without the introduction of a foreign etymological element ('iḳḳêbh 'to cheat'), which became prominent in the subsequent development of the story. The same phenomenon also appears on the domain of the Arabian stories, a region of Semitism which has still to be explored for mythological questions. I have no doubt that the genealogical tables of the Arabs contain names which will be discovered by sound etymology to be Solar designations. This seems to me, for example, to be the case with Hâshim. The story that he and his twin-brother 'Abd Shams were born with their foreheads joined together, or with the forehead of one joined to the hand of the other,[1] resembles the myths of the birth of Jacob and

[1] *Zeitsch. d. D. M. G.*, 1853, VII. p. 28.

Esau, and of that of Perez and Zerah.[1] It was worked out with an object during the later dynastic rivalry between the Hâshimites and Ummayads (descendants of ʻAbd Shams). But Hâshim is 'the Breaker,' thus answering perfectly to Pereṣ (Perez) or Gideʻôn. When the mythical consciousness was lost, a story bearing an obviously apocryphal character was fabricated to give it an etymology. It is this. On occasion of a famine resulting from a bad harvest, Hâshim went to Syria, where he had a quantity of bread baked. This he put into large sacks, loaded his camels with it, and took it to Mekka. There *hashama, i.e.* he broke up the bread into bits, sent for butchers, and distributed it among the people of Mekka. Therefore, it is said, he was called Hâshim, 'the Breaker.'[2] We have here the very same process in the history of etymology which we had occasion to observe in the etymological explanation of Biblical names. Thus, as is obvious in the above-quoted Hebrew examples, it must be admitted that the later etymological conception frequently forced itself into the foreground so much as to obtain recognition as a portion of the narrative.[3] But no entire story, such as that of the Confusion of Tongues at Babel, can be proved to have been formed upon no other basis than an indifferent etymology. So we may with confidence hold to the above-suggested occasion for the origin of this story of the variety of languages. There is good ground for hoping that before very long the recently discovered mythical texts of the Assyrian and Babylonian literature will pour an increasing flood of light on the question discussed in this chapter. The richness of the stores contained in the two latest works of the meritorious scholar George Smith—'Assyrian Discoveries: an account of exploration and discoveries' (1876), and 'The Chaldean Account of Genesis' (1876)—allow us to entertain the best

---

[1] See supra, pp. 133, 183.

[2] Ibn Dureyd, *Kitâb al-Ishtiḳâḳ*, ed. Wüstenfeld, Göttingen 1853, p. 9.

[3] See Ewald, *History of Israel*, I. 19 *et seq.*

hopes of this result. It is greatly to be desired that an unprejudiced conception of the matter of Hebrew mythic stories may be promoted by these discoveries. But to attain to the result of true freedom from old errors, it is essential to put away all fears, and to be guided solely and simply by the interests of the Holiest of Holies, namely, scientific truth, in forming a judgment on the priority or simultaneous origin of such stories in different nations.

EXCURSUS.

A. (*Page* 30.)

Agadic Etymologies.

In another direction also the Agâdâ is wont to supply the omissions of the Scripture. In passages where the Bible itself gives no reason for the choice or origin of a name, the Agâdâ quite independently gives its own etymological reason: this peculiarity occurs excessively often (e.g. in the etymology of the name Miriam in the Midrâsh to the Song of Songs, II. 12, that of the names of the two midwives Shiphrah and Puah, who in addition are identified with Jochebed and Miriam, in the Talmûd Bab. tr. Sôṭâ, fol. 11. b, etc.).[1] Here I will bring forward out of a great number of instances one which affords an opportunity of exhibiting an interesting coincidence between the Jewish and the Mohammedan Agâdâ, and affords a proof how extensive and how far-reaching into the smallest detail are the loans taken by the Mohammedan from the Rabbinical theologians, and on the other hand how independently and how completely in an Arabian spirit these borrowed treasures were worked up.

In Gen. XLVI. 21, Benjamin's sons are enumerated without any etymological observations. The Agâdâ supplies the deficiency, and puts every one of the names of Joseph's nephews into connexion with Benjamin's melancholy remembrance of his lost brother. The interpretations in question are contained in the Talmûd and Midrâsh; and they are found in a different, but probably the most original form in the Targûm Jerus. on the passage; and it is sufficient to refer to this. According to this, Benjamin named his ten sons 'al perishûthâ de-Yôsêph achôhî 'for the separation

[1] I have referred to this in *Zeitschr. d. D.M.G.* 1870, XXIV. 207.

from his brother Joseph :' thus Bela', 'because Joseph was devoured-away (i.e. *torn away*) from him,' de-ithbela' minnêh : Bekher, 'because Joseph was his mother's first-born,' bukhrâ de-immêh : Ashbêl, 'from the captivity into which Joseph fell,' de-halakh be-shibhyâthâ : Gêrâ, 'because Joseph had to live as a stranger in a foreign land,' de-ithgar be-ar'â nukhrâ'â : Na'amân, 'because Joseph was charming and dear to him,' da-hawâ nâ'îm we-yaḳḳîr : Êchî, 'because he was his brother (achôhî) :' Rôsh, because he was the most excellent in his father's house : Muppîm, because he was sold to the land Môph (Egypt) : Chuppîm, because Benjamin had exactly reached the age of eighteen years, that of maturity for marriage (chuppâh) in men :[1] Ard, from yârad 'to go down,' because Joseph had to go down to Egypt.

The Arabic pendant to this Agâdâ I found in a book Zahr al-kimâm fî ḳiṣṣat Yûsuf 'aleyhi al-salâm, by the learned Mâlikite 'Omar b. Ibrâhîm al-Ausî al-Anṣârî. It is the same book as Ḥâjî Chalfâ quotes (V. 381, no. 11386) by the name Majâlis ḳiṣṣat Yûsuf,[2] although the commencement given by him does not agree with the initial words of our Codex (No. 7 of the Supplement, in the Leipzig University Library). The book is divided into seventeen majâlis, or sessions—an arrangement not uncommon in Arabic works of a hortatory character or touching on religious knowledge. Each mejlis contains a portion of the life of Joseph, always introduced by a verse of the Ḳorân, and abundantly mixed with poems and other episodes and intermezzos. It is an instructive source for the legend of Joseph among the Mohammedans. It would take us too far from the subject if I were to give a full characterisation of the book. I will therefore only mention that it betrays a close relation to the Jewish legend, and that the author generally gives frequent occasion for the conjecture that the Bible and the Jewish tradition were not strange to him or to the sources from which he drew. But everything appears here curiously altered. For example, the cry of Isaac when deceived, 'The voice is the voice of Jacob, but the hands are the hands of Esau' (Gen. XXVII. 22), is there given (fol. 5 *recto*) thus : al-lams lams 'Aysau w-al-rîḥ rîḥ Ya'ḳûb 'the touch is the touch of

[1] According to Rabbinical views, Âbhôth V, Mishnâ 21.

[2] The author refers on p. 127 *recto* to his earlier work, *Biġyat al-muta'allim wa-fâ'idat al-mutakallim.* Ḥâji Chalfâ does not know this book of the author's.

Esau, but the smell is the smell of Jacob' (see Gen. XXVII. 27). The passage with which we have to do here occurs fol. 149 *recto.*

The scene is the brothers' dinner in Joseph's house. Each sits beside his full brother; Benjamin alone has none, and begins to weep bitterly. Then Joseph approaches him, and after a long dialogue makes himself known to Benjamin as his full brother, and talks with him. Afterwards Joseph asks him, 'Youth, hast thou a wife?' 'Yes,' replies Benjamin. 'And children?' 'I have three sons.' 'What name gavest thou to the eldest?' 'D̲îb (Wolf).' 'And why didst thou choose this name?' 'Because my brothers were of opinion that a wolf had devoured my brother, and I wished to have a memento of the catastrophe.' 'And what didst thou call the second?' 'I named him Dam (Blood).' 'And wherefore?' 'Because my brothers brought a coat dipped in blood, and I wished to preserve the memory of it.' 'And what is thy third son's name?' 'Yûsuf, that my brother's name may not be forgotten.'

But even names whose etymology occurs in the Bible itself are provided by the Agâdâ with new etymological explanations: so e.g. Yiṣchâḳ, is explained by yâṣâ or yêṣê chôḳ 'A statute has gone or will go forth.'[1]

B. (*Page* 34.)

A Hermeneutical Law of the Agâdâ.

The hermeneutic principle to which we have referred in the text, although not so well known to the Agadists as it was in other circles (for they have nowhere expressly declared it), is to be traced throughout their whole conception of Scripture. It is the principle that *the intensity of the sense of a word increases with the enlargement of its form.* This law was also set up by the Greek etymologists, and applied even to the point of pedantry by one of the oldest grammarians, Tryphon.[2] With the Arabic grammarians it controls the entire grammatical field: ziyâdet al-lafẓ (al-binâ) tadullu 'ala ziyâdet al-ma'na 'the increase of the word (the form) points to increase of the meaning.' In Agadic exegesis also it is

[1] Berêsh. r. sect. 53; see Beer, *Leben Abraham's*, p. 168, note 506.

[2] See Steinthal, *Geschichte der Sprachwissenschaft bei Griechen und Römern*, p. 342.

often accepted as a valid rule of Scriptural interpretation. In the case of reduplicated forms especially, the reduplicated indicates a fuller concept than the unreduplicated: e.g. lêbhâbh compared with lêbh (both denoting 'heart') is treated as signifying a 'double heart,' comprising the good and the evil impulse (yêṣer ṭôbh and yêṣer hâra': Sifrê on Deuter. VI. 5. § 32). So also in shephîphôn compared with shephî, the doubled *ph* is supposed to point to an enlargement of the signification.

But this word shephîphôn contains besides the reduplication of a radical letter an affix *ôn*. This affix is also generally brought into connexion with an enlargement of the signification, exactly as is done by the interpreters of the Ḳorân with the corresponding Arabic affix *ân*.[1] An example from the Agâdâ is as follows: in Berêshîth rabbâ, sect. 97, Yôsê b. Chalaphtâ says, 'The labours of bread-winning are double as laborious as the labours of child-birth, for of these it is said "With pain (be'eṣebh) thou shalt bear children" (Gen. III. 16), while of those it is said, "With painfulness (be'iṣṣâbhôn) thou shalt enjoy it [its fruits] all the days of thy life"' (*ib.* v. 17). Hence the *ôn* affixed to 'eṣeb is taken to indicate a doubling of the pain; just as the *ôn* added to shephî in shephîphôn denoted lameness in both feet.

C. (*Page* 100.)

Pools and Whips of the Sun.

There is no doubt that the ancient idea which associates Pools with the rising and the setting sun was based on the conception that the rising sun emerged from water and the setting sun sank into water. In later times, when the original mythical circumstances had lost their clearness, the conception of the Sun's Pools underwent a considerable modification. On this subject we must notice two different conceptions, both of which sound quite mythical, which are preserved in the Jewish and Arabic tradition. One of these supposed that the Sun exhibited such an eagerness for the performance of his work, that the whole world would be set on fire if its consequences were not moderated by various means for cooling down the heat; and these means are the Pools of the Sun. In the Midrâsh on Ecclesiastes, I. 6, it is said: 'It is

[1] See on raḥmân and raḥîm al-Beyḍâwî's *Comm. in Coranum*, ed. Fleischer, 5. 11.

reported in the name of Rabbi Nâthân that the ball of the Sun is fixed in a reservoir with a pool of water before him; when he is about to go forth he is full of fire, and God weakens his force by that water, that he may not burn up the whole world.' A similar account is found in the Shôchêr ṭôbh on Ps. XIX. 8, and in the same Midrâsh on v. 8 the Talmudic theory of the *upper waters* (mayîm hâ-'elyônîm, which are said to be above the heaven) is brought into connexion with this idea. Another conception is diametrically opposite to this. According to this view, the Sun at first resists the performance of his business, and is only moved to do it by force and violent measures. In the Midrâsh Êkhâ rabbâ, Introduction, § 25, the Sun himself complains that he will not go out till he has been struck with sixty whips, and received the command 'Go out, and let thy light shine.' Among the Arabs the poet Umayyâ b. Abî-ṣ-Ṣalt discourses at length on the compulsion which must be exerted on the Sun before he is willing to bestow the benefit of his light and warmth on mortals:

W-ash-shamsu taṭla'u kulla âchiri leylatin * ḥamrâ'a maṭla'u launihâ mutawarridu.
Ta'ba falâ tabdû lanâ fî raslihâ * illâ mu'a<u>dd</u>abatan wa-illâ tujladu.

'The Sun rises at the close of every night * commencing red in colour, slowly advancing.
He refuses, and appears not to us during his delay * until he is chastised, until he is whipped.'[1]

According to the tradition of 'Ikrimâ seven thousand angels are daily occupied with keeping the Sun in order.[2] The first conception also is represented in Mohammedan tradition. A sentence of tradition quoted by al-Suyûṭî (Tashnîf al sam' bi-ta'dîd al-sab')[3] says that the Sun is pelted every day with snow and ice by seven angels, that his heat may not destroy the earth. This mode of cooling is the Mohammedan equivalent for the Pool of the Sun. Mohammedan tradition speaks, moreover, also of a Pool of the Moon.[4]

D. (*Page* 100.)

Solar Myth and Animal-Worship.

The Egyptian animal-worship, indeed animal-worship in general, can only be traced back to mythical conceptions, which,

---

[1] *Kitâb al-aġânî*, IV. 191. My translation differs from Sprenger's.
[2] Sprenger, *Leben Mohammed's*, I. 112.
[3] MS. of the Leipzig University Library, Cod. Ref. no. 357.
[4] See Sprenger, *ibid.* p. 111.

when the myth passed into theology and the true understanding of it became rare and then ceased altogether, gained a new meaning quite different from the original. Animal-worship is accordingly one of the sources for the discovery of mythological facts. This is especially the case with the Egyptian animal-worship, which, as Plutarch (*De Iside et Osiride*, c. VIII.) says of the religion of the Egyptians, is founded *par excellence* on *αἰτία φυσική*, since the same impulse which is reflected in the figurative portion of the Hieroglyphic system of writing led the Egyptians to employ animals in mythology with equal profuseness. Thus, e.g. the often discussed Cat-worship of the Egyptians is traced back to one point of their Solar myth. The old Egyptian myth unquestionably called the Sun the Cat; of which a clear trace is left in the XVIIth chapter of the Book of the Dead.[1] Like the Sun, says Horapollo, the pupil of the cat's eye grows larger with the advance of day, till at noon it is quite round; after which it gradually decreases again. The Egyptian myth imagined a great cat behind the Sun, which is the pupil of the cat's eye. In the later Edda (I. 96, Gylf. 24) also Freya is said to drive out with two cats to draw her car. In the above-quoted chapter of the Book of the Dead, which Brugsch, who cites the passage of Horapollo, analyses in an interesting essay,[2] it is frequently said that the cat is frightened by a scorpion which approaches on the vault of heaven, intending to block the way of the cat and cover its body with dirt. Brugsch identifies the scorpion with *Sin*; but to me it seems more probable that we have here an echo of the old myth of the Cat, i.e. a Solar myth, in which the Sun does battle against the Dragon or serpentine monster that obscures or devours him. Instead of the mythical expression, that Darkness covers up the Sun, it is said here that 'The Dragon of storms or night covers the Cat's body with dirt.'

I mention here this important argument affecting the origin of animal-worship, not on account of the Cat, but in order to point to an element of the Egyptian animal-worship which hangs together with the mythical mode of regarding the Sun which has been more fully worked out in the text—that he sinks into the water in the evening, so as to come to land again in the morning. It is well known that in many parts of Egypt the Crocodile enjoyed divine honours. Now this worship appears to be connected

[1] See Lenormant, *Premières Civilisations*, I. 359.

[2] *Aegyptische Studien*, in the *Zeitsch. der D. M. G.*, X. 683.

with the fact that in the above respect the Crocodile is, so to speak, a mythological hieroglyph of the Sun, and doubtless figured in the Solar myth as a designation of the Sun. The Crocodile passes the greater part of the day on the dry land, and the night in the water. Herodotus (II. 68) says, *τὸ πολλὸν τῆς ἡμέρης διατρίβει ἐν τῷ ξηρῷ, τὴν δὲ νύκτα πᾶσαν ἐν τῷ ποταμῷ.* Plutarch shows admirable tact, especially in his sober intelligence in relation to the mythical use made of living creatures that abide in the water or grow up out of it, and consequently understands the relation of the Lotus-flower to the Sun in this sense : *οὕτως ἀνατολὴν ἡλίου γράφουσι τὴν ἐξ ὑγρῶν ἡλίου γινομένην ἄναψιν αἰνιττόμενοι* (*De Iside et Osiride*, c. XI.). Yet in treating of the Crocodile he strangely heaps hypothesis upon hypothesis (*ibid.* c. LXXV.), and exhibits superior insight only in so far as he endeavours to find in the nature of the Crocodile the origin of the worship paid to it, whereas Diodorus is satisfied wlth the utilitarian explanation that the Crocodile keeps robbers at a distance from the Nile (I. 89). But on this point he does not, as on many others, hit the nail on the head.

The reverse of the Crocodile-worship is that of the Ichneumon in the country now called Fayûm. According to the classical reporters, this animal was sacred to Buto, who was identified with the Leto of the Greeks. Now Max Müller (*Chips etc.* II. p. 80) has convincingly proved Leto or Latona to be one of the names of the Night. The Ichneumon, accordingly, is likewise a mythical designation of the Night in its relation to the Sun (Cat, Crocodile) ; for the special characteristic of the Ichneumon, with which the worship paid to it is connected, is its peculiar hostility to cats and crocodiles.

The part played by the Cow also in animal-worship must be traced back to the Solar myth as its primary origin. It is well known that one of the very commonest appellations of the Sun in mythology is this—the Cow. The Sun's rays are described as the Cow's milk ; especially in the Vedas this is one of the most familiar conceptions. The worship of the Scarabeus among the Egyptians must also be based on a close connexion with the Solar myth, although the point of attachment to that mythological group is not obvious in this case to us, who are so far removed from the mythical mind. However, even Plutarch[1] endeavours

[1] *De Iside et Osiride*, c. LXXIV.

to discover some point of similarity which might serve as ***tertium comparationis***, and finds it in the Scarabeus' mode of generation.

The animal-worship was not based upon any experience of the usefulness or hurtfulness of the animals, but always stands in close connexion with the Solar myth, of which it is only a theological and liturgical development. This is most conspicuously evident from the fact that, besides real existing animals, there were also imaginary ones that received divine honours, and played a very prominent part, as, for example, the Phenix. But this word also is only an ancient mythical designation of the Sun. The Phenix is 'a winged animal with red and golden feathers;'[1] a description of the Sun from the mythical point of view, as must be sufficiently obvious from what was expounded on p. 116. The Phenix comes every five hundred years—at the end of each great Solar period. When the myth-creating stage had been overpassed, and the name Phenix disappeared from the inventory of names of the Sun, the word, surviving the myth itself, and the remains of a misunderstood mythical conception attached to the word, might produce the superstition of the real existence of the bird Phenix. And it is these very remains that permit and render possible the reconstruction of the mythical significance.[2] Even religious usages may have their source in the ancient mythical circle of ideas. From Herodotus we learn that the Egyptians were forbidden to sacrifice or eat the Cow, but that the Ox was not so protected.[3] This is closely connected with mythical ideas. To the Cow, whose milk and horns are the mythical representatives of the rays, whether of the Sun or of the Moon, extensive divine veneration could more naturally be paid than to the Ox, who less perfectly exhibits what the myth tells of the Sun, inasmuch as he has not the milk; and the veneration would naturally carry with it the idea, that it was forbidden either to kill or to eat of the sacred animal.

---

[1] Herod. II. 73: *τὰ μὲν αὐτοῦ χρυσόκομα τῶν πτερῶν, τὰ δὲ, ἐρυθρά.*

[2] On other animals, rather fantastic than mythological, belonging to Egyptian antiquity, see Chabas, *Études sur l'antiquité historique*, Paris 1873, pp. 399–403.

[3] Herod. II. 41: *Τοὺς μέν νυν καθαροὺς βοῦς τοὺς ἔρσενας καὶ τοὺς μόσχους οἱ πάντες Αἰγύπτιοι θύουσι· τὰς δὲ θηλέας οὔ σφι ἔξεστι θύειν, ἀλλὰ ἱραί εἰσι τῆς Ἴσιος.*

E. (*Page* 109.)

The Sun as a Well.

To the mythical conception discussed in the text, which regards the Sun as an Eye, must be added another parallel view, that of the Sun as a *Well.* Language and myth here show remarkable uniformity, which helps the identification. Many languages have the same name for Well and Eye, as if they followed the mathematical law that when two things are each equal to a third, they are equal to each other. So it is in Semitic ('ayin, 'ayn, etc.); in Persian tsheshm and tsheshmeh; in Chinese ian, which word denotes both *well* and *eye.* The thirty-four wells near Bunarbashi, which was formerly believed to be the site of the Homeric Ilion, are called by the people, using a round number, 'the forty *eyes.*' For the Sun is not only a seeing eye, but also a flowing well. It is possible that the *weeping eye,* which is actually a flowing well (see Jer. VIII. 23 [IX. 1] we-'ênay meḳôr dim'â 'would that my eyes were a fountain of tears'), may serve to mediate between the two senses. Heinrich Heine, in his 'Nordsee-cyclus' ('*Nachts in der Kajüte*') says:

From those heavenly eyes above me,
Light and trembling sparks are falling. . .
O ye heavenly eyes above me!
Weep yourselves into my spirit,
That my spirit may run over
With those tears so sweet and starry.[1]

Freya, an acknowledged solar figure, whose car is drawn by cats, weeps *golden tears* for her lost husband.[2] Here the tears of the Sun's eye are his golden rays.

The Sun being a Well, the light of his rays is the moisture that flows from the well. In the Egyptian Book of the Dead the Sun is called râ pu num âtef nuteru 'the Sun, *the primitive water,* the father of the gods.'[3] Lucretius (*De Rerum Natura,* V. 282) calls the Sun

Largus item *liquidi* fons *luminis,* aetherius, Sol,
Inrigat assidue coelum candore recenti,

---

[1] E. A. Bowring's translation of the *Book of Songs,* where the 'Nordsee' is rendered 'Baltic'!

[2] Later Edda, I. 90, Gylf. 35.

[3] Lepsius, *Aelteste Texte des Todtenbuchs,* Berlin 1867, p. 42.

'who fructifies the heaven with ever-new brilliancy.' The same view prevails also on Semitic ground. In Hebrew and Arabic the root nâhar denotes equally 'to flow' and 'to shine.' Nâhâr (Heb.), nahar (Ar.), is 'a river,' nahâr (Ar.) 'the brightness of the sun by day.' In 'Abd-al-Raḥmân al-Asadî's poem in defence of the tribe of Asad against a satire of Ibn Mayyâdâ of the tribe of Murr, the setting of the Sun is called inṣibâbuhâ[1] 'his pouring himself out,' his condition when he has poured forth all his rays :

If the Sun's rays belonged to one tribe, * then his shining-forth and his concealment would belong to us ;
But he belongs to God, who holds command over him; * to His power belong both his rising and his effusion of himself.

Walau anna ḳarna-sh-shamsi kâna li-ma'sharin * lakâna lanâ ishrâḳuhâ wa'ḥtijâbuhâ ;
Walâkinnahâ lillâhi yamliku amrahâ * li-ḳudratihi iṣ'âduhâ wanṣibâbuhâ.

The poet Ṭarafâ, to express the idea that the Sun *lends* or *spends* his rays, uses the verb to 'give to drink' (saḳat-hu iyât ush-shamsi, Mu'allaḳâ, v. 9.), and the same idiom is used of the light of the stars. The word kaukab, which in Semitic generally denotes *star*, also signifies a well-spring, e.g. 'and may no well-spring (kaukab) irrigate the pasture' (*Aġânî*, XI. 126. 15). Compare a passage in the introduction to the Commentary on the Ḳorân called al-Kashshâf by Zamachsharî (de Sacy, *Anthologie gramm. ar.* p. 120. 8, text), where the two significations of the word occur close together. To this place belongs also a sentence delivered by Rabbi Ami in the Babylonian Talmûd, Ta'anîth, fol. 7 b. He explains the words al-kappayîm kissâôr in Job XXXVI. 32, thus : 'On account of the sin of their hands he (God) holds back the rain,' as by 'light' rain must be meant (ên ôr ellâ mâṭâr), and gives the same interpretation of the word ôr 'light' in another passage, Job XXXVII. 11, 'he also loads the cloud with moisture, *spreads abroad the cloud of his rain*' (yâphîṣ 'anan ôrô). But of what fluid the rays of the heavenly bodies are composed is not fixed and determined by the myth. In the Vendidad, XXI. 26, 32, 34, 'the Sun, moon, and stars are rich in *Milk*.' No less frequent is the idea that the heavenly bodies *make water*.[2] This latter view of the Sun's rays as a liquid is remarkably reflected in the Hungarian language ; and I will therefore note some facts relating to the subject, which will

[1] *Aġânî* II. 118. 7.
[2] See especially Schwartz, *Sonne, Mond und Sterne*, p. 30 sq.

be interesting to the investigators of Comparative Mythology. It is especially noteworthy that in old Hungarian the word hugy, which in the modern language means only 'urine,' was employed for 'star.' In the Legend of St. Francis, an ancient document of the Hungarian language, the Latin *stellarum cursus* is translated *hugoknak folyása* 'the flowing of the *hugyok*.' To the same root belong probably some proper names also, collected by Rev. Aron Szilády (*Magyar Nyelvőr*, I. 223), e.g. Hugdi, Hugod, Hugus (which should be read Hugydi, Hugyad, Hugyos), which must surely signify 'shining,' *fényes*. The same view of light as a fluid is also preserved in the later language, in which with sugár 'ray' the verb ömlik 'to pour itself out' is employed, as in many other languages.

F. (*Page* 113.)

Cain in Arabic.

The names of the first brothers in the Biblical legend of the Mohammedans are Hâbil and Ḳâbil. Even D'Herbelot (*Bibliothèque Orientale*, s.v. Cabil) explains: Ḳâbil, 'Receiver,' as an Arabic diversion of the etymon with which the Hebrew text supplies the name, viz. kânîthî, 'I have gained or received a man for Jahveh.' Still we must doubt whether the name Ḳâbil has any etymological foot-hold in this group. Nor can it, as Chwolson supposes, be traced to a transcriber's error which had been propagated so as to become fixed.[1] It is founded on a peculiar fancy of the Arabs for putting together pairs of names. This process may be observed to take place in one of two modes. First, the Arabs are fond of employing in groups of names various derivatives of the same root: e.g. they call the two angels of the grave Munkar and Nekir; the two armies in the story of Alexander Munsik and Nâsik, a sort of Yâjûj and Mâjûj;[2] and in the story of Joseph the two Midianites who lifted Joseph out of the pit are Bashshâr and Bushrâ.[3] To the same category belong Shiddîd and Shaddâd, the two sons of 'Âd; Mâlik and Milkân, the sons of Kinânâ.[4] This fancy passed from legend into actual life, where it often decided the names to be

---

1 See Gutschmid in *Zeitschr. d. D.M.G.* 1861, XV. 86.

2 See W. Bacher's Nizâmî's *Leben und Werke*, p. 21.

3 MS. of the Leipzig University Library, Suppl. 7. fol. 30 *recto*.

4 Yâḳût, III. 92; Krehl, *Vorislam. Religion des Araber*, p. 12 etc. See also Ewald, *History of Israel*, I. 272. note 4.

given to children, e.g. Ḥasan and Ḥuseyn the two sons of ʻAlî, and larger groups, as the three brothers Nabîh, Munabbih, and Nabahân (*Aġânî*, VI. 101), Amîn, Ma'mûn, and Musta'min the three sons of the Khalif Hârûn ar-Rashîd. The practice is observable not only in the names of contemporaries, but also in genealogical series of names both of prehistoric and of historic times: e.g. Huzâl b. Huzeyl b. Huzeylâ, a man belonging to the ʻAdites (*Commentaire historique sur le poëme d'Ibn Abdoun par Ibn Badroun*, ed. Dozy, Leyden 1848, p. 67. 1 text); the Thamûdite Ḳudâr b. Ḳudeyrâ (Ḥarîrî, *Mak.* p. 201); Sâṭirûn b. Asṭîrûn al-Jarmaḳî, builder of the fortress Ḥaḍr, the conquest of which is bound up with a story full of terrific tragedy (Yâḳût, II. 284. 12), etc. An interesting example of such grouping of nouns in modern popular rhetoric occurs in Burton's *Personal Narrative of a Pilgrimage to Mecca and Medina* (II. 146 of the ed. in two vols.). Secondly, in pairing names, the Arabs are fond of allowing *assonance* to prevail. So we have Rahâm and Rayâm, Hârût and Mârût, Hâwil and Ḳâwil, (see Bacher, *ibid.*), Yâjûj and Mâjûj for the Biblical Gôg and Mâgôg. From the last instance it is evident that the inclination to form assonant pairs of names is not foreign to the Hebrews; another Hebrew instance is Eldâd and Mêdâd, and from Talmudical literature Chillêḳ and Billêḳ. The assonance occurs not only at the end of the words, the initial syllable being indifferent, but also inversely in the first syllable, the end of the word being indifferent. An instance of the latter is found in the names of the orthodox survivors of the ʻAd and Thamûd peoples in the Mohammedan legend, Jâbalḳ and Jâbars (or Jâbarṣ, see Yâḳût, II. 2; but certainly not Jabulka and Jabulsa, as Justi writes in the *Ausland* for 1875, p. 306). Moreover, this love of assonance natural to Arabic writers extends beyond the proper sphere of Arabic legends to foreign parts. An instance is found in the Romance of *ʻAntar*, XXIX. 72. 10, where two Franks, brothers, slain by ʻAntar, are called Saubert and Taubert. No doubt the writer had heard of Frankish names ending in *bert*; he had already mentioned a king Jaubert. The tendency to form such assonant names is so prevalent that the correct sounds of one of the two are unhesitatingly corrupted for the sake of assonance. This was the case with Yâjûj and Mâjûj; another well-known instance is the pair of names Soliman and Doliman for Suleyman and Dânishmand. The Biblical Saul is called in the Mohammedan legend Ṭâlût, for the sake of assonance with Jâlût

(Goliath).[1] It is also noteworthy that the first species of assonance is to be observed not only in personal names, but also in geographical proper names, e.g. Kadâ and Kudeyy, two hills near Mekka (Yâḳût, IV. 245. 15), Achshan and Chusheyn, also hills (*ibid.* I. 164. 12, and see the proverbs referring to them in al-Meydânî, I. 14. 2); Sharaf and Shureyf, localities in Nejd (Ibn Dureyd, 127. 15.)

This phonological tendency produced also the name Ḳâbil as an assonant with Hâbil. The name Ḳayin 'Cain' was originally pronounced by the Arabs in its Hebrew form, which was particularly easy, because Ḳayn is an old Arabic proper name.[2] Through the force of assonance Ḳayin was changed in the mouth of the people into Ḳâbil, and this form made its way at a later time into literature and became general. Mas'ûdî still knows the name Ḳayin, and expressly condemns the form Ḳâbil as incorrect (*Les Prairies d'or*, I. 62); and he quotes a verse from which it appears that the Biblical etymology from ḳânâ, which is equally applicable to the Arabic language, is known to him :

Waḳtanayâ-l-ibna fa-summiya Ḳâyina * wa-'âyanâ nash'ahu mâ 'âyanâ
Fa-shabba Hâbilu fa-shabba Ḳâyin * wa-lam yakun beynahumâ tabâyun.

They (Adam and Eve) gained the son ; so he was called Ḳâyin, * and they saw his growth as they saw it.
So Hâbil grew up, and Ḳâyin grew up, * and there was no dispute between them.

The same is also evident from the fact that Mohammedan tradition makes Ḳâbil live at a place Ḳaneynâ near Damascus (Yâḳût, II. 588. 11), which can only be explained from its phonetic resemblance to Ḳâyin. Moreover, the connexion in which Abulfaraj (*Historia Dynastiarum*, p. 8) puts the invention of musical instruments with the daughters of Cain,[3] affords evidence for the former employment of the Biblical form of the name by the Arabs, since this tradition depends upon the Arabic word ḳaynâ 'female singer.'

In the Oriental Christian Book of Adam, which Dillmann has translated, the word Ḳayin is interpreted 'Hater;' 'for he hated his sister in his mother's womb, and therefore Adam named him Ḳayin.' Dillmann justly conjectures that this idea is sug-

---

[1] See Frankel's *Monatsschrift für jüd. Geschichte*, II. 273. See on assonance of names, *Zeitschr. d. D.M.G.* XXI. 593.

[2] E.g. Ḥamâsâ, p. 221 ; compare *Zeitsch. d. D.M.G.*, 1849, III. 177.

[3] See Gutschmid, l.c. p. 87.

gested by a derivation of the name from kinnê 'to be jealous of some one.'[1]

G. (*Page* 116.)

Grammatical Note on Joel II. 2.

I reserved the justification of the use which I made of the verse Joel II. 2 for a short excursus here. It is well known that in the Semitic languages the passive participle is frequently used instead of the active, similarly to the English *possessed of* instead of *possessing*, and the German *Bedienter* for *Bedienender*. In Arabic (in which the native grammarians call this usage maf'ûl bima'na-l-fâ'il) ḥijâb mastûr 'the *concealed* curtain,' is said for 'the *concealing*,' sâtir (Ḳorân, XVII. 47; compare al-Ḥarîrî, 2nd ed., p. 528. 17) etc., in Aramaic achîd 'âmartâ 'the conqueror of the world,' for âchêd; râphûḳâ 'digger,' for râphêḳ (Talm. Babyl. Sôtâ 9 b.); in Samaritan kethûbhâ 'the writer,' (Le Long, *Bibl. sacra*, p. 117; de Sacy, *Mémoire sur la version arabe des livres de Moïse*, in the *Mém. de l'Acad. des Inscriptions*, 1808, p. 16); in later Hebrew lâḳûach 'buyer' instead of lôḳêach kephûy ṭôbhâ 'one who conceals the good he has received,' hence 'unthankful' (see *supra*, p. 193), instead of kôphe; dôbh chaṭûph 'a tearing bear,' for chôṭêph (Targ. II. Gen. XLIX. 27). So also frequently in Biblical Hebrew, e.g. achûzê cherebh 'holding swords' for ôchazê, Song of Songs, III. 8); 'erûkh milchâmâ 'arranging battle' for 'ôrêkh (Joel II. 5, compare Jer. VI. 23, L. 42, where the verb '-r-kh, when used of drawing up the lines for battle, is followed by the preposition le; this, however, can be omitted, as in kôhên meshûach milchâmâ 'a priest anointed for war,' in the Mishna). I put in the same category the shachar pârûs in the verse now being considered, where in my opinion the passive pârûs stands for the active pôrês.

But to understand my explanation of the verse it must also be noticed that verbs which are regularly employed with a certain noun as subject or object in Hebrew can dispense with the noun, which then is implicitly included in the verb: a very natural proceeding. If I say, for instance, 'he clapped,' the verb contains in itself the notion 'his hands.' It is an elliptic, or rather pregnant construction where a noun is omitted, similar to that which is used

[1] In Ewald's *Jahrb. für bibl. Wissenschaft*, 1853, V. 139. note 53.

to express motion by a verb not in itself implying motion;[1] e.g. Num. XX. 26, we-Aharôn yê'âsêph ûmêth shâm 'Aaron *was gathered* [to his fathers or his people] and died there.' The words 'and died there,' render superfluous the complement el 'ammâw 'to his peoples,' which is added in v. 24. Similarly with s-ph-ḳ 'to clap' the object kappayîm 'the hands' can be omitted (Job XXXIV. 37; perhaps also Is. II. 6), etc. In the same list I put the pârûs or pôrês of our passage: kenâphayîm 'the wings' or kenâphâw 'its wings' being omitted. The expression 'the spreading dawn' is intelligible by itself, as 'the dawn that spreads out its wings.' But the fact that the complementary object after pârûs could be omitted proves how general was the conception of the Bird of the Dawn with outstretched wings, which found this mode of expression.

H. (*Page* 153.)

Hajnal.

The Hungarian language shows how speech wavers in determining the colour of the rising Sun. The Hungarian word for Dawn, hajnal, is etymologically related to hó, which means *snow.* Therefore, the former must have originally denoted 'the white;'[2] and hajnalpir, 'the morning Redness,' is literally 'the Redness of the White.' And the conception of the *redness* of the dawn has overcome that which must have prevailed when the expression hajnal came into use, but which is now only recognisable by the help of grammatical analysis. This is evident also from the fact that in the district of Ermellék people of red complexion are derisively called *hajnal* (i.e. like the *red dawn,* but strictly the *white dawn*).[3]

I. (*Page* 155.)

The Sun growing Pale and the Moon Red.

Although, as we have seen, mythology ascribes a reddish as well as a white colour to the Sun, yet it must be observed that this is so only at the earliest stage of the myth. A later period

---

[1] *Gesenius, Hebrew Grammar,* edited by Rödiger, § 141; Ewald, *Ausführl. Lehrb. der. Heb. Spr.* § 282. c.

[2] Paul Hunfalvy in the monthly magazine *Magyar Nyelvőr,* 1874, III. 202.

[3] Ibid., 1873, II. 179.

prefers to connect the Sun with the conception of a reddish or yellow colour, leaving the white to the Moon, as more appropriate. Lâbhân, 'the white,' has not fixed itself in the language as a name of the Sun, whereas its feminine Lebhânâ has, as a name of the Moon. The conception of colour which the myth attaches to Sun and Moon is well illustrated by a passage in which it is said that both Sun and Moon lose their natural colour through shame, viz., Is. XXIV. 23 wechâpherâ hal-lebhânâ û-bhôshâ ha-chammâ, 'The moon turns red and the sun pale, for Jahveh of hosts rules on Mount Zion and in Jerusalem.' The distribution of the expressions for *shame*, bôsh and châphar, which elsewhere also stand in parallelism, is here not arranged haphazard, since the Sun and the Moon are spoken of—objects which are imagined to be provided with distinct colours of their own—but must correspond to the natural colours of each. Of *men* both verbs are employed without distinction; but 'making white' is the prevalent expression for *putting to shame*, so that in a later age, 'to make white the face of a neighbour' became a fixed formula in that sense (ham-malbîn penê chabhêrô or achwâr appê, Bâbhâ Meṣî'â fol. 58 b; compare Levy, *Chald. Wörterb.* I. 245 a; II. 173 a), and drove the 'causing to blush red' out of the field. The word bôsh for 'to be ashamed' is moreover even in the earlier times commoner than ch-ph-r. The former denotes 'to grow white,' and belongs etymologically to the same group as the Arabic bâḍ, whence abyad 'white;' the latter belongs to the group of the Arabic ḥ-m-r (with a change of the labials *p* and *m*), whence aḥmar 'red.' Accordingly, the expression that the Sun bôshâ 'turns white,' and the Moon châpherâ 'turns red' presupposes the idea of a reddish sun (Edôm) and a white moon (lebhânâ).

The same relation between the colours of the Sun and the Moon is also assumed by the old Persian poet Asadî in his 'Rivalry between Day and Night,' a poem to which we had occasion to refer on p. 95. In it Day says to Night:[2] 'Although the Sun walks yellow, yet he is better than the Moon; although a gold-piece is yellow, yet it is better than a silver groat.'

[2] Rückert, l.c., p. 62. v. 18.

K. (*Page* 155.)

Colour of the Sun.

The following is a literal translation of a passage in the Talmûd, which shows what speculations there were in a late age on the colour of the Sun, and how, even when the technical terms of language were far advanced towards settlement, people were by no means clear what idea of colour was to be attached to the Sun. The passage occurs in the tract Bâbhâ Bathrâ, fol. 84 a. of the Babylonian Talmûd. To enable the reader to understand it, I need only premise that it is a discussion on a word expressing colour, namely, shechamtîth. In the Mishnâ to which this extract of the Talmûd refers, the following words occur:

Shechamtîth we-nimṣâ'ath lebhânâ, lebhânâ we-nimṣâ'ath shechamtîth shenêhem yekhôlîn lachazôr bâhen, 'When the buyer and the seller have come to terms about wheat, which is to have the colour shechamtîth, and the seller delivers white, or *vice versa*, then they can both annul the sale.' Now in the Talmûd it is taken for granted that this colour-word is derived from chammâ 'sun,' and means 'sun-coloured.'

Râbh Pâpâ says, 'As it is said [that the seller delivers] *white* [as the opposite to what was required], it is manifest that the sun is *red* (sûmaḳtî); and in fact it is red at rising and setting; and it is only the fault of our vision, which is not powerful enough, that we do not see it the whole day long of this colour. *Question*: It is said [of one species of leprosy], *A colour deeper than that of the skin* (Lev. XIII. several times), that is the colour of the *sun*, which appears deeper than that of the shade, whereas the passage manifestly speaks of the *white* colour of leprosy? [so that the colour of the sun would be white.] *Answer*: Both is true of the colour of leprosy: it resembles the sun-colour insofar as this is deeper than the shade [and this passage speaks of a species of leprosy in which the colour is deeper than that of the skin]; but it fails to resemble the sun-colour insofar as the latter is red while it is itself white. But the putting of the question [which took for granted the white colour of the sun] assumed the idea that the [originally white] sun takes a red tint at rising and setting only because at rising it passes by the roses of the Garden of Eden, and at setting passes the gates of Gêhinnôm [Hell, and in each case the red tint of the object passed is reflected on the sun itself]. Some assume the inverse condition [and suppose that the colours which lie at the opposite side of the heaven—at rising that of Hell, and at setting that of the roses of Paradise—are reflected on the sun].'

L. (*Page* 189.)

Transformation of Foreign Stories in Mohammedan Legends.

The Mohammedan legends and popular traditions present instances of borrowing stories which in some foreign cycle of legends are connected with favourite heroes of that cycle, by substituting for the foreign heroes those who are well known in Mohammedan tradition. In this manner many Iranian local traditions and stories were changed and interpreted in a Mohammedan sense after the subjection of the mind of Îrân to the dominion of Islâm. This phenomenon meets us at every step in the history of the religions and stories of the East and West. I will here limit myself to the quotation of a single instance. The mountain Demâwend in the region of Reyy plays an important part in the old Iranian story of the war of the great king Ferîdûn with Zohak Buyurasp; to this mountain the conqueror of the demons chained the inhuman monster and made it powerless for evil. Now the Mohammedan cycle of legends borrowed Suleymân (Solomon) from the Jews, and invested him with the characteristics which the Agâdâ narrates of the great king of the Hebrews; which characteristics, by the way, themselves point strongly to the influence of the Iranian story of Ferîdûn. Among these is especially to be reckoned the subjection of the demons by the mysterious ring, which passed from the Agâdâ into the Ḳorân (Sûr. XXI. v. 82) and into Islamite tradition. When Demâwend had become Mohammedan ground, it had to divest itself of memories of the old fabled Iranian king. 'The common people believe,' it is said in Yâḳût, II. 607, 'that Suleymân son of Dâ'ûd chained to this mountain one of the rebellious Satans named Ṣachr, the Traitor; others believe that Ferîdûn chained Buyurasp to it, and that the smoke which is seen to issue from a cavern in it is his breath.' We learn, moreover, from this note that the original story still possessed vitality alongside of the transformation. The preservation of old national memories was promoted partly by the intellectual movement excited in Îrân by the 'King's Book' (Shâh-nâmeh), partly by national historians of a remarkable type, who were at the same time proficient in Arabic philology and interested in the preservation of old memories of their own nation.[1] Appropriation and transformation of Greek myths are probably rarer. The case quoted in the text is an instance of such appropriation, in which the place of the less-known personages of the Greek myth is occupied by the more familiar ones of Nimrod and his family. There are, however, also cases in which the name is changed, although the abandoned one is quite as familiar as that newly imported into the legend. An instance of this, from Yâḳût's *Geographical Dictionary*, IV. 351. 16 *sq.*, is as follows. The writer is speaking of a place called al-Lajûn west of the Jordan, and says: 'In the middle of the village of al-Lajûn is a round rock with a dome (ḳubbâ) over it, which is believed to have been a place of prayer of Abraham. Beneath the rock is a well with abundant water. It is narrated that on his journey to Egypt Abraham came with his flocks to this place, where there was insufficient water, and the villagers begged him to go on farther, as there was too little water even for themselves; but Abraham struck his staff against the rock, and water flowed copiously from it. The rock exists to this day.' No further examination is needed to show that this Mohammedan legend is only a transformation of the Biblical one of Moses striking the rock and providing water for his thirsty people. Yet Ibrâhîm has been substituted for Mûsa, a name equally familiar to Mohammedan legends.

This miracle of making water gush out by striking a hard substance with a staff is, moreover, a very favourite one in legends, and is repeated on other occasions, notably in the legend of King Solomon. It is said that the well at Lînâ, a watering station in the land of Negd in Arabia, was dug by demons in the service of Suleymân. For he once, having left Jerusalem on a journey to Yemen, passed by Lînâ, when his company were seized with terrible thirst, and could find no water. Then one of the demons laughed. 'What makes you laugh so?' asked Suleymân. The demon replied, 'I am laughing at your people being so thirsty,

---

[1] Such as Ḥamzâ al-Iẓfahânî; compare Yâḳût, I. 292–3, 791. 20; III. 925, 629. 18 *sq.*, IV. 683. 10. and my *Beiträge zur Geschichte der Sprachgelehrsamkeit bei den Arabern,* Vienna 1871-3, no. I. p. 45 and no. III. p. 26.

when they are standing over a whole sea of water.' So Suleymân ordered them to strike with their sticks, and water immediately gushed out. (Yâkût, *ibid.* p. 375. 22 *sq.*)

M. (*Page* 212.)

The Origins.

As an example of this, I may mention that, in opposition to the Biblical Myth of Civilisation, which brings the planting of the vine into connexion with Noah, the Rabbinical Agâdâ makes even Adam enjoy the fruit of the vine, which was the forbidden fruit of Paradise.[1] The Mohammedan legend names the Canaanitish king Daramshil, contemporary with Noah, as the first wine-drinker, saying that he was the first who pressed and drank wine: auwal man-i'tasar-al-chamr washaribahâ.[2] I also observe in passing that a feature of the Noah-legend of the Arabs which is mentioned in my article quoted below, viz. longevity, seems to have a connexion with the old Solar myth. Long life distinguishes the posterity of Adam in Genesis, and reaches its maximum in Methuselah. The longevity which in the popular belief, especially in Italy, is ascribed to the Cuckoo (A. de Gubernatis, p. 519) is accounted for by its solar character in the myth. Noah's longevity passed into a by-word in Arabic: 'umr Nûḥ 'the length of life of Noah.' In the writings of the poet Ru'bâ we find—

Faḳultu lau 'ummirtu 'umra-l-ḥisli * au 'umra Nûḥin zaman-al-fiṭaḥli,

'I said, If I were made to live the lifetime of the lizard or the lifetime of Noah at the time of the flood.'[3] Marzûḳ al-Mekkî says, in a poem to Mohammed al-Amîn: Fa'ish 'umra Nûḥin fî surûrin wa-ġibtatin, 'Live the lifetime of Noah in joy and comfort' (Aġânî, XV. 67. 4); and similarly Abû-l-'Alâ (Saḳṭ al-zand, I. 65. v. 4.):

---

[1] Leviticus rabbâ, sect. 12: ôthô hâ-'êṣ sheâkhal mimmennû Âdâm hâ-rîshôn 'anâbhîm hâyâh.

[2] Ibn Iyyâs, in the book Badâ'i al-zuhûr fî waḳâ'i al-duhûr, Cairo 1865, p. 83: see my artitle *Zur Geschichte der Etymologie des Namens Nûḥ* in *Zeitsch. d. D.M.G.*, 1870, XXIV. 209.

[3] Ibn al-Sikkît, p. 19, al-Jauharî, s. v. fṭḥl. On the proverbial longevity of the lizard see Kâmil, ed. W. Wright, p. 197. 18; al-Damîrî, II. 34; al-Jauharî, s. v. ḥsl; Burckhardt's *Reisen in Syrien*, note by Gesenius in the German translation, p. 1077.

Fakun fî-l-mulki yâ cheyra-l-barâyâ * Suleymânan fakun fî-l-'umri Nûḥâ,

'Then be in the government, O best of created beings, a Solomon, and be in length of life a Noah.' And we also find in Ḥâfiẓ: [1]

Come, hand me here the gold-dust, victorious for ever; be it poured,
That gives us Ḳârûn's treasures rich *and Noah's age* for our reward.

But a collateral reason for Noah being made a special example of longevity may be found in the South-Semitic signification of the verb nôch. In Ethiopic Noah is called Nôch, and the verb denotes *longus fuit*. And in an Ethiopic poem (in Dillmann's *Chrestomath. Aethiop.*, III. no. 13. v. 1) it is said of Methuselah's longevity, ôzawahabkô *nûch* mawâ'el la-Matûsâlâ.

N. (*Page* 254.)

Influence of National Passion on Genealogical Statements.

The same tendency which among the Hebrews caused the origin of the Ammonites and Moabites to be referred to the incestuous intercourse of Lot's daughters with their father, produced exactly the same result many centuries later in a different yet related sphere. It is known to students of the history of the civilisation of Islâm that the best Persians, despite their subjection to the sceptre of Islâm, strove long and actively against Arabisation, which they regarded as quite unworthy of the Persian nation, to them the more talented of the two. This reaction caused the publication of many literary documents; and produced especially one very curious and not yet fully appreciated movement, which originated in the circle of the Shu'ûbîyyâ.[2] In order to appear as a member of the great family of Islâm of equal birth with the Arabs, the Persians took care to weave their own early history into the legends of that religion. This was managed in two ways. *First*, they were anxious to trace their genealogy to a son of Abraham, so as to possess a counterpoise to the Arabs and their father Ishmael. Thus it was managed to refer the non-Arabs to Isaac, with a col-

[1] Rosenzweig, III. 465.

[2] See A. von Kremer, *Culturgeschichtliche Streifzüge auf dem Gebiete des Islams*, Leipzig 1873.

lateral intention of representing this descent as nobler than that from Ishmael.[1] And we also meet with an allegation, in the Kitâb al-'ayn, that Abraham had another son besides Isaac and Ishmael, named Farrûch, from whom the non-Arabs (al-'ajam) descend.[2] *Secondly*, the genealogical sacred history is perverted in a sense hostile to the Arabs. Thus, for instance, Ishmael is not allowed to be the son whom Abraham is about to sacrifice to Allâh, but Isaac the ancestor of the non-Arabs, as the Hebrew tradition has it[3]; and the story of the well Zemzem is put into connexion with Sâbûr the Persian king and with other reminiscences.[4] In the *Commentaire historique sur le poëme d'Ibn Abdoun par Ibn Badroun*, published by Prof. Dozy, page 7 of the Arabic text, we find various assertions relative to the derivation of the Persians. The majority of these genealogies trace the Persians back by various ways to Sâm b. Nûḥ (Shem, son of Noah); one derives them from Joseph, son of Jacob. The ethnological derivation of a nation from Sâm in the view of the Arabs certainly involves no idea of special excellence in the nation concerned; for even the enigmatical Nasnâs of the Arabic fables, a sort of monstrous half-men, half-birds (apes are also called so in vulgar Arabic), are allowed to have a Semitic genealogy.[5] But, at all events, no hostile intention lurks in the pedigree from Sâm. Thus the above genealogies, while possessing no tendency directly hostile to the Persians, are far from placing that nation in the foreground, and allow an unexpressed idea of the eminence of the Arabian nation to shine through. The case is very different with another derivation propounded in the same passage. This makes the Persians to belong to the descendants of Lot, their ancestors being the fruit of his incest with his two daughters. The Samaritans say the same of the Druses.[6] I believe this genealogy is based on intention only—like the identical

---

[1] See Kitâb al'ikd, MSS. of the Imperial Hofbibliothek, Vienna, A.F., no. 84, vol. I. pp. 188 *sq*. The data bearing on this subject I have collected and published in a essay on the Nationality-question in Islâm, written in Hungarian, Buda-Pest 1873.

[2] See al-Nawawî's *Commentary on Muslim's Collection of Traditions*, ed. Cairo, I. 124.

[3] Compare al-Damîrî Ḥayât al-ḥaywân, II. 316 *sq*.

[4] Al-Mas'ûdî, *Les Prairies d'or*, II. 148 *sq*; al-Kazwînî, ed. Wüstenfeld, I. 199; Yâḳût, Mu'jam, II. 941.

[5] Al-Maḳrîzî, *History of the Copts*, ed. Wüstenfeld, Göttingen 1847, p. 90.

[6] Petermann, *Reisen im Orient*, I. 147.

story told by the ancient Hebrews of Ammon and Moab. A local tradition, existing at Jeyrûd, a village to the north of Damascus, on the road to Palmyra, speaks of *a tribe of the people of Lot* as having dwelt on the ground now covered by a salt lake (Memlaḥa or Mellâḥa), whose city was destroyed by the wrath of God.[1] This story perhaps originated in some war of the later Mohammedan population against the older inhabitants or against Beduins who had taken up an abode there. It must also be observed that Mohammedan writers exhibit a prevailing tendency to remove far to the north, to Hamâ and Ḥaleb (Aleppo) in Syria, the mu'tafikâ or maḳlûbâ, i.e. the Sodom of the Bible. This follows from Yâḳût, III. 59, 124. In the particular case just mentioned, no doubt the existence of the salt lake cooperated in the creation of the local tradition (in the language of the Talmûd the notion of the Yam ḥam-melach 'Sea of salt' is greatly generalised and becomes almost a figure of rhetoric; see the passages in the Tôsâphôth on Pesâchîm, fol. 28 a. init. 'Abhôdath); on the lake Yammune on the north of Lebanon, see Seetzen's *Reisen*, I. 229, 302, II. 338, referred to by Ewald, *History of Israel*, I. 314. Similarly a later Arabic local tradition localised an episode of the Sodom-story on the transjordanic shore of the Dead Sea. For it is evident that the story of the conversion of Lot's wife into a pillar of salt is the source of the following popular tradition noted by Palmer (*Desert of the Exodus*, p. 483). Not far from the Dead Sea, in the former country of Moab, at a place called El-Yehûdîyyâ 'the Jewess,' there is a great black mass of basalt, said to have been originally a woman, who was thus changed into stone as a punishment for having denied the 'certainty of death'—a somewhat obscure expression.

---

[1] Kremer, *Mittelsyrien und Damaskus*, p. 194.

APPENDIX.

TWO ESSAYS BY H. STEINTHAL,

PROFESSOR AT THE UNIVERSITY OF BERLIN:

I

THE ORIGINAL FORM OF THE LEGEND OF PROMETHEUS.

II

THE LEGEND OF SAMSON.

THE ORIGINAL FORM OF THE LEGEND OF PROMETHEUS:

A REVIEW OF AD. KUHN'S 'HERABKUNFT DES FEUERS UND DES GÖTTERTRANKS.'

By H. STEINTHAL.

THE soundness of a new discovery is attested in various ways, but especially by the circumstance that the new thought is no sooner uttered in speech than it is seized upon and worked out by others besides its author; for the thought in question is thus proved to be really the subject which the intellect of the time is best prepared to take up, and which will lead on the Past to the Future. This is found to be the case with Comparative Mythology, Kuhn's new creation. When a large number of Vedic Hymns—text, translation, and commentary—first appeared in Europe through the instrumentality of a German, Rosen (too early lost to science), Kuhn saw at once not only that they were written in a more ancient language than the classical Sanskrit, but, what was more important, that they opened up a source of mythological views which flowed from a more distant and primeval antiquity than is known to us anywhere else, and that this was the common source of the more important myths and figures of gods of the Aryan nations. He then demonstrated this, in successive essays on Erinnys, Despoina and Athenê, the Kentaurs, Minos, Orpheus, Hermes, and on Wuotan (Odin) in the German mythology, by proving the identity of their names and myths with corresponding ones in the Vedas. Kuhn's acuteness and skilful combinations thus established the fact, of the highest importance to primeval history, that the heathen Aryan nations possessed a belief in gods, the outlines of which dated from the age of their original unity. But Kuhn saw also that two further facts followed from the first, one more important, the other more interesting. By the former I mean the fact, that the Vedic myths still exist in so primitive a form as to point to the ground of their own origin, and thus themselves to furnish their own certain interpretation. The latter is the fact that all Saga-poetry, whether epic or dramatic, artistic or popular, stands in connexion with the oldest myths; and further, that the mythological faith and worship, so far from being extinct even among the civilised Christian nations of Europe, still lives on in the rural classes of the population in spirit and practice, as superstition or sometimes as jest, though of course not without frequent transformations and disfigurements. This last point, however, had already been discovered by the genius of Jacob Grimm, who only wanted the support of the Vedas to become the founder of Comparative Mythology, as he was of Historical Grammar. But this support was necessary to elevate Comparative Mythology into a science based on method, and to give sufficient certainty to the interpretation of myths and gods. The greatest genius—fully entering into the spirit of the ancient Greeks and Germans, and endowed with a lively sympathy with nature—could, without the guarantee of the Vedas, never have produced anything higher than unproved conjectures. It would have remained impossible to demonstrate the original identity of different gods, had not the Vedas given us the connecting terms. And the sense of the myths and gods could only have been vaguely and uncertainly guessed at, had not the language of the Vedas, with a happy transparency both of grammar and of psychology, furnished the means of tracing the development of ideas from the most primitive impressions received by the soul.

Starting from the same fundamental idea as Kuhn,

Roth proved, about the same time, that the heroes of the New-Persian epos are only old mythic figures of the religion of Zoroaster, which are equivalent in names and functions to certain Vedic gods. In the *Oxford Essays* of 1855, Max Müller gave a sketch of Comparative Mythology, drawn in a certain poetical spirit which is quite in harmony with the subject. He endeavoured, very justly, to exhibit the essential connexion between the poetical and the mythic aspect, and to show that all formation of myths was simply poetic invention. Kuhn's idea was immediately and generally accepted and worked out by all those who were engaged on the Vedas—Benfey, Weber, and others. Mannhardt has frequently elucidated German myths with penetrating thoroughness from Vedic-Indian ones.

Thus Kuhn's idea has with rare rapidity become a secure common property of science. In the book, the title of which is given at the head of this article, he now gives an unsurpassable model of careful method in this field of investigation. When the weight of every argument is tested with such accuracy and the conscientiousness of a judge, and exhibited so unvarnished and so entirely free from special pleading, and the conclusion is drawn with such cautiousness, as here, not only scientific but also moral recognition is the writer's due.

We will first attempt to realise the result attained, and then proceed to a psychological analysis of it. I shall, however, here strictly confine myself to the one mythical feature which forms the foundation of *Prometheus*. Kuhn's book contains, besides, an extraordinary multitude of mythological facts, grouped together as belonging to the subject mentioned in his title.

In the earliest times Fire must have been given to man by nature: there was a burning here or there, and man came to know fire and its effects by experience. At the same time he learned also how to keep it in, and very soon he may also have learned how to produce it. He took certain kinds of wood, bored a stick of the one into a stick or disk of the other, and turned the former round and round in the latter till it produced flame. Kuhn has shown elaborately that the Aryan nations' oldest fire-instrument was formed in this way, and that the rotation of the boring-stick was effected by a thread or cord wound round it and pulled to and fro.[1] But man knew also of another sort of fire, that in the sky. Up there burned the fire of the Sun's disk; from thence the fire of the Lightning darted down. The primitive man, in his simplicity, believed the heavenly fire to be like the earthly; its effects were the same, and it went out from time to time like the earthly fire. Therefore, Must not its origin also have been similar? must it not after every extinction have been kindled again in like manner? There was no want of the necessary wood in the sky. In the sky was seen the great Ash-tree of the world,—in a configuration of clouds which is still in North Germany called the *Wetterbaum*, the *storm-tree*.[2] It was supposed, before men believed in gods of human form, that the lightning fell down from this Ash-tree, against which a branch twined round it had rubbed till the fire was produced, as had been observed in forests on earth. The men thought that the earthly fire had its origin in the sky, and was only heavenly fire that had fallen down. They saw how it fell down in the lightning; they recognised in the lightning a divine eagle, hawk, or woodpecker;[3] and many a bird which now flies about in the atmosphere of earth is a fallen flash of lightning, proved to be such either by its colour or by some other circumstance. The wood, too, which when rubbed turns to fire, is similarly a transformed lightning-bird. This is seen sometimes in the fiery-red colour of the fruit, *e.g.* of the mountain-ash (rowan),[4] sometimes in the thorns or in

---

[1] See W. K. Kelly, *Curiosities of Indo-European Tradition and Folk-lore*, London 1863, chap. II.—Tr.

[2] See Kelly, *ibid.*, p. 74.—Tr.

[3] See Kelly, *ibid.*, p. 83.—Tr.

[4] See Kelly, *ibid.*, 163–5—Tr.

the pinnate leaves of the plant, in which the claws and feathers of the lightning-bird are still recognisable. The rubbing merely revokes this transformation: the igneous creature is enabled to take up again its original form.

Originally the bird was probably regarded as being itself the lightning, because inversely the lightning was treated as a bird. Afterwards it was thought that the bird which was at first perched upon the heavenly Ash that produced the fire brought the fire down from the tree to the earth.

But further, Is not Life, too, a fire, burning in the body?—and Death the extinction of the flame? And as fire is kindled by boring with a stick in the hole of a plate of wood, so human life is produced in the womb. And what happens now and always here on earth, happened up there in the Ash-tree of the world at the original creation of man. That Ash produced, first Fire, and then Man, who is also fire. Indeed, strictly speaking, this is still going on: the Soul is a lightning-bird that has come down to earth, and the birds that bear down the fire—such as the Stork [1]—still bring us children too, just as they brought the first man down to earth: in short, the Fire-god is also the Man-god.

Then, at a later stage of the development of ideas, when the divine powers were imagined as personages in human form, the wonderful element of Fire, which drew to itself the attention of men no less by its mysteriousness than by its usefulness, was undoubtedly one of the first divine figures to be personified. Now one of the oldest words for fire was *agni-s*, Lat. *igni-s*. According to Benfey it comes from the root *ag* 'to shine,' by means of the suffix *ni*; *s* is the sign of the nominative. Therefore Agni is the Shining one, the Fire; but in the earliest times the word designated not the element Fire, but the god Fire. He, the god Agni, had his abode in the wood, and was allured forth by the turning.

---

[1] See Kelly, *Curiosities etc.*, p, 89.—Tr.

Agni was fire and light in general, both the absolute element in general and also every special and separate manifestation of it: such as the brilliant sky, the shining sun, the lightning, fire burning here for us, the first man and progenitor of mankind. But alongside of this, the peculiar conception of the Lightning-Bird still continued. That also was converted into a personal divine or heroic figure, which brought fire and man to the earth in the lightning. Sometimes Agni himself was called a 'golden-winged bird,' even in the Vedic Hymns; and sometimes the bird was made into a special god or hero distinct from Agni, bearing a name taken from one of Agni's various epithets. Thus Picus, originally only the woodpecker, was in the belief of the Latins the Fire-Bird. He was Lightning and Man; and it was said later that the first king of Latium was Picus, for the first man and father of mankind frequently appears in localised stories as the first king of the locality. Picus is shown to be a Lightning-Bird and Lightning-Man, not only by his name and story, but also by the manner of his worship: since he was regarded as the protecting deity of women in childbed and of infants.[1]

Less obviously, but not less certainly, a Lightning-Bird was preserved at Argos in Phoroneus. He, and not Prometheus, was said in the Peloponnesian story to have given fire to men; and in his honour a holy flame was kept burning on an altar at Argos. He was at the same time regarded as father of the human race. Having been originally a bird sitting on the celestial Ash-tree, he was made a hero, son of the nymph Melia, 'the Ash.' Now his name is Grecised from the Sanskrit *bhuraṇyu-s*, an epithet of the Fire-god Agni, denoting 'rapid, darting, flying,' thus picturing Agni as a bird. The name Phoroneus, *bhuraṇyu-s*, is in root (*bhar*=φερ) and signification, though not in grammatical form, equivalent to the word φερόμενος.[2]

---

[1] See Kelly, *Curiosities etc.*, p. 83–85, 151.—Tr.

[2] See Kelly, *ibid.*, p. 83, 141–3.—Tr.

It was not possible to stop with the mere conversion of the bird into a person. When the divine beings were once thought of as persons, they were also allowed to appear and act as such. So men no longer imagined the fire in the sky to be self-originated on the World's Tree, but regarded it as produced by gods, who acted similarly to men on earth, and revived the extinct flame of the sun hidden behind a mountain of clouds in the morning or during a storm, by driving a bolt into the sun's disk or into the cloud.

These are mythic conceptions of the very earliest age, but they contain in themselves a motive to further development, to give completeness to the relations subsisting among them, or binding them to the natural phenomenon that they represent. Thus true myths arise.

Now, the most striking peculiarity of fire was obviously the necessity of constantly kindling it again afresh, because when lighted it must go out again sooner or later. This aspect was exhibited in the following very simple myth. Agni vanished from the earth; he had hidden himself in a cave. Mâtariśvan brings him back to men. This myth is easily understood. The existence of the god Agni is assumed to be absolute and uninterrupted: but Fire is often not present; consequently the god must have hidden himself. Where, then, can he be? Afar off, it is sometimes said, quite generally; another time it is said, In the sky—which seems to be regarded as his proper home—or with the gods. But sometimes he is not there either, as at night or in a storm. Where is he, then? Why, where he is found; in the hollow of the cloud, from which he soon shines forth: in the hole of the disk in which the stick is turned round and round. Then, who finds him there, and brings him back to men? He who makes the fire appear, or flame up, and thereby restores to men the god who had withdrawn from them: that is, the Borer, or the Lightning which bores into the cloud as the stick into the wooden disk; it is Mâtariśvan, says the myth.

This is a divine or semi-divine being, of whom but little is known. He seems to be a figure which has never been fully crystallised;[1] regarded as a divine person, he fetches back the Fire-God to men.

Then the following terminology was introduced. The boring, by which man kindled fire and the sun when extinguished was lighted up again, was called *manthana*, from the root *math* (*math-nâ-mi* or *manth-â-mi*, 'I shake, rub, or produce by rubbing'). In German, the corresponding word is *mangeln*, 'to roll,[2] *Mangelholz*, used in North Germany; *manth* here becomes *mang*, as *hinter* is pronounced *hinger*, and *unter unger*. The boring-stick was probably originally called *matha*, from which *mathin*, 'a twirling-stick,' differs only in its suffix. Very soon, however, *matha* appears to have been restricted to another signification,[3] and then the fire-generating wooden stick was designated by a term formed from the same root with the preposition *pra* prefixed, which only gave a shade of difference to the meaning, *pramantha*. But the fetching of the god Agni by Mâtariśvan (the personified *pramantha*) is also designated by the same verb *mathnâmi*, *manthâmi*, as the proper earthly boring. Now this verb, especially when compounded with the preposition *pra*, gained the signification 'to tear off, snatch to oneself, rob.' Thus the fetching of Agni became a robbery of the fire, and the *pramantha* a fire-robber. The gods had intended, for some reason or other, to withhold fire from men; a benefactor of mankind stole it from the gods. This robbery was called *pramâtha*; *pramâthyu-s* is 'he who

---

[1] See Kelly, *Curiosities etc.*, pp. 37, 43.—Tr. The literal meaning of his name is *qui in matre tumescit vel praevalet*, i.e. a boring-stick like the lightning.

[2] In English *mangle*, substantive and verb. The verb *mangle* 'to tear' is probably the same, derived from the action of *boring*. To *mantle*—to winnow corn, to rave, to froth, may be from the same original root, represented by the Sanskrit, *math, manth*, in the sense 'to shake.' See Halliwell, *Dict. of Archaic and Provincial Words*. The Greek *μόθος* 'tumult' is connected with the same root by G. Curtius, *Grundzüge der griech. Etymologie*, No. 476.—Tr.

[3] The penis. The Latin *mentula*, as Prof. Weber reminds me, is clearly the same.

loves boring or robbery,' a Borer or a Robber. From the latter word, according to the peculiarities of Greek phonology, is formed Προμηθεύ-ς, Prometheus. He is therefore a Fire-God, very like Hephaestos, whose functions he often assumes. Mâtariśvan, who is quite synonymous with him in meaning, derives his name still more directly from the Fire-God; for mâtariśvan is originally a mere epithet of Agni; for the boring-stick itself bursts into flame, and in so doing reveals itself as Agni. Originally a mere epithet, mâtariśvan was subsequently separated from Agni and made into a distinct person; but, as already observed, without clearly-defined characteristics. Prometheus is the fire-generator, and as such the creator of the human race.[1] This relation to men explains the affection for them which prompts him to give them fire against the will of Zeus. He hid the spark of fire in a stem of Narthex,—one of the kinds of wood which were used for the production of fire, and were regarded as transformed fire.

Fire on earth was the Fire-God descended from heaven; the first man was only the same god in another form; consequently the first men—the representatives and benefactors of the human race—the first kings—the founders of the great sacerdotal families among the priest-ridden Indians—all were designated by attributes of the Fire-God. The family of the Aṅgiras-es acknowledges its descent from *Aṅgiras.* But Agni himself is often called by this name; and indeed these two names, Agni and Aṅgiras, come from the same root *ag* or *aṅg*, and have the same meaning—'shining.' Thus, in the mythical view Fire existed in three forms: first, as actual fire, i.e. as the Fire-God; secondly, as generator, rubber, fetcher, and robber, of fire, i.e. as Pramantha, Mâtariśvan, Prometheus; and thirdly, as those for whom it exists, and to whom it is given, i.e. as men. After the Fire-God has

[1] The boring-stick and the penis.

come down from heaven as man, he as man or as god fetches himself as god or divine element to earth, and presents himself as element to himself as man.

In the view of primitive man the mediating term between heaven and earth lay in the Lightning. In the lightning he saw the Fire—the god, the man—fall from heaven. *Bhṛgu*,[1] originally *bhargu*, from the root *bharg*, from which the Latin *fulgeo*, *fulgur*, and the Greek φλέγω also come, signifies 'the Shining,' 'the Lightning;' German *blitz*, which latter word comes from the identical German root (Old High German *plih*, Middle High German *blic*).[2] Bhṛgu was said to be the ancestor of the Bhṛgu-s, a sacerdotal family. To them, as representatives of the human race born from the lightning, Mâtariśvan is said to have given the fire. But as the Bhṛgu-s are the lightning, and consequently the Fire-God himself, the myth could be so turned round as to make Mâtariśvan fetch the god from the Bhṛgu-s as divine beings, or to make the Bhṛgu-s go after the traces of Agni, find him in the hole, take him among men, and cause him to display his fire.

It is also told of the above-mentioned Aṅgiras that *they* found Agni hidden in the cave. They are, indeed, only the same god broken into fragments: the fire separated into individual cases of burning, flame flashing at various places.

Thus there is a mythical identity, on the one hand, between Prometheus and Mâtarisvan as fire-god and fire-fetcher, and on the other, between Prometheus and the Bhṛgu-s in the same capacities, except that the latter are also representatives of mankind. And their relation to Prometheus can be authenticated in Greek myths as well. Bhṛgu is Lightning in his very name. His son *Ćyavana*

[1] ṛ in Sanskrit is pronounced as *r* with a very short vowel, *e.g.* like *ri* in *merrily*.—Tr.

[2] Halliwell, *l.c.*, gives in provincial English *bliken* 'to shine,' *blickent* shining.' and *blink* 'a spark of fire.'—Tr.

'the Fallen' (from *ćyu* 'to fall' [1]) is the Lightning again. Hephaestos, also, is well known to have fallen down. The name Iapetos appears most likely to express the notion of 'the Fallen'; only he is not the son, but the father, of Prometheus. Prometheus created men of clay, and the earth which he used for the purpose was shown near Panopeus in Phokis, the seat of the Phlegyans; the Phlegyans, therefore, considered themselves the first men: they are the Bhṛgu-s, Grecised regularly. The Indians had, moreover, other ideas connected with the Bhṛgu-s which closely coincide with those held by the Greeks concerning the Phlegyans; especially the conception that Bhṛgu, the ancestor of the Bhṛgu-s, like Phlegyas that of the Phlegyans, was hurled into Tartaros for pride and insurrection against the gods. The same characteristics, pride and opposition to Zeus, as well as the punishment, are also found in Prometheus, who is identical with the other two.

The identity of the Indian Mâtariśvan with the Greek Prometheus, and the explanation of the latter thereby gained, are accordingly based on such a coincidence of several mythical features and so similar a combination of these features, as cannot possibly be the work of chance; as well as on several interpretations of names, which are intrinsically more or less certain. If we knew more of the Indian Mâtariśvan, or if the word *pramâthyu-s*, corresponding to the Greek Prometheus, could be authenticated in the Vedas, then the certainty of all that has been said above of the Greek Titan would force itself upon us. In compensation for what has not yet been found, and is perhaps lost for ever, it may be serviceable to learn about a host of divine beings described in the epic poems of the Indians, who have some connexion with the Fire-God and are called *Pramatha*-s or *Pramâtha*-s; they appear to be only the one original Pramâtha or Pramâthyu-s broken up into fragments.

[1] ć in Sanskrit is the English *ch* in *church*.—Tr.

This is, in Kuhn's profound exposition, the simplest and the pure form of the Story of Prometheus. Later, in Greece, it was brought into relation to other stories in Hesiod's poetry; and again, with peculiar profundity, into new combinations by Aeschylos. Prometheus received his higher mental signification mainly through the fact that the Greek verb *μανθάν-ω*, with which the name of the Titan was correctly assumed to be connected, had taken a more mental meaning than the Sanskrit *mathnâ-mi* or *manthâ-mi*. The two verbs are obviously originally absolutely identical; only the nasalisation of the root *math* is effected differently in each language. We might suppose that the meaning 'to learn,' which the root *μαθ* has in Greek, had grown out of the fundamental sense 'to shake'; for learning is a shaking up, a movement, of the mind to and fro. Yet such a mode of conception might be scarcely possible to the mind of the primeval age in which that signification must have grown up; the primitive act of learning was not such violent exertion as ours in modern times, but rather a simple *hearing*, a mental *reception*. Now as the Sanskrit word *mathnâmi* grew into the meaning 'to take' (as has been observed), it is more probable that the notion of *learning* was formed by the Greeks from this ('snatching to oneself, taking'[1]), as Kuhn supposes. Then the physical sense of *μαθ* was lost altogether to the Greeks; it was, indeed, still known that Prometheus was a fire-*taker*, but not that the name indicated this. So they attempted to understand his name in a strictly mental sense, and remodelled the nature of the Titan accordingly.

Accordingly, the answer to the question of the nature of the etymology of the name Prometheus must be this: Prometheus comes from a root *pra + math*, which had the same meaning as the simple verb *μανθάνω*. But the form-

[1] This is supported by the analogy of the French *apprendre*. It should also be noted that Plato, in defining the signification of *μανθάνειν*, says that it means *πράγματός τινος λαμβάνειν τὴν ἐπιστήμην* (Euthyd. 277. e.).

ation of the name from the verb is older than the appearance of any specific Hellenism; for Prometheus was not formed by the Greeks. With the verb *mathnâ-mi* the name *pramâthyu-s*, without any verb *pramathnâ-mi*, was also delivered to them; and so there were in Greek μανθάνω and Προμηθεύς, but not προμανθάνω. The knowledge of the mutual connexion of the two former words continued vivid in the language; and when the sense of μανθάνω was spiritualised, the same change came over that of Prometheus also. Besides this, the preposition προ was understood, according to the usual Greek analogy, as 'beforehand'; and the verb προμανθάνω was then formed on Greek ground. Thus Prometheus came finally to denote to the Greeks 'the Fore-learner, the Provident.' I shall have more to say presently on this development. Let us pause for a while here, and attempt the psychological analysis of the simpler form of the myth exhibited above.

The following definitions must be given in advance:

Every simple act of the soul and every simple occurrence in the soul shall be termed a *Motion*, that we may have a general word to embrace all psychological data and designate, so to speak, a psychical atom.

Simple Motions *combine* together for very various reasons and in various ways, which I need not enumerate here; e.g. a colour, a form, and a matter. Thus they form a *Combination* of motions, e.g. 'a black round disk.'

Simple Motions, or single Combinations of them, in case they are not distinct or distinguished from other simple motions or single combinations on account of the similarity or equality of their contents, *coalesce* with the latter into one motion or combination of motions, as the case may be. For instance, to one who has not a clear sight, or has no sense of colour, or is looking at too great a distance, two colours that are but little different will appear one and the same. If one sees a ribbon today, and tomorrow sees at the same place another scarcely differing from it in colour, length, and breadth, one will suppose it to be the same. Thus, Coalescence produces a loss of contents (for in the place of two or more motions only one remains, whereas distinction brings an enrichment of contents), but the loss is compensated by the force of the motion.

Not simple motions, but certainly combinations, can be *interlaced* (*sich verflechten*) with one another. Interlacing of combinations occurs when certain motions belonging to two or more combinations coalesce, whilst the other motions belonging to them remain apart. The interlacing of the combinations approximates more or less to a coalescence of them in proportion to the number and value of the motions that coalesce. On this more accurate definitions may be given presently. Here I will only allude to a frequently occurring instance: two words of similar sound in a foreign language are easily interlaced, even to the point of perfect coalescence, i.e. they are confounded with each other. So also two persons closely resembling each other. The coalescing members of the combinations here so greatly exceed in number and force those that remain separated, that there is no consciousness of the latter.

When something presents itself to the mind to be perceived, estimated, or in the most general sense received, a certain procedure or negotiation takes place between this something on the one side, and certain older ideas, through the instrumentality of which the reception is to be effected, on the other. This procedure is *Apperception*: it is obviously far from a primary occurrence in the consciousness; it depends upon Coalescences, Interlacings, and Combinations of all sorts.[1]

The primitive man saw fire on the earth and in the sky; or, to express it more precisely, he saw something

[1] On all this see my *Einleitung in die Psychologie und Sprachwissenschaft.*

burning, shining. From the conception of burning things the idea of Burning or Shining was extracted. The difference between Conception (*Anschauung*) and Idea (*Vorstellung*) must now be carefully noted.[1] The former is an undivided sum-total of many elements, corresponding to the object or occurrence presented to the senses. The thought of it is expressed in language by a plurality of ideas, every one of which corresponds to one single element of the conception; so that the ideas are equal in number to the separate elements which are recognised and distinguished in the conception. Thus, to a single conception corresponds a combination of many separate ideas. The two combinations of ideas concerning the heavenly fire and concerning the earthly, contained elements (ideas) which coalesced together; and thus they became interlaced with one another. The conceptions of the two fires (as aggregate unities, in opposition to the ideas, into which they are broken up by the analysis of their elements) would not, indeed, easily coalesce; for as such aggregates they appear to the observer too different from each other. But when the conceptions are converted into combinations of ideas, which conversion is effected by language, then the related elements in the two combinations come into prominence and coalesce, and thus produce an interlacing of the combinations. But it must not be imagined that in this interlacing only those elements are affected which coalesce, and those which do not remain entirely unaffected by them; on the contrary, while the one set of elements press on towards coalescence, they are held back by their connexion with the others. The coalescence is therefore not quite perfect. Now, when on the one side even the not-distinguished elements are protected against the coalescence to which they incline, on the other the distinct elements which keep the two combinations asunder are

---

[1] It is explained by Lazarus, *Leben der Seele*, II. p. 166, and by me in *Grammatik, Logik und Psychologie*, pp. 319–340, and in *Charakteristik der Typen des Sprachbaues*, pp. 78 *et seq.*

themselves drawn in to the inclination towards coalescence. Thus the mutual relations of the combinations as aggregates are disturbed by their interlacing; they do not become identical, and yet are not severed: they become analogous.

The one is analogous to the other, the one gives the measure by which the other is measured: the one is the more powerful, the ruling, that which gives the means of apperception; the other the weaker, the ruled, the apperceived. How is this relation divided between the combinations of ideas of the earthly and the heavenly fire?

No doubt the heavenly fire is by far the greater and more effective, and therefore also the more penetrating into the soul of man. Man soon recognises the Sun as the source of the daylight and the origin of growth, and consequently as the giver of all wealth and all joy; and learning, on the one hand, what the sun procures him, he also experiences, on the other, by night and in winter, what it is to be deprived of it. At its rising and setting, but most impressively in the thunderstorm, the sun surprises him by the grandest sights. Thus it might be thought that the heavenly fire must give the measure for the apprehension of the earthly, and therefore for that of fire in general. But the matter demands more careful consideration.

Only the more powerful combination of ideas can give the measure and be the organ of apperception. Now a physical occurrence which works more powerfully, i.e. with greater force, upon our senses, will indeed arouse stronger feelings; but we cannot speak of stronger sensations. For instance, the vibrations of the air produce in the organ of hearing both the sensation of a tone and a feeling of pleasure or pain. Stronger commotions of air produce stronger and more painful feelings in the ear, but not stronger sensations, only sensations of louder, stronger tones. In memory we distinguish louder and softer tones merely in defining their contents, without meaning that the memory of the one is stronger than that of the other. The sensation of a louder tone is not a louder sensation. Therefore, from the mere fact that the sun is brighter and speaks louder to men in the thunder than the earthly fire, no greater power in human consciousness accrues to men's ideas of the heavenly fire.

The more important and impressive idea, too, is not necessarily also the more powerful; for this quality also, importance and force of impression, works in the first instance only on the feeling, not on the course of ideas also at the same time. A number or a name may be very important to us, and yet we forget it very soon.

Therefore the power which an idea can exert on the consciousness, e.g. in an apperception, essentially depends on conditions which flow simply from the nature of our consciousness. I hope that the following exposition will meet with assent. Power, or influence on the consciousness, is obtained by a combination of ideas through the number of its elements, through familiarity with it as an aggregate, and yet more through accurate acquaintance with its separate elements by themselves and in their relations both to one another and to elements belonging to other combinations, and through the number and variety of such relations. Greater clearness in our consciousness of something is only another mode of expression for more manifold distinction of the elements contained in it; and this implies increase of knowledge, but also sharp definiteness and thoroughness.

There is a curious contrast between feeling and theory. In the latter clearness, careful assortment, delicate distinction, and reference, give preponderance; whereas it is the masses of unclearness that work most powerfully on the former.

We will measure by this principle the force of the ideas concerning the heavenly and of those concerning the earthly fire. The latter must be much more numerous, clear, definite, and certain, as man has the earthly fire nearer, and works in company with it, and work is a copious source of knowledge. The earthly fire is the only one that he knows; a heavenly fire he only infers. The earthly fire enlightens the darkness of his night, which surrounds him as soon as ever it goes out; by it he learns the operation of warmth: this first leads him to seek the cause of the brightness and warmth of the day in the place where he sees something similar to his fire—in the sun; especially as, when he sees no sun, darkness and cold prevail just as when there is no fire. It is then the knowledge of the earthly fire that helps him to apprehend the kosmic fire; from the former he transfers his ideas to the latter. He experiences the former only; he constructs or images to himself the latter. Therefore, in the theoretical consciousness the ideas of the earthly fire are the more powerful and creative, and they give the measure; those of the heavenly are formed in conformity to them. The feeling, on the contrary, is more powerfully affected by the heavenly than by the earthly fire, because that is grander in its activity, mysterious in its appearance and disappearance, and independent of man. It surprises, stirs, and troubles the mind in a higher degree, and excites a more lively attention.

Now the power exerted by ideas upon the feeling is certainly not without influence even on their theoretical connexion and distinction, on their prominence and their formation. Further, much as man may have to do with fire, often as he may kindle it and put it out, variously as he may employ it, still he never fully understands it as to its appearance, mode of working, and essence. Now it always seems that the great must be the generator of the small, the strong the point of departure for the weak, the worthy and impressive more original than the mean and ineffective. If therefore, on the one hand, the ideas of the celestial fire are formed by analogy with those of the terrestrial, on the other hand, the latter are complemented by being put into connexion with the former. First of all the question is asked, What is there above?—and the answer is, The same as here below. But then comes the question, Whence comes this that is here below, and what is it?—and the answer is, It comes from above, and is the same as what is above. There above is the great, the self-subsisting, the adorable; it has descended to earth to do us good. Thus the idea of the heavenly is attained through the earthly; but the origin of the latter removed to the upper regions.

Thus it comes to pass that, although the ideas of the earthly fire are prior in psychological perception and give rise to those of the heavenly, still man holds the heavenly fire to be the original and creative one, from which the other is derived. He is so overpowered by the grandeur, wonder, and unapproachableness of the celestial element, that he regards the fire which he kindles for himself as fallen down from on high and given to him.

Man receives certain visual sensations of the Sun; and he converts these into a conception, or an object, by apperceiving them with the ideas that he has of fire. Thus he makes of them a fiery wheel. The ideas of this wheel are partly the same as those of the earthly fire, partly different; for they are distinct in the elements of place, size, effect, and dependence or independence. Thus arises an interlacing of the two combinations of ideas, as has been already observed. The disturbance produced among the ideas by this relation impels to a double apperception of the two combinations, first on the part of what is alike in them, and next on the part of what is different. The first apperception results in the comprehension of the two combinations as fire; the other in the separate conceptions of a divine and an earthly fire. This latter separation contradicts the first comprehension; and this contradiction is composed by a new process of apperception, in which both the likeness and the difference are regarded as the consequence of the relation of originality or derivation, in which the earthly fire stands to the divine.

They are both really the same, namely, the god Agni, who lives above and descends to men.

For the separation of the combination of ideas of the celestial fire from that of the terrestrial, is not sufficiently supported to offer an effectual opposition to the coalescence to which the most essential elements tend. All the difference that declares itself here resolves itself ultimately into one point only; for the differences of nearness and distance, of greatness and smallness, and whatever else may be added to these, all unite in the one point of the independence of the celestial fire and the dependence of the terrestrial. But this point is very weak. For even the terrestrial fire is observed by man to be not dependent on him, and seems to him to be even less so than it is in fact. The primitive man does not think he actually generates the fire by boring: he regards his action as scarcely more than a petition to the fire to appear. And if the fire then does appear, it does so as a free and kindly being that has an independent existence. Where, then, could it live in its own character, if not on high? It lives there for itself and for ever; here it comes down out of kindness.

Having thus discovered the psychological foundation for the fact that the primitive man regarded the fire as a god, we will endeavour to make clear to ourselves also the first forms of mythical conceptions.

We must imagine the primitive man placed as he was freely in the midst of nature. He saw the sky, the sun, clouds, and in the storm the lightning, and likewise heard thunder. He saw, he heard:—this means only 'he received sense-impressions.' These may no doubt have formed themselves into an image; still the image was not yet an object placed before his mind,—not yet a conception. When we see something strange to us, we ask, What is it? Yet we see clear, and have a definite image of the thing; then what more can we have to ask about it? We want to know also the purpose, origin, and regulation of what we have seen, so as to be able to find a place for it in the series of things previously known, or, if there is no suitable place, at least to find out its relation to that series. Nothing less will satisfy us; then it is no longer an isolated image, but a conception, an object; then we have apperceived it. It remains therefore for the mind to convert the image into an object through apperception. But certain means are demanded by the mind for all its creations, *i.e.* for everything that it makes its own by thought. The sensations—all that is presented by the senses: tones, colours, touch—are merely matter which the mind appropriates to itself. The means whereby this appropriation is rendered possible are not delivered to it by the organs, nor yet innate in it and ready for use. On the contrary, as in trade and commerce possession is multiplied by possession, so also the mind enriches itself every time by means of that which has been already gained; every acquisition is made a means towards its own enlargement. Thus then the primitive man apperceived the descent of the lightning and the sun's rays by means of that which his mind already possessed. But I must insist on the necessity of caution. In speaking here of the 'descent of the lightning and the sun's rays,' I have presented and apperceived a certain physical occurrence in the way in which we are now wont to do in conversation. But that is not the way in which the primitive man spoke; and we have still to enquire how he did speak. For him there was as yet no sun, no lightning, no ray; of all these he knew nothing. He saw at first only *something shining*, in various forms and movements. But he had not set himself the task of working further with his mind at this presentment of the senses: his consciousness passively received motions, out of which mythical ideas grew up. He apperceived unconsciously, and of course with the ideas that he already had; his mind built with the materials that it possessed. What, then, was likely to be the result of his building?

Which, of all the creatures known to man, passed through the sky like the sun, darted down and cut through the air like the lightning and the ray of light? Only the Bird. This comparison of the bird with the manifestations of light, was made immediately and unconsciously. Among the ideas about the bird, motion through the air was the most prominent; so when this motion was perceived, the aggregate of ideas about the bird was instantly ready to operate as a means towards the apperception that 'What moves in the air is a bird.' It comes down from the heavenly tree. Thus then the Fire-god Agni, as god of the lightning, is invoked as a fiery, golden-winged bird. The bird in general is next individualised into an eagle or falcon—a strong, swift bird, that darts down with might and majesty.

This apperception was one of the simplest, and was made unconsciously, as has been said. The idea of motion through the air presented by the lightning, and the same idea derived from the combination of ideas of the bird, coalesced and became one. The mere smallness of man's knowledge of the lightning caused the entire combination of ideas of the lightning to be drawn into that of the bird, whereby the latter combination was enriched so far as to admit the existence of a most wonderful divine bird beside the earthly ones. Thus no conscious comparison between lightning and bird took place; but immediate coalescence of the two was effected by the single conception of the lightning-bird, in which men were not conscious of any dualism. What we call lightning, was to the primitive man a bird, not lightning at all.

But also conversely, what we call a bird of this or that kind—eagle, vulture, or woodpecker—was to him lightning. The original meaning of the name φλεγύας, given by the Greeks to a kind of eagle or vulture—which, as has been noticed, has a connexion with *Blitz*, the Phlegyans and the Bhṛgu-s—was not 'a bird as swift as lightning,' but 'lightning' itself.

Thus, then, a multitude of mythical conceptions exhibit the lightning as some kind of bird, or a bird in general. So Phoroneus, 'the quickly descending' (p. 368), is in origin only an epithet of the powerful bird, and the Sabine goddess Feronia presents the corresponding feminine form; and numerous superstitions are founded on the recognition of lightning in a bird.

Still there is a difference between lightning and a bird flying; and this did not escape the notice of the primitive man. Nevertheless, so far from this difference having power to cancel, when once accomplished, the coalescence of the ideas of lightning and bird, and the unconscious apperception of the former through the latter; the difference itself was rather apperceived only in conformity with this coalescence. The difference was without any reflexion explained thus: when the bird has once descended flashing with lightning, it flashes no more; it is now only a lightning that has become weakened and earthly. Or it may also be said: the bird is not itself the lightning, it has brought the lightning down.

But where, then, has the lightning gone? It has shone for a moment, and vanished. It shone as if it were fire (*fulgeo* = φλέγω). Or perhaps it hit and fired something—then, whether it be bird or no, it is clearly fire. We must figure it to ourselves thus. In the sky, at the farthest limits of the space which the eye can reach, the primitive man saw light, radiance, brightness, in an overpowering degree; there he saw the sun and stars. He knew only the things on earth; only ideas of earthly things formed the possessions of his mind; and on the dark earth he knew nothing similar to those things of the upper world, except fire; only by his idea of this could he apperceive those. Now fire darts down from above before his very eyes. Now all is explained: the earthly fire comes from above, and the upper fire, having descended, conceals itself at once, by a transformation, in the body from which he extracts fire—in wood.

But now the relations are becoming more complicated; and already they are so far complicated that the original idea of the Lightning-Bird cannot be retained in its simplicity. Alongside of it the idea of the deity, or of the divine essence, has been everywhere developed; and the fire, the lightning, the golden-winged bird, has become the god Agni. Now the ideas of fire also take a new and less simple form.

The flame breaks forth from the wood: consequently, it must have been in it for a long time. The boring and rubbing in a certain way move Agni to appear: such action is therefore loved by the god, he allows himself to be drawn forth by it. If he loves it, it cannot be indifferent to the man who yields himself to the god in fear and thankfulness. It is a holy action. The pieces of wood which he stirs hold the god concealed. All appears divine to him, and his consciousness tarries in a world of gods. For the slight separation which he can make between the fire on high and that below, consists merely in the distinction between essence and manifestation. But wherever the god manifests himself, why there he is for certain. Consequently, during the holy act of kindling fire the two combinations of ideas of the God-Fire and of the earthly fire coalesce completely; there only remain ideas of one fire. But it was the ideas of the divine fire that completely absorbed those of the earthly. Unresisted, they exert an exclusive power over the consciousness and entirely fill it. Man is removed in spirit from the earth into the world of gods. He has forgotten everything sensuous and earthly, and sees and touches only gods and divine things. And every perception received from his senses is directly laid hold of by the ideas respecting the world of gods of which his consciousness is full, and has a place and significance assigned to it among them. The pieces of wood are no longer wood; the borer, the really active piece that draws the god forth, is a divine being that fetches the god. The god is concealed in the hole of the disk, but this is transformed in conception into a locality in the country of the gods—a hollow, in which the god is found. It is an occurrence that took place among the gods: the divine Pramantha fetches Agni out of the hollow.

The flaring of the flame, however, brings the consciousness back to the earth: Pramantha has brought the god to earth. We must realise the revolution effected in the consciousness by the fire breaking out. The combination of ideas concerning the earthly fire, which had coalesced with the other combination concerning the divine fire, is, by the present perception, again introduced into the consciousness as a special power, and its coalescence with the other conception is thereby cancelled. Against the sensuous impression of the present actual fire the circle of ideas of the divine one cannot maintain its supremacy. It retires and leaves the foreground of the consciousness to the circle of ideas of the earthly fire. But all this appeared to the primitive man not a psychological, but a real procedure; not a shifting of ideas, but an actual shifting of the imagined reality. When attention was shifted from the one circle of ideas to the other, guided by the idea of fire, which bound the two together, then it appeared to the primitive man as if the actual fire had removed from the one into the other, and had come from heaven to earth; and the already-begun fancy that the god Pramantha had fetched Agni, is accordingly carried on to the further point of saying that he put him among men.

Man soon observed in the sky on an enlarged, divine scale, the identical process which he had learned when producing fire by rotation. Agni dwells in the bright, clear, light sky. But the sky is overcast and darkened by a thunder-cloud: Agni has concealed himself; he has hidden himself in the hollow of the cloud. He breaks forth from it, being fetched by a divine Pramantha, Mâtariśvan, the Lightning. The lightning bores into the cloud as the earthly borer into the wooden disk: Prometheus, or Bhṛgu and his descendants the Bhṛgu-s, fetch the god from his hiding-place. They go down to the earth with him and take him to men.

The primitive man does not ask, Where does the fire come from? what becomes of the fire that has fallen from heaven? Before he asks this, and without his asking, he sees, and the lightning tells him, that the fire comes from heaven, and the wood tells him that the lightning (Agni) is concealed in the wood. Neither does the primitive man ask, Where does man come from? He sees it, and practises it.[1] The birth of man is a generating of fire. When the primitive man sees a tree, he does not ask, What is it? but by the sight of the tree present before him the combination of ideas respecting trees which is already formed in his mind is without his observation recalled into his consciousness; and this combination appropriates to itself the present sight, the perception coalescing with the combination of ideas through the similarity of their contents: and thereby what is seen is apperceived as a tree. Similarly, when the primitive man figures to himself the act of copulation, it is the combination of ideas of producing fire by rubbing that enters into his consciousness on account of the similarity of the movement, and gives him an apperception of that act. The similarity of the two acts seems to the primitive man greater than to us. On the one hand, the production of fire is to him a religion and a divine energy; on the other, man is already regarded by him as a fire-creature, lightning-born quite as much as a bird. The two combinations of ideas do not, indeed, coalesce; but yet are greatly interlaced with each other in some of their essen-

---

[1] The male is the Pramantha, the female the ἐσχάρα (the lower piece of wood and the female pudenda).

tial elements. The opposition between the partial difference which separates the combinations and the partial similarity which unites them, leads to a solution in a double and reciprocal apperception: first, that the divine rubber, Pramantha or Prometheus, created man, or that lightning, Bhṛgu, Yama, or the lightning-bird Picus, was the first man; secondly and conversely, that the production of the flame by rubbing is the production of the Fire-God Agni, and that the wood is the cradle of the new-born god. Thus Agni remains always the 'new-born' and the 'youngest,' as he is called in the Vedas; and Dionysos, also a fire-god, appears as λικνίτης, a god in a cradle.

The primitive man was convinced that man was fire. Indeed, his wonder at his own lightning-nature was aroused every time that he produced the god; and when sacerdotal families had gained the exclusive privilege of kindling fire, these families traced their origin to Bhṛgu or Agni, and called themselves Bhṛgu-s, Aṅgiras-es, etc. For they continued to do just what their ancestor, the Lightning, had done before them.

This is, as far as I can give it, the psychological explanation of the original forms of the stories of the Descent of the Fire. The superstition attached to these stories, in ancient as well as in modern times, would be more fittingly considered separately. The peculiar formation of the character of Prometheus among the Greeks however, may still engage our attention a little longer.

Prometheus is a god and yet a Titan also. He is the greatest benefactor of the human race. Yet in all other cases the mythical idea is that whoever does good to man is also friendly to God, and that only those who do harm to man rebel also against God. For the elucidation of this most peculiar and contradictory position, the following points seem to me worth pondering.

All the forces and occurrences of nature show two sides; one beneficial to man, and one hostile to him. So also the myth almost always discovers in the one and the same natural event, a good and a bad god. The bad god is hostile at once to men and gods. The development of a myth frequently takes the course of converting one of the epithets of the god who represents some process of nature, into a good god, and another into a bad god. The course to be followed in such a case is frequently determined by the nature or significance of the epithets themselves. Now it is certain that Hephaestos and Prometheus are identical in their origin, as indeed is shown in the story of the birth of Athene, in which the head of Zeus is cleft by either one or the other of them. But both Hephaestos and Prometheus are Agni in different forms. We have seen what Prometheus signifies. Somewhat of the physical signification must have still clung to this name even when it came upon Greek ground. Hephaestos, on the other hand, possessed from its very origin the finest signification of Agni; for it probably represents Agni as a home-god, guardian of the family, as a god of the hearth. And Hephaestos was still worshiped by the Greeks as a hearth-god. It surely seems natural, then, that the ideas of the beneficent action of fire should fasten themselves to him. But, on the other side, to make Prometheus, the Fire-stealer, an actual enemy of the gods, was impossible, for the very reason that he had been a benefactor of men by giving them fire, and was also the creator of men. Thus, he, as a god, became the champion of mankind against the injustice of the gods. It must be added that, perhaps even in the age of the unity of the Aryan race, the Fire-god, in his capacity as god (creator) of mankind, was also a god of Thought, who among primeval circumstances could scarcely be anything else but a god of Prudence, or foreseeing caution—an idea which gave the Romans their Minerva, but which might very naturally be attached to a god of fire, since prudence is exhibited nowhere more plainly than in the use of fire. At all events, even in the Vedas, Agni has the epithet *pramati*, which would yield something like προμῆτι-ς in Greek. Epic story made Pramati an independent personage, a son of Çyavana (*supra*, p. 373), the 'Fallen,' who is a son of Bhṛgu, the Lightning. Thus in sense, if not in name, the Indian Pramati is equivalent to Prometheus.

Prometheus is Fire-god, Man-god, God of human energy in thought. In this capacity he comes into collision with the supreme god. So he appears in Hesiod, and also in Aeschylus, except that the latter was able to give a far deeper meaning to the guilt of Prometheus, to his entire relation to Zeus, and therefore also to his ultimate reconciliation.

Thus then in Prometheus is comprised the whole essence of heathenism: deification of Man and Nature. He was the most characteristic figure of that mode of conception which created gods in the image of man. But the opposite mode of conception, according to which man was created like one single god, and was expected to make himself like God in life, produced a figure opposed to that of Prometheus—Moses. I speak here not of the historical, but of the mythical Moses; and I hope that the reader will be inclined to distinguish the two as clearly as we distinguish the historical and the legendary Charlemagne. Now the mythical Moses may be compared in meaning with Prometheus. Prometheus ascended to heaven and fetched down fire from the altar of Zeus for men. Moses also went up and brought back the Tables of his God with the fundamental laws of all common human moral life; for this act Moses could not come into conflict with God. But the original heathen myth respecting Moses was different. Moses struck water out of the rock with his staff: the staff is the lightning, the rock the cloud, the water the rain. Kuhn has shown at length what a close connexion subsists between the procuring of water, wine, honey, mead, and soma, and the bringing down of fire,[1] (like the connexion between

[1] See Kelly, *Curiosities etc.*, pp. 35-38, 137-150, 158.—Tr.

rain and lightning), and that they are so to speak, mythical synonyms. And this water did cause a difference between Moses and God. Now the reconciliation is brought about by Aeschylus by making both Prometheus and Zeus purify themselves and bind themselves by moral elements. But the monotheistic spirit of the Prophet transfigured the entire myth, and put in the place of the water and the fire the Word of God; and then no reconciliation was needed, for God spoke with Moses as his servant and messenger. Yet alongside of this monotheistic myth of Moses who brings down the Word of God, there remained also the old heathen one, which said that he brought water. It was a correct feeling, or a lingering consciousness which had been retained, that declared that Moses had sinned in the matter of the water, although it was no longer known in what the sin consisted.[1] Therefore I interpret and clear up the obscured remembrance or suspicion of the author of the Book of Numbers, by saying that, forasmuch as Moses strikes water out of the rock with his staff, he is a heathen god, a Mâtariśvan, a Pramantha, and therefore in opposition to the one true God, and must die; but forasmuch as he gives the Word of God to men, he is the Prophet without his equal.

THE LEGEND OF SAMSON.

By H. Steinthal.

When an author can presume that his readers share his views on things in general, and also accept like principles respecting the special sphere to which his subject belongs, it may be fitting to descend from the general to the particular. But when, as is now more frequently the case, no such assumption can be made, the opposite course, from the particular to the general, is preferable for the

[1] Num. XX. 12, XXVII. 13, 14.—Tr.

sake of both the matter and the manner of the investigation itself. I shall therefore adopt it.

I shall, therefore, at the outset leave out of the question what view it is possible to hold respecting the growth of the people of Israel, and especially of their monotheism. I shall not proceed on the assumption that any particular view is proved true, but try whether, after the consideration of our subject in its details, any result affecting general questions is reached. I also for the present leave undetermined the value of the Biblical Books as sources of history, the period of the composition of the separate books, and even their relative age—i.e. the earlier or later compilation of one with reference to others. For all these are still disputed points; and I desire not to build upon any unproved assumption, but to see how much can be contributed to the solution of the questions that arise. Even the question, whether, and how far, we are justified in treating the history of Samson in the Bible as legend,[1] may be left to be answered only from the result of the following enquiry. If, on comparing these stories with other nations' stories, similarities are discovered alongside of much that is dissimilar, nothing shall, in the first instance, be decided about the cause and significance of such similarities, but new investigation shall be made on the subject.

I. THE ADVENTURE WITH THE LION, AND THE RIDDLE.—THE FOXES.

I pass over the narrative of the birth of Samson for the present, intending to come to it only after the contemplation of his actions. The reason for this arrangement will then become apparent. I therefore commence with Samson's first action.

[1] *Sage*, a 'saying' or legendary story, which may have no historical foundation, but be produced out of mythic matter. Where, as here, it is sharply distinguished from history, I render it *legend*; elsewhere *story*, which is generally the best English equivalent, notwithstanding its derivation from *historia*.—Tr.

It is narrated (Judges XIV.) that Samson was attacked by a lion when on the way to see his bride, and killed him. When he went by the same road to his wedding, he looked at the carcase of the lion, and found a swarm of bees and honey in it. This occurrence suggested the following riddle, which he put forth at the wedding-feast: 'Out of the Eater came forth Meat, and out of the Strong [Wild] came forth Sweetness.' By his bride's treachery the riddle was solved: 'What is sweeter than honey? and what stronger than a lion?'

Samson's riddle is still a riddle even to us now. It has never yet been solved, as far as I know; certainly not in the Bible itself, for the answer there given is a still greater riddle than the riddle itself, which seems not to have been observed. Only look closely at the pretended solution. It looks as if the question had been: 'What is the sweetest, and what the strongest?' But the actual problem was: 'Out of the wild eater comes sweet food;' how that came to pass, was the question—and still is a question. For even the story of the slain lion and the honey found in his carcase cannot contain the solution, because it involves a physical impossibility. Bees do not build in dead flesh; their wax and honey would be spoiled by putrefaction. In no such wise can honey come out of the lion. Besides, Samson would be very foolish to base a riddle on a mere personal experience known to no one; it would then be absolutely insoluble. We cannot credit the original narrative with so gross an ineptitude. Then what is the position of the affair?

It is certain that a riddle like the one in question was in circulation among the ancient Hebrews, and that Samson was believed to have proposed it. It is equally certain that its solution lay in the words transmitted from antiquity: 'What is sweeter than honey, what stronger than a lion?' But it is not only to us at the present day that this solution is as obscure as the riddle itself; it was quite as unintelligible to the latest elaborator of the

Book of Judges. So he attempted a solution on his own responsibility. He had two data in his possession: the riddle, and the story of the lion-killing. Well, he concluded, Samson must have found honey in the carcase of this lion. What he had wrongly inferred, he narrated as a fact which ought to yield the solution of the riddle. But we must guess better. If it is certain that Samson cannot have found honey in the lion's carcase, yet, on the other hand, the pretended solution at least proves that by the strong eater the lion is to be understood, and by the sweet food the honey. And if this was solution sufficient for the legend, it follows that at the time when the riddle arose some connexion between lion and honey was so definitely and clearly present to the consciousness of every individual, because held by the mind of the entire people, that it came into prominence as soon as ever lion and honey were named together: somewhat as among us when we speak of bear and honey together, though with reference to something else.[1] But there must have been some known connexion which made it evident how honey came out of the lion. It is our task now to discover this connexion if we are to attempt the solution of the riddle—one which is more than thirty centuries old, and the unriddling of which has been forgotten for some twenty-five. Can there be any other riddle of equal interest? In the following remarks I endeavour to solve it.

When once we know that the Eater in the riddle is the Lion, of course it is natural to think of the lion killed by Samson; and the compiler of the Book of Judges would not have fancied that the honey was in its carcase, but for an obscure memory that this particular lion had something to do with it. Now to us this lion is not a real but a mythological one, i.e. a symbol. And we know the meaning of the symbol. Herakles also, it is well known, begins

---

[1] The allusion is to the story of Bruin the bear and the honey, in Reynard the Fox: see *Reinhart*, v. 1533–1562, *Reinaert*, v. 601–706, in Jacob Grimm's edition, Berlin 1834; and Goethe's modern German version, canto 2.—Tr.

his labours by killing a lion. The Assyrians and Lydians, both of them Semitic nations, worshipped a Sun-god named Sandan or Sandon; he also is imagined to be a lion-killer, and frequently figured struggling with the lion or standing upon the slain lion. The lion is found as the animal of Apollon on the Lycian monuments as well as at Patara.[1] Hence, it becomes clear that the lion was accepted by the Semitic nations as a symbol of the summer neat. The reason of the symbol was undoubtedly the light colour, the colour of fire, the mane, which recalled Apollon's golden locks, and also the power and rage of the wild beast. The hair represents the burning rays. So we have here to do with the sign of the Lion in the zodiac, in which the sun is during the dog-days. At this season the sky is occupied by Orion, the powerful huntsman—of whom I shall presently have a few words to say—and Sirius, who in Arabic is designated 'the Hairy' in reference to his rays.

'Samson, Herakles, or Sandon kills the lion,' means therefore, 'He is the beneficent saving power that protects the earth against the burning heat of summer.' Samson is the kind Aristaeos who delivers the island of Keos from the lion,[2] the protector of bees and hives of honey, which is the most abundant when the sun is in the Lion. Thus sweet food comes out of the strong eater.

Very possibly and probably, however, there was a superstition to the effect that bees are generated out of the lion's carcase, in the same way as they are believed by some nations to spring from an ox's carcase.[3] But such a superstition must have some basis, and no other basis is easily conceivable but the mythological one which I have mentioned. What was true in symbol, that the Lion produced honey, was taken as true in fact. For I must

---

[1] Welcker, *Griechische Götterlehre*, I. 478.

[2] Welcker, *ibid.*, 490.

[3] Studer, *Buch der Richter*, p. 320; Sachs, *Beiträge zur Sprach- und Alterthumsforschung*, II. p. 92.

insist on the fact that, according to the literal meaning of the Hebrew, no mere taking of the honey from outside a lion's skeleton is meant, but its being actually produced by the lion.

However, when we try to clear up to our own minds what has been said, we stumble upon a difficulty. It is after all the Sun that produces the summer-heat; Apollon sends the destructive shafts. Therefore, if the Sun-god does battle against the summer-heat, he is fighting against himself; if he kills it, he kills himself. No doubt he does. The Phenicians, Assyrians, and Lydians attributed suicide to their Sun-god; for they could only understand the sun's mitigation of its own heat as suicide. If the Sun stands highest in the summer, and its rays burn with their devouring glow, then, they thought, the god must burn himself; yet does not die, but only gains a new youth in the character of the Phenix, and appears as a gentler autumn-sun. Herakles also burns himself, but rises out of the flames to Olympos.

This is the contradiction usual in the heathen gods. As physical forces they are both salutary and injurious to man. To do good and to save, therefore, they must work against themselves. The contradiction is blunted when each side of the physical force is personified in a separate god; or when, though only one divine person is imagined, the two modes of operation—the beneficent and the pernicious—are distinguished by separate symbols. The symbols then become more and more independent, and are ultimately themselves regarded as gods; and whereas originally the god worked against himself, now the one symbol fights against the other symbol, one god against the other god, or the god with the symbol. So the Lion represents as a symbol the hostile aspect of the Sun-god, and the latter must kill him lest he should be burned himself.

Samson also unites both aspects in himself. The Hebrew story makes him operate even on the pernicious side, but against the foe. To the foe he is the scathing Sun-god. This is the sense of the story of the Foxes, which Samson caught and sent into the Philistines' fields with firebrands fastened to their tails, to burn the crops. Like the lion, the fox is an animal that indicated the solar heat; being well suited for this both by its colour and by its long-haired tail. At the festival of Ceres at Rome, a fox-hunt through the Circus was held, in which burning torches were bound to the foxes' tails: 'a symbolical reminder of the damage done to the fields by mildew, called the "red fox" (*robigo*), which was exorcised in various ways at this momentous season (the last third of April). It is the time of the Dog-star, at which the mildew was most to be feared; if at that time great solar heat follows too close upon the hoar-frost or dew of the cold nights, this mischief rages like a burning fox through the corn-fields. On the twenty-fifth of April were celebrated the Robigalia, at which prayers were addressed to Mars and Robigo together, and to Robigus and Flora together, for protection against devastation. In the grove of Robigus young dogs of red colour were offered in expiation on the same day.'[1] Ovid's story of the fox which was rolled in straw and hay for punishment, and ran into the corn with the straw burning and set it on fire,[2] is a mere invention to account for the above-mentioned ceremonial fox-hunt; still it has for its basis, though in the disguise of a story, the original mythical conception of the divine Fire-fox that burns up the corn.

The stories of Samson hitherto discussed seem to me so similar to the Eastern and Western ones that I have compared, their interpretation so certain, and their sense so essential to the character of the Sun-god, that I am of opinion that even the coincidence of collateral points cannot be treated as accidental. The Bible says that Samson killed the lion with his bare hands: 'there was nothing

---

[1] Preller, *Römische Mythologie*, p. 437–8.
[2] Ovid, *Fasti*, IV. 679 *et seqq.*

in his hand.' But Herakles also kills the Nemean lion without his arrows, by strangling him with his arms. This feature, too, is probably significant. The Greek myth says that the reason why Herakles could not use any weapons was because the lion's hide was invulnerable; but this is pure invention. The truth seems to me to be, that the weapons possessed by the Sun-god are actually his only in so far as his symbol is the lion; for they consist of the force and efficacy of the Sun. Now when the Sun itself is to be killed, that cannot be done with the very weapons which are its strength. The god is forced to catch the burning rays in his own arms; he must extinguish the Sun's heat by embracing the Sun, i.e. by strangling or rending the lion.

The following point is less clear, but surely not without significance. The Philistines avenge the destruction of their cornfields, vineyards, and olives by Samson, by burning his bride and her father. This causes Samson to inflict a great defeat on his enemies; but after the victory he flies and hides in a cavern.[1] What means this behaviour, for which no motive is assigned? What had Samson to fear in any case, but especially after such a victory? But let it be remembered that Apollon flies after killing the dragon; so also Indra after killing Vrtra, according to the Indian legend in the Vedas; and that even Êl, the Semitic supreme god, has to fly. Thus Samson's retreat, mentioned, but not very clearly expressed because not understood, by the Biblical narrator, appears to indicate this often-recurring flight of the Sun-god after victory. In the tempestuous phenomena, in which two powers of nature seemed to be contending together, men felt the presence of the good god; but after his victory, when all was quiet again, he seemed to have withdrawn and gone to a distance.

But if on the last-mentioned point the story is seen to

---

[1] Judges XV. 8.

be shrouded in much obscurity, this is the case in even a higher degree with the two next-following deeds of Samson.

2. THE ASS'S JAWBONE.

We come to Samson's heroism displayed with the ass's jawbone. There is much difficulty here, and it will be impossible to be certain as to the interpretation. But it must be noticed at the outset that the story belongs strictly to a certain locality. Its field of action is a district between the Philistine and the Israelite territories, which was called 'Jawbone,' or perhaps in full, 'Ass's Jawbone,' and doubtless received this name from the peculiar conformation of the mountains. Pointed rocks probably formed a curved line, and thus presented the figure of a jawbone with teeth. Between these teeth of rock there may have been a cauldron-shaped depression, which had the appearance of an empty place for a tooth; and just there a spring, no doubt a well-known and perhaps a particularly healing one, must have risen.[1] So, although the story wishes to derive the name from Samson's feats, the truth is rather that the name and the territorial conditions produced the transformation of the story.

Now I must first remind the reader of the tongue of land in Lakonia close to the promontory of Maleae, which stretches out into the Lakonian gulf opposite the island Kythera: it bears the very same name as the place where Samson performed his feat, Onugnathos ('Ass's Jawbone'). The name is certainly only the Greek translation of an original Phenician name. From Strabo[2] we learn little or nothing of this peninsula. Pausanias[3] reports that there had been on it a temple of Athene without image and without roof. Now this Athene was probably identical with a modification of the Astarte of Sidon, Athene Onka, who was worshipped at Thebes also. And it

---

[1] Judges XV. 15–19.

[2] VIII. 5. 1, p. 353.

[3] III. 22. 8.

may be significant, that there was in that temple a monument to Menelaos' steersman, who was called Kinados ('Fox'). At all events *Onugnathos* proves a myth, known also to the Phenicians, of which an ass's jawbone was an essential part.

But the ass, like the fox, was in many nations sacred to the evil Sun-god, Moloch or Typhon, on account of his red colour, from which his name in Hebrew is taken. The Greeks say that in the country of the Hyperboreans, hecatombs of asses were offered to Apollon. But he was also ascribed to Silenos, the demon of springs, on account of his wantonness; and this may perhaps furnish the explanation of the celebrated spring at this place, which has its rise in the Jawbone. Perhaps formerly there was at this spring, which was called 'Spring of the Crier,'[1] a sanctuary where the priests of the Sun-god gave out oracles, as those of Sandon, the Lydian Sun-god, did at a spring in the neighbourhood of Kolophon. And the ass is a prophetic animal: I need only refer to Balaam's ass.

To ancient tradition must undoubtedly be ascribed the exclamation which Samson is said to have uttered on this occasion: 'With an ass's jawbone a heap, two heaps—with an ass's jawbone I slew a thousand men.'[2] Now Bertheau conjectures[3] that this short verse had originally '*at* the place called *Ass's Jawbone* I slew,' and that the story of Samson gaining a victory with an ass's jawbone arose solely from false interpretation of it; and no doubt the Hebrew preposition *be* can denote 'in, at' quite as well as 'with.' The same scholar observes further, that according to the story the rocks called 'Jawbone Hill'[4] are, themselves, the very ass's jawbone that was thrown away by Samson after his victory; for only so is it intelligible that a spring should gush out of the cast-away jawbone, as the story goes on to relate.[5] To this I must add, that

---

[1] Judges XV. 19: 'Ên haḳḳôrê.

[2] Judges XV. 16.

[3] *Buch der Richter*, p. 185.

[4] Judges XV. 17: Râmath Lechî.

[5] v. 19.

the throwing of the jawbone seems to me the most essential and original feature in the whole story, from which the name and origin of the locality, and the victory with the jawbone also, were developed. For surely the jawbone cannot be anything but the Lightning, just as in Aryan mythology the head of an ass, or still more that of a horse, denotes a storm-cloud, and a tooth, especially the tusk of a boar, signifies the lightning.[1] Here then we have a thunder-bolt thrown down in the lightning—the instrument with which the Sun-god conquered, and at the same time formed the locality.

I have two more observations to make here. We nowhere find Samson armed with the weapons which we see almost everywhere else in the hands both of the Greek and of the Oriental Herakles – the mortar-club (pestle) or the bow and arrows. The club had the appearance of a mortar with the pestle in it, or of a tooth in its cavity; and in Hebrew one word[2] denoted both a mortar and the cavity of a tooth.[3] The second remark relates to the Spring. The Bible tells that Samson, wearied out by the murderous contest, at length sank down, faint with thirst, and prayed to God, saying 'Thou hast given this great deliverance into the hand of thy servant, and now I shall die for thirst and fall into the hand of the uncircumcised!' upon which God made the spring burst forth. This might be a fiction, in which Samson was depicted under human conditions; and the story of the spring given to relieve Hagar and Ishmael might in that case serve as a model for it. But perhaps the following combination will not

[1] Schwartz, *Ursprung der Mythologie.*

[2] Makhtêsh, v. 19.

[3] I formerly saw in the Jawbone the representative of the Harpe (toothed sickle), with which Herakles cuts off the heads of the Hydra, and which Kronos and Perseus also employ—the latter when he beheads Medusa. I have changed my view in favour of that here propounded, through consideration of the 'throwing,' which undoubtedly is significant. But complete certainty is unattainable. What meaning can be attached to the circumstance that the jawbone is called a 'fresh' (new) one (v. 15)?

be found too far-fetched. The Solar hero wages war with the mischief done to nature by an excess of heat. Thus the battle of Herakles with Antaeos is only the form localised in the deserts of Libya, of the story of the contest against the stifling heat, against the simoom which gains its strength from the sandy soil, as Movers, who also sees in the Erymanthean boar only a variant of Antaeos, has ingeniously explained. In Tingis, i.e. Tangier, the grave of Antaeos was shown, *with a spring beside it.* A similar legend among the Hebrews might perhaps assume in time the above strictly Jahveistic form. In that case the national instinct of Israel would have retained only the spirit and sense of the old story, while putting off all the heathen form and substituting a Jahveistic one for it. This would require no reflexion indeed, but undoubtedly much creative power of popular imagination. The fact, that in the Hebrew story the spring is put into combination with the jawbone, would seem to me, connecting it with my conception of the latter as Lightning, to indicate that the spring is the Rain, which breaks forth from the cloud with the lightning.

3. SAMSON AT GAZA.

It is related[1] that to escape out of the Philistine town of Gaza by night, Samson pulled up the city-gates with their posts and bars, and carried them to the top of the hill opposite the city of Hebron; which seems an utterly senseless practical joke, though quite in keeping with Samson's overweening jovial character. It will probably be difficult to make out with any certainty what is the foundation of this legend. It seems probable to me, however, that we have to do here with a disfigured myth, of the same import as that of the descent of Herakles into

---

[1] Judges XVI. 1–3.

the nether-world,[1] which originally declared that Samson broke open the gates of the well-bolted (πυλάρτης) Hades. As in the Greek story of Herakles the fight at the *gate* of the nether-world, ἐν πύλῳ ἐν νεκύεσσι, was transformed into a fight at Pylos,[2] by a mere play on words; so in the Hebrew story, instead of the gates of the nether-world or of death (sha'arê mâweth), those of the city called the Strong (Gaza, or properly 'Azzâ) might be named. The cause for which Samson went down into the nether-world was forgotten, and a new motive was invented by the legend for his visit to Gaza, in keeping with the licentiousness of his character. The fact that he starts at midnight, and does not sleep till morning, is certainly not without significance, but contains a remembrance of the circumstance that the deed took place in the darkness, i.e. in the nether-world. And the feature of the story which tells that Samson carries the gates to the top of a hill, must have been suggested by some local peculiarity in the form of the rock. But very probably the recollection of a myth which made the Solar hero bring something up from the nether-world had also some influence on the story.

4. SAMSON'S AMOURS.

The circumstance that Samson is so addicted to sexual pleasure, has its origin in the remembrance that the Solar god is the god of fruitfulness and procreation. Thus in Lydia Herakles (Sandon) is associated with Omphale the Birth-goddess, and in Assyria the effeminate Ninyas with Semiramis; whilst among the Phenicians, Melkart pursues Dido-Anna.

The beloved of the god is the goddess of parturition and of love. She is, in general terms, Nature, which is fructified by the solar heat, conceives and bears; or is

---

[1] Welcker, *Griech. Götterlehre*, II. 776; Preller, *Griech. Mythol.*, II. 154, 167; Movers, *Phönizier*, I. 442.

[2] Welcker, *ibid.*, II. 761.

specially identified with the Moon, or even with the Earth, but more frequently with Water—originally rain, and subsequently the sea and rivers also, and finally (the rain being regarded as mead or wine) the vine, caressed by the sun. Thus Venus rises out of the sea; and Semitic goddesses have fish-ponds dedicated to them. Iole, whom Herakles woos, is the daughter of Eurytos, the 'Copiously Flowing.' Of the three Philistine women whom Samson approaches, only one—the one who brings about his ruin—is named. Her name, Delîlâ, denotes, according to Gesenius, *infirma, desiderio confecta*, i.e. the 'Longing, Languishing,' and according to Bertheau the 'Tender;' at all events, it refers to love. She lives in the 'Vine-Valley,'[1] and consequently appears to represent the vine itself, which the Sun-god is so zealous in wooing; indeed, even the name Delîlâ might denote a Branch, a Vine-shoot. Deianeira, also, is the daughter of Oeneus the 'Wine-man,' or, as others say, of Dionysos. Orion, who stands so near to the Sun-god, woos the daughter of Oenipion the 'Vine.' But even supposing—what is very possible—that Delîlâ originally denoted a Palm-branch, we know that the palm was sacred to Asherah.

But yet another combination appears admissible. Delîlâ may also signify the 'Relaxed, Vanishing,' as a Moon-goddess. This goddess is indeed originally a chaste virgin; but in Tyre and Assyria she also assumes the character of Birth-goddess, and is variously served by strict chastity, by sacrifice of children, and by prostitution of virginity.

The coalescence of the chaste and cruel goddess with the luxurious one is exhibited in Semiramis, who is said to have killed her husband and all her numerous lovers. This might have given to the story of Samson its present form, which represents his ruin as brought about by a woman. But this leads to the following point.

---

[1] Judges XVI. 4: Nachal Sôrêḳ, *i.e.* Valley of the Vine.

5. SAMSON'S END.

Looking back, we find that we may probably regard as certain the proposed interpretation of the killing of the lion, of the foxes carrying firebrands, and of Samson's sexual passion: while the deeds with the jawbone and the gates must be termed uncertain. Now Samson's end brings us back into perfect clearness; it refers again to the Solar god. If the hair is the symbol of the growth of nature in summer, then the cutting off of the hair must be the disappearance of the productive power of Nature in winter. Samson is blinded at the same time, like Orion: this again has the same meaning, the cessation of the power of the Sun. Again, Samson and the other Sun-gods are forced to endure being bound: and this too indicates the tied-up power of the Sun in winter.

The final act, Samson's death, reminds us clearly and decisively of the Phenician Herakles, as Sun-god, who died at the winter solstice in the furthest West, where his two Pillars are set up to mark the end of his wanderings. Samson also dies at the two Pillars, but in his case they are not the Pillars of the World, but are only set up in the middle of a great banqueting-hall. A feast was being held in honour of Dagon, the Fish-god; the sun was in the sign of the Waterman; Samson, the Sun-god, died.[1]

---

[1] I formerly took Delîlâ, *i.e.* the 'Worn out,' to be a personification of Nature, worn out and no longer productive in the winter-season. Then the name Delîlâ might be compared with that of Aphrodite *Morpho*, supposing Movers (p. 586) to give the right interpretation of the latter, in discovering it to be the Syriac word for Fatigue, Flagging. Then Delîlâ would be the Winter-goddess, and might be a peculiar phase of Derketo, who was worshiped in conjunction with the barren Sea-god Dagon (see Stark, *Gaza*, p. 285). Pausanias (III. 15. 8) relates that there was at Sparta an old temple with an image of Aphrodite to whom it belonged—*i.e.* Astarte, Semiramis, etc. This temple (alone of all the temples that Pausanias knew) had an upper story, in which was an image of Aphrodite Morpho. She was represented sitting, veiled, and with her feet bound. Pausanias himself interprets the fetters to indicate women's attachment to their husbands; but this reading is not binding on us. I regard this Morpho as a picture of Nature fettered and mourning

6. SAMSON THE HEBREW SOLAR HERO = HERAKLES, MELKART.

The above comparison and interpretation of all Samson's deeds and the manner of his end has yielded so clear and decided a result, that the answer to the question, 'Who or what was Samson originally?' has necessarily

---

in winter. Similarly, and also at Sparta (*ibid.* 5) the bound Enyalios signifies the restrained solar heat of Mars. However, this interpretation of Delîlâ as Winter stands in no contradiction to what is said in the text. Moon-goddess, Love-goddess, Chaste goddess, and Winter, are only different aspects of the same mythological figure, to which a name capable of many interpretations is very suitable. Stark (*Gaza*, p. 292) is right in asserting the hostility of Herakles to the descendants of Poseidon, the gloomy sea-god, who according to Semitic conceptions I believe to have been also the Winter-god (Dagon). But Movers (p. 441) appears to be also right in showing how, besides combating the creatures of Typhon, Melkart-Herakles is also hostile to the evil Moon-goddess. For she is only the female figure corresponding to the male Moloch, Typhon and Mars. In the Greek myth the place of the Semitic Lunar Astarte is occupied by Hera, the adversary of Herakles. She is confounded both with Ashêrâ the goddess of Love, and with Astarte. Thus there was in Sparta an Aphrodite Hera (Paus. III. 13. 6). To her goats were sacrificed at Sparta, and only there, as to the Semitic Birth-goddess; and she was called 'Goat-eater' (Ἥρα αἰγοφάγος, *ib.* 15. 7; Preller, *Griech. Myth.*, p. 111; but I am of opinion that the goats have not the same meaning in her case as in that of Zeus). In the character of Astarte, as an evil Moon-goddess, a female Moloch or Mars, she appears when she sends the Nemean lion, the Solar heat, into the land, and on other occasions when she is put into connexion with the powers of evil (Preller, p. 109). The conception which unites opposite natural forces in the same divine person, which then appears under a modified form, could not be better expressed in architecture than it is in the above-mentioned temple of Aphrodite. The lower story is a temple of the Armed Aphrodite; the upper a temple of Aphrodite Morpho: thus the whole is a temple of the strict goddess, below of the Summer, above of the Winter. The fact that a deity of the Solar heat and the Fire is regarded as also a deity of the Sea, may be explained not only by the equal barrenness of the Desert—a sea of sand, and the Sea—a desert of water, but perhaps also by the opinion, attributed by Plutarch (*de Is. et Os.* c. 7) to the Egyptians, that the sea is not an independent element but only a morbid emanation from fire. To Morpho or Winter corresponds Hera, as one at variance with Zeus, or as a widow (Preller, p. 108). Thus then it will be clear that Delîlâ may be both the Birth-goddess (Ashêrâ) and the evil Moon-goddess (Astarte), or more accurately the Winter-goddess (Derketo). If Semiramis exhibits a combination of Ashêrâ with Astarte, then Delîlâ shows a similar combination of Ashêrâ with Derketo, who is only a modification of Astarte.

been already anticipated. I therefore now only combine together what has been discovered, and say: Samson was originally a Sun-god, or his vicegerent a Solar hero—the Sun being conceived as the representative of the force of Heat in nature, whether vivifying and salutary, or scorching and destructive.

To this result we are brought, finally, by the name of our hero. For Samson, or more accurately Shimshôn, is an obvious derivative from the Hebrew word for 'Sun.'[1] As from dâg 'fish' Dâg-ôn,[2] the name of the Fish-god of the Philistines, is formed, so from shemesh 'sun' we have Shimsh-ôn, the Sun-god.

Now, to recur to Samson's hair, our thoughts turn most naturally to Apollon's locks. But this comparison appears to me not quite accurate. For Apollon's locks are connected with his arrows, and are, like them, a figure of his rays. But Samson is not the shining god, but the warming and productive god. His hair, like the hair and beard of Zeus, Kronos, Aristaeos, and Asklepios, is a figure of increase and luxuriant fulness. In winter, when nature appears to have lost all strength, the god of growing young life has lost his hair. In the spring the hair grows again, and nature returns to life again. Of this original conception the Biblical story still preserves

---

[1] The derivation from the root *shmn* is impossible, that from the root *shmm* far-fetched. The simple derivation from shemes 'sun' appears to be rejected by Bertheau (*Buch der Richter*, p. 169) only 'because the long narrative concerning Samson presents no reference to a name of any such signification' (as 'the Sunny,' the Solar hero), and because, as he says, 'we do not expect to find a name of this kind anywhere in Hebrew antiquity.' But the matter appears to us now in a very different light, and the connexion with the Sun which Bertheau did not expect to find has now become clear.

[2] That Dagon really had the form of a fish, which Movers denies, surely appears certain from 1 Sam. V. 4 (see Stark, *Gaza*, p. 249). And it would be an excess of diplomatic accuracy, such as we are not justified in ascribing to the Hebrew writer, to suppose that his only reason for writing dâgôn was that the Hebrew dâgân 'corn' was pronounced Dâgôn in Phenician. Moreover, such a word as 'Corn' (dâgân) cannot well be a proper name. The formation of proper names of men and places by the termination *ôn* is excessively common, and requires no citation of examples.

a trace. Samson's hair, after being cut off, grows again, and his strength comes back with it.[1]

This Sun-god was, moreover, regarded as the beneficent power that destroyed all powers and influences injurious to man and to life in general,—the chivalrous hero, who wandered over the earth from the east to the furthest west, everywhere ready to strike a blow to deliver the earth from the creatures of Typhon, the Hydra, etc., the defender and king of cities, leader of emigrants and protector of colonies—in short, as *Herakles*.

This character of the Herakles-Melkart of the Phenicians appears in Samson in greatly shrunken proportions. The Hebrews sent no colonies to Mount Atlas; the supernatural monsters become a natural lion; and Samson's strength was required only against the Philistines. It is also seen, moreover, from the above comparison, not only that it is correct, but also how far it is correct, to call Samson the Hebrew Herakles. The one as well as the other is a martial Sun-god. And this makes it clear also that we are equally justified in classing Samson with Perseus and Bellerophon, with Indra and Siegfried,—in short, with all the mythological beings and legendary heroes whose nature is related to sun, light, and especially warmth, like Orion, Seirios, Aristaeos, and Kronos. In mythology, as in language, there are synonyms; e.g. Apollon and Helios, Herakles and Perseus; indeed, the two latter are both synonymous with Apollon. Now two words belonging to different languages, though similar in meaning, still scarcely ever call up absolutely the same conception, but are a little different from one another as synonyms. So also mythological beings and names in two nations, especially where the difference is so great as it is between the Hebrews and the Greeks, and between the Semites and the Aryans in general, are probably never perfectly identical, but never more than synonyms.

---

[1] Judges XVI, 22.

Therefore we must not indulge the caprice of trying to make Samson as similar as possible to Herakles: for instance, there is not the slightest reason to assign to Samson twelve labours, and the less so as that number even in the case of Herakles is only derived from a late age and forms too contracted a sphere. And, on the other hand, in finding analogies to Samson, we are nowise compelled to rest satisfied with Herakles. But now we must look closer into Samson's birth and the position ascribed to him in the Biblical narrative.

7. SAMSON'S BIRTH AND NAZIRITISM.

The birth of the hero of a legend is always the last circumstance to be invented concerning him, when his life and character are already settled; just as an author writes his preface only after the completion of his book. This comparison is here particularly apposite, since the narrative of the appearance of the angel who announces to the parents of Samson after a long period of childlessness, the birth of a son who is to be dedicated to God,[1] is not invented by popular imagination, but produced by the writer.

This introduction to the history of Samson is capable of two comparisons. It may be put side by side with the birth of Samuel,[2] or with the law of Naziritism.[3] In either case several differences appear. Samuel is not described by the Biblical narrator as a Nazirite (nâzîr). But from this it does not follow that at the time of the composition of the Book of Samuel this word had not yet come into use, but only that in the signification which it then had, it did not seem appropriate to Samuel as he was then fancied. Samuel was called one Lent to God.[4] In consequence of this, he lived in the Tabernacle, waiting on the High Priest and Judge Eli; he wore a priest's

---

[1] Judges XIII.
[2] I Sam. I.
[3] Num. VI. 1-21.
[4] I Sam. I. 28.

dress, and, as is stated with great emphasis, no razor came upon his head.[1] The latter is said of Samson also. The expression 'Lent to God,' seems not to have been a technical word or fixed designation, but only an etymological interpretation of the name Samuel. The life in the Tabernacle and the priest's dress were certainly not essential to the position of a Nazirite any more than to that of a Prophet, and are also out of accord with the narrative of Samuel's later life; they must be only a later invention.

The narrative of Samuel's dedication is perfectly simple, concerned only with universal human conditions and feelings, deeply and fervently religious. Deeply troubled and vexed at her childlessness, the wife prays God for a son, vowing, if only her prayer be answered, to dedicate the child to God for all the days of his life. With the impulse of true piety, after the fulfilment of her prayer, she performs a voluntary vow, to which she is compelled by no law. This story is older than that of Samson, who becomes a Nazirite, not in fulfilment of a vow, but by reason of a Divine command.

The term Nazirite is first found used by the prophet Amos,[2] who couples together the Nazirite and the Prophet; but he makes no mention of the hair, only of the prohibition of wine. But it does not follow from this fact that in the time of Amos the Nazirite did employ the razor on his head. Samson's parents received a command to dedicate their son: he was to be a Nazirite from his mother's womb to the day of his death. But to the prohibition to shave off the hair and to drink wine was added a prohibition to eat anything unclean; this was a later addition. The written law on the subject was the latest and also the severest and most fully developed; for it adds to the previous prohibitions another against defilement by dead bodies. On the other side, however, the Law

---

[1] 1 Sam. II. 11, 18, III. 3, I. 11. [2] Amos II. 11, 12.

knows nothing of any life-long Nazirites, who were to live like Samuel all their days in the Temple before God; for, in the later view represented by the Law, only the Priest, the son of Aaron, lived in the Temple; he was then the truly dedicated person, and wine was denied him not absolutely, but at the time of his service in the Temple.[1] And the Law had no need expressly to forbid the Nazirite to touch unclean food, since it was already forbidden to every Israelite. But to defile himself by the touch of a corpse, even of that of his father or mother, brother or sister, was forbidden to the Nazirite.[2]

Thus we discover three or four stages in the development of Naziritism among the Israelites, exhibited, (1) by the passage in the prophet Amos, (2) by the narrative of the birth of Samuel, (3) by that of the birth of Samson, and lastly, (4) by the Law. Before the time of Amos there were Nazirites—that is, as appears from their being classed next to Prophets, people who by a voluntary resolve consecrated their lives to God and the establishment of religion in the nation, and as a symbol of their resolve denied themselves the use of wine and did not cut their hair. There might be many prophets living as Nazirites because such a mode of life seemed to them appropriate to their intercourse with God. At the time of the construction of the narrative of Samuel's birth the Nazirite's abstinence was regarded as something intrinsically meritorious, rewarded by the special favour of God. Hence arose the idea that Samuel, a man whom tradition allowed to have possessed extraordinary greatness, had been a Nazirite, not only at a mature age, but from his very birth, although tradition did not call him such, but represented him only as a Prophet and Judge. It was supposed that Naziritism from birth had qualified him for his subsequent greatness. At the time when the narrator of the birth of Samson lived, this idea was pro-

[1] Lev. X. 9. [1] Num. VI. 6, 7.

bably so firmly established, that God could be imagined to bestow his special favour on an individual only by means of Naziritism, which was demanded at his very birth as a condition of that favour. Naziritism, which to Amos had been only a peculiar mode of working for the cause of the religion and morality of the nation, was degraded by the above process into a personal mode of life which was thought to be especially well-pleasing to God. And then any one could adopt it at any moment, and keep it up for a certain time only, longer or shorter; and the Law then prescribed the conduct of such as took a vow to live as Nazirites for a certain period.

But how does the author of this narrative of Samson's birth stand in relation to the subsequent popular legends? and what do these legends know of Samson's Naziritism? Little, not to say Nothing. The contradiction cannot be obliterated, and seems to have been observed by the narrator of the birth himself. He was the first who called Samson a Nazirite. If even his mother was to observe abstinence during her pregnancy, it seemed to follow as a matter of course that Samson himself as a Nazirite ought to pass his life in no less abstinence. But the legends reported the fact to be the reverse. The narrator observed this. So when Samson's father prayed earnestly that the angel who had appeared to his wife and given her a rule of conduct, might appear to him also and say how they should do unto the child, the angel gave no answer, but only repeated the rule for the mother. Thus the narrator did not venture to allow a degree of abstinence to be prescribed for Samson, which in the legends he never practised.

There is, however, one feature of the Nazirite which is known even to the legends: the uncut hair. The legend knows for certain that Samson's hair is the seat of his strength. But in the legend the hair is not represented as a mere ideal sign of divine consecration, but as the real source of strength. And therefore Samson, having trifled away his hair and thereby lost his strength, gets his strength back as soon as his hair has begun to grow again. Thus the loss of the hair is not in the legend a symbol of a falling away from God, nor the weakness that attends it produced through being deserted by God; but the hair itself is the strength, and to cut it off is the same thing as to curtail the strength, as we have already seen.

There must, at all events, have been a time in Israel when hair and fulness of physical energy formed one identical idea: it was the heathen time. When the people had gained a knowledge of the true God, the old legend had to be modified. Then the uncut hair was treated as a consecration of its possessor to the service of Jahveh. But the modification was not fully carried out: one heathen feature remained unaltered—the idea that with the growth of Samson's hair his strength also grew up again.

8. GENERAL CHARACTER OF SAMSON, THE HEBREW HERO.

The very distinctness and clearness with which it has been found possible to invest the conception and interpretation of Samson as a hero of heathen mythology, proves the justice and certainty of such an interpretation. And the justice of the mythical conception of Samson's deeds may be demonstrated also by another consideration. The difference between Samson's position and that of the other Judges makes it obvious enough that his history is mere legend through and through. All the other Judges, Barak, Gideon, Jephthah, fight at the head either of a large force or of a small and picked company: Samson always appears alone, and beats hundreds and thousands alone, and this too without arms. If the other Judges receive Divine apparitions by which they are impelled to action for the deliverance of their people, yet they act with perfectly human forces and means, in human fashion: Samson acts with supernatural force, and is a miracle from beginning to end. In spite of this, Samson's action is not only destitute of any proper result, but also—what is more significant and far worse—devoid of even the consciousness of any aim, devoid of plan or idea. He—Samson the Nazirite consecrated to God!—looks for wives and mistresses among his own and his people's enemies.[1] He teases, irritates, injures his enemies, and kills many of them. But there appears nowhere the consciousness of any mission which he had to fulfil for the good of his native land against his enemies. He is inspired by no idea of Jahveh, driven forward by no impatience of a shameful yoke. He is roused only by pleasures of the senses and the caprice of insolence. Samson is utterly immoral. He is exactly an old heathen god, and therefore immoral, like all idols. Idols must be so, for they are only personifications of the forces and occurrences of nature; now nature as such is indifferent towards morality, and consequently, though not moral, still not immoral either; but when the mechanical force of nature is pictured as a person, and removed into the conditions of ethical life, it cannot but appear absolutely immoral. This is what all heathendom does, that of Greece not excepted.[2]

If, on the one hand, Samson wants all the qualities necessary to an historical hero, he is on the other, viewed from the esthetic point, a most admirable phenomenon, quite unique in Hebrew literature. It is really wonderful with what tact, and what firm and delicate esthetic feeling, the gigantic, Herculean, Samson is delineated in the Hebrew legend. His behaviour evinces nothing uncouth or vulgar, a fault from which even the Greek Herakles is

---

[1] The circumstance that this was 'of Jahveh' (Judges XIV. 4) is a fiction interpolated into the legend by the systematising author.

[2] It will be seen from the above, that I am far from subscribing to the judgment on the heathen religions which has in recent times been widely diffused among philosophers and philologians. I agree essentially with the judgment of the natural mind, which always sees delusion and superstition in heathendom. But it does not follow from this that the heathens were absolutely immoral: they invested with their own morality gods who were intrin sically representations of nature only.

not free. Herakles, though adored as a god, has to put up with being scorned and derided for his greediness; he is a standing character in the Greek comedy, and a butt against which all jests are levelled. Samson, on the contrary, is himself the jester and scoffer, who adds the jest of insult to the injury he does his enemies. A native merriness encircles him; and in the very hour of death, at his self-prepared destruction, he maintains his humour, which here assumes a sarcastic tone.

We have now to take in hand two more considerations of a general character, which will determine the true import of the preceding detached ones and set them on a firm basis. We must first enquire: What means the above demonstrated accordance of the Hebrew legend with the legends of other nations?—what is to be inferred from it? The answer to this will assign the cause of the accordance. And then the field for the development of the legend of Samson in the popular mind, and the connexion of the legend with the progress of religious life in the course of centuries, must be more fully discussed.

9. THE MUTUAL RELATIONSHIP OF THE COMPARED LEGENDS.

In the preceding comparisons, I have in the first instance proved Samson's relationship to the Semitic Sun-gods. The Hebrews being Semites themselves, and living in the midst of Semitic nations, there can be no doubt that the similarity of the Story of Samson to those of the Semitic Sun-god is founded on original identity. But, on the other hand, the Hebrew form of the story exhibits sufficient peculiarity to negative the idea of its being simply borrowed from other Semitic nations. Samson is not exactly the Tyrian Melkart, nor the Assyrian and Lydian Sandon, but a peculiar modification of the conception which lies at the base of both of them. It is, moreover, quite inconceivable that myths and stories heard from strangers could yield materials for tales about a national hero such as Samson. If we knew the Semitic myths and stories more completely, there would probably be not a single feature in the story of Samson left without some mythical conception of the Semites corresponding to it; yet every feature would have undergone a peculiar Hebrew modification. In the absence of such knowledge, we were obliged to proceed to a comparison with Greek and Roman legends. Now how are we to understand the similarities discovered there?

In the abstract, three cases may be assumed as possible. First, there may have been borrowing; and if so, we should probably be inclined without hesitation to assume that the Greeks borrowed from the Phenicians and the Semitic nations of Asia Minor. Secondly, there may have existed an original similarity in certain mythical conceptions between Semites and Aryans, whether by reason of original historical unity, or because both races had, independently of one another, hit upon the same conception. Then thirdly, a combination of borrowing and unity is conceivable, by which the Greeks regained by borrowing some element which had been lost out of their memory, or obtained by borrowing from strangers an idea synonymous with a preexisting native one. Which of these possibilities is the reality, cannot be decided all at once with reference to Herakles in general; but even after some result has been reached respecting that hero's personality, the above enquiry must be instituted afresh concerning every one of his acts.

Now as to the general aspect of Herakles, I think we have at the present day advanced far enough to be able summarily to reject as absurd the idea that the Greeks had borrowed him from the Phenicians. The hero exhibits so decidedly the character of the Aryan Sun-god and Solar hero, and moreover appears in so specifically Greek a form, that there can be no doubt but that in him we see the peculiar Greek modification of a possession held in common by all the Aryans.

The fact, however, of Herakles being originally Greek, does not exclude the possibility that the Greeks, if they heard of a Semitic god whom they believed to be their Herakles, might claim the deeds of the foreign god as belonging to their own hero. This was a perfectly natural and simple process in the mind, such as may occur now to any one of us. Suppose that some one tells us news of a certain person whom we think we know, because we know a person of the same name and position living at the same place; then we shall immediately attribute what is told us of the stranger to the one known to us. Thus the Greeks could, and could not but, ascribe unconsciously to their Herakles what were really Semitic stories of Solar heroes.

Accordingly, it seems to me beyond doubt, that the Greeks borrowed the killing of the lion from the Semitic god. For the Lion is a mythical symbol that recurs among all Semitic nations, whereas he is scarcely ever, if ever, found in the original Aryan mythology. In the original seats of the Aryan races there can scarcely have been any lions. Moreover, it is only after the seventh century B.C. that Herakles was figured with the lion's hide. His original arms were those of Apollon, the bow and arrows.

We touch here on a characteristic distinction between the Semitic and the Aryan Sun-god. The former kills a lion, the latter a dragon. The Lion is a symbol of solar heat; the Dragon was originally a symbol of winter, rain, mist, marshy vapours. The Semitic god has to combat chiefly with the burning sun, the Aryan with clouds. In India, no doubt, Indra does battle with the 'Scorcher,' 'the Drought' (*śushṇa*); but this is surely a later, peculiarly Indian, accretion. On the other side, however, as we shall see further on, the Semites were not ignorant of the Cloud-Dragon. The distinction just indicated, therefore, must be understood as meaning only that here the one, there the other, of the two characteristics is the more widely spread and important; or that the one or the other is the more fully developed.

With this may be combined another interesting feature. The Semitic Sun-god represents chiefly the procreative warmth and the scorching heat; the Aryan rather the illuminating light and the fire, which latter however, in connexion with the rain, is no doubt regarded as productive of fertility. The two races also appear in general to be similarly distinguished: the Semite has greater heat, the Aryan more light; the former is more passionate, the latter more sanguine. But this is not a suitable place to follow out this train of thought.

As to the foxes with fire-brands, that feature is probably also borrowed. Among all the Aryan nations, it is only the Latins, as far as I know, with whom this feature assumes any prominence; and with them it appears only in the form of sport, derived from a legend already enfeebled, and scarcely at all in religious rites; for in the latter we find the red dog with the same signification; and the dog also is Semitic. It is possible that the fox is also preserved in the Fox of Teumessos;[1] but the latter belongs to Boeotia, where much Phenician influence is visible.

If the adventure with the gates of Gaza is correctly interpreted above, the corresponding descent of Herakles into the nether-world can still scarcely be regarded as borrowed. The interpretation of the adventure at Gaza, however, is not certain enough to build any further theories upon, any more than the story of the ass's jawbone, which moreover is very different from the boar's tusks.

---

[1] See Preller, *Griech. Mythol.* II. 97; Gerhard, *Griech. Mythol.* § 711.

10. THE DEVELOPMENT OF MYTHS AMONG THE ISRAELITES IN CONNEXION WITH THAT OF MONOTHEISM.

We have convinced ourselves that the mythical mode of looking at things indicates a distinct stage in the development of the intellectual life of nations. The substance, which is looked at in the myth, is very various, and by no means bound to a polytheistic system. Without offending the dignity of Monotheism, it must be affirmed that not only Genesis, but also the narrative portion of the other Books of Moses, of Joshua and Judges, and isolated passages in all other books of the Old and the New Testament, are mythical. The primeval history comprised in the first ten chapters of Genesis, sublime above the cosmogonies and theogonies of all other nations, contains also sublimer myths.

But these Israelite myths, in the form in which we have them now, are framed throughout on a monotheistic principle. This form is for the most part not the original one, but a conversion out of a polytheistic form. My exposition of the legend of Samson might be considered to have sufficed to prove the existence of a primeval heathenism among the Hebrews, which of course rested on a Semitic foundation. But this conclusion may be further confirmed by the following considerations.

I believe myself justified *a priori*, i.e. by reflections of a general nature, in relying on the concession, that the notion of Revelation, in the sense that at a definite point of time and by a special Divine contrivance, Monotheism was taught to a whole nation, and immediately handed down by them in the sharpest, fullest, and most elaborated antagonism to all heathen ideas, is philosophically untenable, since it is in accordance neither with psychology nor with history. This leads directly and necessarily to the assumption, that the Israelites freed themselves gradually from their inherited Semitic heathenism, and passed over to a Monotheism which increased in purity with time.

In opposition to these ideas, some have very recently renewed the attempt to establish Monotheism as the belief of primeval mankind, from which the nations passed into Polytheism, either, as some assume, through a growing dulness of spirit (a Fall), or, as others think, through the very opposite process, a higher development of mind; whilst the Israelites preserved the old original Monotheism, which is reckoned to their credit by the first, and to their blame by the latter, theorists. It suffices here to remark that this primitive Monotheism is absolutely incapable of proof from history, that at the outset it turns history upside down, and especially that it is conjoined to a very loose and mean notion of the nature of Monotheism. Moreover, the Semitic race did not possess Monotheism as an inheritance from its birth.[1]

Now if history is unable to prove Monotheism to have existed from the beginning in the Semitic race, even the monotheistic literature of the Israelites contains evidence

[1] For this assertion I must for the present refer to what I have said in an article, *Zur Charakteristik der semitischen Völker*, in the *Zeitschr. für Völkerpsychologie etc.* Vol. I. p. 328 *et seqq.* In Liebner and others' *Jahrbücher für deutsche Theologie*, V. p. 669 *et seqq.*, there is a long article by Diestel, *Der Monotheismus des ältesten Heidenthums, vorzüglich bei den Semiten.* He also declares himself averse to the assumption of a primitive Monotheism, because it is destitute of all historical proof. He brings many points judiciously into the light, especially the absence of an accurate conception of Monotheism (p. 684). But when he objects to me, that in the above-quoted article (p. 330) I am too hard on the expression *Instinct* used by Renan, inasmuch as it is to be understood as implying only an individual disposition of the religious mind, not a momentum of half-animal physical life, I must observe in reply, that I can scarcely imagine how else instinct can be understood but as a 'half-animal momentum'; and even reason, taken as an instinct, is *eo ipso* degraded to a momentum of *half*-animal physical life. And if Diestel here means by instinct a 'disposition of the mind,' I can see in such dispositions scarcely anything more than momenta of half-animal physical life. Moreover, I cannot admit any such 'dispositions of the religious mind,' which have the special object of their belief determined beforehand. A disposition to reasonableness in general, or to religiousness in general, does dwell in the human mind; but not a disposition so defined as to its object that a limited idea, such as Monotheism, could be *a priori* inherent in it.

on the other side, exhibiting a mythical Polytheism that extended from high antiquity down into those writings. For this Polytheism, as was natural, impressed on the language a stamp so distinct as to be still recognisable in various views and phrases belonging to the Prophets and sacred poets.

I will begin with the Book of Job. We need not here discuss the age of the composition of this wonderful poem. No one will now think of placing it before Solomon's time; and Schlottmann's view, that it was produced at the end of Solomon's reign or under his successor, has probably but few adherents. Now in this poem occur many personifications, which, although mainly based on lively poetical views and forming simply the poet's language, often also betray the existence of decidedly mythical persons. Although the author was undoubtedly a monotheist and a Jahveist, yet in his ideas of the world heathenism was still not far removed from him. This appears precisely in the passages in which he tries to portray the omnipotence of Jahveh; for there he sometimes slips into expressions which look as if intended to picture the power of Indra and Zeus or Apollon. So e.g. (XXVI. 11–13): 'The pillars of heaven tremble, and are frightened at his rebuke; by his strength he shakes the sea, and by his wisdom he crushes Rahabh; by his breath he brightens the heaven, his hand pierces the flying Dragon.' To understand these words in the poet's own sense, I think we must make very delicate distinctions. He appears to me to occupy a position in the middle between the pure Heathenism of a Vedic bard, and Prophetism, and no doubt nearer to the latter than to the former; yet a position from which the myth still almost looked like a myth, and was not a mere poetic figure. I must explain my meaning more fully.

Ewald's view, that Rahabh was originally a name of Egypt, and then became the mythological designation of a sea-monster, is an exact inversion of the fact, and requires no refutation—especially as it has been already answered.[1] *Rahabh*, etymologically denoting the Noisy, Defiant, was originally the name and description of the Storm-Dragon. In the storm it was believed that Jahveh was fighting with a monster that threatened to devour the sun and the light of the sky. I should claim this well-known myth of Indra for the Semitic race, were it supported only by the above verses, and should consequently regard it as a primeval feature of the mythical aspect of nature, common to Semites and Aryans, even if we were not so fortunate as we are, through Tuch's and Osiander's investigations, in finding the same myth repeated among the Arabs and Edomites, who have the divine person Ḳuzaḥ, a Cloud-god, who shoots arrows from his bow.[2] Here it is clear at the same time that the Bow is the Rainbow, and the Arrow the Lightning.[3] I see no reason for the supposition that the Storm-monster was fettered to the sky. But I think we may gather from Is. XXVII. 1, that the Semitic Storm-Dragon[4] was imagined in three forms: coiled up ('aḳallâthôn), i.e. the Cloud; flying (bârîach), i.e. the Lightning, or the dragon flying from the lightning, and lastly stretching himself, extended (Tannîn), i.e. streaming Rain. By the downpour of the rain the sea in heaven produced a sea on earth, and the tannîn was removed from the sky into the ocean. As a sea-serpent he is called Rahabh, the Noisy.

Of this nothing was known even to Isaiah, and no later Prophet or Psalmist understood this mythical view; these names of mythical beings had been imperceptibly converted into names of hostile nations, having been probably first used to designate great and notorious beasts living in the territories of the nations. Thus in Ps. LXXXVII. 4, Rahabh indisputably stands for Egypt; and two passages in Ezekiel (XXIX. 3, and XXXII. 2),

---

[1] By J. Olshausen in Hirzel's *Hiob*, p. 60 note.—But Ewald says expressly (*Ijob*, 1854, p. 126) that Rahab is everywhere *a mythological name for a sea-monster*, even where it stands for Egypt.—Tr. [2] See pp. 73, 169.

[3] See *Zeitsch. d. D. M. G.*, 1849, III. p. 200 *et seq.*

[4] Hebrew livyâthân, nâchâs; Sanskrit Vṛtra, Ahi.

exhibit clearly the supposed transition, since Pharaoh, that is Egypt, is in the latter compared to the Tannîn, that is the Crocodile, and in the former actually addressed as such. Thus the Tannîn or Rahabh became first any kind of sea-monster, then specially the crocodile, and finally Egypt. Similarly it is said in Ps LXVIII. 31 [30], 'Rebuke the beast of the sedge,'[1] i.e., the crocodile, meaning Egypt.

But there is a general connexion between this dragging down of mythical beings into the life on earth and the conversion of mythical actions in heaven into terrestrial history. Passages are not wanting in which a wavering between the mythic signification and that of legendary history, or the absorption of the former in the latter, is evident. Thus it is said in Ps. LXXXIX. 10–12 [9–11], 'Thou rulest the pride (elevation) of the sea; when it raises its waves, thou stillest them; thou treadest under foot Rahabh as one that is slain; with the arm of thy might thou scatterest thy enemies. Thine is the heaven, thine also the earth, etc.' Here the parallel to Rahabh in the preceding member is gê'ûth 'elevation, pride, defiance,' and in the succeeding one 'thy enemies.' The writer's general attention is directed to physical phenomena, which yielded to him the old heathen conception of Rahabh; but Rahabh had already gained a historical signification, and consequently suggested in the following member an historical reference.

This appears still more beautifully, and in a way which lays open to us the origin of the legendary history, in the following passage, Ps. LXXIV. 12–17: 'But God my king, from the olden time working deliverances in the middle of the earth. Thou cleavest with thy might the sea, breakest the heads of the Tannîns over the water.

[1] The literal and only possible translation of the first three words of the verse, ge'ar chayyath ḳaneh, rendered correctly in the Septuagint and Vulgate; for which the English A.V. unaccountably substitutes 'Rebuke the company of spearmen,' while the Prayer-book version goes even further astray.—Tr.

Thou crushest the heads of Livyâthân, givest him for food to beasts of the desert. Thou splittest open (i.e. makest to burst forth) spring and stream; thou driest mighty rivers. Thine is the day, thine also the night, thou hast appointed light and sun. Thou settest all the borders of the earth; summer and winter, thou formest them.' Here, again, we have a picture of the natural world, and one taken from the mythical point of view. God cleaves the cloud with the lightning, and by that act kills the upper Dragon above the water, so that the rivers of rain stream down out of cloud-rocks. But this mythical act, which is repeated for ever in every thunderstorm, had been converted first into a single act, performed once in ancient time (miḳḳedem), and subsequently into a cleaving of the sea at the Exodus out of Egypt. It is this which the poet intends to depict in these six verses, which he probably took from an ancient song. Thus he sings of Israel's passage through the sea and the desert in words which were intended to picture the Semitic Storm-myth; and thus we see how the latter was transformed into the former. This transformation was facilitated on the part of the language by the circumstances that in the verses just quoted the verbs may be understood as well as in a preterite as in a present sense ('thou cleavest' or 'thou cleavedst'), and that ḳedem denotes either 'past time, antiquity,' or 'the beginning of all time.'

The case is exactly the same with the Prophet, Is. LIX. 9, 10: 'Awake, awake, put on strength, O arm of Jahveh; awake, as in the days of the beginning (ḳedem), in the generations of olden times ('ôlâmîm)! Is it not thou that dost (or 'didst') cut Rahabh, that piercest (or 'piercedst') Tannîn? is it not thou that didst dry the sea, the water of the great abyss, that didst make the depths of the sea a way for the ransomed to pass over?' Here also it is clear how the Prophet's consciousness passed imperceptibly from the myth into the legend, or, if you prefer to call it so, history.

From these passages it appears that the conversion of the legend into history was already so firmly fixed in the minds of men, that, when they began with depicting nature, and in so doing had recourse to the stereotyped expressions that originally had a mythical meaning, they were involuntarily drawn into historical contemplation. This is not the case with the writer of Job: he remains within the mythical contemplation of nature. So full of life are the mythical pictures in his writings that we must suppose them to have been to him more than a mere matter of constructive fancy. The Pillars of Heaven are not to him mere mountains poetically described, but also convey a full-toned echo of the Pillars of Hercules that supported the heaven.[1] The stars and constellations are to him still actually living beings. In his work Rahabh cannot signify Egypt, but is still really the Sea-serpent. It is true that in other passages of the Prophets and Psalms Jahveh walks over the water of the clouds, which is by Habakkuk (III. 15), in a chapter containing many references to mythology, actually called 'Sea' (yâm): but only the writer of Job still speaks of the 'heights of the sea,'[2] which in mythology are the clouds; even Amos, one of the earliest Prophets, substitutes for it 'the heights of the earth' (IV. 13). Isaiah mentions the 'heights of the clouds,'[3] a decidedly mythical phrase; but the Prophet appears in that passage to have intentionally adopted heathen conceptions, as the words are put into a heathen mouth. Amos (V. 8) names the constellations Orion and the Pleiades, but he knows only that Jahveh 'made' them; whereas the writer of Job (XXXVIII. 31) speaks of their fetters. From the speech which he puts into the mouth of Jahveh it may probably be inferred that he regarded the mythical acts as acts that took place at the Creation. Thus, as I have already remarked, he takes a middle position between pure myth as such and myth transformed

[1] Ba'al kûn, see Movers, I. 292.
[2] Job IX. 8; bâmothê yâm.—Tr.
[3] Is. XIV. 14; bâmothê 'âbh.—Tr.

into legendary history. Altogether, he never directs his attention to History and the revelation of God in history: to his mind God is only a wise creator and upholder of Nature, and within this nature lies Man, i.e. the individual whom God created thus, and whose destiny he determines in wisdom and grace. The poet of Job does not possess the world-embracing glance of the Prophet.

Still, though in his mythology he stands nearer to heathenism than the Prophets, and his mind falls short of the breadth and greatness of the prophetic soul, he may yet be a contemporary of theirs, only one who lived in a retired circle, and had, so to speak, a one-sided education. And his whole phraseology possesses a somewhat sensuous and materialistical character, which becomes strikingly obvious on the comparison of certain expressions and certain passages expressing the same thought. Orion is in Job still really the fettered Giant (Kesîl 'the Strong,' not 'the Fool'); but Isaiah (XIII. 10) forms from this word the plural kesîlîm, 'the bright-shining stars.' Then the word had ceased to be a proper name, which it was still in Job. Similarly Tannîn is here a proper name; but later it denotes a great sea-animal in general (e.g. in Ps. LXXIV. 13, quoted above), and therefore can have a plural. See also Is. XIX. 13, 14: 'The princes of Zoan are become fools, the princes of Noph are deceived; the heads of her tribes have led Egypt astray. Jahveh pours into their midst a spirit of perverseness, and they lead Egypt astray in all her action, like a drunken man tumbling into his vomit;' and compare with this Job XII. 24: '[God] taketh away the heart of the chief of the people of the earth, and leads them astray in a pathless waste; they grope in darkness without light, and he leads them astray like a drunken man.' Here we have not, as in Isaiah, the abstract 'Spirit (rûach) of perverseness,' but the concrete 'Heart' lêbh); and the 'Going astray' also is depicted more sensuously.[1]

[1] It will be inferred from the above reasoning, that I should be inclined to

Now that we have thus learnt that the Storm-myth existed among the Hebrews and the Semites in a form similar to that which it had among the Aryans, to such an extent that it indelibly permeated their views of nature and their language, we have not only gained a greatly increased justification for regarding the story of Samson as a myth, but we can now venture also on other mythological combinations and interpretations, which taken singly possess but little security and may pass for mere conjectures, but which almost certainly have a general mythic character. Thus we may find in the Bible a copious source of knowledge of Semitic Mythology. While only calling to memory in general terms the numerous accordances with Semitic mythology contained in the Bible, which Movers has in many cases made quite certain, I will here select a few narratives which seem to have a connexion with the above discussed Storm-myth.

I have before[1] pointed to the fact that myths of a Sun-god are embodied in the life of Moses. Now all of these correspond to wide-spread Aryan myths of the Sun-god or Solar hero. Immediately after his birth Moses is put into a chest and placed on the water. A similar fate befalls nearly all the Solar heroes: e.g. Perseus, and heroes of the German legends. As Moses sees a burning bush which does not burn away, so the grove of Feronia[2] is in flames without burning away. I have already shown[3] that the staff by which Moses performs his miracles is the

assign an early age to the writer of the Book of Job. But I can find no reason for making him older than Amos; indeed, he may have lived into the lifetime of Isaiah. I must further remark that Schlottmann (*Das Buch Hiob verdeutscht und erläutert*, pp. 69–105, especially 101 *et seqq.*) has expressed ideas similar to those propounded by me, though starting from assumptions utterly different in principle. To the passages of Job which he places side by side with corresponding ones of Amos (p. 109), the following may be added: Amos V. 8 and IX. 6, 'who calleth to the water of the (Cloud-) Sea,' and Job XXXVIII. 34, 'wilt thou lift up thy voice to the Cloud?'

[1] *Prometheus*, p. 391.

[2] Kuhn, *Herabkunft des Feuers etc.*, p. 30.

[3] P. 392.

Pramantha. Like Moses, Dionysos strikes fountains of wine and water out of the rock.[1] Moses, by throwing a piece of wood into bitter water makes it sweet (Ex. XV. 25). This must be the same as the churning of the Amṛta, Soma, Nectar, the divine mead. Moses has no dragon to kill, but he kills an Egyptian, and immediately flies, like all Solar heroes;[2] and like Apollon, Herakles and Siegfried, he becomes a servant. And the sea, over which Moses stretches out his hand with the staff, and which he divides, so that the waters stand up on either side like walls while he passes through, must surely have been originally the Sea of Clouds;[3] and I have consequently little inclination to look for the spot of the earth where, and the conditions under which, the passage might have taken place. A German story presents a perfectly similar feature.[4] The conception of the Cloud as sea, rock and wall, recurs very frequently in mythology. Moses feeds the Israelites with quails. By means of a quail Iolaos wakes the dead Melkart from death. And the quail appears to have had a close connexion with Apollon and Diana; for Ὀρτυγία is an old name of Delos, the island of Apollon; and the nurse of Apollon and Diana, and even Diana herself, are called by the same name. Moses causes manna, sweet as honey, to be rained down with the dew; this again reminds us of the nectar and the mead of the gods.

Thus we see that almost all the acts of Moses correspond to those of the Sun-gods. We have here not only similar mythical features, but features which in both cases unite to form one and the same cycle.

The Book of Judges, as well as the Books of Moses, exhibits ancient elements preserved from the heathen times, also in conformity with Aryan myths. So Shamgar (Judges III. 31), who slew six hundred Philis-

---

1 Preller. ib. I. 438; Kuhn, ib. p. 24, 243.

2 See p. 399.

3 See p. 425.

4 Schwartz, *Ursprung der Mythologie*, p. 251.

tines with an ox-goad, is only Samson in another form. And his name points to the Sun-god; for it seems to me to denote 'He that circles about in the sky.' We must pay attention to the fact that Barak denotes 'Lightning,' even though Barcas is a Carthaginian name. With Barak is associated Deborah, the 'Bee.' Now if rain and dew are treated as Honey, then the Bee must stand for the rain-cloud. A third name occurs in this connexion—Jael (Yâ'el), the 'Wild Goat,' which is also a symbol of the Cloud. The Melissae (bees) and the goat Amalthea, among the Greeks take each others' places. Lastly, the manner in which Sisera is killed, by a hammer and nail, reminds one of the God of Lightning. The mode in which David kills Goliath reminds us of Thor's battle with Hrungnir, in which he throws his hammer into Hrungnir's forehead.

The germ of these various agreements ought in fact probably to be referred to an original identity in the mythical views of the Semites and Aryans, who were not separated till later. The Fire and (connected therewith) the Sun, and then the Storm also, may well have led to the formation of the same myths by the two races while they still lived together. The separation of the races then produced distinct developments out of the common germ, which developments, however, naturally had many points of agreement.

II. ANALOGY WITH OLD HEATHEN ELEMENTS IN THE POPULAR IDEAS OF THE LATER AGE.

It results from the preceding historical investigation that the oldest Hebrews were heathens, and that elements belonging to heathen mythology are even present in the Bible. To gain a clearer idea of the nature of this fact, I will refer to a precisely similar case—the relation of our age to the old German heathen times.

The Germans had originally gods, worship, myths and

legends—in short, a heathen faith, of their own. But for more than a thousand years all the German tribes have been Christian. Nevertheless, heathen practices still survive among them everywhere and in most various forms; and are so closely interwoven with Christian practices as to be almost ineradicable. I will only select a few instances. The old German gods still live in the names of the days of the week.[1] Churches and convents were founded at places which had been heathen sanctuaries; Christian feasts were fixed on days sacred to heathen deities, and thus the heathen name 'Easter' has maintained its existence as a designation for the highest Christian feast. Heathenism is preserved chiefly in the popular legends both of the hills and of the lowlands, in popular customs, usages, games and superstitions; all which has been lately collected in special books and periodicals. Kuhn's collections made in North Germany and Westphalia are of especial scientific value. The gods, however, have been converted into devils and monsters, the goddesses into night-hags and witches. But religious stories, Christian legends, are also often utterly heathen; there are deeds and occurrences belonging to gods and heroes, which are attributed to the Saints and to Christ himself. Thus the killing of the Dragon, which is known as a myth to all the Aryan nations, is ascribed to Saint George. The office of the god Thor, who pursued and bound giants, is filled in Christian Norway by Saint Olave. Christ and Saint Peter wander about unrecognised in human form, to reward virtue and punish vice, as the heathen gods did before them. Mary, especially, had a multitude of lovely and charming features ascribed to her, which under heathenism were attributes of Freyja, Holda, and Bertha. A great number of flowers, plants and insects, the older names of which referred to Freyja and Venus, are called after Mary, e.g. Maiden-hair

[1] In English Tues-day, Wednes-day, Thurs-day, Fri-day, Satur-day, from Anglo-Saxon names of gods, Tiu or Teow, Wôden, Thunor, Frige, Sætern.—Tr.

(i.e. the Virgin Mary's hair), otherwise Capillus Veneris;[1] and Holda who sends snow becomes Mary: Notre Dame aux neiges, Maria ad nives. In short, 'now Christian substance appears disguised in a heathen form, now heathen substance in Christian form,' as Jacob Grimm says, in whose *Deutsche Mythologie* the reader will find much relating to this mixture of old heathen and Christian ideas in the spirit of the 'simple folk that have a craving for myths.'

With the Hebrews it must have been much the same as with the Germans. We know that no less time than the entire period from Moses to Ezra—a thousand years of all manner of struggles and of the exercise of the greatest intellectual and moral forces—was requisite to develop the faith in One God, and make it a common and permanent possession of the people, pervading the whole spiritual consciousness.

But the fact that the Germans' monotheism was brought to them from outside, while that of the Israelites sprang up among themselves, must surely have been favourable to the preservation of heathen characteristics among the latter. Whilst in Germany a systematised Christianity, fully conscious of the issues involved, contended against Heathendom; among the Hebrews, Monotheism unfolded all its inevitable consequences only by degrees, gradually gaining a knowledge both of itself and of the antagonism in which it was implicated towards all

---

[1] E.g. the Lady-bird, in German Marienkäfer; its Danish name, Marihöne, was, according to Grimm, anciently Freyjuhöna 'Freyja's hen.' So Venus' Looking-glass (Speculum Veneris) is also called Lady's Glass; Pecten Veneris is Lady's Comb. There are very numerous plants named after Our Lady, which were probably originally dedicated to Freyja or Venus, as Lady's Mantle; Lady's Thistle or Lady's Milk (Carduus Marianus: 'distinguished at once by the white veins on its leaves. . . . A drop of the Virgin Mary's milk was conceived to have produced these veins, as that of Juno was fabled to be the origin of the Milky Way.' Hooker and Arnott, *British Flora*, p. 231); Lady's Smock (Cardamine); Lady's Bower or Virgin's Bower (Clematis); Lady's Fingers (Anthyllis); Lady's Tresses (Spiranthes or Neottia); Lady's Slipper (Cypripedium).—Tr.

phases of the heathen faith, worship and life. The Germans knew that their ancestors were heathens; they endeavoured as far as possible to break with their heathen past; and yet, knowingly or unknowingly, they retained a great deal of heathenism; and the pride of the Old German popular poetry, the *Nibelungen*, has a primeval myth for its subject. But the contrast between the heathen and the modern age was not at all firmly fixed in the mind of the Israelites, precisely because the transition was gradual. Only exceptionally do we find any reminiscence of the old heathenism, which is put back into the most ancient times. As far as the people were able to trace their history backwards, that is, to their supposed ancestor Abraham, they put back the faith in Jahveh; or indeed still farther, to Adam. The only true God Jahveh was soon treated as the only one worshiped in the beginning, from whom mankind fell away, intentionally defying him. Abraham alone remained faithful, and therefore Jahveh elected Abraham's descendants to be his people. Thus the Israelite fancied the faith in Jahveh to be the primitive and inalienable possession of his people, which had been only temporarily weakened, but never really lost. Even to other nations the knowledge of Jahveh could never be wanting; for they worshiped false, non-existent, gods from folly and malice, and the Israelite took for granted that they must know all that he knew. Now if even the Christian of the middle ages, although he knew that his ancestors were heathen, nevertheless often described them as acting like Christians, because he had no knowledge of heathendom, and no power of imagining a past age, except in the likeness of his own; how much more would the monotheistic Israelite picture his past ages, in which he acknowledged no heathenism at all, in a Jahveistic light? His whole history was unconsciously transformed. The heathen myths, which must have something in them, else they could not be told at all, were converted into events of the earth, closely coalescing with historical facts, what the heathen gods were said to have done was ascribed to Jahveh himself or one of his human ministers. The old Semitic gods, if not utterly forgotten, were made by the Hebrew into men of the primeval age, powerful heroes, or Patriarchs. I can invoke the authority of Ewald and Bunsen, for the assertion that no Biblical name before Abraham has any historical significance, and that of Movers for saying that Abraham is only the ancient national god of the Semites, El, who was also their first king or their ancestor, and that Israel, Abraham's grandson, was the Semitic Herakles Palaemon. The Israelite knew no longer how his forerunners had lived and thought in those ages, while they were still heathen; and he flooded his past history with the light which shone for him, but was of recent origin. He unconsciously falsified the facts of the history, because he did not care particularly for facts. Everything heathen received a Jahveistic sense, the heathen form a Jahveistic significance, the heathen substance a Jahveistic form. Only under these conditions could the past history of Israel be made intelligible to the mind of the people.

And then, when priests and prophets came to reduce the popular stories to writing, they could certainly only complete what the populace had already begun. They also were not historians or investigators at all; instead of transporting themselves into a past age, they raised the past age to the light of the present. No doubt they were more consistent and more inventive than the populace; for they wrote with an intelligence which marks and attempts to explain inconsistencies; and even in the interest of a certain political or religious object. The heathenism, which they could not understand, seemed to them impossible; they discovered everywhere at least Jahveistic motives.

Thus, I think, the Biblical narrative of Samson was an old heathen story, transformed by a Jahveistic colouring, given to it first by the Israelitish populace, and subsequently by the author of the narrative. I have endeavoured, by the aid of parallel instances, to trace the mode of this transformation and to recover the original form and meaning of the old story.

12. GENERAL PSYCHOLOGICAL REFLECTION.

We must now attempt to realise the psychological relations and processes upon which is based the preservation and transformation of heathen ideas within the range of Monotheism, the fact of which has been exhibited above.

We require here to see clearly, at least in broad outline, what relations ideas of recent growth, especially on religion and morals, bear to older representations. For from this it will then be easy to make the application to the special case before us, the relation of the monotheistic Jahveistic ideas to the older heathen representations among the Israelites. The story of Samson will then present only a special instance of this relation.

Among the ideas and thoughts, either of a nation or of an individual, a certain harmony prevails, which is in its nature not logical but psychological, not based on the law of Contradiction, but yielding that law as a specially rigorous result; in itself, however, much broader and more delicate, and indeed through its very breadth losing in stringency. The laws of logic have a double basis, a metaphysical one on the objective side, and a psychological on the subjective. That is, the logical law must be observed, because, if it be not, there arises, on the one hand, a disturbance of the metaphysical relation under which things in their reality have to come into thought, and on the other, an insoluble problem for our psychological function of Consciousness. Of course, in logical error or offence against logical law, so far as it actually occurs, there is nothing psychologically impossible. For example, a logically improper association of two ideas in the mind is possible—but only through the absence from the mind of the third factor, which logically makes it an error: if it were present, it would infallibly have prevented the improper association. That which is logically wrong is thus incapable of being thought. No one can think that $7+4=12$. We may certainly make such a false reckoning, if we happen not completely to spread before us the contents of the numbers in this succession: then such an association of ideas, such a summation of the series, may be formed. But as soon as the set of numbers is fully counted out, our passage from $7+4$ to 12 is stopped, and no effort would avail to connect them as equals. That which in the logical sphere is 'right' or 'wrong' takes, in the psychological, the form of 'complete' or 'incomplete.' Accordingly, if without knowing logic men can think right, and tell right thinking from wrong, it is because, when once the elements of a case are all clearly present to the mind, wrong thinking is psychologically impossible. This impossibility in the first instance only forces us to drop the wrong combination; but this is the first inducement to search for the right one. But, supposing no free movement of search and a total absence of reflection, then we shall simply have such range of combination as may be compatible with the psychological conditions; and, provided the necessary factors are all clear in the mind, this can be no other than the right one, viz., that which accords with the aggregate view of things.

This congruity among the ideas of particular nations or individuals is no doubt tantamount in the end to an avoidance of logical contradiction; and into this we might in all cases resolve such concord, could we exactly trace all the threads or intermediate members. But where the most we can do is to *feel* such threads of connexion, the congruity takes the shape of some Characteristic pervading the circles of ideas—some common stamp.

According to this, we ought to be able to discover in the mind of every nation a system of ideas intrinsically bound together and never self-contradictory. And this will so far prove to be the fact, that a certain national type will be everywhere present. But it is possible for contradictions to occur in the national life; for, if only they do not clash against one another in the consciousness, the contradictory ideas do not operate with their force of contradiction. Even every individual doubtless bears about with him unconsciously many ideas in harshest contradiction; contradictions, however, they are, in virtue not of any objective force proper to the ideas in themselves, but of an act of judgment which sets them forth as mutually contradictory. The contradictions are often hidden very deep, and only brought to light by a methodical search. When, however, new ideas, proclaimed everywhere in the streets, conflict with the old ones, the contradiction is at once brought to the light of day. What will be the result?

A conflict will arise, without doubt: will it be one with physical weapons? Such a conflict, though it may be inevitable, and though it has often given occasion for the exhibition of high and noble virtue, is nevertheless of no value to the real cause, the true victory, the victory of truth; and the chief point gained by the physical victory has generally been only the conviction of its worthlessness.

The conflict within the mind, where Ideas *en masse* confront Ideas in rank and file,—this forms the substance of the History of Mankind: a Conflict of Souls.

Mind rules and moulds, Matter is ruled and moulded: this relation repeats itself within the consciousness. Whatever consciousness owes to impressions of sense, serves as material to be moulded by mental activity. For the purpose of this moulding, the mind, impelled partly by this material itself and partly by its own nature, forms representations, notions, forms i.e. modes of apprehension, and ideas, namely, the general conceptions of genera and species, the metaphysical categories, and the moral ideas. In accordance with the moral ideas are formed principles of action, judgments on the acts of others, even of God, insofar as man believes himself acquainted with the acts of God. Conversely, acts are declared to be or not to be God's, insofar as they do or do not accord with the moral standard and the conception of God. In accordance with the general class-conceptions the world of things divides itself before the view: and while by certain esthetic and moral ideas these things are brought under a rule of valuation, in metaphysical aspects they are put into a causal relation. Finally, religious ideas form the foundation and the summit of all these curious constructions of a world and judgments passed on a world.

Accordingly, the conflict shows itself in two forms. Sometimes a certain domain of materials, in which new relations and connexions have become prominent, requires a new form of thought to dominate it; sometimes a new form of thought strives to supplant the old one, and to reshape, in accordance with its new laws, the matter which had been shaped by the former one. An example will make this clear. The thought 'God' forms the apex of the pyramid of ideas; it possesses the highest and widest dominion—for this very reason unfortunately often the weakest—and therefore shapes every province of consciousness in accordance with what it contains. Now, let an altered character come over the contents of one of these domains, say of the ideas concerning our relation to our fellow-men, or concerning causality in nature; then that domain can no longer tolerate to be ruled and moulded by the thought previously connoted in the word 'God,' standing as it now does in contradiction to that thought. It sets up the sway of a new form of thought, which fits its new contents, because growing out of them; there arises a new conception of God, a new Theology. But the old Theology has still its seat in all the other provinces of consciousness; so that, before any further advance, the new Idea has still to bring all these other provinces under its sway, to dissolve the shape given them by the old principle, and replace it by one which is congenial with itself. This may, nay must, produce a long conflict, which demands much labour. Of many a concept the intension will have to be entirely cancelled,—of all to be at least remodelled. Yet with many ideas the association has through long habit become quite fixed. Severed they must be, the new God requires it; but it can only be done very gradually. A thousand forbidden combinations find lurking-places and remain; they maintain themselves in contradiction to the new order of things, and perhaps half accommodate themselves to it in order to avoid a shock.

Imperfectly as I have expounded the point in question, I hope, nevertheless, that what I have said will suffice for the present purpose. What it wants in transparency and clearness may yet be added by the application of the general remarks to the particular case.

There existed for a long time, as I have remarked, monotheistic and heathen ideas in the national mind of the Israelites side by side—the former being the newer, the latter the older. But yet the former were the ruling ideas, and always gaining strength and clearness and coming to the brightest foreground of the consciousness, whereas the latter were constantly losing ground and clearness. Thus the nation lost the true consciousness of its heathen past history and the understanding of its former condition and experiences. For no nation as such possesses that true sense for history, by which it would conceive of itself and its present existence in conscious contrast to the past, and strive to gain an objective view of the mind and nature of past ages. The consciousness of a nation is only the active present age, and knows nothing of history. Therefore, whenever a radical revolution, extending over many important domains of ideas, has come over the nation, it no longer understands its own past history which lies on the other side of the revolution. Yet the old words, sayings and stories are transmitted all the same, and they contain accounts of bygone events and conditions, ancient ideas and ancient faith. But the stories which refer to obsolete and forgotten states of things are unintelligible; the names and sayings of forgotten gods, things and ideas are empty; typical figures and phrases based on those legends and gods, though still living on the lips, have become senseless. The nation always thinks that the word must have an idea behind it. So what it does not understand, it converts into what it does; it transforms the word until it can understand it. Thus words and names have their forms altered: e.g. the French *écrevisse* becomes in English *crawfish*, and the heathen god *Svantevit* was changed by the Christian Slavs into *Saint Vitus*, and the Parisians converted *Mons Martis* into *Montmartre*. And what was reported of persons or beings represented like persons, that are no longer known, is now told of persons whose acquaintance has been newly made. In Germany it was told of the god Wuotan, that he was called Long-beard, and as such fell asleep inside a mountain; now when Wuotan was utterly forgotten, a new subject had to be found; and the legend was transferred to the heroic kings Charles [the Great] and Frederick [Barbarossa]. Moreover, the myth that forms the groundwork of the poem of the *Nibelungen*, which was originally told without mention of any definite time or place, was assigned to a well-known locality, and its heroes received the names of historical kings.

Every nation must of necessity act similarly; for the legends which it tells must be its own legends, and reflect its own life and present circumstances; if they have ceased to do so because its life has changed, then they are changed in accordance with the change in the life. Even the future beyond the grave is to the popular mind only the present life somewhat gilded; then how is it likely that the past shall be thought of as different from the present?

And precisely because these transformations and transferences are necessary, they take place unconsciously and unintentionally. The mind of the nation does not make them; they are an occurrence in that mind, which makes itself by itself. The nation has subjects and predicates, sounds and meanings, given to it in the legend. Now if the stream of time carries off the subjects and meanings into the ocean of oblivion, then by the psychological law the unattached predicates and sounds must fasten themselves on to any other subjects and meanings by which they can be supported. This takes place without any one intending it, and without any one observing it.

The words, names and phrases which a nation uses have to be apperceived in the moment when they are employed. This is true both of the hearer and of the speaker. But the apperceptions are dependent on the previously formed associations of ideas. Now if a German heard 'Sinfluth,' or if, when speaking, this word known to him by tradition presented itself to his consciousness in the course of speech, then the second part of the word, *Fluth* 'flood,' found the idea with which it was associated, and which was reproduced by being brought into consciousness by the word; but the first part, *Sin*, stood in no association and roused no idea. But by material relationship and partial identity of sound, *Sin* is associated with *Sünde* 'sin,' and the latter idea (that of sin or guilt) was at the same time associated with the word *Sinfluth* as a whole; thus then this idea of sinfulness was strongly lifted into prominence on two sides, much more strongly and quickly than the German *Sin* itself. This latter was ultimately raised into prominence only through its traditional combination with *Fluth* 'flood,' and this only as a sound; consequently in its advance it was overtaken by *Sünde* 'sin,' which was lifted into prominence partly through it (*Sin*), and partly also through *Fluth*, and therefore with double force. Consequently people spoke and thought *Sünd*, instead of saying without thinking *Sin;* and this was the direct result of a simple psychological process.[1] Similarly in all analogous cases. Among the Ossetes of the Caucasus the Dies Martis, Tuesday, is unconsciously converted into George's Day; and the Dies Veneris, Friday, into Mary's Day. In many nations the gods form a circle limited to twelve immortals; the thirteenth in a society was then a mortal, one destined to die. Similarly, even at the present day, Christians fear that out of thirteen one will die, referring it however to the company of thirteen formed by Jesus and the twelve Apostles. Again, there was a legend widely spread among Teutonic nations, of an Archer, who shot an apple from his own little boy's head, and answered the despot at whose command he had done it, when asked about his other two arrows, that they were intended for him, in case the first had killed the child. Who was the Archer? Who was the Despot? where and what was the motive? All this was forgotten; there only remained a dim echo of the legend of the shot. But when Switzerland, a nation of archers, had shaken off the yoke of a despot, all the features of the story recovered definite names, places, time, and motive. As the stone flying through the air falls to the earth by the law of attraction, so the old legend fell into the Liberation-time.

---

[1] As this German example will not be familiar to all English readers, it is necessary to give a few words of explanation. The great Deluge (Gen. VI.–VIII.) is called in modern German *Sünd-fluth*, which seems to be Sin-flood = Flood on account of sin. But in Old High German it is written Sin-vluot and Sint-vluot, which cannot be identical with the assumed meaning of the modern word, since *sin* (peccatum) is in Old High German *sunta*. Moreover, *sin* is a prefix well known to most of the Teutonic languages, denoting (1) always, (2) great. In the former sense we have it in the Old English *singrene* 'evergreen;' in the latter in the Anglo-Saxon *sinhere* 'great army.' Hence it is assumed that the word in German altered its pronunciation when the prefix *sin* became obsolete, being then supposed to be intended for *Sünd-fluth*, as is shown in the text. See Grimm, *Deut. Gram.* II. 554, Graff, *Althochd. Sprachschatz*, VI. 25, Ettmüller, *Lex. Anglosax.* p. 638, Vigfusson, *Icelandic English Dict.* s. v. Sí. Prof. Steinthal appears now (in a letter to the translator) to doubt whether this history of the word is tenable; but the assumption that it is so may at least be allowed, in order to retain this excellent example of the psychological progress.—Tr.

Sometimes we forget something, but yet retain a small part of it in the memory, as when we say, I have really forgotten his name; but I am sure it begins with B. The same thing happens to nations. The name of Venus, or Holda, was forgotten; but people were sure that she was a divine woman. Now to the Christians of the middle ages 'Divine Woman' and 'Mary' were one single idea; consequently, the name Mary, unobserved, took the place of the heathen goddesses in the numerous appellations and legends which are now connected with Mary. Of Mars it was only remembered that he was a warrior; so Tuesday, which was sacred to him, could only become Saint George's Day.

Similar was the history of the Israelites when they became monotheistic. The heathen cosmogony, and the heathen idea of the activity of the gods in physical occurrences, contradicted the new idea of the One Almighty God, before whom Nature is nothing. But even though the idea that this God alone created the world, had been long accepted and established, yet there were still, preserved in stereotyped expressions of language, many ideas which preserved from oblivion and ruin features of the old modes of thought alongside of the new. They remain, so long as attention is not drawn to the contradiction in which these separate words stand to the new general system. When the clouds were no longer regarded as a sea, as they once were, people ceased to understand the meaning of 'the heights of the sea;' this expression no longer finds any organ of apperception, because 'Sea' is no longer associated with the idea of the clouds. Therefore, the expression is sustained only by its traditional connexion with 'heights.' But 'heights' are very closely associated with earth and with the idea of mountains; and thus with the Prophet Amos[1] this association supplanted the older one—the living took the place of the dead. We will now, in conclusion, return to Samson.

---

[1] See *supra*, p. 426.

13. HISTORY OF THE MYTH OF THE SUN-GOD.

We will now review the entire history of the old Semitic God of the Sun or of Heat, as he was present to the national consciousness of Israel.

I wonder whether I am mistaken? I flatter myself that I know the particle by which was expressed the greatest revolution ever experienced in the development of the human mind, or rather by which the mind itself was brought into existence. It is the particle 'as' in the verse[1] 'And he [the Sun] is *as* a bridegroom, coming out of his chamber; he rejoices *as* a hero to run his course.' Nature appears to us *as* a man, *as* mind, but is not man or mind. This is the birth of Mind, the generation of Poetry. This 'as' is unknown not only to the Vedas, but even to the Greeks. This does not mean that the Greeks had no poetry at all, but only that there is an inherent defect in their poetry, which is connected with the deepest foundation of their national mind. Helios, driving along the celestial road with fiery steeds, is not poetry, but only becomes poetical when we tacitly insert the 'as' of the Psalmist. He to whom Helios is a conscious being is childlike, if not childish: the Psalmist is poetical.

Now when such psalms were being spread abroad increasingly in Israel; when Jahveh was acknowledged as the being that brings up the sun, the stars and the rain-clouds, that builds the house and guards the city; then the old Sun-god or Herakles was forgotten; that is, his divinity, and that only, was forgotten. His deeds were still recounted; but deeds demand an agent. And thus out of the god, who could exist no longer in the presence of Jahveh, a man was made, who with Jahveh's force to aid him performed superhuman things, but in other respects lived among men and within human conditions, worked quite as a man, and even enjoyed his superhuman

[1] Ps. XIX. 6 [5].

power only on human terms, namely the terms of Naziritism.

Deeds were reported of some one who had long hair. But who wore his hair long, but the Nazirite consecrated to Jahveh? Deeds were told, which no one could accomplish unless exceptionally endowed with strength by Jahveh; and Jahveh would give such privilege only to the Nazirite consecrated to him. Consequently, when Samson was no longer a god, he must be a Nazirite. Nevertheless, he was distinguished beyond all other Nazirites: he was so from his very birth, like Samuel, to whom with Naziritism was granted Prophecy, a gift vouchsafed to others only later in life and occasionally. The strictly mythical character, the allusion to a religion of nature, was entirely lost from the stories about Samson. Whatever happened to him took a purely human character.

There was also a dim memory of the same forgotten god, that he was Melkart, i.e. 'king or guardian of the city.' Samson, now reduced to humanity, could have been such a guardian only in a human sense, though perhaps in an extraordinary degree. Now Israel preserved from the first half of its political existence the memory of no other enemy so dangerous, so difficult to withstand, and again in its subsequent weakness so hateful, as the Philistines: against them Samson must have fought. No other foe had laid on Israel so hard a yoke or such bitter degradation as the Philistines: but Samson must have avenged this on them. He must not only have conquered them, but likewise have given them a taste of his great physical and intellectual superiority: the Nazirite consecrated to Jahveh could scoff at the Philistines. Thus Samson was in the end a Judge, Shôphêṭ; for in the age of the Judges, the wars with the Philistines had begun, and after Eli and Samuel, Saul and David, or even beside any of them, Samson could not have lived. These were not deliberations, but unconscious impulses, which shaped the legend of Samson in the national mind of Israel.

No feature of the Solar hero has suffered a more characteristic conversion than his end, as is seen by a comparison with the corresponding polytheistic legends. Orion is blinded by the father of his lady-love, and Samson had his eyes put out. But Orion kindled the light of his eyes again at the rays of Helios, whereas Samson remains blind, and only prays to be endowed with strength to avenge the loss of one of his two eyes.[1] It is true, his hair grows again and brings back his strength: after the winter comes a new spring. But all in vain—Samson dies, notwithstanding. He dies like Herakles: but there is no Iolaos to wake him to a new life, no Athene and Apollon to lead him to Olympos, no Zeus and Here to present to him Hebe, the personification of the enjoyment of perpetual youth. Samson dies and remains dead; he dies, and tears down with him his own pillars—the pillars on which he had built the world—to find a grave beneath them. The heathen god is dead, and draws his own world down with him into his own nothingness; his battles were a play of shadows. Jahveh lives, 'he hath established the world by his wisdom,' 'he giveth rain, the autumn and the spring showers, each in its season, and keepeth to us the prescribed weeks of harvest,' 'cold and heat, summer and winter, day and night;'[2] he lives, the Lord of the world, the King of the earth, and his hero is Israel.

---

[1] Judges XVI. 28: 'Give me strength only this once, O God, and I will avenge myself with *the vengeance of one of my two eyes* on the Philistines.' This is the only possible meaning of the very simple Hebrew words nekam achath mishshethê 'ênay, which were misunderstood by the LXX and Vulg.; and the German and English versions have merely followed the latter.—Tr.

[2] Jer. X. 12, V. 24; Gen. VIII. 22.

INDEX.